How to use

GW00370613

The goal of eBizguides is to offer extensive economic and investment information on a country, with a focus on the top companies, while offering the best tourism and leisure information for your spare time. With this, we believe that our readers can get fully acquainted with the country, before investing in it long term.

This book comprises three major sections, which deal with general information, the country's economy and leisure.

General Information

Background information on the country is coupled with the main business resources available to you.

The Angolan Economy

This section of the book starts off with an in-depth look

nd the rviews with the most important business people in the country, we then provide our readers with privileged information and sector analysis, including introductions written by key decision-makers in the sector, such as government ministers.

You will also find fact files of all the major corporations, outlining their business activities, key projects and any investment opportunities. We consider this to include some of the most invaluable information for business globetrotters.

Leisure

For you to fall in love with the country, we also showcase the best spots to visit, essential areas to discover, the top hotels and restaurants, and much more.

Icons

eBiz Recommended

These companies were particular favourites of our team during their stay; this stamp is mostly given to restaurants, hotels, and so on.

eBiz Recommended Partner

Our team has been interviewing the heads of many companies; when they choose to allocate this stamp to a company, it is because they themselves have received reliable service from the company.

Notice

This indicates that the information is important and something to take notice of when planning, or during, your stay.

B.eBiz & L.eBiz

These are the two mascots of eBizguides. B.eBiz is always thinking about the best business opportunities and L.eBiz is more relaxed and wants to enjoy life. They are unseparable companions and they had visited all the places they are portraying you in eBizguide collection

Legends

Proverbs

These local phrases will help you to understand the popular culture in the country better. Perhaps you can even use them yourself.

Top Companies

This is a listing of the top companies that eBizguides encountered during their time in the country.

Blue Boxes

This is useful insider information that will help you to assess the country, do business and enjoy your stay.

eBizguides

ANGOLA

CREDITS

It is always good to know who worked hard for this Guide.

Many talented people and many wonderful stories have gone into making it. Here is the list of those involved:

PRODUCTION

Producer: Pascal Belda

Regional Project Director: Melanie Rose Hardiman

Post Production: Tatjana Vetter-Blanckenstein

Local Project Director: Maria Cruz Ferreira Costa

Associate Production: Luis Aparicio Garcia, Carlos Aparicio Belmonte, Julia Miralles Rodríguez and Adrien Germain-Thomas

Advertising Agencies: EAL - Edições de Angola, DG: Mr. Carlos Alberto Arques Santos; FEPEL, DG: Mr. Estevão Cauanda

EDITION

We appreciate the support and information provided by KPMG Angola, A.N.I.P.Agência Nacional para o Investimento Privado, D.N.A.T. Direcção Nacional de Actividades Turisticas and INFOTUR Instituto de Fomento Turístico

Edited by: Margaret Hunter.

Design and Layout: Iria Salgado.

Photos: All pictures by eBizguides; Dreadlocks Agency; Mr. João Pedro G. Pinheiro; Mr. Miquel Barti; Ulyses, Henrique Santos (surrenders of photo image copyrights).

ACKNOWLEDGEMENTS

We would like to thank the following people for their contribution and support:

Hon. Eng. Gilberto Buta Lutukuta, Former Minister of Agriculture and Rural Development; Hon Dr. Antonio Manuel Rebelais, Minister of Social Communication; Hon. Dr. Eduardo Donatão S. Chingunji, Minister of Tourism; Hon. Eng. Pedro Canga, Minister of Agriculture and Rural Development; Hon. Dr. Manuel Vicente Inglês Pinto, President of the Angolan Bar Association; Dr. Emanuel Maria Maravilhoso Buchartts, Head of Office of the Minister of Finances; Dr. José Luis de Matos, Director of the Ministry of Social Communication; Hon. Ambassador Javier Vallaure, Hon. Ambassador António da Costa Fernandes; Hon. Ambassador Hubert Cooreman; Dr. Rui Jose Veiga Pinto, Dr. Fernando Cruz, Eng. Abilio Sianga and Eng. Fernando Roberto, Dr. Gilles Bernard, Dr. Paixão António Junior, Dr. Paul de Sousa and Dr. Décio Gaspar and especially to Dr. Rui Luís Falcão Pinto de Andrade.

We would also like to thank the heads of the following companies for their sponsorship and support and without whom this eBizguide would not have been possible: Clínica Sagrada Esperança; Físico Estética e Saúde; Sistec; Eurostral; Fepel; Dreadlocks; Ango Atenta; Teleservices; Protector; Mamboji; Copebe; Prismatur; Alfa 5; W.A.P.O.; Expresso; Madiba; Lince; AP Services; Rest Veneza; Facar; Sogec; iL; SML; DSL; Soclimedic; BPC; Infotur; Angases; Arena Direct; Nexus; Mstelcom; INSS; KPMG; Atlas; Mangais; Citelfónica; Ango Patrulha; Securitas de Angola; SDV-AMI; Hull Blyth; Cargo Team; Fitness Club; Escritório de Advogados Inglés Pinto & Associados; IDA; ATS; Clidopa; EAL; Rest Tambarino; Bamboo Imperial; Odebrecht; TAAG; ANIP; Transcontinental; Sonangol; IDIA; Unitel; Movicel; Chevron; Grupo Chicoil; Petrobrás; Endiama and Panalpina.

We want as well to show our appreciation to our many friends in Angola, especially: Manuela Ganga, Francesca Bonelli, Shay, Mikel Barti, Ulyses, João Pedro G. Pinheiro and Angélica Xinda Martins. We also demonstrate our special gratitude to John Savage, Sarah Wood, Ana Fernández, Jean-Claude, Marcel, Rachid, Andrezza and Dilherman, Débora, Betty, Stephanie, Quick and Dany, Santos, Patrick, Héctor, Iván, Jacobo, Maria, Denise, Djamila, Marineth, Jessica, Rosa Cruz, Wanda Freire, Carla Soares and the whole Committee of Miss Angola, Bella, Sofia, Joana, Mayte, Mo, Marc and Leyla, Augusto, Daniel, Kenya, Almeida, Pin, Mary, Fina, Sofia, Sara Tiago, Lurdes, Nuno, Engª Bernarda. Thanks to the whole team of Mangais, to Luis Salgado, Rest. Tambarino, and to the team of Veneza, Abdeson, and Bamboo Imperial.

DISCLAIMER

While every effort has been made to ensure the accuracy of the information contained in this publication, this cannot be guaranteed and neither eBizguides nor any related entity shall have any liability to any person or entity who relies on the information contained in this publication. This publication is not a substitute for professional advice on services, and it should not be acted on or relied on or used as a basis for any decision or action that may affect you or your business. Any such reliance is solely at the user's risk.

World Investment News Inc

Customer Service: Tel: + 34-91-787 38 70, Fax: + 34-91-7873889

Email: info@ebizguides.com, www.ebizguides.com

Printed by: Imprenta Roal

ISBN: 84-933978-8-1

D.P.L.: M-41534-2009

Contents

i Did You Know?...7

i Angola Fact File..9

i General Information...11

Business Resources..37

The Angolan Economy...59 to 310

Investment & Legal Framework..59

Angolan Economy..81

Agriculture & Fisheries...95

Energy & Oil..111

Finance..151

Industry & Trade..173

Mining 201

Public Services..217

Works & Housing...251

Tourism..263

Transport & Communication..285

Leisure...311 to 364

Travel Agencies...353

i Basic Vocabulary...354

i Useful Websites...356

i Company Index..359

Did You Know?

Angola was the world's fourth largest producer of diamonds before 1975 and is one of the world's largest and least explored mineral treasure troves. Substantial deposits of gold, iron ore, manganese, phosphates, quartz, copper, lead, marbles, gypsums, beryl, black granite, zinc and numerous base and strategic metals are found.

Angola has considerable valuable timber resources that have been untapped since independence. The valuable tree species include rosewood, ebony, African sandalwood, mahogany, tola and mulberry. Nearly 150,000 hectares of eucalyptus, cypress and pine plantation are waiting to be rehabilitated.

When Portuguese mariner Diego Cão landed at the mouth of the Congo River in 1483, two distinct Kingdoms ruled the region. The Kingdom of the Bakongo reigned in the north. The Quimbundos Kingdom, also known as Ndongo, dominated in the western and central areas. The king of the Quimbundos was called Ngola. The region, taking its name from the king, became Angola.

Giant sable (*Hippotragus niger variani*) is a beautiful animal that is unique to Angola. This animal was named palanca negra in 1916, but the natives had named it *sumbakaloko* long before. It is believed that a white giant sable antelope can be found in central Angola, although we haven't been able to capture it in a photograph!!

The welwitschia is a unique plant that grows only in southern Angola and Namibia. The Portuguese General Army Command of Angola (Comando Geral Militar de Angola) used the *Welwitschia mirabilis* as its coat of arms.

Angola is forecast to become Africa's number one sub-Saharan oil producer by 2015.

Angola changed from a one-party Marxist–Leninist system to a formal multiparty democracy following the 1992 elections.

The Zambezi River and several tributaries of the Congo River have their sources in Angola.

Capoeira was brought to Brazil by captured slaves from Angola. In this foreign land the Angolan people developed their practice into a method of defending themselves against their violent overlords. Because of their predicament, these enslaved people had to disguise their training as recreational song and dance.

Angolans generally trace their descent through their mothers.

Portuguese is one of the few (if not the only) languages in the world where the weekdays are numbered instead of named. However, the days of the working week run from *segunda-feira* (Second day) to *sexta-feira* (Sixth day). Surprisingly "Second day" is Monday and not Tuesday as one might have expected.

Angola Fact File

Land Area:	1,246,700 km²
Population (000s):	15,116
Province of Bengo	240
Province of Benguela:	913
Province of Bié:	1.625
Province of Cabinda:	254
Province of Cuando-Cubango	176
Province of Cunene	324
Province of Huambo:	2,197
Province of Huíla:	1,215
Province of Cuanza Norte:	559
Province of Cuanza Sul:	901
Province of Luanda:	2,566
Province of Lunda Norte	405
Province of Lunda Sul	208
Province of Malanje	1,296
Province of Móxico	457
Province of Namibe:	194
Province of Uíge:	1,252
Province of Zaire	334
Population Growth Rate:	2.45% per year
Capital:	Luanda
Other Main Cities:	Huambo, Benguela and Lubango.
International Airports:	1 (Airport 4 de Fevereiro in Luanda)
Main Ports:	Luanda, Lobito, Namibe and Zaire
GDP:	$45,93 billion (2005 est.)
GDP Per Capita:	$3,200 (2005 est.)
Inflation:	17.7%
Government System:	Multiparty Democracy – Republic, with a strong Presidential System
Head of State:	Eng. José Eduardo Dos Santos
Official Languages:	Portuguese.
Climate:	Semiarid in the south and along the coast to Luanda. Has cool, dry season (May to October) and hot, rainy season (November to April)
Measures:	Metric System
Fiscal Year:	January 1st to December 31st
Time:	GMT + 1 Hour
Electricity:	220 volts AC50HZ
Currency:	Kwanza

"The father of the ants lives in a cave, a person lives in a house"
Angolan proverb

INTRODUCTION

The message most Angolan politicians and businesspeople like to convey about their country is definitely: "Angola has big potential". Seen from the outside, this may sound surprising for a nation so often associated with landmines, conflict diamonds and a virtually uninterrupted civil war that has plagued its people since they won independence from Portugal in 1975.

The Old Fortress of São Miguel overlooks Luanda Island beyond the Port

Take a closer look and Angola's potential rapidly becomes apparent. Not surprising for a country forecast to become Africa's number one sub-Saharan oil producer by 2015. In fact, few African countries have such a favourable natural endowment as Angola. Besides the oil industry, which has rapidly become the country's economic lifeline since the first offshore discoveries were made in the sixties, Angola is blessed with extensive stretches of fertile land and some of the largest and mostly unexplored diamond deposits in the world.

But Angola's spectacular rise as a petro-diamond state also raised the stakes in a civil war that stemmed from a fragmented independence movement in the seventies to one of the most disputed hotspots of the cold war throughout the eighties. More recently, the wave of democracy that swept across Africa in the nineties, coupled with large oil discoveries, has given Angola a second chance of achieving peace and prosperity.

HISTORY

The first inhabitants of the area that is now Angola are thought to have been members of the hunter-gatherer Khoisan group. Bantu-speaking peoples from West Africa arrived in the region in the thirteenth century, partially displacing the Khoisan and establishing a number of powerful kingdoms. The Portuguese settled in 1483 at the river Congo, where the Kongo State, Ndongo and Lunda existed. The Kongo State stretched from modern Gabon in the north to the Cuanza River in the south. In 1575 Portugal established a colony at Luanda based on the slave trade. The Portuguese gradually took control of the coastal strip throughout the sixteenth century by a series of treaties and wars. They formed the colony of Angola. The Dutch occupied Luanda from 1641–48, providing a boost for anti-Portuguese states.

In 1648 Portugal retook Luanda and initiated a process of military conquest of the Kongo and Ndongo states that ended with Portuguese victory in 1671. Full Portuguese administrative control of the interior didn't occur until the beginning of the twentieth century. In 1951 the colony was restyled as an overseas province, also called Portuguese West Africa. When Portugal refused a decolonization process three independence movements emerged:

• the Popular Movement for the Liberation of Angola (Movimento Popular de Libertação de Angola MPLA), with a base among Kimbundu and the mixed-race intelligentsia of Luanda, and links to communist parties in Portugal and the Eastern Bloc;

• the National Liberation Front of Angola (Frente Nacional de Libertação de Angola, FNLA), with an ethnic base in the Bakongo region of the north and links to the United States and the Mobutu regime in Zaire; and

• the National Union for Total Independence of Angola (União Nacional para a Independência Total de Angola, UNITA), led by Jonas Malheiro Savimbi, with an ethnic and regional base in the Ovimbundu heartland in the centre of the country.

After a 14-year guerrilla war, and the overthrow of Portugal's colonial rule by a military coup, Angola's nationalist parties began to negotiate for independence in January 1975. Independence was to be declared in November 1975. Almost immediately, a civil war broke out between MPLA, UNITA and FNLA, exacerbated by foreign intervention. South African troops struck an alliance of convenience with UNITA and invaded Angola in August 1975 to ensure that there would be no interference (by a newly independent Angolan state) in Namibia, which was then under South African control. Cuban troops came to the support of the MPLA in October 1975, enabling them to control the capital, Luanda, and hold off the South African forces. The MPLA declared itself to be the de facto government of the country when independence was formally declared in November, with Agostinho Neto as the first President.

In 1976, the FNLA was defeated by a combination of MPLA and Cuban troops, leaving the Marxist MPLA and UNITA (backed by the United States and South Africa) to fight for power. The conflict raged on, fuelled by the geopolitics of the Cold War and by the ability of both parties to access Angola's natural resources. The MPLA drew upon the revenues of offshore oil resources, while UNITA accessed alluvial diamonds that were easily smuggled through the region's very porous borders.

In 1991, the factions agreed to turn Angola into a multiparty state, but after the current president José Eduardo dos Santos of MPLA won UN-supervised elections, UNITA claimed there was fraud and fighting broke out again.

A 1994 peace accord (Lusaka protocol) between the government and UNITA provided for the integration of former UNITA insurgents into the government. A national unity government was installed in 1997, but serious fighting resumed in late 1998, rendering hundreds of thousands of people homeless. President José Eduardo dos Santos suspended the regular functioning of democratic processes due to the conflict.

On February 22nd 2002, Jonas Savimbi, the leader of UNITA, was shot dead and a ceasefire was reached by the two factions. UNITA gave up its armed wing and assumed the role of major opposition party. Although the political situation of the country seems to be normalizing, president dos Santos still hasn't allowed regular democratic processes to take place. Among Angola's major problems are a serious humanitarian crisis (a result of the

prolonged war), the abundance of minefields, and the actions of guerrilla movements fighting for the independence of the northern enclave of Cabinda (Frente para a Libertação do Enclave de Cabinda).

NATIONAL SYMBOLS

FLAG

The national flag of Angola is split horizontally into an upper red half and a lower black half. The red is for the blood spilt by Angolans during their independence struggles, while the black is for the continent of Africa. The symbol in the middle is of a crossed cogwheel and machete with a yellow star, representing the workers. It was adopted during a time when Angola had a Marxist government, and it thus supposed to evoke the image of the hammer and sickle found on the flag of the former Soviet Union, a common symbol of Communism.

COAT OF ARMS

The coat of arms of Angola reflects the recent past of the new nation. There is heavy Marxist imagery found on the coat of arms, expanded from what is found on the national flag.

In the centre is a machete and hoe, representing the revolution through which the nation gained independence and the importance of agricultural workers. Above both emblems is a star that is often found in many socialist images. The star is taken to represent progress. The rising sun is the traditional symbol of a new beginning. These emblems are all enclosed within a circle formed by a half cogwheel, which represents the industrial workers, and half vine of coffee leaves, which represents the coffee industry.

At the bottom is an open book, which represents education. A banner reads "Republic of Angola" at the bottom in Portuguese.

NATIONAL ANTHEM

Portuguese:

Pátria, nunca mais esqueceremos
Os heróis do quatro de Fevereio.
O Pátria, nós saudamos os teus filhos.
Tombados pela nossa Independência,
Honramos o passado e a nossa História,
Construindo no Trabalho o Homem novo,

CHORUS
Angola, avante!
Revolução, pelo Poder Popular!
Pátria Unida, Liberdade,
Um só povo, uma só Nação!

Levantemos nossas vozes libertadas
Para glóriados povos africanos.
Marchemos, combatentes angolanos,
Solidários com os poroso primidos.
Orgulhosos lutaremos Pela Paz
Com as forças progressistas do mundo.

English:

O Fatherland, we shall never forget
The heroes of the Fourth of February.
O Fatherland, we salute your sons
Who died for our Independence.
We honour the past and our history
As by our work we build the New Man.

CHORUS
Forward, Angola!
Revolution through the power of the People!
A United Country, Freedom,
One People, one Nation!

Let us raise our liberated voices
To the glory of the peoples of Africa.
We shall march, Angolan fighters,
In solidarity with oppressed peoples.
We shall fight proudly for Peace
Along with the progressive forces of the world.

GOVERNMENT

Angola changed from a one-party Marxist–Leninist system ruled by the MPLA to a formal multiparty democracy following the 1992 elections. President dos Santos won the first round election with more than 49% of the vote to Jonas Savimbi's 40%. A run-off never has taken place. The subsequent renewal of civil war and collapse of the Lusaka Protocol have left much of this process dead, but democratic forms exist, notably the National Assembly. Currently, political power is concentrated in the Presidency.

EXECUTIVE POWER OF THE GOVERNMENT

The executive branch of the government is composed of the President, the Prime Minister and Council of Ministers. Currently, political power is concentrated in the Presidency. The Council of Ministers, composed of all government ministers and vice ministers, meets regularly to discuss policy issues. Governors of the 18 provinces are appointed by and serve at the pleasure of the President. The Constitutional Law of 1992 establishes the broad outlines of government structure and delineates the

Angolan National Assembly

Angolan independence was declared in 1975

rights and duties of citizens. The legal system is based on Portuguese and customary law but is weak and fragmented, and courts operate in only a limited number of municipalities outside of Luanda. A Supreme Court serves as the appellate tribunal; a Constitutional Court with powers of judicial review has never been constituted despite statutory authorization.

THE LEGISLATIVE PROCEDURE

The National Assembly is the highest governmental body in Angola and represents the sovereign will of the Angolan people. It promotes the implementation of the objectives of the state, and legislates and makes decisions on basic questions relating to the state.

The Assembly's jurisdiction includes making changes in the constitutional law, approving laws, and proposing the government, the National Plan and the general state budget. The National Assembly also monitors, at supreme level, the actions of the government and of the other state organs. The National Assembly also authorizes the government to contract and grant loans, approves international treaties, grants amnesties and authorizes the President to declare war and make peace.

It is the legislative branch of the government of Angola, and is a unicameral body, with 220 members: 130 members elected by proportional representation and 90 members elected by provincial districts. Theoretically, the Assembly sits for a four-year term, but in reality the last election was held in 1992. The following election, scheduled for 1997, was put off indefinitely, although President José Eduardo dos Santos announced the government's intention to organize elections (presidential and legislative alike) in 2006.

Summary of the 29 and 30 September 1992 National Assembly of Angola election results			
Parties		%	Seats
Popular Movement for the Liberation of Angola (Movimento Popular de Libertação de Angola)		53.7	129
National Union for the Total Independence of Angola (União Nacional para a Independência Total de Angola)		34.1	77
National Front for the Liberation of Angola (Frente Nacional de Libertação de Angola)		2.4	5
Liberal Democratic Party (Partido Liberal Democrático)		2.4	3
Social Renewal Party (Partido Renovador Social)		2.3	6
Democratic Renewal Party (Partido Renovador Democrático)		0.9	1
Democratic Alliance of Angola (Aliança Democrática de Angola)		0.9	1
Social Democrat Party (Partido Social-Democrata)		0.8	1
Party of the Alliance of Youth Workers and Farmers of Angola (Partido da Aliança da Juventude, Operários e Campesinos de Angola)		0.4	1
Angolan Democratic Forum (Fórum Democrático Angolano)		0.3	1
Democratic Progress Party/Angolan National Alliance Party (Partido Democrático para Progreso/Aliança Nacional Angolano)		0.3	1
Angolan National Democratic Party (Partido Nacional Democrático Angolano)		0.3	1
Total (Turnout 93.5 %)			220

Source: Electionworld

THE JUDICIAL SYSTEM

The judicial system includes municipal and provincial courts at the trial level and a Supreme Court at the appellate level. Municipal court judges are usually laymen. In theory, the Ministry of Justice administers provincial courts located in each of the 18 provincial capitals. The Supreme Court nominates provincial court judges. The judge of the provincial court, along with two laymen, acts as a jury.

In 1991, the constitution was amended to guarantee an independent judiciary. In practice, however, the President appoints the 16 Supreme Court judges for life upon recommendation of an association of magistrates, and he appoints the attorney general. Confirmation by the General Assembly is not required.

GOVERNMENT OFFICES

President of the Republic
Presidência da República
Cidade Alta - Luanda
Tel: +244-222-394541 / 397251
Fax: +244-222-352083 / 392737

Cabinet of the Prime Minister
Primeiro Ministro – Gabinete
Cidade Alta - Luanda
Tel: +244-222-397071
Fax: +244-222-469381

National Assembly
Assembleia Nacional
Rua Amilcar Cabral - Luanda
Tel: +244-222-393534 / 335921
Fax: +244-222-470091

President of the National Assembly
Presidência da Assembleia Nacional
Rua Amilcar Cabral - Luanda
Tel: +244-222-395636 / 335438
Fax: +244-222-392386

Secretariat of the Council of Ministers
Secretariado do Conselho de Ministros
Cidade Alta - Luanda
Tel: +244-222-323359 / 397826
Fax: +244-222-392271 / 323359

Ministry of Agriculture and Rural Development
Ministério da Agricultura e Desenvolvimento Rural
Avenida Comadante Gika, n° 8, Largo do Ministerios
PO Box 527, Luanda
Tel: +244-222-322694 / 5
Fax: +244-222-320553 / 323650 / 320710

Ministry of Commerce
Ministério do Comércio
Avenida 4 de Fevereiro, Palácio de Vidro - Luanda
Tel: +244-222-310335 / 338619
Fax: +244-222-311195
Website: www.dnci.net

Ministry of Defence
Ministério da Defesa Nacional
Rua 17 de Setembro, Cidade Alta - Luanda
Tel: +244-222-518728
Fax: +244-222-330819

Ministry of Internal Administration
Ministério do Interior
Luanda
Tel: +244-222-395133 / 398743
Fax: +244-222-398754

Ministry of Education & Culture
Ministério da Educação e Cultura
Largo Antonio Jacinto, Avenida Comandante Gika
PO Box 1281, Luanda
Tel: +244-222-320582
Fax: +244-222-322466

Ministry of Energy and Water
Ministério da Energia e Aguas
Avenida 4 de Fevereiro, n° 105, 4th Floor
PO Box 2229, Luanda
Tel: +244-222-393681 / 335039
Fax: +244-222-393687

Ministry of External Relations
Ministério das Relações Exteriores
Rua Major Kanhangulo, n°35 - Luanda
Tel: +244-222-396038 / 397490
Fax: +244-222-395778 / 396776

Ministry of Family & Promotion of Women
Ministério da Familia e Promoção da Mulher
Largo 4 de Fevereiro, Palácio de Vidro, 2nd Floor - Luanda
Tel: +244-222-311171
Fax: +244-222-310182

Ministry of Finance
Ministério das Finanças
Largo da Mutamba – Prédio das Finanças
PO Box 592, Luanda
Tel: +244-222-396843 / 332069
Fax: +244-222-338548
Website: www.minfin.gv.ao

Ministry of Fisheries
Ministério das Pescas
Avenida 4 de Fevereiro, Prédio das Pescas
PO Box 83, Luanda
Tel: +244-222-310759 / 310560
Fax: +244-222-338548 / 310199
Website: www.angola-minpescas.com

Ministry of Former Combatants
Ministério dos Antigos Combatentes e Veteranos de Guerra
Avenida Comandante Gika, 2° - Luanda
Tel: +244-222-330876
Fax: +244-222-322234

Ministry of Geology and Mining
Ministério da Geologia eMinas
Avenidade Comandante Gika, 260 - Luanda

17

Tel: +244-222-321655 / 322766 / 326724
Fax: +244-222-395778 / 321655

Ministry of Health
Ministério da Saúde
Rua 17 Setembro, Coqueiros
PO Box 1201, Luanda
Tel: +244-222-391281
Fax: +244-222-391281

Ministry of Hotels & Tourism
Ministério da Hotelaria e Turismo
Largo 4 de Fevereiro, Palácio de Vidro - Luanda
Tel: +244-222-338211 / 310899 / 310609
Fax: +244-222-337624

Ministry of Industry
Ministério da Indústria
Rua Cerqueira Lukoki, n°25
PO Box 594, Luanda
Tel: +244-222-392400 / 338049 / 334700
Fax: +244-222-392400

Ministry of Interior
Ministério do Interior
Avenida 4 de Fevereiro
PO Box 2732, Luanda
Tel: +244-222-395139 / 1049/79
Fax: +244-222-391133/75

Ministry of Justice
Ministério da Justiça
Rua 17 de Setembro
PO Box 2250, Luanda
Tel: +244-222-330327
Fax: +244-222-339212

Ministry of Petroleum
Ministério dos Petróleos
Avenida 4 de Fevereiro, 105 Prédio dos Petróleos
PO Box 1279, Luanda
Tel: +244-222-337440
Fax: +244-222-395847

Ministry of Planning
Ministério do Planeamento
Largo da Cidade Alta, Palácio do Povo
PO Box 1205, Luanda
Tel: +244-222-338686 / 396482
Fax: +244-222-366845 / 390188 / 2731

Ministry of Postal Works & Telecommunications
Ministério dos Correios e Telecomunicações
Rua do Faninga - Luanda
Tel: +244-222-337777 / 311803
Fax: +244-222-396144 / 310165/4

Ministry of Public Administration, Employment & Social Security
Ministério da Administração Pública, Emprego e Segurança Social
Rua 17 de Setembro, 32
PO Box 1986, Luanda
Tel: +244-222-336095/6 / 338654 / 3339257
Fax: +244-222-339796
Website: www.mapess.gv.ao

Ministry of Public Works
Ministério das Obras Públicas
Rua Federico Engles, 92, 5th Floor
Bairro Ingombota, Mutamba
PO Box 1061, Luanda
Tel: +244-222-336715 / 337478
Fax: +244-222-392539 / 398431

Ministry of Science & Technology
Ministério da Ciência e Tecnologia
Luanda
Tel: +244-222-309794 / 5
Fax: +244-222-398891

Ministry of Social Assistance & Reintegration
Ministério da Reinserção Social
Avenida Hoji Ya Henda, 117
PO Box 102, Luanda
Tel: +244-222-342949 / 340370
Fax: +244-222-343606

Ministry of Social Communication
Ministério da Comunicação Social
Av. Comandante Valódia, 1° e 2° andar
PO Box 2608, Luanda
Tel: +244-222-343495
Fax: +244-222-446818

Ministry of Sports & Youth
Ministério da Juventude e Desportos
Avenida Comandante Gika
PO Box 5466, Luanda
Tel: +244-222-323090 / 321117/8/9
Fax: +244-222-321118

Ministry of Transport
Ministério dos Transportes
Avenida 4 de Fevereiro 42, 7th Floor
PO Box 2732, Luanda
Tel: +244-222-311303 / 330799
Fax: +244-222-311582 / 337699

Ministry of Territorial Administration
Ministério da Administração do Território
Avenida Comandante Gika, n° 8
PO Box 1241, Luanda
Tel: +244-222-321072 / 321791 / 320729
Fax: +244-222-3272 / 321072

Ministry of Urbanism and Environment
Ministério do Urbanismo e Ambiente
Avenida Comandante Gika, n° 8
PO Box 1241, Luanda
Tel: +244-222-310517
Fax: +244-222-334683

GEOGRAPHY

Angola is located on the south Atlantic coast of West Africa between Namibia and the Republic of the Congo. It also is bordered by the Democratic Republic of the Congo and Zambia to the east. The country is divided into an arid coastal strip stretching from Namibia to Luanda; a wet, interior highland; a dry savanna in the interior south and south-east; and rain forest in the north and in Cabinda. The Zambezi River and several tributaries

of the Congo River have their sources in Angola. The coastal strip is tempered by the cool Benguela current, resulting in a climate similar to coastal Peru or Baja California. There is a short rainy season lasting from February to April. Summers are hot and dry, while winters are mild. The interior highlands have a mild climate, with a rainy season from November to April followed by a cool dry season from May to October. Elevations generally range from 3,000 to 6,000 feet (900 to 1,800 m). The far north and Cabinda enjoy rain throughout much of the year.

The coast is for the most part flat, with occasional low cliffs and bluffs of red sandstone. There is but one deep inlet of the sea – Great Fish Bay (or Baía dos Tigres). Farther north are Port Alexander, Little Fish Bay and Lobito Bay, while shallower bays are numerous. Lobito Bay has water sufficient to allow large ships to unload close inshore. The coastal plain extends inland for a distance varying from 30 to 100 miles (48 to 165 km). This region is in general sparsely watered and somewhat sterile. The approach to the great central plateau of Africa is marked by a series of irregular terraces. This intermediate mountain belt is covered with luxuriant vegetation. Water is fairly abundant, though in the dry season obtainable only by digging in the sandy beds of the rivers. The plateau has an altitude ranging from 4,000 to 6,000 feet (1,200 to 1,800 m). It consists of well-watered, wide rolling plains and low hills with scanty vegetation. In the east the tableland falls away to the basins of the Congo and Zambezi, and to the south it merges into a barren sandy desert. A large number of rivers make their

Quedas de Kalandula Malange - Kalandula Malange Falls

i

way westward to the sea; they rise mostly in the mountain belt and are unimportant, the only two of any size being the Cuanza and the Cunene.

The mountain chains that form the edge of the plateau, or diversify its surface, run generally parallel to the coast – Tala Mugongo (4,400 ft or 1,350 m), Chella and Vissecua (5,250–6,500 ft or 1,500–2,000 m). In the district of Benguela are the highest points of the province – Loviti (7,780 ft or 2,370 m) at 12° 5′ S, and Mt Elonga (7,550 ft or 2,300 m). South of the Cuanza is the volcanic mountain Caculo-Cabaza (3,300 ft or 1,000 m). From the tableland the Cuango and many other streams flow north to join the Kasai River (one of the largest affluents of the Congo), which in its upper course forms for fully 300 miles (490 km) the boundary between Angola and the Congo State. In the south-east part of the province the rivers belong either to the Zambezi system or, like the Okavango, drain to Lake Ngami.

NATURAL RESOURCES

Angola has been blessed with very rich natural resources. While oil is undoubtedly the biggest wealth of the country, Angola also has a very rich soil. Gold, diamonds, quartz and copper are among the many various minerals that can be found in the inner provinces of the country. But the country also has the chance of benefiting from extensive forests and Atlantic fisheries. Due to a lack of irrigation and technical knowledge, agriculture isn't yet mechanized.

WILDLIFE

The 25-year civil war in Angola has taken a heavy toll on the country and its people and it has also nearly wiped out Angola's wildlife, which has been killed in crossfire, by landmines or deliberately hunted down by poachers.

Game reserves are a huge tourist attraction and they bring in thousands of holidaymakers and their hard cash every year, so many projects are being run, in collaboration with regional neighbours and the government, in order to repopulate Angola's wildlife.

CLIMATE

Like the rest of tropical Africa, Angola experiences distinct, alternating rainy and dry seasons. In the north, the rainy season may last for as long as seven months – usually from September to April, with perhaps a brief slackening in January or February. In the south, the rainy season begins later in November and lasts until about February. The dry season (*cacimbo*) is often characterized by a heavy morning mist. In general, precipitation is higher in the north, but at any latitude it is greater in the interior than along the coast and increases with altitude.

Temperatures fall with distance from the equator and with altitude and tend to rise closer to the Atlantic Ocean. Thus at Soyo, at the mouth of the Congo River, the average annual temperature is about 26 °C, but it is under 16 °C at Huambo on the temperate central plateau. The coolest months are July and August (in the middle of the dry season), when frost may sometimes form at higher altitudes.

PEOPLE

The demographics of Angola consist of three main ethnic groups, each speaking a Bantu language: Ovimbundu 37%, Kimbundu 25% and Bakongo 13%. Other groups include Chokwe (or Lunda), Ganguela, Nhaneca-Humbe, Ambo, Herero, and Xindunga. In addition, mixed racial (European and African) people amount to about 2%, with a small (1%) population of whites, mainly ethnically Portuguese. Portuguese make up the largest non-Angolan population, with at least 30,000 (though many native-born Angolans can claim Portuguese nationality under Portuguese law).

In 1975, 250,000 Cuban soldiers settled in Angola to help the MPLA forces to fight for its independence. These Cubans are of European and Asian (mostly Chinese) descent, while others include those of pure African and mulatto descent, who have ancestors in Angola. But in 1989, almost all Cubans left the country after a peace agreement had been signed between Angola, Cuba and South Africa. Cubans speak Spanish, but almost none of their descendants speak it. Portuguese is both the official and predominant language.

The great majority of the inhabitants are of Bantu-Negro stock with some admixture in the Congo district with the pure negro type. In the south-east are various tribes of Bushmen. The best known of the Bantu-Negro tribes are the Ba-Kongo (Ba-Fiot), who dwell chiefly in the north, and the Abunda (Mbunda, Ba-Bundo), who occupy the central part of the province, which takes its name from the Ngola tribe of Abunda. Another of these tribes, the Bangala, living on the west bank of the upper Cuango, must not be confused with the Bangala of the middle Congo. In the Abunda there is a considerable strain of Portuguese blood. The Ba-Lunda inhabit the Lunda district. Along the upper Cunene and in other districts of the plateau are settlements of Boers, the Boer population being about 2,000. In the coast towns, the majority of the white inhabitants are Portuguese.

The Mushi-Kongo and other divisions of the Ba-Kongo retain curious traces of the Christianity professed by them in the sixteenth and seventeenth centuries and possibly later. Crucifixes are used as potent fetish charms or as symbols of power passing down from chief to chief; whilst every native has a Santu or Christian name and is dubbed 'dom' or 'dona'. Fetishism is the prevailing religion throughout the province. The dwelling-places are usually small huts of the simplest construction, used chiefly as sleeping apartments; the day is spent in an open space in front of the hut protected from the sun by a roof of palm or other leaves.

LANGUAGES

Although Portuguese was Angola's official language, the great majority of Angolans (more than 95% of the total population) used languages of the Bantu family – some closely related, others remotely so – that were spoken by most Africans living south of the equator and by substantial numbers north of it.

Angola's remaining indigenous peoples fell into two disparate categories. A small number, all in southern Angola, spoke so-called Click languages (after a variety of sounds characteristic of them) and differed physically from local African populations. These Click speakers shared characteristics, such as small stature and lighter skin colour, linking them to the hunting and gathering

Mumuila Mother and Son

bands of southern Africa sometimes referred to by Europeans as Bushmen. The second category consisted of mestiços, largely urban and living in western Angola. Most spoke Portuguese, although some were also acquainted with African languages, and a few may have used such a language exclusively.

RELIGION

The constitution provides for freedom of religion, and the government generally respects this right in practice. The government at all levels strives to protect this right in full and does not tolerate its abuse, either by governmental or private actors.

Christianity is the religion of the vast majority of the country's population, with Roman Catholicism as the country's largest single denomination. The Roman Catholic Church claims five million adherents, but such figures could not be verified. The major Protestant denominations also are present, along with a number of Brazilian Christian and indigenous African denomina-

tions. The largest Protestant denominations, which include Methodists, Baptists, Congregationalists (United Church of Christ) and Assemblies of God, claim to have three to five million adherents. The largest syncretic religious group is the Kimbanguist Church, whose followers believe that a mid-twentieth century Congolese pastor named Joseph Kimbangu was a prophet. A small portion of the country's rural population practises animism or traditional indigenous religions. There is a small Islamic community, less than 1% of the population, comprising mainly migrants from West Africa. There are few declared atheists in the country.

PUBLIC HOLIDAYS

Date	Holiday
1st January	New Year
4th January	Day of the martyrs of the Colonial Repression
4th February	National Day for the Armed Forces
8th March	International Day of the Woman

Catholic church - The vast majority of Angolans are Catholic

Children playing in Gabela

4th April	Peace Day
1st May	Work Day
1st June	International Day for Children
17th September	Day of the National Heroes and of the Founder of the Nation
2nd November	Saints Day
11th November	Independence Day
25th December	Christmas
31st December	St Sylvester

BUSINESS WORKING HOURS

Most offices open from 0830 to 1700 with a two-hour break between 1200 and 14:00.

MONEY MATTERS

CURRENCY

The local currency is the Kwanza. At the time of publication US $1 amounted to roughly 138 Kwanzas.

BANKS

Banks are mainly open:

Monday–Friday: 0830–1500
Saturdays: 0900–1100 on the first and last Saturday of the month only.

Many banks have different opening hours, depending on their branches. Check with the bank for details.

FOREX BUREAUS

Banks offer foreign currency exchange services, and there are also private Forex bureaus dotted all over Luanda. The Forex bureaus tend to give better rates than the banks, but it is worth checking the rate in advance and any commissions that may be charged. When changing money, be sure to calculate the money you expect to receive and to count it completely. At no point should you feel rushed to complete the transaction. US dollars is the preferred currency for exchange. It is worth bearing in mind that larger denomination notes, like US $100, often receive a better exchange rate than the smaller notes, such as US $10.

NOTICE! See the Business Resources section for Forex Bureau listings.

CREDIT CARDS

As no major international credit cards are accepted in Angola (VISA, American Express, Master Card), it is strongly advised to carry cash at all times. Some of the local banks have their own network of ATMs, but these work only with local credit cards. There are very few places in which credit cards are accepted. Only top-end hotels might provide this service.

National Bank of Angola

Restaurant in "Ilha do Cabo", Luanda

COMMUNICATIONS

FIXED LINES

Four main companies share the market for fixed lines. The most important one is the historical public company Angola Telecom, but through the years other private companies have been competing to gain their share of the market. The most important ones are Nexus, Mercury and Wezacom.

The international country code for Angola is 244.

Main area codes are:

Baia Farta	72
Bela Vista	72
Benguela	72
Cabinda	31
Catete	34
Catumbela	72
Caxito	34
Cubal	72
Cunene	65
Dombe Grande	72
Ganda	72
Huíla	61
Huambo	41
Kuito	48
Lobito	48
Luanda	2
Lubango	61
Lucapa	52
Luena	54
Malange	51
Menongue	49
Namibe	64
Ndalatando	35
Ondjiva	65
Saurimo	53
Sumbe	36
Tombwa	893
Uíge	64
Xangongo	65

SOME INDICATIVE PRICES

Not surprisingly, Angola is a very expensive country. Here are some indicative prices about the cost of life in Angola.

Renting a house	between US $2,500 and 4,500 per month
Restaurant	usually over US $50 per person
Pizza	US $20
A drink out	US $10
Taxi	US $20 for 5 to 10 minutes
Mobile phone	US $200–400

Curiosity: Bread is US $0.10 = 10 Kwanza

Imported products are usually US $10 more expensive than in Europe.

NB If you phone from abroad, you have to dial +244-2-[tel. no.] to get an Angolan number. However, if you call from within Angola or from an Angolan mobile phone to

i

24

Competition is growing in both the fixed lines and mobile communication markets

a landline, you have to dial an extended Luanda area code, for example: 222-[tel. no.].

Standard prices (per minute) of international calls from Angola go from US $0.90 to US $1.80, depending on the country

INTERNATIONAL CALLING CARDS

There are very few international calling cards available in Angola. The best way to call at a cheap price is via the Internet using VOIP.

MOBILE PHONES

At the time of publication, there were two main mobile operators in Angola, Movicel and Unitel. Movicel is the cellular division of Angola Telecom. Unitel is a private entity. Many shops sell SIM cards from these two companies as well as scratch recharge cards. The SIM cards are around US $24, and the recharge cards are available in a variety of denominations. These pre-paid scratch cards are the most common and efficient way of calling within Angola.

RECOMMENDED PARTNER Movicel
Customer service centre: 191
Headquarters Movicel:
Rua Mãe Isabel, n°1,

Prédio da Movicel - Luanda
Tel: +244-222-692000
Fax: +244-222-692090
Website: www.movicel.com

RECOMMENDED Unitel
Customer service centre: 19192
Headquarters Unitel:
Rua Kwame N'Krumah
Prédio da UNITEL, Maianga - Luanda
Tel: +244-222-447784
Fax: +244-222-447783
Website: www.unitel.co.ao

SATELLITE PHONES

As in many parts of the world, satellite phones can prove to be very useful in remote parts of the country. As the overall mobile phone coverage is still in expansion, a sat phone will be needed for urgent communications.

INTERNET SERVICES

There are several Internet service providers in Angola, some offering high-speed Internet connections.

NOTICE! See the Business Resources section for ISP listings.

BEFORE AND AFTER YOU ARRIVE

HEALTH AND SAFETY

Before You Arrive

Before entering Angola, make sure that all your vaccinations are up to date. Your family doctor can best advise you on which vaccinations are recommended; however, it is essential that you have the yellow fever vaccination, as you may be asked to present the certificate of vaccination on arrival in Angola.

It is also worth considering having vaccinations or boosters for polio, typhoid, tetanus, hepatitis A and B, and cholera. All travellers should visit their personal doctor or a travel health clinic four to eight weeks before departure.

Malaria is a common disease in Angola. There is no vaccination for malaria and precautionary measures should be taken to minimize the risk. For a short stay, it is highly advisable to take anti-malaria tablets. For a longer stay, tablets can be harmful to the liver and it is preferable to take all the preventive measures possible, such as through sprays and mosquito nets. The most common symptoms of malaria are high fever, headache, stiffness, pain in the joints and deep fatigue. At any sign of the above symptoms, you should go for a malaria test and go to see a doctor as soon as possible (please see Business Resources section).

As malaria is endemic to Angola, you should take anti-malaria tablets especially if you are travelling to the coast or to some game parks. There are a variety of options available, and the choice will depend on your length of stay, how soon you need to travel, your medical condition and so on. Some anti-malaria drugs like Lariam (Mefloquine) only need to be taken once a week, but many people have reported them to have neuropsychiatric side effects. Doxycycline is an antibiotic prophylaxis that is taken daily, and only needs to be started one day before you travel. It is also widely available in the pharmacies locally, and can also protect you against traveller's diarrhoea. However, in a few cases it can increase your skin's sensitivity to the sun. A new drug, Malarone, can also be started the day before you travel, and is currently recommended by many doctors as it does not have the side effects of the others. However, it is the most expensive option.

On Arrival

It is recommended that you have your accommodation booked before you arrive. If you are staying at a hotel you can arrange for a driver to collect you from the airport; write your name on a placard so you can be identified easily.

Travellers should only drink mineral water, or in an emergency boiled water, since the water is untreated and therefore tap water is not safe.

AIDS and HIV are very prevalent in Africa, so at all costs, avoid having unprotected sex.

HEALTH SERVICES

In Luanda, hospitals offer good facilities in comparison with neighbouring countries. As in many countries, the cost of medical services or hospital care must be paid in cash. Most places will accept payment by the patient's private health insurance, although there are exceptions to the rule. There are pharmacies in Angola, and they are open during normal trading hours. In case of a serious medical emergency, it is recommended that you contact your embassy.

 See the Business Resources section for medical services and pharmacy listings.

EMERGENCY CALLS

In the event of an emergency call:

Emergencies SADC 112
Ambulance: 116
Ambulance Clinica Sagrada Esperança: +244-222-309687 / 309034
Ambulance Clinica Clidopa: +244-222-391587 / 391488
Customs Airport: +244-222-350777
Customs Port: +244-222-310625
Customs Post: +244-222-337067
Electricity 24 hours: +244-222-440267

i   **26**

Fire Service: 115
Fire Service Operative Unit: +244-222-323333
Police: 113
Police Central Unit: +244-222-391479
Red Cross Centre: +244-222-333991/31
Water 24 hours: +244-222-441447

ENTRY VISA REQUIREMENTS AND EXTENSIONS

People of all nationalities must get a visa prior to arrival. It is not possible to obtain a visa upon arrival. You can only obtain a visa in advance from the Angolan embassy or consulate in your country of residence.

Passports must have a validity of at least six months and two blank pages.

Application forms can be photocopies but must be of a high standard, and the applicant's signature must be original otherwise the forms will be returned.

The following items are basic requirements when applying for an ordinary visa to enter Angola:

- Completed application form
- International passport valid for at least six months
- Four recent passport photographs
- Return ticket
- A letter of invitation from Angola
- Company letter from you requesting the visa.

The ordinary visa takes up to eight working days to process and the length of stay may not exceed 30 days. Ordinary visas are valid for stays not exceeding one month. However, it is possible to renew an ordinary visa twice. After three months you will have to return to your country of citizenship or residency if you wish to be granted another entry visa.

 Renewing your Visa takes a long time. We recommend to go to the DEFA very early in the morning to avoid queues

DIPLOMATIC VISA:

- Two colour passport-size photographs
- Application form
- Note from embassy or official body
- Passport and three copies of passport.

RESIDENCE VISA:

- Three colour passport-size photographs
- Application form
- Fax invitation from Angola (faxed directly to the embassy of Angola in the UK)
- Written undertaking to comply with Angolan laws
- Means of subsistence
- Letter addressed to the Consular Sector explaining the reason for establishing residence
- Name and address of relatives living in Angola or abroad
- Address in Angola
- Criminal record.

TRANSIT VISA:

- Application form
- Passport
- Two color photographs
- Company letter, ticket or itinerary.

WORK VISA:

- Application form
- Passport and three copies of passport
- Three colour passport-size photographs
- Fax invitation and copy of documents of the Angolan company (sent directly to the embassy of Angola in the UK)
- Company or personal letter (original and two copies)
- Three copies of contract (translated into Portuguese)
- Three curriculum vitae certificates (three copies translated into Portuguese)
- Written undertaking to comply with Angolan laws
- Criminal record (original and two copies translated into Portuguese and authenticated by the Foreign Office and to be stamped by the consulate)
- Medical records (original and two copies, authenticated by the Foreign Office and to be stamped by the consulate)

An aerial view of Huambo

- Immunization card
- Return ticket or itinerary.

A work visa will take more than a month to be issued.

To renew your visa you must go the Angolan Directorate for Immigration and Customs (DEFA) in Luanda, purchase a prorogation form and provide them with your passport and three photos. Your visa extension will be granted within a week.

VISA ENQUIRIES

DEFA / Direcção de Emigração e Fronteiras de Angola
Luanda
Tel: +244-222-330314 / 330019
Fax: +244-222-3127
As requirements tend to change and vary from country to country, and depending on the type of visa you are applying for, we strongly advise you contact your nearest Angolan mission for all entry requirements well in advance.

NOTICE! See the end of this section for listings of Angolan embassies abroad.

GETTING THERE AND AROUND

BY AIR

Luanda 4 de Fevereiro Airport is situated only 4 km outside Luanda. There are no public phones or bank facilities at the airport.

TAAG Angolan Airlines has flights between Luanda and some states in Africa, for example to South Africa (Johannesburg), Namibia (Windhoek), Zimbabwe (Harare), Democratic Republic of Congo (Kinshasa) and the Republic of Congo (Brazzaville). TAAG also connects Angola to South America with its twice-weekly flight to Rio de Janeiro in Brazil.

SAA South African Airways operates from Johannesburg to Luanda. British Airways offers direct connections between London and Luanda, Air France between Paris and Luanda and TAP Air Portugal flies from Lisbon to Luanda. Ethiopian Airways flies from Addis Ababa to Luanda.

TAAG, Air Gemini and other smaller charter or air taxi companies provide domestic flights.

When travelling within Angola it is recommended to use internal flights as the infrastructure is basic. Airport departure taxes are generally included in the price of the ticket.

Airport Information: +244-222-354614
Airport Protocol: +244-222-350804/14
Angolan Airlines TAAG: +244-222-393098 / 351750
Air France: +244-222-352515 / 350412
Air Gabon: +244-222-310614 / 310878
Air Gemini: +244-222-355064/65
Air Namibia: +244-222-336726
British Airways: +244-222-399679 / 355266
Ethiopian Airways: +244-222-316615 / 353981
SAA South African Airways: +244-222-350032
SN Brussels: +244-222-311447 / 353886
TAP Air Portugal: 222-331697 / 351051

Houston Express is a private charter service operated by US-based World Airways for the national oil company's subsidiary Sonair, and is available only to members of the US Africa Energy Association.

Sonair/World Airways – Houston Express

Todd Liggett,
Ground Security and Operations Coordinator,
Avenida 4 de Fevereiro
PO Box 1316, Luanda
Tel: +244-222-310972 / 912-517726
Fax: +244-222-310717
Email: sonair@support.ebonet.net
Website: www.sonairsarl.com

BY BUS

There are no bus links between Angola and other nations.

BY BOAT

No organized river-borne passenger transport companies operate in Angola today. There are no official ferry links between Angola and other nations. As of 2003 it was at least possible to enter Angola via a small passenger ferry near Rundu in Namibia. There was both an Angolan and Namibia border official present. The crossing was mostly used by Angolans for the purposes of acquiring food and other supplies in Namibia.

Kwanza bridge

International shipping can reach Angola via the ports of Luanda, Lobito, Namibe and Cabinda. Shipments bound for Angolan ports require a Certificado de Embarque, the loading certificate, to unload cargo upon arrival. It is the responsibility of the shipper to obtain the document prior to the cargo leaving port from the Conselho Nacional de Carregadores (CNC) representative at the port of origin. Most major shipping ports have a CNC representative from whom a loading certificate can be obtained.

BY CAR

Before driving into Angola, check with the Angolan embassy in your country which papers you need to show at the border. At the land borders you will not be able to get a visa, so it is better to obtain it from the appropriate embassy before travelling. You can enter from Namibia at the border post near Oshikango (Namibia)/Ngiva (Angola). Entering from the north was, as of 2002, via Luvo, a small town on the Kinshasa–Matadi 'road'.

Concerning road transportation, it is very important to highlight that of 72,000 kilometres of road, less than 20,000 is paved. Even some of the paved roads are unusable due to collapsed bridges and landmines, though most of the major roads linking provincial capitals have been de-mined. The general condition of all roads and related infrastructure is poor, even within the city limits of Luanda. Petrol is available in most urban areas. Rental cars are available for hire in Luanda and some major provincial cities. Driving outside of metropolitan areas can be dangerous due to poor road conditions, especially at night. Angolan car rental agencies have price schedules that vary depending upon length of rental and class of car. Most prices include insurance. An international driver's licence is not required but recommended. Hiring a local driver is highly recommended, as driving through unmarked streets, confusing routes and dangerous traffic can be a daunting task for a visiting traveller.

BY TRAIN

Little of the once extensive railway infrastructure currently functions due to war damage and destruction. The rail link to the port of Luanda is not currently operational; rehabilitation work is currently under way and temporarily interrupts service from Luanda to Viana (35 km). The Benguela railroad, which formerly ran 1,340 km from the Lobito port to the Zambian border, currently runs only 154 km between the cities of Lobito, Benguela and Cubal. Only the service between Namibe and Matala (320 km) comes close to pre-war levels. Rehabilitating the lines is a priority for the government of Angola.

RENTING A CAR

To rent a saloon car for one day costs approximately US $65–100, while hiring a 4x4 car can range from US $100–160. All car rental companies provide drivers for an additional US $30.

 For car rental companies please check the Business Resources section under Rent a Car.

ANGOLAN EMBASSIES ABROAD

Algeria
Rue Mohame Khoudi
Villa 12, El Bihar - Argel
Tel: +213-21-925337
Fax: +213-21-920418

Argentina
Ancoreta 1314 esq. Charcas
PO Box 1425, Buenos Aires
Tel: +54-11-48213999 / 48219559
Fax: +54-11-48213233 / 48210909

Austria
Seilerstätte 15, 1 stock Tür 10 A
PO Box 1010, Vienna
Tel: +43-1-7187488
Fax: +43-1-7187486 / 7148866

Belgium
Rue Franz Merjay, 182 - Brussels
Tel: +32-2-3461872 / 3468748
Fax: +32-2-3440894 / 3792809

Botswana
2715 Phala Crescent - Gaborone
Tel: +267-3900204 / 3905724 / 3974106
Fax:+267-3181876 / 3975089 / 3184599

Brasil
Shis Qi 09 Conjunto 16, House 23 Lago Sul - Brasilia
Tel: +55-61-2484489 / 6880
Fax: +55-61-2581567 / 3640291

Canada
Av. Laurier Av. East Ottawa - Ontario
Tel: +1-613-2341152
Fax: +1-613-2341179

Cape Verde
Av. da Oua Meio da Achada de Santo Antonio
PO Box 78-A, Praia, Ilha de Santiago
Tel: +2382-623235/6 / 613412 / 8825
Fax: +2382-623234 / 621503

China
Tayuan Diplomatic Office Building, 1-8-1/2
PO Box 100600, Beijing
Tel: +86-10-65326968/839 / 65327143
Fax: +86-10-62326990/69/92

Congo – Brazzaville
PO Box 388, Brazzaville
Tel: +242-814721 / 811561
Fax: +242-815287 / 394495

Congo – Kinshasa
Avenue du Boulevard du 30 Juin Nr. 44/13
Zona Gamboe - Kinshasa RDC
Tel: +243-12-33003 / 13-98972
Fax: +243-13-98971/ 8809376

Côte d'Ivoire
Commune de Cocody, Quartier 2, Plateaux Vallon
Rue des Jardins, Lot n° 2327 – 148 16
PO Box 1734-16, Abidjan
Tel: +225-22-413879 / 410343
Fax: +225-22-412889 / 418242

Cuba
5ª Av. N °s 1012/1008
PO Box 10/12, Miramar, La Habana
Tel: +537-2042474 / 2275 / 4391
Fax: +537-2040487 / 4390

Egypt
12 Midan Fouad, Mody Eldine, Mohandiseen - Cairo
Tel: +20-2-3377602 / 7498259
Fax: +20-2-3378683 / 3354968

Ethiopia
Bole Road, Woreda 18, Kebele 26, House N.006 - Addis Ababa
Tel: +25-11-510085 / 8114
Fax: +25-11-514922 / 528909

France
19 Avenue Foch
PO Box 75016, Paris
Tel: +33-1-45015820 / 45019496
Fax: +33-1-45003371 / 45000497

Gabon
Trois Quartier
PO Box 4884, Libreville
Tel: +241-730426 / 736855
Fax: +241-73724 / 1433

Germany
Wallstrasse, 58/59
PO Box 10179, Berlin
Tel: +49-30-2408970
Fax: +49-30-24089712

Great Britain
Dorset Street - London
Tel: +44-20-72999850 / 83479674
Fax: +44-20-74869397

Greece
Rua Elefterio venizelo n° 24, Zona de Filothei,
PO Box 15237, Athens
Tel: +30-210-6811811 / 994 / 6898681/2/3
Fax: +30-210-6898683

Hungary
Alkotas Utca 50
PO Box 1123, Budapest
Tel: +36-1-3253000 / 3253080
Fax: +36-1-3253006

India
5/50F, NyayaMarg, Chanakyapuri
PO Box 110-021, New Delhi
Tel: +91-11-26882680 / 26110701 / 5063480
Fax: +91-11-24673787 / 26882750 / 26113512

Israel
8, Shaul Hamelech Blvd, 13th Floor
PO Box 64733, Tel Aviv
Tel: +972-3-6912093 / 6912101 / 99510080
Fax: +972-3-6912094 / 2101 / 99518449

Italy
Via Filippo Bbernardoini, n° 21 - Roma
Tel: +39-06-39366902/941 / 30880957
Fax: +39-06-39366570 / 39388221

Japan
2-10-24, D aizawa, Setagaya Ku 155
PO Box 0032, Tokyo
Tel: +81-3-54307879/2/3/4/ 54307883
Fax: +81-3-57127481 / 57127482

Mexico
Schiller 503, Polanco
PO Box 11560, Méjico DF
Tel: +525-55-52943085 / 52024421
Fax: +525-55-5452733

Morocco
Route de Zares Km 45 Surissi - Rabat
Tel: +212-37-659239 / 756588
Fax: +212-37-653703 / 659238

Mozambique
Av. Kennete Kaunda n° 770 - Maputo
Tel: +258-1-493691/139 / 493271
Fax: +258-1-493930 / 499086 / 493928/30 / 485066

Namibia
Private Bag 12020-Ausspannplatz - Windhoek
Tel: +264-61-227535/1330 / 221339
Fax: +264-61-221498 / 229979 / 271444 / 220978

Nigeria
Plot-9, Pope John Paul II, off Ghana Str-Maitama - Abuja
Tel: +234-9-4134164/5 / 4135121
Fax: +234-9-4134082 / 4134136

Poland
Ul Balonwa 20
PO Box 02–635, Warsaw
Tel: +48-22-6467272/3529/9039 / 6465584
Fax: +48-22-8447452

Slovakia
Mudronova 47

81103, Bratislava
Tel: +421-2-54412164/5
Fax: +421-2-54412182

South Africa
1030 Schoeman Street, Hatfield 0083
PO Box 8685, Pretoria
Tel: +27-12-3420049 / 50
Tel: +27-12-3423671 / 3696 / 3424404
Fax: +27-12-3427039

Spain
C/Serrano, 64, 3° floor
PO Box 28001, Madrid
Tel: +34-91-4356430 / 168 / 64355150
Fax: +34-91-5779010 / 6501081

United States of America
12th Street NW 2100-2108
PO Box 20009, Washington DC
Tel: +1-202-7851156 / 7859584
Fax: +1-202-7851258 / 8229049

125 East 73rd Street
PO Box 10021, New York City
Tel: +1-212-8615656 / 8615787/8/9
Fax: +1-121-8619295 / 7256307 / 5355261

FOREIGN EMBASSIES IN ANGOLA

Algeria
Rua Joaquim Figueiredo n°34 - Luanda
Tel: +244-222-332881
Fax: +244-222-334785

Belgium
Av. 4° de Fevereiro n° 93, 3rd Floor - Luanda
Tel: +244-222-336436
Fax: +244-222-336337

Brazil
Rua Houari Boumedienne n°132, Miramar - Luanda
Tel: +244-222-430707 / 442871
Fax: +244-222-443275

i

Bulgaria
Rua Fernão Mendes Pinto n°35 - Luanda
Tel: +244-222-324094 / 324213
Fax: +244-222-321010

Cape Verde
Rua Oliveira Martins n° 3 - Luanda
Tel: +244-222-320412 / 321765
Fax: +244-222-320832

China
B° Alvalade - Luanda
Tel: +244-222-322803 / 444658
Fax: +244-222-444185

Congo
Av. 4° de Fevereiro n° 3 - Luanda
Tel: +244-222-310293
Fax: +244-222-31029

Côte d'Ivoire
Rua Eng° Armando Andrade n° 75 - Luanda
Tel: +244-222-440897 / 440878
Fax: +244 222-440997

Cuba
Rua Cmdt. Che Guevara n°42 - Luanda
Tel: +244-222-334275 / 330586
Fax: +244-222-339165

Czech Republic
Rua companhia de Jesus n° 43-35, Miramar - Luanda
Tel: +244-222-430646 / 441547
Fax: +244-222-447676

Democratic Republic of Congo
Rua Cesário Verde n° 23-25 - Luanda
Tel: +244-222-261953 / 263146
Fax: +244-222-263233

Egypt
Rua Cmdt. Stona n° 247, Alvalade - Luanda
Tel: +244-222-321590 / 320568
Fax: +244-222-323285

France
Rua Ver. Pedro Agostinho Neto - Luanda
Tel: +244-222-338035 / 330065
Fax: +244-222-334533 / 291949

Women of the Ilheus tribe

Gabon
Rua Engº Armindo Andrade nº 149 - Luanda
Tel: +244-222-449289
Fax: +244-222-449402

Germany
Av. 4 de Fevereiro nº 120 - Luanda
Tel: +244-222-334516 / 334773
Fax: +244-222-396358

Ghana
Rua Cirilo C. Silva nº 5 - Luanda
Tel: +244-222-339249 / 339222
Fax: +244-222-338235
Email: embassyghana@ebonet.net

Greece
Rua Rª Ginga nº 37 - Luanda
Tel: +244-222-335864
Fax: +244-222-335864

India
Rua Marques das Minas nº 18 - Luanda
Tel: +244-222-371060 / 371089
Fax: +244-222-371094
Email: indembluanda@ebonet.net

Israel
Rua Joaquim Figueiredo Ernesto nº 34 - Luanda
Tel: +244-222-397331 / 397901
Fax: +244-222-396366

Italy
Rua Americo Boavida - Luanda
Tel: +244-222-331245 / 393533
Fax: +244-222-333743 / 331245
Email: utl.luanda@esteril.it

Japan
Rua Samuel Bernardo - Luanda
Tel: +244-222-330834 / 330908

Mali
Rua Alf. Felner - Luanda
Tel: +244-222-430376 / 430716

Fax: +244-222-430716
Email: ambamali@netangola.com

Morocco
Rua Joaquim Figueiredo nº 34 - Luanda
Tel: +244-222-393708 / 310847
Fax: +244-222-338847

Mozambique
Rua Amilcar Cabral nº 102 - Luanda
Tel: +244-222-332883 / 331158
Fax: +244-222-34871
Email: embamoc.lda@netangola.com

Namibia
Rua dos Coqueiros nº 37 - Luanda
Tel: +244-222-339235 / 394730
Fax: +244-222-339234
Email: embnam@netangola.com

Nigeria
Rua Pres. Houari Boumedienne nº 120 - Luanda
Tel: +244-222-440084 / 440861
Fax: +244-222-440089

Norway
Rua de Cambambe nº 2 - Luanda
Tel: +244-222-447922 / 449248 / 449936

Poland
Rua Cmdt. N'Zanji nº 21, Alvalade - Luanda
Tel: +244-222-323086 / 323088
Fax: +244-222-323086

Portugal
Av. Portugal nº 50 - Luanda
Tel: +244-222-333443 / 390545
Fax: +244-222-390392

The Netherlands
Av. 4 de Fevereiro nº 110 - Luanda
Tel: +244-222-310686 / 311808
Fax: +244-222-310966

Slovakia
Rua Amilcar Cabral nº 5 - Luanda
Tel: +244-222-336229 / 331098
Fax: +244-222-333539

Romania
Rua Ramalho Ortigão nº 30, Alvalade - Luanda
Tel: +244-222-321076 / 322234
Fax: +244-222-321076
Email: ambromania@ebonet.net

Russia
Rua Pres. Houari Boumedienne nº170 - Luanda
Tel: +244-222-445028 / 449984
Fax: +244-222-445320 / 440041
Email: russemb@netangola.com

São Tomé e Príncipe
Av. Cmdt. Nzaji - Luanda
Tel: +244-222-326224 / 326251
Fax: +244-222-445677

Serbia & Montenegro
Rua Cmdt. nº 2 - Luanda
Tel: +244-222-320393
Fax: +244-222-321724

Spain
Av. 4 de Fevereiro nº 95, 1st Floor - Luanda
Tel: +244-222-391166 / 391187
Fax: +244-222-396993 / 392780

South Africa
Rua Kwamme N'Krumah nº 31 - Luanda
Tel: +244-222-333830 / 339566
Fax: +244-222-399126

South Korea
Rua Cabral Moncana nº 116, Alvalade - Luanda
Tel: +244-222-395575 / 323037
Fax: +244-222-323033

Swaziland
Rua da India nº 3 - Luanda
Tel: +244-222-442213 / 442934
Fax: +244-222-442934

Sweden
Rua Garcia Neto nº 9 - Luanda
Tel: +244-222-440424 / 440706
Fax: +244-222-443460 / 443476

Taiwan
Rua Murtala Mohamed nº 28 - Luanda
Tel: +244-222-398173
Fax: +244-222-398173

United Kingdom
Rua Diogo Cao nº 4 - Luanda
Tel: +244- 222-392991 / 334582
Fax: +244-222-333331
Email: postmaster.luanda@fco.gov.uk

United States of America
Rua Major Kanhangulo nº 136 - Luanda
Tel: +244-222-371645 / 371697
Fax: +244-222-446924

Vietnam
Rua Engrácia Fragoso - Luanda
Tel: +244- 222-390769 / 322828
Fax: +244-222-323389

Zambia
Rua Rei Katyavala nº 106/108
PO Box 1496, Maculusso, Luanda
Tel: +244-222-441634 / 47496
Fax: +244-222-441763
Email: embzambia@netangola.com

Zimbabwe
Av 4 de Fevereiro nº 42 - Luanda
Tel: +244-222-3118 66 / 310125 / 310683

BUSINESS RESOURCES

"Whoever runs can get a dinner"
Angolan proverb

ADVERTISING AGENCIES

Dread Locks
Avenida Comandante Gika, n° 199
Predio da OMA - Luanda
Tel: +244-222-320381 / 320399
Fax: +244-222-320399
Email: dreadlocks@snet.co.ao

 EAL - Edições de Angola
Rua Vereador Prazeres, n° 41-43
Bairro de São Paulo - Luanda
Tel: +244-222-442899 / 442109
Email: edicoesdeangola@yahoo.com

Fepel
Rua Gil da Liberdade, n° 7
Bairro Comandante Valodia - Luanda
Tel: +244-222-442190 / 449324
Fax: +244-222-448 640
Email: fepel@nexus.ao.fepel
Website: www.fepel.net

Imprima
Rua Conego Manuel das Neves, n° 160, 1st Floor
Luanda
Tel: +244-222-447729
Fax: +244-222-446806
Email: imprima@snet.co.ao

Link
Rua Emilio M'bidi, n° 199 / 121 - Luanda
Tel: +244-222-325584 / 325462
Fax: +244-222-325606
Email: marketinglink@netangola.com

Movimento
Largo Che Guevara, n° 18 - Luanda
Tel: +244-222-37351 / 394019
Fax: + 244-222-4867
Email: movimento@snet.co.ao

 Orion
Rua Praceta Farinha Leitão, n° 27, 3rd Floor
PO Box 10100, Luanda
Tel: +244-222-339-442/3/4
Fax: +244-222-392703
Email: orion@netangola.com

Ponto Um
Rua Sebastiao Desta Vez, n° 55 - Luanda
Tel: +244-222-430506
Fax: +244-222-448315

Silnor
Rua Francisco Necessidades Castelo Branco, n° 51-A
Luanda
Tel: +244-222-331868

AIR CHARTER

AAC Angola Air Charter
Aeroporto 4 de Fevereiro - Luanda
Tel: +244-222-320773 / 321290 / 323559
Fax: +244-222-320773 / 320105
Email: ang-aircharter@ebonet.net

Angolan Air Service, Lda.
Terminal Doméstico - Aeroporto
Airport of Luanda - Luanda
Tel: +244-222-327087
Fax: +244-222-327710

Air Gemini
Rua Guilherme Pereira Ingles, n° 43, 3rd Floor
Bairro Largo da Ingombota - Luanda
Tel: +244-222-355511 / 355779 / 336405 / 336426
Fax: +244-222-335511 / 336199 / 336495
Email: arigemini@ebonet.net
Website: www.airgemini.com

SAL Sociedade de Aviação Ligeira
Aeroporto 4 de Fevereiro
PO Box 2590, Luanda
Tel: +244-222-351044 / 354987 / 351162
Fax: +244-222-395477
Email: sal@snet.co.ao

SonAir

Aeroporto Internacional 4 de Fevereiro - Luanda

Tel: +244-222-633502

Fax: +244-222-633600

Email: sonair@sonabgol.co.ao

Website: www.sonangol.co.ao/info_sonairsarl_p.html

RECOMMENDED PARTNER TAAG - Linhas Aerias de Angola

Aeroporto 4 de Fevereiro

Rua da Missão, n° 123, 11th Floor - Luanda

Tel: +244-222-633614 / 327112 / 633663 / 334889

Fax: + 244-222-327494 / 327314 / 327494

BANKS

In general banks are open Monday–Friday, from 800 a.m to 1500 p.m, and sometimes on Saturday mornings. (Please check with your local branch)

BAI - Banco Africano de Investimentos

Rua Major Kanhangulo, n° 34

PO Box 6022, Luanda

Tel: +244-222-335127 / 335749 / 336579

Fax: +244-222-335486 / 393780

Email: baisede@bai.ebonet.net

Website: www.bancobai.co.ao

BCA - Banco Comercial Angolano

Avenida Comandante Valódia, n° 83ª - Luanda

Tel: +244-222-449548 / 449517

Fax: +244-222-449516

Email: bca@snet.co.ao

BCI - Banco de Comércio e Indústria

Rua Rainha Ginga, Largo do Atlético, n° 78/79 - Luanda

Tel: +244-222-331174 / 331498

Fax: +244-222-331498

Email: secretariado@bci.ebonet.net

BES - Banco Espírito Santo Angola

Rua Guilherme Pereira Inglês, n° 43, 1st Floor

Largo das Ingombotas - Luanda

Tel: +244-226-693600

Fax: +244-226-693698

Email: besangola@angola.bes.pt

BFA - Banco de Fomento de Angola

Rua Amílcar Cabral n° 58, Maianga - Luanda

Tel: +244-222-638900 / 638900

Fax: +244-222-638970

Website: www.bfa.ao/ www.bfanet.ao

Banco BIC

Rua Cerqueira Lukoki, n° 79/81 - Luanda

Tel: +244-222-391816

Fax: +244-222-391274

Website: www.bancobic.ao

Banco Millenium - BCP

Rua Rainha Ginga, n° 83 - Luanda

Tel: +244-222-397946 / 335399

Fax: +244-222-335237 / 397397

Website: www.millenniumbcp.pt

Banco Mundial em Angola

Rua Alfredo Trony, Prédio da BPC 15 - Luanda

Tel: +244-222-394677/4727

Fax: +244-222-394784

Email: worldbank@ebonet.net

BNA - Banco Nacional de Angola

Avenida 4 de Fevereiro, n° 51

PO Box 1243, Luanda

Tel: +244-222-339143/41

Fax: +244-222-390579

BNP Paribas

Rua Dr. Alfredo Tróni, Prédio da BPC, n° 18

PO Box 1385, Luanda

Tel: +244-222-391890 / 390877

Fax: +244-222-392339

RECOMMENDED PARTNER BPC - Banco de Poupança e Crédito

Largo Saidy Mingas

PO Box 1373, Luanda

Tel: +244-222-390241

Fax: +244-222-393790

Email: bpc@bpc.ebonet.net

Website: www.bpc.ao

Banco Regional do Keve
Rua Rainha Ginga, nº 77 - Luanda
Tel: +244-222-394100
Fax: +244-222-394812
Email: servicoscentrais@bankeve.com
Website: www.bankeve.com

Banco Sol
Rua Amilcar Cabral, nº 133 - Luanda
Tel: +244-222-440340
Fax: +244-222-394968

Banco Totta de Angola
Avenida 4 de Fevereiro, nº 99
PO Box 1231, Luanda
Tel: +244-226-670800
Fax: +244-222-372710
Email: agencia.sede@tottang.co.ao

 In general the Banks are open Monday to Friday from 0800 to 1500. Be aware of the huge queues. Take your time!

CARGO

Air Cargo Center Angola – ACCA
Rua Mártires do Kifangondo, nº 74 - Luanda
Tel: +244-222-324583/84/85
Fax: +244-222-324586
Email: voangol@ebonet.net

ATS
Rua Amílcar Cabral, nº13 (247) - Luanda
Tel: +244-222-398252
Fax: +244-222-390275
Email: airsea@snet.co.ao

Cargo – Sociedade de Transportes, Lda.
Estrada do Cacuaco, Km. 7 - Luanda
Tel: +244-222-840011

Cargo Team
Rua Amílcar Cabral, nº 23
PO Box 5589, Luanda

Tel: +244-222-394800/805/807/903
Fax: +244-222-394900

Central Freight & Cargo Services
Aeroporto 4 de Fevereiro
PO Box 3889, Luanda
Tel: +244-222-264662
Fax: +244-222-264662

ETRAM Air Wing
Avda. Revolução de Outubro, nº 16
Rua da Missão, n º 93 r/c - Luanda
Tel: +244-222-350039 / 353594
Fax: +244-222-350042
Email: etram@snet.co.ao

Hull Blyth Angola
Avd. 4 de Fevereiro, nº 23-24
PO Box 1214, Luanda
Tel: +244-222-310621
Fax: +244-222-310029
Email: hbs1@hullblyth-angola.com

Maersk - Sealand
Rua Major Kanhangulo, nº 290 - Luanda
Tel: +244-222-395114 / 395630 / 394281
Fax: +244-222-399388 / 399237
Email: angsal@maersk.com
Website: www.maersk.com

Miraset
Rua Amilcar Cabral, nº 1 - Luanda
Tel: +244-222-372458
Fax: +244-222-372455

NDS - Nile Dutch Africa Line
Rua Cirilo Conceição Silva, nº 13 - Luanda
Tel: +244-222-339187 / 339340
Fax: +244-222-395729
Email: nds@ebonet.net

 Panalpina
Rua Kima Kienda, nº 106, Boa Vista,
PO Box 3682, Luanda
Tel: +244-226-691000

Luanda Port

Fax: +244-222-310034
Email: ladcy@panalpina.com

Porto de Luanda
Av. 4 de Fevereiro
PO Box 1229, Luanda
Tel: +244-222-310655 / 310074 / 335972
Fax: +244-222-311178 / 310355

SDV - AMI
Estrada do Cacuaco, n° 288 - Luanda
Tel: +244-222-840936 / 841266 / 840688
Fax: +244-222-840535 / 840585 / 840760
Email: ami@ami.ebonet.net
Website: www.sdv.com

CATERERS

Many of the main hotels have an outside catering facility; just call the banqueting department of the hotel of your choice for more information.

(For hotel listings see Leisure Section)

Cafago - Catering
Esplanada do Teatro Avenida - Luanda
Tel: +244-222-449543
Cell phone: +244-923-937085

Casa 70
Rua da Liberdade, n° 70, Vila Alice - Luanda
Tel: +244-222-265004
Fax: +244-222-260467
Email: casa70@netangola

NOTICE! Portions are really big. Be careful about how much you order!

Catering – Hotel Continental
Rua Rainha Ginga, n° 18/21
PO Box 5150, Luanda
Tel: +244-222-334243 / 396599
Fax: +244-222-392735
Email: reservas@hcontinental.org
Website: www.hcontinental.org

Catering - Hotel Forum
Rua Ho Chi Min - Luanda
Tel: +244-222-321858/82
Fax: +244-222-322193
Email: hotelforum@netangola.com

Catering - Radio Vial
Rua Mãe Isabel, n° 8, Ingombota - Luanda
Tel: +244-912-501440 / 923-400151
Fax: +244-222-316380/217/049

RECOMMENDED PARTNER Catering - Restaurante Tambarino
Rua Amilca Cabral, n° 23 r/c - Luanda
Tel: +244-222-397343 / 396884
Cell phone: +244-924-549156

RECOMMENDED Catering - Restaurante Veneza
Rua Comandante Che Guevara,
n°116 / 20 - Luanda
Tel: +244-222-320 954 / 328184
Fax: +244-222-320954
Cell phone: +244-912-200135
E-mail: rest.veneza@netangola.com

Catering S.A.
Rua Moisés Alves Pinho, n° 6/7 - Luanda
Tel: +244-222-320593 / 352181
Fax: +244-222-390933

Catermar Angola
Rua Pedro Félix Machado, n° 51, 2nd Floor
PO Box 1716, Luanda
Tel: +244-222-330668 / 391235

Fax: +244-222-330982
Email: catladsec@aol.com

Complexo Hoteleiro da Endiama – CHE
Rua Houari Boumediene, n° 66/68, Miramar,
PO Box 5589, Luanda
Tel: +244-222-447954/9852
Fax: +244-222-446937

CONFERENCE FACILITIES

Most of the main hotels have conference facilities available, with a variety of packages. Call the sales department of the hotel of your choice for further information.

(For more hotel information, see Leisure)

There are conference facilities at the following centres:

Hotel Alvalade
Avenida Comandante Gika - Luanda
Tel: +244-222-327470
Fax: +244-222-327480
Email: geral@halvalade.mstelcom.com
Website: reservas@halvalade.mstelcom.com

RECOMMENDED Hotel Continental
Rua Rainha Ginga, n° 18/21
PO Box 5150, Luanda
Tel: +244-222334243 / 396599
Fax: +244-222-392735
Email: reservas@hcontinental.org
Website: www.hcontinental.org

Hotel Forum
Rua Ho Chi Min - Luanda
Tel: +244-222-321858/82
Fax: +244-222-322193
Email: hotelforum@netangola.com

Hotel Presidente
Largo 4 de Fevereiro - Luanda
Tel: +244-222-330041
Fax: +244-222-331141

Hotel Tivoli
Rua da Missão, n° 85
PO Box 2049, Luanda
Tel: +244-222-392292 / 393890 / 393897
Fax: +244-222-335644 / 391128

Hotel Trópico
Rua da Missão,n° 103 - Luanda
Tel: +244-222-370070
Fax: +244-222-393330 / 391798
Email: tropico@netangola.com

Restaurante Tamariz
Rua Mortala Mohamed, Ilha do Cabo - Luanda
Tel: +244-222-309485

COURIER EXPRESS

Correios de Angola
PO Box 3202, Luanda
Tel: +244-222-337575
Fax: +244-222-337628
Email: encta.sec@ebonet.net

The Angolan postal service is cheap but not very reliable. If you want something a little faster and more secure try one of the following express courier services:

DHL Express
Rua Kwame Nkrumah, n° 274 / 276, Luanda
Tel: +244-222-395180
Fax: +244-222-390326
Email: ladreq@dhl.com
Website: www.dhl.co.ao

Federal Express
Represented by Saga Expres c/o AMI - Luanda
Tel: +244-222-447575
Website: www.fedex.com/ao

Make sure the courier will take care of clearing customs for your merchandise. This is not an easy task in Angola!

Secil Marítima
Avenida 4 de Fevereiro
PO Box 5910, Luanda
Tel: +244-222-311334 / 310950
Fax: +244-222-311784
Email: secilmar@snet.co.ao

Tropicana
Av. Comandante Valódia, n° 199 - Luanda
Tel: +244-222-444099
Fax: +244-222-440283
Cell phone: +244-912-506330
Email: tropicana@ebonet.net

World Travel Agency
Avenida 4 de Fevereiro, n° 39 - Luanda
Tel: +244-222-310772 / 310972 / 310496
Fax: +244-222-310717
Email: wta.resa@netangola.com

DENTAL SERVICES

Anglodente Policlínica
Rua de Karipande, 1 trav., Maianga - Luanda
Tel: +244-222-337919 / 336445
Fax: +244-222-398007
Email: anglodente@netangola.com

Biodente Clínica
Largo Che Guevara n°4, Maculusso - Luanda
Tel: +244-222-396095
Fax: +244-222-391201

Clínica Clidopa
Avenida Rainha Ginga, n° 98/106
PO Box 10449, Luanda
Tel: +244-222-391488
Fax: +244-222-332933
Email: clidopa@snet.co.ao

Clínica Multiperfil
Rua Morro Bento - Luanda
Tel: +244-222-469447 / 469450
Fax: +244-222-469446
Email: clinicamultiperfil@yahoo.com

RECOMMENDED PARTNER Clínica Sagrada Esperança

Avenida Mortala Mohamed,
Ilha do Cabo - Luanda
Tel: +244-222-309688 / 309034
Fax: +244-222-309033
Email: sagradaesp@ebonet.net

DRY CLEANERS

RECOMMENDED A Lavandaria
Rua Rei Katiavala, nº 87-B - Luanda
Tel: +244-222-444733
Fax: +244-222-370630
Email: alavandaria@netangola.com

CBS – Mexicana
Also shoe repairs
Av. Portugal, nº 77, Ingombotas - Luanda
Tel: +244-222-334872

Eco Seco
Rua Che Guevara, nº 65, Maculusso - Luanda
Tel: +244-222-397585

Nalseb
Jardins de Talatona-T.Amarela-C/D - Luanda Sul
Tel: +244-222-460501
Cell phone: +244-923-406178

FOREX BUREAUS

Casa de Cambios de Luanda
Rua Rainha Ginga, nº 9
PO Box 3185, Luanda
Tel: +244-222-331357
Fax: +244-222-336107

Lider
Rua Rei Katyavala, nº 160 - Luanda
Tel: +244-222-335040
Fax: +244-222-335040

Novacambios
Rua Comandante Valodia, nº 24 - Luanda
Tel: +244-222-448426 / 442653
Fax: +244-222-442653

RECOMMENDED Universal Cambios
Rua da Missão 87 - Luanda
Tel: +244-222-370419 / 333747 / 392482
Fax: +244-222-335500
Cell phone: +244-923-557650
Email: universalcambios@nexus.ao

Western Union
Banco BCI
Avenida 4 de Fevereiro, nº 86
PO Box 1395, Luanda
Tel: +244-222-330372
Fax: +244-222-391184

Xamisso
Rua Comandante Che Guevara, nº 61 - Luanda
Tel: +244-222-331711
Fax: +244-222-395477

HAIR & BEAUTY

Any
Avenida Lenin, nº 86 - Luanda
Tel: +244-222-331020
Cell phone: +244-912-510624

As Freitinhas
Rua Fernando Pessõa, nº 108-B - Luanda
Tel: +244-222-322514
Fax: +244 222-322514
Cell phone: +244 923-509669

RECOMMENDED Bamboo Imperial
Hair - Beauty & Massages
Rua General Roçadas, nº 43 - Luanda
Tel: +244-222-394716
Fax: +244-222-394673
Cell: +244-923-546385
Email: bambooimperial@snet.co.ao

 Better to book in advance, especially during weekends.

Belita
Rua Rainha Ginga, n° 18, 2nd Floor
PO Box 923, Luanda
Tel: +244-222-337439

Carpoli Cabeleireiro & Boutique
Rua Joaquim Rodrigues da Graça, n.° 39 - Luanda
Tel: +244-222-355796
Fax: +244-222-355796
Email: carpoli@nexus.ao

Deana Beleza e Lingerie
Rua Joaquim Kapango, n° 53 - Luanda
Tel: +244-222-395567

Madrid
Rua Capelo Ivens, n° 22-Apart 11
Luanda
Tel: +244-222-331108

Matos
Rua Massacres, n° 90
PO Box 16117, Luanda
Tel: +244-222-442330

HEALTH CLUBS

Fisico, Saúde & Estética
Rua Alyone Blond Eye,
Miramar - Luanda
Tel: +244-222-430754
Cell phone: +244-923-503978

Fisico, Saúde & Estética
Gym

Fitness Club
Rua do Massangano, Anangola - Luanda
Tel: +244-222-446361 / 448449
Cell phone: +244-923-416646 / 923-304749
Email: fitness@netcabo.co.ao
Website: www.fitnessangola.com

Gym - Trópico Hotel
Rua da Missão, n° 103 - Luanda
Tel: +244-222-370070
Fax: +244-222-393330 / 391798
Email: tropico@netangola.com

Outdoor sport is a popular pastime

Konceito

Rua Ho Chi Minh, Bairro Militar - Luanda

Cell phone: +244-923-710001 / 912-240884

HOTELS

 (See Leisure section)

INSURANCE

A.A.A. – Seguros e Pensões

RECOMMENDED PARTNER Rua Lenine, nº 58

PO Box 505, Luanda

Tel: +244-222-691283 / 691336

Fax: +244-222-370709 / 691342

Website: www.aaa.ao

ENSA - Seguros de Angola

Avenida 4 de Fevereiro, nº 93 - Luanda

Tel: +244-222-671671 / 332948

Fax: +244-222-671674

Email: segurado@ensa.co.ao

G+A – Global Alliance

Avenida 4 de Fevereiro, nº 79, 1st Floor - Luanda

Tel: +244-222-330368/0425

Fax: +244-222-398815

Email: rlewis@globalalliance.co.ao

GF - Gestão de Fundos, SARL

Avenida 4 de Fevereiro, nº 95, 1st Floor - Luanda

Tel: +244-222-334990

Fax: +244-222-333391

Email: gfundos@ebonet.net

NOSSA

Avenida 4 de Fevereiro, nº 111 - Luanda

Tel: +244-222-399909 / 399929

Fax: +244-222-399153

Website: www.nossaseguros.com

To stay longer term, renting a house is also an alternative

INTERNET PROVIDERS

ACS - Angola Comunicações & Sistemas, Lda.
Avenida de Portugal, nº 14, Mutamba - Luanda
Website: www.acs.ao

Jembas – Multichoice
JAT - Assistência Técnica, Lda.
Largo do Soweto, nº 88
PO Box 10013, Luanda
Tel: +244-222-637000 / 638376
Fax: +244-222-637038
Email: jembas@jembas.com
Website: www.jembas.com

Nexus - Mstelcom
Rua do Enganos, nº 1, 1st Floor, Kinaxixi - Luanda
Tel: +244-222-740020 / 397540 / 397471
Fax: +244-222-390995
Website: www.nexus.ao

Pacon
Rua dos Enganos, nº 23 - Luanda
Tel: +244-222-334329 / 336533
Fax: +244-222-390995
Email: ebonetdg@ebonet.net
Website: www.ebonet.net

Sistec
RECOMMENDED PARTNER
Avenida Che Guevara, nº 189-195
PO Box 3245, Luanda
Tel: +244-222-333140 / 325350
Fax: +244-222-325372
Email: netangola@netangola.com
Website: www.netangola.com

LANGUAGE CENTRES

Alliance Française
Largo Sagrada Familia - Luanda
Tel: +244-222-321993 / 320635
Email: afluanda@ebonet.net

English School Community
Rua Cambambe nº 21-23 - Luanda
Tel: +244-222-443416 / 443020
Fax: +244-222-443326
Cell phone: +244-912-505945
Email: escola@netangola.com

Gestinfor
Rua Rainha Ginga, nº 30, r/c
PO Box 1136, Luanda
Tel: +244-222-395199 / 394009
Fax: +244-222-396999 / 395199
Email: centroformacao@gestinfor-ao.com
Website: www.gestinfor-ao.com

Instituto de Linguas

iL Institute of Languages Luanda

RECOMMENDED PARTNER
Rua Amílcar Cabral, Maianga
PO Box 3488, Luanda
Tel: +244-222-394887
Fax: +244-222-394484
Cell phone: +244-912-519011
Email: ilinguas@snet.co.ao

J.I. Training Centre
Av. Comandante Valódia nº 147 - Luanda
Tel: +244-222-440321
Fax: +244-222-449706
Email: kwanganet@eclipse.ao

Luanda Communication Centre
Largo do Kinaxixi, nº 14 - Luanda
Tel: +244-222-444525
Fax: +244-222-444525
Email: lcc@ebonet.net

LEGAL SERVICES

A Ordem dos Advogados de Angola – OAA
Angolan Bar Association
Rua Ho Chi Min, Edf. da Estatística, 1st Floor - Luanda

Tel: +244-222-322777 / 326330
Fax: +244 222-322777
Email: ordemadvogadosangola@netangola.com
Website: www.oaang.org

Ana Paula Godinho
Rua Marechal Brós Tito n° 90 r/c - Luanda
Tel: +244-222-446174 / 442457
Cell phone: +244-912-501420
Email: agodinho@netangola.com

Carlos Freitas
Rua Samuel Bernardo, n° 13/15 - Luanda
Tel: +244-222-399423
Cell phone: +244-912-500792

Escritório de Advogados
Orlando Ferreira, Teresa Azenayda Cardoso Canda
Largo Matadi Radista, n° 22, 1st- Ingombotas - Luanda
Tel: +244-233-4038
Fax: +244-239-8940
Email: teresazenayda@snet.co.ao

Faria de Bastos
Rua dos Enganos, n° 1 - Luanda
Tel: +244-222-397073
Cell phone: +244-923-405899

Francisco Queiros
Rua Marien N'Guabi, 101 r/c B - Luanda
Tel: +244-222-332466
Cell phone: +244-912-502925

Graça Pitra Costa
Boulevard Nelito Soares,
Rua Baltazar de Aragão, n° 77/79 - Luanda
Tel: +244-222-395050
Cell phone: +244-912-507131

 Inglés Pinto & Associados
Avenida Comandante Valódia
Ex-Combatentes, n° 182, 1st Floor - Luanda
Tel: +244-222-441955
Fax: +244-222-441955

Cell phone: +244-923-595092
Email: inglespinto@snet.co.ao

Manuel Gonçalves
Rua Rainha Ginga, n° 80, 1st Floor 677 - Luanda
Tel: +244-222-337914 / 343177
Cell phone: +244-923-311600

Pulqueria Van-Dunem
Rua Padre Manuel Ruela Pombo, n° 24, 1st Floor, Apt.13- Luanda
Tel: +244-222-357227 / 356721
Cell phone: +244-912-50403 / 923-486548

Terezinha Lopes
Rua Comandante Gika n° 199-E - Luanda
Tel: +244-222-339379 / 370370
Cell phone: +244-912-500950

Victorino Hossi
Rua Dr. José Pereira do Nascimento, n° 30/32 - Luanda
Tel: +244-912-505699

MEDIA

ANGOP – Agência Angolana Press
Rua Rei Katyavala, n° 16, 3rd Floor - Luanda
Tel: +244-222-447331 / 447504
Fax: +244-222-446848
Email: angop@netangola.com
Website: www.angolapress-angop.ao

Ajeco – Associação de Jornalistas Económicos de Angola
Rua Robert Chields, n° 25 - Luanda
Tel: +244-222-393480
Fax: +244-222-370749
Email:ajecoangola@yahoo.com.br

Inacom – Instituto Angolano das Comunicações
Avenida de Portugal, n° 92, 7th Floor
PO Box 1459, Luanda
Tel: +244-222-337011 / 338352
Fax: +244-222-339356
Email: inacom.dg@netangola.com
Website:www.inacom.og.ao

48

 **Jornal de Angola**
Rua Rainha Ginga, nº 18/24
PO Box 1312, Luanda
Tel: +244-222-338947 / 335531
Fax: +244-222-333342
Email: jornaldeangola@netangola.com
Website: www.jornaldeangola.com

Radio Ecclésia
Rua Comandante Bula, nº 118 - Luanda
Tel: +244-222-445484 / 446105
Fax: +244-222-443093
Email: ecclesia@snet.co.ao

Radio Luanda
Avenida Comandante Gika - Luanda
Tel: +244-222-320575 / 324436
Fax: +244-222-326872

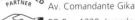 **Radio Nacional de Angola**
Av. Comandante Gika
PO Box 1329, Luanda
Tel: +244-222-321258 / 321056
Fax: +244-222-324647 / 323172

Press Center- Aníbal de Melo
Centro de Imprensa
Rua Cerqueira Lukoki - Luanda

TPA - Televisão Pública de Angola
Avenida Ho Chi Min
PO Box 2604, Luanda
Tel: +244-222-320025/26
Fax: +244-222-326359 / 323622
Cell phone: +244-912-504362
Email: tpa.angola@netangola.com
Website: www.tpa.ao

MEDICAL SERVICES

 Clínica Clidopa
 Avenida Rainha Ginga, nº 98/106
PO Box 10449, Luanda
Tel: +244-222-391488
Fax: +244-222-332933
Email: clidopa@snet.co.ao

Clínica da Mutamba
Rua Engrancia Fragoso, 1 Prédio Fiscal, Mutamba - Luanda
Tel: +244-222- 394086
Fax: +244-222- 393783
Email: medigroup@netangola.com

Clínica Espiritu Santo
Rua da Liberdade 15, Vila Alice - Luanda
Tel: +244-222-321608 / 324135
Fax: +244-222-322888
Cell phone: +244-912-246090
Email: ves@netangola.com

Clínica Sagrada Esperança, Luanda

Clínica Fisiomed
Rua Eduardo Mondlaine n° 41 /43, Maianga - Luanda
Tel: +244-222-396924

Clínica Grande Muralha da China
Travesa Alexandre Peres, n °12-14 - Luanda
Tel: +244-222-376240
Fax: +244-222-370240

Clínica Meditex
Rua da Missão, n° 52, Ingombotas - Luanda
Tel: +244-222-392803
Fax: +244-222-331753

Clínica Multiperfil
Avenida 21 de Janeiro, Futungo de Belas
Morro Bento - Luanda
Tel: +244-222-469447 / 469449
Fax: +244-222-469446 / 469446
Email: clinicamultiperfil@yahoo.com

Clínica Muserra
Rua João Seca, n° 12, Maianga - Luanda
Tel: +244-222-393367 / 370209
Fax: +244-222-331569 / 370240
Email: clinicamusserra@snet.co.ao

Clínica Privada do Alvalade
Rua Emilio M'Bidi, n° 20
PO Box 2687, Luanda
Tel: +244-222-323540 / 324557
Fax: +244-222-324757 / 323753
Email: clinica@netangola.com

RECOMMENDED PARTNER **Clínica Sagrada Esperança**

Avenida Mortala Mohamed, Ilha do Cabo
- Luanda
Tel: +244-222-309688 / 309034 / 309379 / 309687
Fax: +244-222-309033
Email: sagradaesp@ebonet.net

Clínica Soclimedic
Rua Marqués das Minas, n° 9 Baixo - Luanda
Tel: +244-222-338498

Hospital Américo Boa Vida
Avenida Hoji Ya Henda - Luanda
Tel: +244-222-383362 / 383462
Fax: +244-222-380117

Hospital do Gamek
Estrada de Viana, Km 9 - Luanda
Tel: +244-222-677112
Fax: +244-222-446836
Email: hospitalgamek@msn.com

Hospital Maria Pia - Josina Machel
Rua Amílcar Cabral - Luanda
Tel: +244-222-336346 / 336133 / 338174
Fax: +244-222-336349

Hospital Militar Principal/Instituto Superior
Rua do Hospital Militar
Tel: +244-222-322235 / 322220
Fax: +244-222-322315/17
Email: hosmilp@netangola.com

OFFICE SUPPORT

ECIL
Av. 4 de Fevereiro, n° 35/36 - Luanda
Tel: +244-222-310411 / 311799
Fax: +244-222-310961
Email: ecil@ecil.angola.com

ENCISA
Rua Major Kanhangulo, n° 99 - Luanda
Tel: +244-222-332385 / 332331
Fax: +244-222-391991
Email: encisa@ebonet.net

FAMO
Rua Cirilo da Conceição e Silva, n° 88 - Luanda
Tel: +244-222-339963
Fax: +244-222-331713
Email: famo@ebonet.net
Website: www.famo.pt

Gestoffice, Lda.
Largo do Lumege, n° 11/13 - Luanda
Tel: +244-222-334338
Fax: +244-222-335346
Email: gestoffice@acs.ao

Livraria Lelo
Rua Rainha Ginga, n° 7 - Luanda
Tel: +244-222-395730
Fax: +244-222-370809

NCR – Material de Escritório e Informática
Rua do 1° Congresso do MPLA, n° 7/9 - Luanda
Tel: +244-222-338641
Fax: +244-222-338642

 Papelaria Fernandes
Largo da Lumeji, n° 11-13 - Luanda
Tel: +244-222334338 / 335398 / 336598
Fax: +244-222-335346

Rocha Monteiro Lda.
Rua Rainha Ginga, n° 69
PO Box 2815, Luanda
Tel: +244-222-334394/95
Fax: +244-222-332979 / 335145
Email: romo@ebonet.net

Socotec
Avenida Comandante Valodia, n° 72
PO Box 5579, Luanda
Tel: +244-222-441459 / 442065 / 446605
Fax: +244-222-441459

PHARMACIES

Farmácia Boa Vida
Rua Dr. Américo Boa Vida, n° 131 - Luanda
Tel: +244-222-331867
Fax: +244-222-394826
E-mail: sogec@snet.co.ao

Farmácia Coqueiros
Rua Rainha Ginga, n° 33 - Luanda
Tel: +244-222-333073

Farmácia do Cruzeiro
Rua Cónego Manuel das Neves, n° 208 - Luanda
Tel: +244-222-441782
Fax: +244-222-446453

Farmácia Kalandula
Rua Comandante Che Guevara, n° 51-B - Luanda
Tel: +244-222-399429

Farmácia Kinaxixi
Rua Comandante Valódia, n° 23, r/c - Luanda
Tel: +244-222-448588
Fax: +244-222-449443

Farmácia Maianga
Rua Kwame N'kruma, n° 38/40
PO Box 921, Luanda
Tel: +244-222-332177

Farmácia Novic
Rua Amílcar Cabral, n° 19-A - Luanda
Tel: +244-222-332175
Fax: +244-222-393045

Farmácia Pague Menos
Rua da Samba, n° 20 - Luanda
Tel: +244-222-358925 / 396120
Cell phone: +244-923-328746

Farmácia Sarita
Rua Liga Nacional Africana, n° 58 - Luanda
Tel: +244-222-447102

NOTICE! Please be aware that some very specific medicines are difficult to find. It will help if you can bring the generic names with you!

REAL ESTATE

Caninvest
Rua Helder Neto, n° 10 B - Luanda
Tel: +244-222-321431
Fax: +244-222-321431

Grupo Polangol
Avenida Amílcar Cabral, n° 165, r/c - Luanda
Tel: +244-222-390502
Website: www.polangolimobiliaria.com

Imobiliaria Atlántico
Casa do Desportista, 3ª Porta, 1st Floor - Luanda
Tel: +244-222-309049
Fax: +244-222-309050

Imogestin
Rua Amílcar Cabral, n° 40, 1st Floor - Luanda
Tel: +244-222-370795 / 370728
Fax: +244-222-370684
Cell phone: +244-912-511701
Email: imogestin@ebonet.net

Loangos Associados
Rua Rainha Ginga, n° 16-1 - Luanda
Tel: +244-222-331403
Fax: +244-222-338932

 Real State: while renting or during be aware of the extremely High Prices!

REMOVALS

Antonio O. Madaleno
Av. 4 de Feveiro, 16, 2nd Floor - Luanda
Tel: +244-222-311123
Fax: +244-222-311629

David José de Moura
Avenida da Independência, n° 75, r/c - Luanda
Tel: +244-222-222386
Fax: +244-222-225085
Email: davidmoura@netangola.com

Eduardo Pitta-Grós
Rua 28 de Maio, n° 54 - Luanda
Tel: +244-222-336185
Fax: +244-222-331647
Email: pitta-gros@ebonet.net

Fausto Mesquita Morais
Av. 4 de Feveiro, n° 50, 1st Floor - Luanda
Tel: +244-222-337103
Fax: +244-222-397352
Email: fmorais@snet.co.ao

Pedro Hespanhol
R. Major Kanhangulo, 147, 1st Floor - Luanda
Tel: +244-222-311550
Fax: +244-222-354700

RENT A CAR

Avis
Av. Comandante Che Guevara, n° 250
Maculusso - Luanda
Tel: +244-222-321551 / 323182
Fax: +244-222-321620 / 323515
Email: avis.angola@netangola.com
Website: www.avis.com

Boa-Boa
Rua Dr. Antonio Saldanha, n° 1/3, Ingonbotas - Luanda
Tel: +244-222-396105
Fax: +244-222-371068

Equador
Largo Tristão da Cunha, n° 10/11
PO Box 2430, Luanda
Tel: +244-222-330746 / 390720 / 332889
Fax: +244-222-330747
Email: equador@netangola.com

Europcar

 RECOMMENDED PARTNER Rua Domingos Tchekahanga n° 18 - Luanda
Tel: +244-222-396995 / 390837 / 397342
Fax: +244-222-394080

Eurostral

Rua Marechal Broz Tito, n° 27, 1st Floor, Kinaxixi - Luanda

Tel: +244-222-441617 / 449525 / 444865

Fax: +244-222-443022

Mobile: +244-923-301453

Email: eurostral@snet.co.ao

Hertz

Rua Pedro Felix Machado, n° 51, 2nd Floor

PO Box 1716, Luanda

Tel: +244-222-330668 / 330669

Fax: +244-222-330982

Mãe Mena

Rua 4 de Fevereiro, n° 95, 2nd Floor, Door 25 - Luanda

Tel: +244-222-391261 / 338578

Email: mae.mena@nexus.ao

 NOTICE! We recommend renting a Car & Driver. Let's say that it is not an easy task to drive in Angola

SECURITY SERVICES

Alfa 5

Rua da Missão, nª 74, Kinaxixi - Luanda

Tel: +244-222-333588 / 334922 / 3338022

Fax: +244-222-371556

Email: alfa5dg@ebonet.net

Ango Atenta

Rua Martin Luther King, n° 25

PO Box 3572, Luanda

Tel: +244-222-443725

Fax: +244-222-448177

Email: angoatenta@multitel.co.ao

Ango Patrulha

Rua Nicolau Gomes Spencer, n° 92, Maculusso - Luanda

Tel: +244-222-321469 / 396370

Cell phone: +244-923-61958 / 923-396978

RECOMMENDED PARTNER — AP Services

Rua António Feijó, n° 5, Vila Alice - Luanda

Tel: +244-222-320986

Fax: +244-222-326284

Email: fernando.eduardo.manuel@apservices-online.com

Website: www.apservices-online.com

Copebe

Rua N'dunduma, n° 38/44 - Luanda

Tel: +244-222-448814

Fax: +244-222-448814

Email: copebe-security@netangola.com

RECOMMENDED PARTNER — DSL

Rua Marqués da Minas, n° 11/13 - Luanda

Tel: +244-222-396680 / 396598 / 395974

Fax: +244-222-394749

Email: dsl@netangola.com

dan@netangola.com

RECOMMENDED PARTNER — Lince

Avenida 4 de Fevereiro, n° 95, 2nd Floor, Door 25 - Luanda

Tel: +244-222-332509 / 332497 / 358574

Fax: +244-222-332501

Email: lince.dirt@nexus.ao

Lince.dg@netangola.com

Mamboji

Rue Hélder Neto, n° 42

Tel: +244-222-445132 / 322048

Fax: +244-222-445132

Email: mamboj@netangola.com

Protector

Rua de Moçambique, n° 20 - Luanda

Tel: +244-222-447741 / 449919

Fax: +244-222-447741

Cell phone: +244-912-500742

Email: protector@snet.co.ao

Securitas de Angola
Segurança e Vigilância, Lda.
Rua Dr. António Agostinho Neto, nº 67/68
Kinanga - Luanda
Tel: +244-222-398269
Fax: +244-222-395549
Email: info@securitas-angola.com

Teleservice
Av. 4 de Fevereiro, 208 - Luanda
Tel: +244-222-390765 / 390739
Fax: +244-222-339237
Email: teleservice.geral@netangola.com

Security Service: better to have ONE!

SHOPPING

Bellas Shopping
Big Shopping Centre
All kind of shops, restaurants and cinema,
Morro Bento, Talatona - Luanda Sul
Tel: +244-222-678470
Cell phone: +244-924-253972
Website: www.belasshopping.com

Boutique Ana Isabel
Rua Aires de Menezes nº 95 - Luanda
Tel: +244-222-334522
Cell phone: +244-923-507479

Boutique Sónia
Rua Frederick Welwitschia, nº 3ª - Luanda
Tel: +244-222-446133

Boutique Kilamba
Rua do Lobito, Prédio 4, Door 8 - Luanda
Tel: +244-222-449876

CAS – Video & Disco
Rua Luther King, nº 8, Ingombotas - Luanda
Tel: +244-222-444709

Casa Paris
Rua Rainha Ginga nº 51
PO Box 227, Luanda
Tel: +244-222-339953
Fax: +244-222-390075

Gift – Special Gifts
Largo Kinaxixi, nº 20 - Luanda
Tel: +244-222-443250
Fax: +244-222-445237

Karibrinca – Toys for Kids
Rua Cerqueira Lukoki, nº 100/104 - Luanda
Tel: +244-222-396260 / 449774

Kiss Me
Largo Lopes Cerqueira nº 3B , Largo do Atlético - Luanda
Tel: +244-923-828349

LSM-Vestuário e Modas, Lda.
Rua Marien N'Gouabi, nº 30, Maianga - Luanda
Tel: +244-222-330255 / 331287

Stromp Music & CDs
Largo Amílcar Cabral, nº 18 - Luanda
Tel: +244-222-338342

SPORT ACTIVITIES

A Delegação Provincial da Juventude e Desportos
Rua Rei Katyavala, nº 128 - Luanda
Tel: +244-222-447246

Aerobics & Aerobox
Outdoor activities at Fisico, Saúde & Estética
Rua Alyone Blond Eye, Miramar - Luanda
Tel: +244-222-430754
Cell phone: +244-923-503978

Aqua Gym - Club Náutico da Ilha de Luanda,
Rua Murtala Mohammed
PO Box 1146, Ilha do Cabo - Luanda
Tel: +244-222-309689

Capoeira - Fitness Club

Rua do Massangano, Anangola - Luanda
Tel: +244-222-446361 / 448449
Cell phone: +244-923-416646 /
923-304749
Email: fitness@netcabo.co.ao
Website: www.fitnessangola.com

Baseball & Football & Rugby

Club Desportivo 1° de Agosto, Maianga - Luanda
Tel: +244-222-331178
Fax: +244-222-332180
Website: www.cdagosto.com

Boats Renting for Sailing & Fishing

Club Desportivo e Recreativo Marítimo da Ilha
Rua Murtala Mohammed, n° 282, Ilha do Cabo - Luanda
Tel: +244-222-309136

Diving

Foz do Rio Cunene, Namibe Province
Tel: +244-264-230400
Fax: +244-264-230401

Praia da Caota & Baías de Santo António
Farta & Praia Morena & Ponta da Restinga no Lobito
Benguela Province
Tel: +244-272-231742

Fishing

Albufeira do Kuando & Barragem do Gove
Huambo Province
Tel: +244-241-220984

Bengo–Dande–Kwanza–Longa and Onzo, Bengo Province
Tel: +244-222-391-563

Gymnastics for Pregnancy & Kids Special - Fitness Club

Rua do Massangano, Anangola - Luanda
Tel: +244-222-446361 / 448449
Cell phone: +244-923-416646 / 304749
Email: fitness@netcabo.co.ao
Website: www.fitnessangola.com

Golf

Clube de Golfe – Mangais - Eco-Turismo
Barra do Kwanza , Luanda/Bengo Province
Tel: +244-222-391653 / 394825
Fax: +244-222-336633
Email: mangais@mangais.com
Website: www.mangais.com

Scout Movement

Associação dos Escuteiros de Angola (AEA)
PO Box 1479, Luanda
Tel: +244-222-447587 / 924-04380
Email: aea@scoutangola.com.
Website: www.scoutangola.com

Shooting at Calulo

Sumbe, Cuanza Sul Province
Tel: +244-236-230137

Spinning - Fitness Club

Rua do Massangano, Angola - Luanda
Tel: +244-222-446361 / 448449
Cell phone: +244-923-416646 / 304749
Email: fitness@netcabo.co.ao
Website: www.fitnessangola.com

Tennis - Tennis Club of Luanda

Rua Francisco C.Branco - Luanda
Tel: +244-222-330733
Fax: +244-222-330733

Tennis, Swimming and Shooting

Club Antiguos Caçadores
Rua Alyone Blond Eye, Miramar - Luanda
Tel: +244-222-430754

Tennis & Squash - Hotel Trópico

Rua da Missão, n° 103 - Luanda
Tel: +244-222-370070
Fax: +244-222-393330 / 391798
Email: tropico@netangola.com
Book in advance!

Walking & Trekking

Parque Nacional da Kissama, Bengo Province

Tel: +244-222-440855

 While making outdoor sports: we recommended you to do not ever walk or run alone!

TAXIS

 It is not recommended to take the Blue Taxis, so-called "Candungueiros". Better try Macom Taxi, but please be aware of their high prices and be patient when calling for one in order to pick you up.

Associação dos Taxistas de Luanda

Rua Fernando Brique, nº 73 - Luanda

Tel: +244-222-330694

Cell phone: +244-912-200300 / 212163

Candungueiro, the popular Angolan Taxi

Auto Taxi do Palanca
Rua H 16 - Luanda
Tel: +244-222-442012

Empresa de Taxis de Luanda
Avenida Revolução de Outubro - Luanda
Tel: +244-222-351333

Macon Taxi
Estrada do Golf, Bº Golf II - Luanda
Tel: +244-222-470520
Fax: +244-222-470660
Email: macon@macon.netangola.com

Marine
Rua 28 de Maio, nº 30
PO Box 6887 - Luanda
Tel: +244-222-397049 / 397717 / 397606
Fax: +244-222-397997

THEATRES & CINEMAS

 The Angolan culture is very rich and interesting. You cannot miss going to some Local Theatres!

Cine Atlántico
Rua Dr. Américo Boavida - Luanda
Tel: +244-222-321699
Fax: +244-222-333302

Cine Karl Marx
Rua Oliveira Martins, nº 19/21 - Luanda
Tel: +244-222-323456
Fax: +244-222-323456

Cine Miramar
Av. Pres. Houari Boumediene - Luanda
Tel: +244-222-445204

Cine Nacional
Rua 1º Congresso MPLA - Luanda
Tel: +244-222-390936

Teatro Avenida
Rua Rainha Ginga - Luanda
Tel: +244-222-397233
Fax: +244-222-320969

Teatro Lounge Elinga
Rua Largo do Tristão - Luanda

Teatro Nacional
Rua Congresso MPLA

TRAVEL AGENCIES

See Leisure section

Popular dance mixes with modern shows

INVESTMENT & LEGAL FRAMEWORK

"When the stone is aimed at an animal, a person is not lapidated"

Angolan proverb

WHY DO BUSINESS IN ANGOLA?

Angola ranks among the countries with the highest growth potential in Africa. It produces 800,000 barrels of oil daily and has estimated reserves of 10 billion barrels. It also has diamonds, three million hectares of arable land, many valuable minerals, and one of Africa's largest water reserves, which gives it massive potential for producing electric energy and fishing.

This country was once the world's fourth-largest coffee producer, a major iron ore producer and an exporter of high-quality marble, food and sisal. The industrial sector produced food, beer, textiles, cement and much more. Now, following the advent of peace, the government wants to resume development in order to rebuild and restore Angola to its former position in the business world. Inflation has been kept in check in recent years, and there is a confirmed downturn. The government is carrying out a programme to privatize state-owned companies and opening up the oil business to international firms.

DOMESTIC LAWS

The minimum amount of foreign investment (defined as capital from outside Angola) is set at US $100,000; the minimum amount for domestic investment (capital from Angola) is set at US $50,000.

When the amount of foreign investment is not greater than US $5,000,000, the investment proposal is to be submitted by filling an Advance Declaration of Foreign Investment, to be found at the National Agency for Private Investment (ANIP). The declaration must be accompanied by the following documents:

Luanda offers the perfect scenario to develop your business

DOCUMENTS NEEDED FOR THE SUBMISSION OF DOMESTIC INVESTMENT PROJECTS FOR THE PRIOR DECLARATION REGIME (DECLARAÇÃO PREVIA)

• Draft by-laws of the company to be incorporated.
• Certificate of corporate denomination issued by the Ministry of Trade.
• Certified copy of the by-laws and commercial registration of the proponents, duly authenticated in the case of corporations or a copy of the Resident Card in the case of individuals.
• If shares of an existing corporation are acquired, aside from the by-laws of the corporation, proponents must submit certified copies of the minutes of board meetings reflecting approval of the acquisition of those shares (Minutes of the General Assembly).
• Fiscal certification, proving no moneys are owed to the fiscal authorities (for existing Angolan corporations).
• Social Security Certificate proving no moneys are owed to Social Security (for existing Angolan corporations).

Two copies of the above documents are required if the investment is greater than US $5,000,000.

DOCUMENTATION FOR PRESENTATION OF FOREIGN INVESTMENT PROJECTS IN THE PRIOR DECLARATION REGIME:

• Draft by-laws of the company to be incorporated.
• Certificate of corporate denomination issued by the Ministry of Trade.
• Certified copy of the by-laws and commercial registration of the proponents duly authenticated by the Consular Services of the Republic of Angola in the country of origin or in the country where authorization to enter Angola was obtained in the case of corporations or a copy of the passport in case of individuals.
• If shares of an existing corporation are acquired, aside from the by-laws of the corporation, proponents must submit certified copies of the minutes of board meetings reflecting approval of the acquisition of those shares

(Minutes of the General Assembly).
• Police records for non-resident individuals (foreign investors) issued by the authorities in the country of origin or residence.

Two copies of the documents must be submitted if the investment is not greater than US $5,000,000.

CONTRACTUAL REGIME

• Investments equal to or greater than US $5,000,000.
• Whatever their value, in accordance with the legislation, investments that can only be undertaken through the concession of exploration rights.
• Whatever their value, in accordance with the legislation, investments that can only be undertaken with the participation of public enterprises.

ADDITIONAL DOCUMENTATION FOR THE SUBMISSION OF INVESTMENT PROJECTS:

• Financial, economic and technical feasibility studies.
• Draft investment contract.

FOR DOMESTIC INVESTMENT:

• Draft by-laws of the corporation to be created.
• Certificate of corporate denomination issued by the Ministry of Trade.
• Certified copy of the by-laws and commercial registration of the proponents, duly authenticated in the case of corporations or a copy of the Resident Card in case of individuals.
• If shares of an existing corporation are acquired, proponents must submit not only the by-laws of the corporation, but also certified copies of the minutes of board meetings reflecting approval of the acquisition of those shares (Minutes of the General Assembly).
• Fiscal certification, proving no moneys are owed to the fiscal authorities (for existing Angolan corporations).
• Social Security Certificate proving no moneys are owed to Social Security (for existing Angolan corporations).

FOR FOREIGN INVESTMENT:

• Draft by-laws of the company to be incorporated.

• Certificate of corporate denomination issued by the Ministry of Trade.

• Certified copy of the by-laws and commercial registration of the proponents duly authenticated by the Consular Services of the Republic of Angola in the country of origin or in the country where authorization to enter Angola was obtained in the case of corporations or a copy of the passport in case of individuals.

• In case of acquisition of participation in an existing corporation, the by-laws of the corporation must be submitted together with a certified copy of the minutes of the board meetings (Minutes of the General Assembly).

• Police records for non-resident individuals (foreign investors) issued by the authorities in the country of origin or residence.

Three copies of the documents must be submitted if the investment is greater than US $5,000,000.

INVESTMENT LEGISLATION

This law sets forth the general basis of the private investment to be carried out in the Republic of Angola and defines the principles to be followed in the procedure of access to the incentives and aids to be granted by the state to such private investments.

SPECIAL INVESTMENT REGIMES

The regime of investment and access to incentives and aids to be granted to private investments in the oil industry, diamond extraction and financial institutions is governed by separate legislation and in other situations to be specially determined by the state.

The entities competent to approve the investments referred to in the preceding paragraph must submit to the Agência Nacional de Investimento Privado (ANIP), within 30 days, information on the relevant overall value, place of investment, form, regulations, number of jobs to be created, and remaining material information for purposes of registration and centralized statistical control of the private investment concerned.

The provisions laid down in this law are also applicable to various other investments

INVESTMENT POLICY GENERAL PRINCIPLES

The private investment policy and the granting of incentives and aids are carried out in observance of the following general principles:

• Free initiative, except in state reserved areas, as defined by law.

• Guarantees of safety and protection of the investment.

• Equal treatment to national and foreign citizens and protection of the rights of economic citizenship of Angolan nationals.

• Respect for and full compliance with international agreements and treaties.

PRIVATE INVESTMENT PROMOTION

The government shall promote the private investment policy, in particular the investment in fields of activity highly conducive to the economic and social development of the country and to the general well-being of the population.

The Agência Nacional de Investimento Privado (ANIP) is the body entrusted with the enforcement of the national policy as far as private investments are concerned, as well as with the promotion, coordination, direction and supervision thereof.

ADMISSIBILITY OF PRIVATE INVESTMENT

All kinds of private investment may be carried out, provided the same are not contrary to the legislation and formal procedures in force.

Luanda is growing rapidly

Private investment may take the form of domestic or foreign investment.

FOREIGN INVESTMENT OPERATIONS

Under the terms and for the purposes of this law, the following acts and contracts carried out without resorting to the foreign exchange reserves of the country shall, inter alia, be deemed as foreign investment operations:

• Introduction of freely convertible currency in national territory.
• Introduction of technology and know-how.
• Introduction of machinery, equipment, accessories and other tangible fixed assets, as well as inventories or stocks.
• Corporate holdings in Angolan companies and firms domiciled in national territory.
• Financial means raised by foreign loans.

• Creation and expansion of branches and other forms of representation of foreign companies.
• Creation of new companies wholly owned by the foreign investor.
• Acquisition of the whole or part of the capital of existing companies and groups of companies and holding or acquisition of a corporate interest in new or existing companies and groups of companies, under any form whatsoever.
• Execution and amendment of consortium, joint venture and participation agreements or any other form of association agreement permitted by international trade laws, though not foreseen in the legislation in force.
• Total or partial takeover of commercial or industrial establishments, by means of acquisition of the relevant assets or execution of business lease agreements.
• Total or partial takeover of agricultural companies, by means of execution of lease agreements or any other agreements whereby the investor gains possession or operation of such companies.

Luanda is renowned for its busy traffic

FORMS OF REALIZATION OF FOREIGN INVESTMENT

• Operation of real estate developments, in tourism activity or otherwise, of whichever legal nature.

• Provision of supplementary payments of capital, partners' loans and, in general, loans related to profit sharing.

• Acquisition of real estate located in national territory within the scope of private investment projects.

The temporary charter of vessels, aircraft and other means capable of being hired, leased or otherwise temporarily used in national territory, in return for a given freight, is not deemed as foreign investment.

Capital investments of less than the equivalent to US $100,000 do not require prior consent from the Agência Nacional de Investimento Privado (ANIP) and do not benefit from the right to repatriate dividends, profits and other advantages foreseen in this law.

Foreign investment acts may be carried out, separately or cumulatively, by means of:

• Transfer of funds from abroad.

• Investment of liquid assets in foreign currency bank accounts held by non-residents in Angola.

• Import of machinery, equipment, accessories and other tangible fixed assets, as well as inventories and stocks.

• Integration of technology and know-how.

The foreign investment operations listed in the subparagraphs above must be carried out together with a transfer of funds from abroad, in particular to cover incorporation and start-up expenses.

INVESTMENT INCENTIVES AND BENEFITS

Imports of tax-exempt machinery and equipment:

A Certificate of Registration for Private Investment (CRIP) must be submitted, together with the authorization for customs tax incentives, a copy of which is sent to the Customs Authority by ANIP, in conjunction with a list of the equipment to be incorporated into the project.

The entry of machinery, equipment, accessories and other materials is documented on the basis of its CIF (cost, insurance and freight) value in foreign currency, and its equivalent value in Angolan currency, at the exchange rate of the date of arrival in Angola.

Proof of the prices declared for machinery and equipment must be provided in the form of authorized documentation approved by the pre-shipment inspection agency.

There is a 50% reduction for used machinery, equipment and accessories, instead of a customs tax exemption. There is a 100% exemption for new and unused goods.

OTHER ADVANTAGES OF INVESTING IN ANGOLA:

Exemption for up to six years from payment of customs tariffs and other taxes on goods and equipment, including heavy and technological vehicles, from the date of arrival until the beginning of operations for investments. Investors are only required to pay the tax stamp and service charges.

Five-year exemptions from customs tariffs for merchandise incorporated into or directly consumed in the act of producing other products, including during the test stage. This does not include equipment, accessories, surplus parts and raw materials produced in Angola. For these goods, investors are only required to pay the tax stamp and service charges.

Up to 15 years' exemption from industrial tax for profits on investments, as well as the industrial tax on the price of the venture and subcontractors employed to carry out the investor's business activities.

Expenses incurred to build roads, railroads, install telecommunications facilities, water supply systems and social infrastructure facilities for workers, their families and communities, as well as expenses for professional training and investments in the arts and culture, in addition to the purchase of works of art from Angolan artists, will be considered tax-deductible expenses.

INVESTMENT GUARANTEES

STATUS OF PRIVATE INVESTMENT

The companies and firms incorporated in Angola for purposes of obtaining aids and incentives to private investment operations, though with foreign capital, have the same legal status as Angolan companies and firms and, unless otherwise stipulated in the Law or in specific legislation, shall be governed by Angolan general law.

EQUAL TREATMENT

Under the terms of the constitution and of the principles laid down in the juridical, political and economic system of the country, the Angolan state shall give, regardless of the origin of the capital, fair, non-discriminating and equitable treatment to incorporated companies and firms and to property, affording them protection and safety and not hindering the management, maintenance and operation thereof.

Any discrimination among investors is strictly forbidden. Foreign investors benefit from the rights attached to the ownership of the invested means, in particular the right to freely dispose thereof, under the same conditions enjoyed by national investors.

PROTECTION OF RIGHTS

The Angolan state warrants that all private investors shall have access to Angolan courts for purposes of defending their rights and resorting to the appropriate legal proceedings.

In the event of the assets object of private investment being expropriated for important and duly justified reasons of public interest, the state shall pay a fair, prompt and effective indemnity, in such amount as shall be determined in accordance with the applicable legislation. The assets of the private investors must not be nationalized.

Should there occur a change in the Angolan political and economical regime and exceptional measures regarding nationalization be adopted, the state shall pay a fair and prompt cash indemnity for the property nationalized thereunder.

The state shall afford full protection to and respect the professional, banking and trade secrecy of the companies and firms incorporated for investment purposes.

The rights granted to private investments are ensured without prejudice to other rights laid down in agreements and conventions to which the Angolan state is a party.

Should there occur adverse economic and tax alterations, the investments in progress will not be affected thereby for a period of no less than three years and not exceeding five years, under the terms to be laid down in a separate statute.

SPECIFIC GUARANTEES

The rights over industrial property as well as over any intellectual creation are secured pursuant to the legislation in force.

Title to land and to other domain resources is guaranteed by the legislation in force and by any other legislation that may be enacted.

The state shall not interfere in the management of private companies and in the setting of prices, except as otherwise expressly required by law.

The state warrants that no licence shall be cancelled without the competent judicial or administrative proceedings.

The state authorizes the direct import of goods from abroad and the separate export of products manufactured by private investors.

CREDIT

Private investors may raise internal and external credit aids under the terms set forth by law.

DUTIES

General Duties of the Private Investor

Private investors must respect the laws and regulations in force and comply with their contractual covenants, and shall be subject to the penalties therein defined.

Specific Duties of the Private Investor

The private investor shall, in particular:

• Meet the deadlines for the import of capital and for the implementation of the investment project, in accordance with the contractual commitments undertaken.
• Promote the training of domestic workers and the progressive holding of managerial offices by Angolan citizens, without any kind of discrimination whatsoever.
• Create funds and reserves and make provisions under the terms of the legislation in force.
• Follow the national plan of accounts and accounting standards.
• Respect the rules governing environment protection, hygiene, protection and safety of workers against industrial hazards and death and other contingencies foreseen in social security laws.

66

• Take out and keep valid insurance policies against industrial hazards and death of the workers, as well as a liability insurance policy against injuries to third parties or to the environment.

INTERNATIONAL LAWS AND AGREEMENTS

Angola is a member of a number of international organizations and conventions that protect private investments and has enacted a number of other domestic laws and regulations that provide additional security for investors.

Angola is a member of the Multilateral Investment Guarantee Agency (MIGA), which provides private sector investment guarantees and dispute settlement assistance. In addition, Angola's National Assembly recently approved the Voluntary Arbitration Law, which, once promulgated, will provide for non-judicial arbitration of disputes, except for cases expressly excluded by the law.

Angola's new Land and Urban Planning Law clarifies land ownership and tenure, providing security to property investment. Under the law all land ultimately belongs to the state, but the law establishes clear regulations providing for land occupation, leasing and land use for private purposes.

To protect the environment, Angola recently approved regulations that require an Environmental Impact Study for investment in areas such as petroleum, mining and construction of roads or power stations.

Angola is a member of the World Intellectual Property Organization (WIPO) and adheres to its international classification of patent and trademark registration. To further protect intellectual property (patents, copyrights and trademarks) Angola's National Assembly also recently approved the Paris Convention for the Protection of Industrial Intellectual Property, and the convention is now before the President for approval.

New licensing regulations in the energy sector provide stronger legal protection for private investment in electrical infrastructure, such as building dams, power plants or electricity distribution grids.

Angola's General Labour Law outlines responsibilities of employers and employees. Regulations also favour the hiring of Angolan nationals ('Angolanization') and require that Angolan and expatriate staff with the same job functions and responsibilities receive equal salaries. Expatriate staff may only account for up to 30% of a company's workforce in Angola.

Angola has signed bilateral investment treaties with Portugal, South Africa, the United Kingdom, Italy and Germany, and these agreements, once ratified, will provide additional incentives and protection to investors from these countries. A bilateral investment agreement with Cape Verde is already in force.

To promote Angolan free trade, Angola has adopted the Southern African Development Community's (SADC) free trade protocol, which will harmonize trade and customs regimes and reduce tariffs among the 14 SADC member states. Angola has signed customs cooperation agreements with Portugal and São Tomé and Príncipe and is in discussions with South Africa, the community of Portuguese Speaking States (CPLP), Namibia, Zambia, and the democratic Republic of Congo on similar agreements.

Industry is booming in Luanda

TAXATION IN ANGOLA

Companies carrying out industrial and commercial activities in Angola are subject to Industrial Tax (Income Tax) on all profits derived from Angola. If the company has its head office or effective management control in Angola, it is subject to Industrial Tax on its profits derived from Angola and one-third of its gross income earned abroad.

Under the new tax legislation, all the income obtained abroad by an Angolan company operating overseas will be fully taxable.

Foreign entities with a permanent establishment in Angola are subject to Industrial Tax only on profits derived from the permanent establishment.

All companies, regardless of whether they have a permanent place of business in Angola, that perform contracts or subcontracts or render services in Angola, are subject to Industrial Tax if the amounts paid to such companies are considered expenses for Industrial Tax purposes.

This provision is likely to be changed as a consequence of the new definition of permanent establishment. This new definition also considers as permanent establishment the mere rendering of services if made by the presence in Angola of hired personnel for more than 90 days within a year. This implies that those companies that render services will be taxable under the general rules of the Industrial Tax Code.

The Capital Income Tax imposed on taxable dividends was raised to 10% under the new legislation. An exemption, on the same conditions as the exemption from Industrial Tax, can be obtained from the Minister of Finance for new industries and investment projects in fundamental areas.

The tax year is the calendar year. Companies other than Angolan companies operating abroad must file tax returns together with their financial statements by 31st May in the year following the tax year. Advance payments of at least 50% of the prior year's tax liability must be made by 10th December of the tax year. Final payment of tax is due on 15th September of the following year.

The Luandan Coast is beautiful at night

SETTING UP COMMERCIAL COMPANIES

All companies must be registered at the Guichet Único da Empresa (see Business Resources for all contacts).

Before forming a company, foreign non-residents have to go to ANIP to make the following applications:

• Licence for Capital Importation
• Articles of Association stamped by ANIP
• Private Investment Certificate.

Steps to legalize a company at Guichet Único da Empresa (GUE):

1. The initial capital to form a limited partnership (Ltd) must be of a minimum of Kw 100,000 or the equal amount in USD. The partnership must be of two people minimum. The initial capital required to form an anonymous partnership (SA) is of US $20,000 and five people minimum.
2. Customers must buy and fill in a form to apply for the certificate of Social Denomination of the Company. The form costs Kw 400 and the certificate Kw 16,500.
3. A fee of US $300 or the equal amount in Kwanza will be charged for the services that the institution (GUE) offers.
4. Required documentation:
• 7 copies of the Articles of Association
• Certificate of social denomination
• A copy of the identification of each partner
• Foreigners with non-residence card – a copy of the passport
• Foreigners with residence card – copy of the passport and residence card
• Angolans – copy of the ID.
5. The payment of taxes to the Registry Office and to the Commercial Registry depends on the company's initial capital.

Please pay special attention to this issue

TRANSFER OF CAPITAL AND PROFITS

Transfer of Profits and Dividends

Upon implementation of the private foreign investment and against evidence of its execution in accordance with the rules set out in the law, the foreign investor may transfer abroad, under the conditions laid down in the law and in the foreign exchange law:

• The distributed dividends or profits, after deduction of the legal amortizations and taxes levied thereon, taking into account the relevant holding in the equity capital of the company or firm concerned.
• The liquidation proceeds of its investments, including capital gains, after deduction of the taxes levied thereon.
• Any credits, after deduction of the relevant taxes, arising out of acts and contracts considered as private investment operations under the law.
• The proceeds of indemnities pursuant to paragraphs 3 and 4 of Article 15.
• Royalties and other income obtained from indirect investment revenues associated with the assignment of transfer of technology.

Taxes on Transfers of Funds

Transfers abroad and the sales and other transactions made by the private investor, within the scope of the rights set forth in the law, shall be subject to withholding capital gains tax, under the terms of the tax laws in force and the tax regulations governing private investment.

IMPORT AND EXPORT RULES AND REGULATIONS

For goods exceeding US $5,000 an import licence is required. The Angolan customs also demand an import permit (BRI), to be issued specifically for the goods to be imported by the Angolan Ministry of Commerce. It is, however, expected that this document, currently the gov-

Agostinho Neto's Mausoleum

ernment's basis to obtain statistical data on imports, will eventually – and in line with increasing computerization – be abolished. Furthermore a Clear Report of Findings – issued by an internationally operating company called BIVAC – is required. The report will be issued after export goods have undergone a pre-embarcation/loading inspection, in order to confirm international standards in respect of price, quality, quantity and other characteristics. As from February 2003, for instance, labelling of all goods entering Angola has to be in Portuguese. The report will be issued free of charge. It is expected that BIVAC will open an office in Oshikango soon. A fine of 100% – based on the payable customs duties – will be levied on goods entering the country without a clear report of findings. In that case the inspection will be made locally.

In return for a fee, of not more than 2% of the value of goods to be imported, private clearing agents (*despachantes*) will carry out customs clearing. The use of a clearing agent has in the past been compulsory. The new regulation allows importers to carry out clearing by themselves. Regular training courses are offered by the Angolan customs in Luanda. The private sector is welcome to send members of their staff to participate.

The clearing process is currently being simplified. The so-called Documento Unico (Unique Document) is replacing the confusing multitude of previous documentation. This document is already in line with efforts to harmonize customs regulation within SADC countries.

Import costs mainly consist of import duties and a consumer tax (VAT). There are six different categories for import duties (2%, 5%, 10%, 20%, 30%, 35%), and six categories for consumer tax (exempted, 2%, 5%, 10%, 20%, 30%). A total of 2% import duty (+ zero VAT) is being charged for essential goods, such as basic food items. A total of 15% (10% + 5%) is to be charged for vehicles, 50% (30% + 20%) for beverages, such as beer and soft drinks, and as much as 65% (35% + 30%) for spirits and liquors.

Import duties and import taxes can be looked up in the Pauta Aduaneira, which is currently being actualized. This document, which distinguishes among 376 different commodities, is based on international commodity coding (HS code). The book is available at Angolan customs offices for the amount of US \$27. In addition to duties and taxes, a few minor fees will be added, plus of course the above-mentioned cost for the clearing agent, in the case that an agent is to be used. Not all clearing agents have been honest and reputable in the past. Some are believed to have abused their own advantage in knowing the complex import regulations. Due to the new regulations, competition amongst clearing agents is expected to become more pronounced, which will hopefully result in a more transparent and efficient process of clearing goods.

Additional information regarding the Angolan customs can be obtained under: www.minfin.gv.ao, and http://www.minfin.gv.ao/alfan/arqalfan/dou.pdf is the link to the import unique document – Documento Único.

CUSTOMS DUTIES

The National Management of the Customs of the Ministry of Finance, within the framework of a vast programme of modernization of the customs (presented in 2002), implemented the use of a new document of importation, named Documento Único (DU). This document is held and filled in by the Despachante (official agent of the Angolan customs), simplifying all the formalities the importer was confronted with until the change: a multitude of forms to fill in, a slow process, administrative annoyances and corruption. This document is now used for all types of trade such as: imports, exports, re-importation, temporary importation, internal transit, etc. Angola, a member of the SADC, is the first country of this African organization to introduce and apply this new formula and to accept the principles and the rules that other regional entities already use (Mercosur, EU, World Customs Organization), following several studies and agreements with the commercial ministers of the southern area.

The DU, whose basic format, characteristics and standards were imposed by the SADC (but adapted to Angola), enables international use for clearance of goods. The information required in its 53 codified fields follows the uniform codes of the World Customs Organization. Drafting the DU required consultation of various organizations: the Ministry of Finance, the National Bank of Angola, Ministry of Trade & Industry, Plan, Transport, the Police Force of the Borders and the National Institute of Statistics, as well as the World Trade Organization and the World Customs Organization.

The introduction of the Double Channel at the airport, a declaration to be filled for taxable and non-taxable goods, has also helped in monitoring the customs process. It is therefore the end of Zero Tolerance, which implied the physical checking of any goods. From now on, a system of luggage risk analysis will be carried out, making the distinction between registered luggage, unattended luggage and taxable luggage (the fine being able to go up to four times the value of the goods). This information on database is also available inside the country.

 NOTICE While waiting for customs to clear, just be patient!

LABOUR PROVISIONS

LENGTH AND ORGANIZATION OF WORKING TIME (ART 96 OF THE ANGOLAN LABOUR LAW)

1. Except as otherwise provided by law, the normal period of work shall not exceed the following limits:
• 44 hours per week
• 8 hours per day
2. The normal period of work per week may be extended up to 54 hours where the employer adopts shift work patterns or modulated or flexible hours, where a recovery schedule is in effect or where the work is intermittent or simply requires presence.
3. The normal period of daily work may be extended:
(a) up to 9 hours per day where the work is intermittent or simply requires presence, where the employer concentrates the normal period of weekly work into five consecutive days;
(b) up to 10 hours per day where the work is intermittent or simply requires presence, where the employer adopts

modulated or flexible hours, or a recovery schedule is in effect.
4. The maximum limits on normal daily and weekly working time may be reduced under a collective agreement or by a joint order of the Minister of Labour and the Minister for the activity concerned, in activities where the work is performed in particularly unpleasant, tiring or dangerous conditions or which entail risks to workers' health.
5. The reduction in the maximum limits of normal working time shall not entail a reduction in wages of the workers or any alteration to the conditions of work to the detriment of the workers.
6. Working time shall be counted from the time when the worker is present at his place of work until the time he leaves it.

OVERTIME

Exceptions

The following shall not be considered overtime:

(a) work performed within the normal working day by workers exempt from the working time rules;
(b) work performed to recover from previous suspensions of activity or other situations contemplated in paragraphs 2 and 3, subject to the limits and conditions established in the respective regulations;
(c) temporary and unforeseen occurrence of an abnormal volume of work;
(d) substitution of workers who do not report for work at the beginning of the respective work period when this coincides with the end of the previous work period;
(e) movement, transformation or processing of easily perishable products;
(f) performance of preparatory or complementary work which must necessarily be executed outside the working hours of the workplace;
(g) extension of work up to 30 minutes after closure, of establishments selling to the public or providing personal or public services, to complete transactions or services in progress, for cleaning, tidying and preparing the establishment for the activity during opening hours.

Limits

The maximum limits on overtime are:

- 2 hours per normal working day;
- 40 hours per working month;
- 200 hours per year.

Remuneration

1. Each hour of overtime shall be remunerated with an additional 50% of the value of each hour of normal work up to a limit of 30 hours per month.
2. Overtime in excess of the limit established in the previous paragraph shall be remunerated with an additional 75%.
3. The additional remuneration established in the previous paragraphs shall be supplementary to other additions due to workers, specifically that established in paragraph 1 of article 99.
4. For the purposes of payment of overtime:
- fractions of time of less than 15 minutes shall not be considered;
- fractions of time from 15 to 44 minutes shall be counted as half an hour;
- fractions of time of 45 to 60 minutes shall be considered one hour.
5. For the purposes of remuneration of overtime, the day or half day of additional weekly rest shall be considered normal working time.

Administrative Requirements

1. The employer shall be required to maintain an overtime register in which, every day, are recorded the start, end and reason for overtime performed by each worker.
2. Total overtime for each worker shall be calculated each week and signed by him.
3. The register may follow the model approved by order of the Minister of Labour, which may require the inclusion of other elements.
4. The register must be presented to the Inspectorate General of Labour whenever it so requires.

Exemption from Working Time Rules

1. Workers who perform administrative or managerial functions shall be exempt from the working time rules, and the daily and weekly limits set out in article 99 shall not apply to them.
2. The following may also be exempt from working time rules, subject to authorization by the Inspectorate General of Labour: workers who perform functions of trust on behalf of the employer or control functions, and workers who regularly work outside the fixed workplace, in varying places, such that their work is not directly supervised or controlled.

Authorisation

1. Requests for authorization of exemption from the working time rules shall be submitted by the employer to the Inspectorate General of Labour together with the worker's declaration of consent, as well as the necessary supporting documents to justify the functions performed.
2. The authorization of exemption from the working time rules, except where a shorter period is established, shall be valid for one year, and may be renewed by a new request accompanied by the declaration of consent.

Limits on Exemption

1. Workers exempt from the working time rules shall be entitled to a weekly rest day, holidays and an additional day or half day of rest per week.
2. Workers exempt from the working time rules by authorization of the Inspectorate General of Labour shall not work, on average, more than 10 hours per day and shall be entitled to a rest and meal break of one hour during the daily working time.

Remuneration of Exempt Work

1. Workers exempt from the working time rules by authorization of the Inspectorate General of Labour shall be entitled to a wage supplement to be fixed by collective agreement or, failing that, the amount of one hour of overtime per day.

2. On cessation of the exemption from the working time rules, the wage supplement referred to in the previous paragraph shall cease to be payable.

Special Working Time Arrangements

Arrangements considered to be special working time arrangements are set out in the following articles of the present law:

- shift work;
- working time to recover from suspension of activity;
- modulated working time;
- flexible working time;
- part-time work;
- standby arrangements;
- alternating working time and rest time;
- other special working time arrangements established by regulatory decree or collective agreement, which shall always fix the respective arrangements and conditions.

Recovery After Interruption of Work

1. When a stoppage of the activity with a general interruption of work in the workplace or part thereof occurs for reasons of force majeure which are not the result of a strike or other instances of industrial dispute, or holidays, the lost working hours may be recovered within the following six months subject to the following conditions:
(a) the recovery shall only be possible if the employer continued to guarantee the workers' wages during the period of the interruption;
(b) under the recovery arrangements, the weekly and daily length of normal work may not exceed the limits fixed in paragraphs 2 and 3(b) of article 96;

(c) payment for work performed in the context of recovery arrangements is incorporated in basic wages, and increased by additional remuneration of 50%;
(d) before the recovery of working time begins, the employer shall send to the Inspectorate General of Labour a copy of the communication affixed in the workplace informing the workers of the causes and length of the general interruption of work, and the start, arrangements and length determined for the recovery, and the changes introduced into normal working time during that period.

2. The provisions of the previous paragraph shall apply, without, however, entitlement to the additional remuneration envisaged in subparagraph (c) in cases where, by agreement between the employer and the workers' representative organization, the suspension of activity occurs on a working day between a weekly rest day and a holiday.

Modulated Working Time

1. By collective agreement or agreement between the employer and the workers' representative organization, the working time may be arranged on a modular system, with an unequal distribution of working hours from week to week.

2. The modulated working time system shall be subject to the following rules:
(a) the normal period of working time may not exceed the maximum limits fixed in paragraphs 2 and 3(b) of article 96, and on average may not exceed the limits defined in paragraph 1 of that article;
(b) the average length of normal weekly working time shall be calculated by reference to a maximum of six months;
(c) the excess of working time in relation to the limits defined in paragraph 1 of article 96 shall be offset by a corresponding reduction in working time in other weeks within the reference period or by granting the workers paid compensatory rest time;
(d) wages shall be kept level throughout the entire reference period established in accordance with paragraph 2(b);
(e) in the month following the end of the reference period, the time exceeding the average limit of normal

working time for the same period shall be paid as over-time;

(f) excluded from the provision of the previous subparagraph is working time which each day exceeds 10 hours and in each week 54 hours, which shall be paid as overtime in the month it is performed;

(g) where the employment contract ceases or is terminated before the reduction of time or grant of compensatory rest periods referred to in subparagraph (c), the provision of subparagraph (e) of this article shall apply immediately;

(h) the Inspectorate General of Labour shall be informed in advance of the characteristics of the modulated working time introduced.

3. The arrangements set out in paragraph 3 of article 30 shall be considered modulated working time.

Flexible Working Time

1. In workplaces where the worker's activity is not directly and immediately conditioned by the activity of others, the employer may agree an individual flexible working time arrangement with him.

2. Flexible working time must satisfy the following conditions:

(a) it must on average comply with the daily limit established in paragraph 3(a) of article 96 (above mentioned) and shall be performed within the period of the employment contract;

(b) it must consist each day of at least two hours in the morning and in the afternoon when the workers must be present in their respective workplaces.

(c) the remaining working time may be freely performed by the worker before or after the period of compulsory presence according to the worker's wishes, such that at the end of four weeks, the normal working time has been completed.

(d) where the work is not completed by the end of the reference period established in the previous subparagraph, it shall be considered absence from work and deducted from the wages, and work in excess shall be considered as overtime, subject to the limits established in paragraph 1 (b) and (c) of article 103.

3. The rules for flexible working time must be sent to the Inspectorate General of Labour not less than two weeks before it comes into effect.

Part-time Work

1. Part-time employment of workers may be compulsory for the employer in the cases expressly laid down by law, specifically concerning workers with family responsibilities, reduced capacity to work and those attending intermediate or higher education establishments.

2. Provided that the activity of the workplace so allows, the employer may allow workers to work part-time.

3. The performance of part-time work may occur, specifically, in cases where it is desirable for compelling reasons such as the lack of a canteen, the lack of adequate catering services close to the workplace and the absence, breakdown or remoteness of public transport.

4. In the cases referred to in the previous paragraph, the performance of part-time work shall be subject to the following rules:

(a) it is decided by the employer after consultation with the workers' representative organization and prior notification to the Inspectorate General of Labour;

(b) except for compelling technical problems, workers shall be divided into two teams which work mornings and afternoons respectively;

(c) the length of part-time work may not be less than five hours per day;

(d) the performance of part-time work shall be understood to be temporary and shall cease as soon as the reasons for it cease to pertain.

Standby Arrangements

1. Standby arrangements may only be operated in workplaces which provide permanent services to the public, specifically transport and communications, collection, transport and distribution of water and production, transport and distribution of power and enterprises that operate continuously for essential technical reasons, maintaining the regularity and normality of operation of plant and machinery.

2. Except as specially provided by regulatory decrees of collective agreements, standby arrangements shall be

subject to the following rules:

(a) the worker shall be assigned to a standby scheme on a schedule to be fixed at least two weeks in advance;

(b) the worker may not be scheduled for standby on consecutive days;

(c) the standby period may not exceed the normal working day;

(d) a worker on standby must not remain at the workplace, must keep the employer informed of his location, in order to be called for immediate performance of overtime;

(e) the worker shall be entitled to additional remuneration of 20% of his basic wage, on days when he is on standby;

(f) if during the period of standby the worker is required to work, this shall be considered overtime due to force majeure and remunerated as such.

Alternating Working Time

1. By agreement with the workers, employers may adopt a system of alternating working time consisting of a maximum period of four effective working weeks followed by an equal period of rest.

2. The system of work referred to in the previous paragraph shall be subject to the following rules:

(a) the period of rest shall include time spent travelling to and from the workplace;

(b) the weekly rest days, additional weekly rest and holidays included in the effective work period shall be normal working days, and the enjoyment thereof transferred to the subsequent period of rest;

(c) the period of annual holidays shall be imputed to the periods of rest provided that they are not less than 15 consecutive days in length;

(d) the length of normal working time may be up to 12 hours per day, including two periods of rest of 30 minutes each, considered as working time, provided that the working time is organized in shifts and the condition referred to in the last part of paragraph 2 of article 113 pertains;

(e) if, as a consequence of this working arrangement, the annual length of work is exceeded, calculated as 44 hours per week and after deducting normal holidays and public holidays, the excess time shall be considered as overtime and remunerated as such.

Closure and Weekly Rest

1. Industrial, commercial and service establishments must suspend work or close for one complete day per week, which shall be Sunday, except in the case of continuous processing or where the activities undertaken cannot be suspended on that day, for reasons of public interest or technical reasons.

2. Authorization for continuous processing shall be granted by joint orders of the Minister of Labour and the Minister responsible for the activity, following consultation with the trade unions and employers' associations concerned.

ACCESS TO LAND

A proposal for a new land law is currently being discussed in Angola. The land issue has become a sensitive issue in some parts of Africa and has to a certain extent been used by potential investors as an instrument to judge the credibility of governments and accordingly to judge the political risk involved in respect of possible investments.

The new law is expected to grant access to land not only to nationals, but also to foreigners. While urban land is expected to be for sale, access to rural (agricultural) land will mostly likely be granted by means of renewable 50-year concessions. Angola's farming land is not divided into commercial and communal areas. Before a title is granted to an investor, the traditional local authorities of the region will have to be consulted.

INVESTMENT DIRECTORY

NOTICE! Angola offers really great opportunities, so DO NOT miss out!

ANGOP – Agencia Angola Press - Angolan Press Agency
Rua Rei Katiavala, n° 120–122 - Luanda
Tel: +244-222-447343
Fax: +244-222-447434
Email: angop@netangola.com

AAVOTA – Associação das Agências de Viagens e Operadores Turísticos de Angola - Association of Travel Agencies and Tour Operators of Angola
Rua da Missão, n° 93, 1st Floor, Suite 12
Tel: +244-222-372259
Fax: +244-222-372259
Email: geral@aavota.com
Website: www.aavota.com

ADRA – Acção para o Desenvolvimento Rural e Ambiente Action for Rural and Environmental Development
Praceta da Farinha Leitão, n° 24, 1st Floor - Luanda
Tel: +244-222-396683
Fax: +244-222-399312

AIA – Associação Industrial de Angola - Industrial Association of Angola
Rua Manuel Caldeira, n° 6,
PO Box 61227, Luanda
Tel: +244-222-330624
Fax: +244-222-338650
Email: aia@netangola.com
Website: www.aiaangola.com

ANIP – Agência Nacional para o Investimento Privado National Agency for Private Investment
Rua Cerqueira Lukoki, n ° 25, 9th Floor, Luanda
Tel: +244-222-391434 / 331252
Fax: +244-222-331252
Email: iie@multitel.co.ao
Website: www.investinangola.com

AGENANG – Agência Nacional Maritima de Angola Angolan National Maritime Agency
Rua Engracia Fragoso, n° 47–49, Luanda
Tel: +244-222-393988
Fax: +244-222-391444

ASSOMEL – Women Entrepreneurs Association
Largo do Kinaxixi, n° 14, 3rd Floor, Luanda
Tel: +244-222-346742
Fax: +244-222-346742

BNA – Banco Nacional de Angola - National Bank of Angola
Av. 4 de Fevereiro, n° 151
Tel: +244-222-399125
Fax: +244-222-390579 / 394986
Email: bna.gvb@ebonet.net
Website: www.bna.ao

Cámara de Comêrcio e Indústria de Angola - Angolan Chamber of Commerce and Industry
Largo do Kinaxixi, n° 14, 1st Floor - Luanda
Tel: +244-222-444541
Fax: +244-222-444629
Email: ccira@ebonat.net
Website: www.cccia.ebonat.net

Correios de Angola
Largo Fernando Coelho da Cruz, n° 12,
PO Box 1400, Luanda
Tel: +244-222-337700
Fax: +244-222-337628

Direcção Nacional das Alfandegas - Angolan Customs Directorate
Largo das Alfandegas - Luanda
Tel: +244-222-330331 / 339492
Fax: +244-222-339490
Email: alfandegadeangola@hotmail.com
Website: www.alfandegas.com

Direcção Nacional de Aviação Civil - National Directorate of Civil Aviation
Rua Miguel de Melo, n° 96, 6th Floor - Luanda
Tel: +244-222-338596 / 338594 / 339413
Fax: +244-222-390529

Direcção Nacional de Agricultura, Pecuaria e Florestas - National Directorate of Agriculture, Fisheries and Forestry
Avenida Comadante Gika, n° 8, Largo do Ministerios
PO Box 527, Luanda
Tel: +244-222-321429
Fax: +244-321429

Empresa Portuaria de Cabinda – Port of Cabinda Company
Rua do Comércio
PO Box 68, Cabinda
Tel: +244-231-222464 / 222474
Fax: +244-231-222464

Empresa Portuaria de Lobito – Port of Lobito Company
Avenida da Independência,
PO Box 16, Lobito, Benguela
Tel: +244-272-222711 / 222718
Fax: +244-272-222718

Empresa Portuaria de Luanda – Port of Luanda Company
Avenida 4 de Fevereiro, Marginal,
PO Box 1229, Luanda
Tel: +244-222-310074 / 311774
Fax: +244-222-311178

Empresa Portuaria de Namibe – Port of Namibe Company
Avenida do Porto,
PO Box 49, Namibe
Tel; +244-264-261921 / 260190
Fax: +244-264-261510

Empresa Provincial de Agua de Luanda - Luanda Water Company
Rua Frederich Engels, n° 3 - Luanda
Tel: +244-222-335001
Fax: +244-222-330380
Email: epalsdg@snet.co.ao

Empresa Nacional de Exploração de Aeroportos e Navegacão Aerea - National Airport Company
Rua Amilcar Cabral, n° 110
PO Box 841, Luanda
Tel: +244-222-330791
Fax: +244-222393626

ENEL – Empresa Nacional de Electricidade - National Electricity Company
Edificio Geominas, 6–7
PO Box 772, Luanda
Tel: +244-222-321499
Fax: +244-222-323433
Email: enepdg@netangola.com

FDES – Fundo de Desenvolvimento Económico e Social Economical & Social Development Fund
Tel: +244-222-370484
Fax: +244-222-370484
Email: fdes@ebonet.net

Guichê Único de Empresas
Largo António Correia de Freitas/ Marginal, n° 120, Luanda
Tel: +244-222-372320
Fax: +244-222-371076

IANORQ – Angolan Institute of Standardization and Quality
Rua Cerqueira Lukoki 25,
PO Box 594, Luanda
Tel: 244-222-337294
Fax: 244-222-392400
Email: ianorq@netangola.com

Instituto Angolano de Propriedade Industrial - Angolan Institute of Industrial Property
Rua Cequeira Lukoki, n° 25, Luanda
Tel: +244-222-336391 / 336428 / 336479
Fax: +244-222-332974
Email: iapidg@ebonet.net

IDA – Instituto de Desenvolvimento Agrario - Angolan Agrarian Development Institute
Avenida Comadante Gika, n° 8, Largo do Ministerios
PO Box 527, Luanda
Tel: +244-222-321446 / 323326 / 323351
Fax: +244-222-324902
Email: ida@minade.com
Website: www.ida-minader.com

IDIA - Instituto de Desenvolvimento Industrial de Angola Angolan Industrial Development Institute
Rua Cerqueira Lukoki, n° 25, Luanda
Tel: +244-222-338492
Fax: +244-222-338492
Website: www.idiadgov.ao

Instituto de Desenvolvimento da Pesca Artesanal Development of Traditional Fishing Institute
Rua Aires de Almeida Santos, nº 82 - Luanda
Tel: +244-272-234696
Email: ipescartesanal@snet.co.ao

INFOTUR – Instituto de Fomento Turistico - Promotion & Tourism Development Institute
Avenida Ho Chi Min, nº 410 - Luanda
Tel: +244-222-444400 / 444493 / 448787
Fax: +244-222-448726

Instituto Geográfico e Cadastral de Angola - Angolan Geografical Institute
Largo Bressane Leite, nº 29 - Luanda
Tel: +244-222-336385
Fax: +244-222-336385
Email: igca@nexus.ao

Instituto Geológico de Angola - Angolan Geological Institute
Avenida Commandant Gika, 4th Floor - Luanda
Tel: +244-222-324866 / 324852 / 324860
Fax: +244-222-322569

Instituto Médio Comercial de Luanda - Commercial Institute of Luanda
Rua Ho Chi Min, Luanda
Tel: +244 222-326895 / 327113 / 329452
Email: imcl@nexus.com

Instituto Médio Industrial de Luanda - Industrial Institute of Luanda
Rua Gregorio Jose Mendes, Luanda
Tel: +244-222-443200 / 442389
Email: imil@yahoo.com

INAPEM – Instituto Nacional Angolano para Pequena e Mediana Empresa - Institute for Small and Medium Enterprises
Rua Mota Fêo, nº 18 - Luanda
Tel: 244-222-310706
Fax: 244-222-310147
Email: inapem@ebonet.net

Instituto Nacional de Administração Pública - National Institute of Public Administration
Estrada do Futungo, Costa do Sol
Tel: +244-222-469428 / 469429
Fax: +244-222-469427
Email: inap@snet.co.ao

Instituto Nacional de Bolsa e Estudios - National Institute for Scholarships and Studies
Rua Eça de Queiros, nº 24–26
Tel: +244-222-321227
Fax: +244-222-321210

Instituto Nacional do Café - National Institute for Coffee
Avenida 4 de Fevereiro, nº 107
Tel: +244-222-332896 / 332888 / 334743
Fax: +244-222-338678
Email: madias@snet.co.ao

INE – Instituto Nacional de Estatísticas - National Institute of Statistics
Rua Hô Chi Minh, nº 8 - Luanda
Tel: +244-222-325109
Fax: +244-222-325109

INSS – Instituto Nacional de Segurança Social - National Institute of Social Security
Rua Cirilo da Conceição, 1st Floor - Luanda
Tel: +244-222-332048 / 337736 / 337930
Fax: +244-222-3377736

PRESTIGIO – Young Entrepreneurs Association
Rua da Liga Africana, nº 17 - Luanda
Tel: +244-222-447216 / 449689
Fax: +244-222-447216
Email: prestigio@snet.co.ao

SDM – Sociedade de Desenvolvimento Mineiro de Angola
Estrada do Futungo
Av. Pedro de Castro Van-Dúnem 'Loy', s/n, Block D, Luanda Sul
Tel: +244-226-676772 / 676782
Fax: +244-226-676729
Website: www.sdm.net

ANGOLAN ECONOMY

"The eyes are not prevented from seeing by a hedge"
Angolan proverb

OVERVIEW

Angola has an abundance of natural resources, particularly petroleum and diamonds, as well as iron, manganese, copper, phosphate, granite and marble.

The main petroleum exploration areas are situated near the coast, in the provinces of Cabinda, Zaire (Soyo) and Luanda. Oil production in Angola currently accounts for about half of GDP and about 75% of government revenue. With oil production forecast to double over the next three years, projections for the government's fiscal position in the medium term are dependent on both the value of oil production and the proportion that will accrue to the government.

The diamond-rich Lunda zone is considered to be one of the world's most important diamond production areas.

Angola is the fourth-largest producer of rough diamonds in the world. Angola has considerable potential to further increase diamond output, and benefits from a high proportion of its production being of gem quality. Angola's diamond deposits include kimberlite deposits and alluvial deposits. Diamond production in Angola is divided between the formal sector, with companies operating under licences issued by Endiama, and an informal sector, comprised of artisan diggers, many without a licence.

Fishing is an important resource for Angola. With 1,650 km of coast, Angola is rich in fish, molluscs and crustaceans. Fishing is concentrated in the province of Namibe, where cold-water species are predominant. Tropical species appear in the south, in the province of Benguela, where fishing also plays an important role.

More and more multinational companies are setting up a base in Luanda, susch as SDV-AMI Angola

Forests are situated mainly in Cabinda (Mayombe forest) where there are abundant stocks of great economic value such as blackwood, ironwood, ebony and African sandalwood.

Angola is potentially a wealthy country, with enormous resources of oil, gas and diamonds, as well as considerable hydroelectric potential, varied agricultural land and adequate rainfall. Despite these resources, the effects of decades of war have resulted in economic performance below potential in the industrial, manufacturing and agriculture sectors, where most of the population has traditionally been employed.

Since peace in 2002, the process of demobilization and reintegration of former combatants has been proceeding successfully, and the government has turned its attention to the challenges of post-conflict reconstruction. With much of both national and local infrastructure destroyed during more than 30 years of conflict, the challenge is enormous.

Despite substantial and varied natural resources, Angola remains one of the poorest countries in the world. Although growing revenues from oil and diamonds have boosted per capita income to over US $3,200, human development indicators are poor, reflecting the heavy toll of nearly three decades of conflict. For example:

• In 2003 only 38% of the population had access to clean water.
• Infant mortality is high and decreased only marginally, from 172 per 1,000 in 1995 to 154 per 1,000 in 2003.
• The prevalence of HIV/AIDS has increased from 2.1% in 1997 to 5.74% in 2004.
• Primary school enrolment has increased slowly, from 72% in 1995 to 74% in 2000.
• Female primary school enrolment was only 69% in 2000, while male primary school enrolment was 78% in the same year.

Since peace, the performance of Angola's economy at the macroeconomic level has improved, resulting in a more stable economy. The improvement has been praised by the International Monetary Fund.

Economic Indicators

	2000	2001	2002	2003	2004	2005
GDP Growth (%)	3	3.1	14.4	3.4	11.2	15.5
Inflation (%)	268	116	106	77	31	18
Exchange rate (Kwz/Usd)	16.1	30.5	57.09	78.48	85.99	89.8
Exchange depreciation (%)	n.d.	-47%	-47%	-27%	-9%	-4%
Budget deficit (%)	-8.4	-3.9	-9.3	-7.9	-1.9	-2.7
External debts /GDP (%)	81.3	81	69.9	66.4	48.1	37.6

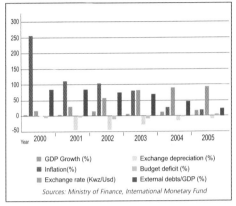

■ GDP Growth (%)   ▨ Exchange depreciation (%)
■ Inflation(%)   ■ Budget deficit (%)
■ Exchange rate (Kwz/Usd) ■ External debts/GDP (%)

Sources: Ministry of Finance, International Monetary Fund

This stability has been achieved by a strategy of macroeconomic adjustment, mostly through inflation reduction and exchange rate stabilization. Macroeconomic stability continues to be one of the most important objectives of Angola's government.

The implementation of these measures benefited from the high international oil prices, which have generated an important increase in foreign currency inflow into Angola, with consequent improvements in the national accounts and balance of payments accounts.

The Angolan government is focusing on public investment, namely in basic infrastructure, to enhance the economic conditions for the development of the non-oil sector.

The main objective of this investment programme is to reduce the strong dependence of the Angolan economy on oil, decrease its vulnerability to an eventual oil price reduction, and simultaneously support the recovery of other sectors of the economy. The investment plan has two main objectives:

• Build infrastructure to support the normal development of economic activities.

• Direct investment promotion in key sectors such as agriculture, fishing and animal husbandry farming and industry.

ECONOMIC GROWTH AND ECONOMIC REFORM STRATEGY

In recent years the low GDP growth (based on formal sector statistics) has been due essentially to bad agricultural harvests and weak industrial performance. Agriculture has been highly affected by the war and resultant social and political environment. Other constraints, imposed by the incipient macroeconomic environment, such as high inflation and interest rates, exchange rate fluctuations and the problem of unpaid government internal national debt, have also affected the economy, particularly sectors such as industry, building and the production of goods and services.

The economy is still deeply dependent on the oil sector. However, no more than 1% of the nation's workforce is employed in the oil industry. It is imperative that other sectors improve their relative importance, providing new jobs, increasing and diversifying the internal markets and increasing manufactured exports. The implementation of appropriate policies is necessary to accelerate the development of industry, agriculture, construction and services so that the current GDP structure can be diversified away from oil and significant increases in domestic production can be achieved.

The government intends to achieve the following general objectives of economic and social policy:

• Achieve and consolidate military and political stability.
• Maintain and consolidate the current macroeconomic stability.
• Revive the national production of goods and services.
• Reform the administration of the state.
• Continue the National Humanitarian Assistance Programme.
• Improve social services (education and health).
• Improve productive and social infrastructure.

The expected oil industry production increases – in 2008 oil production is expected to reach 2 million barrels a day, doubling the existing production – and the maintenance of current high oil price levels are likely to allow for relatively fast-track growth of the Angolan economy in the next few years and the rebuilding of its social and economic infrastructure, creating conditions for the accelerated development of non-oil economic sectors and the consolidation of the peace process started in 2002.

For the period 2005 to 2007, the IMF predicts an average growth of over 20% per annum for the Angolan economy. Nevertheless, this growth will not be uniform, as the non-oil sector economic expansion is forecast to be 11.9% in 2006.

Oil production growth and the consequent increase in foreign currency inflows will allow the maintenance of the present exchange rate stability policy. This stabilization is likely to be helped by reduced inflation, which was estimated to come down to 10% by the end of 2006.

In spite of the strong growth in oil income, the government forecasts a budget deficit of 6.9% of GDP in 2006 (vs. the 2005 excess of 2.5%), given the investment in rebuilding Angola's infrastructure.

Additional obstacles to Angolan economic growth include the absence of support services and the ineffectiveness of legal mechanisms that support economic progress such as the protection of private property.

The World Bank estimates that efforts being made by Angola to rebuild its infrastructure will cost US $15–20 billion. For the 2005–2006 period, the total investment was planned to be US $1.9 billion.

Angolan Economic Projections

	2005	2006	2007	2008	2009
GDP Growth (%)	17	25.8	20.5	7.1	6.3
Oil Sector	22.4	34.3	28	4.2	3.1
Non Oil Sector	10.4	11.9	11.4	10.9	10.1
Inflation (%)	18.5	10	5	3	2
Average Exchange Rate (Kwz/ Usd)	80.7	81.6	81.7	83.3	85
Current Accounts (% GDP)	3.7	4.8	3.5	2.8	3
External Debt GDP (%)	37.6	28.8	22.2	20.3	20.7

Sources: Ministry of Finance, International Monetary Fund, Angola's Catholic University

Angola is blessed with fertile land, ideal for Agriculture

GROSS DOMESTIC PRODUCT

Angola has one of the highest development potentials in Africa, mainly because of its oil reserves, abundant mineral resources and its high potential for electric energy production. Angola also has many other economic sectors that are currently under-explored, such as animal husbandry, fishing and forestry.

The economic importance of the country's manufacturing sector is low. Angola is highly dependent on its extractive industries, particularly the oil sector, which represents almost 50% of the country's GDP, and on the diamond sector to a lesser extent.

Real GDP Growth Rates

	2000	2001	2002	2003	2004	2005	2006E	2007E
Agriculture, Foresty and Fishing	9.3	18	13.4	11.7	14.1	27,40%	34.30%	17.40%
Oil and Byproducts	0.4	-1	20.6	-2.2	13.1	43.70%	34.30%	17.40%
Diamonds and others	12.8	19.5	-2.1	19.8	0.8	36.00%	55.30%	10.80%
Manufacturing	8.9	9.8	10.3	11.9	13.5	22.80%	34.30%	17.40%
Electricity	0.8	10	21.3	0.2	11.5	-28.10%	34.30%	17.40%
Construction	7.5	8.5	10	12.6	14	19.30%	34.30%	17.40%
Trade	3.4	6	11.6	9.9	10.4	56.20%	34.30%	17.40%
Services	1.5	1	2.5	1.9	2.5	63.90%	30.30%	18.90%
GDP	3.7	5.2	13.2	5.2	11.3	16.1	24.4	25.6

Sources: Ministry of Planning and INE (National Statistics Institute)

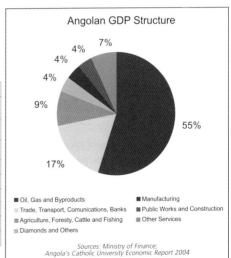

Angolan GDP Structure

7%
4%
4%
4%
9%
55%
17%

- Oil, Gas and Byproducts
- Manufacturing
- Trade, Transport, Comunications, Banks
- Public Works and Construction
- Agriculture, Foresty, Cattle and Fishing
- Other Services
- Diamonds and Others

Sources: Ministry of Finance;
Angola's Catholic University Economic Report 2004

INFLATION AND COST OF LIVING

Angola has experienced significant economic problems in recent years, including high levels of inflation, primarily attributed to the war, which ended in 2002. This situation has resulted in a very high cost of living for the Angolan population.

More recently the Angolan government has successfully put in place tight monetary policies to stabilize Angola's macroeconomic indicators. A major anti-inflationary initiative was put in place in September 2003 following a number of administrative measures affecting monetary policy that were implemented earlier in the year.

Angola has made important progress in reducing inflation since 1999, after two decades of high or hyperinflation. Between 1999 and the peace agreement of April 2002, consumer price inflation fell from over 300% p.a. to around 100% p.a., around which level it then oscillated for over a year. Inflation then decelerated sharply, following the adoption of a stabilization programme in September 2003. By December 2004, the 12-month inflation rate had fallen to 37% and the December 2005 inflation rate had fallen to 23%.

EMPLOYMENT

In 2000 48% of the Angolan population was economically active, as shown below:

Year	Population (million)	Population Growth rate	Economically Active Population 15-64 (million)
1996	13,009	2.76%	6,733
1998	13,766	2.90%	7,152
2000	14,602	3.01%	7,604

*Source: Manuel José Alves da Rocha
"Os limites do crescimento económico em Angola"*

There is a need to urgently develop the non-mineral sectors because of the potential to create more employment.

The public administration sector is the most important employer in Angola, with 44.5% of the total labour force. The education sector has the highest number of employees (53.4%), followed by the health sector (19%) and justice with 1.3%.

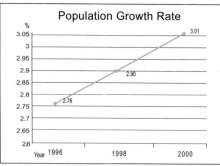

Population Growth Rate

The informal sector also plays a major role in terms of total employment in Angola.

Angola does not have accurate data concerning unemployment. The only information available is related to supply and demand of employment, as shown in the table below:

Employment Supply and Demand

(1,000s)	1998	1999	2000	2001	2002	2003	2004
Demand	23,143	15,135	17,989	16,728	25,602	23,930	26,832
Supply	9,748	6,847	4,661	4,630	7,748	8,606	9,122
Number of people employed	8,053	6,611	4,464	4,561	5,978	8,118	8,150
Ratio supply/demand	42%	45%	26%	28%	30%	36%	34%
Growth rate: supply	8%	-30%	-32%	-1%	67%	11%	6%
Growth rate: demand	18%	-34%	17%	-7%	53%	-7%	12%
Ratio n° people employed/supply	83%	97%	96%	99%	77%	94%	89%
Ratio n° people employed/demand	35%	43%	25%	27%	23%	34%	30%

Source: Direcção Nacional de Emprego e Formação Profissional – Mapess

BALANCE OF TRADE

The Angolan macroeconomic situation is gradually recovering since 2002, when peace was established, after three decades of civil war.

The balance of payments is an element that provides information on the commercial and financial relations of Angola with other countries.

The structure of the economy shows a high dependence on oil revenues, representing over 90% of total exports, not only because of its influence on the balance of trade, but also because oil earnings are used as collateral to obtain loans.

Ships uploading cargo at Luanda Port

The current account balance changed from a deficit of 6.4% of GDP in 2003 to a surplus of 4.5% in 2004. Despite the positive influence of trade balance, the balance of payments is affected in large measure by external debt cost.

BALANCE OF PAYMENTS (USD MILLIONS)

The statistical data shows, for 2004, a current account surplus of US $686 million, which represents a rapid increase when compared with the deficit of the previous year. The trade surplus was due to the vast oil revenue resulting from the high oil prices in the international market and rise in oil production.

The national currency has become more stable in relation to the dollar from 2003 onwards, reflecting government macroeconomic stabilization measures.

TRADE ANNUAL VARIATION (IN PERCENTAGE)

As shown in the table above, exports have increased 41.7% in 2004 while imports became more controlled with a lower variation of 6.4%.

Balance of Payments (Usd Millions)

	1999	2000	2001	2002	2003	2004
Exports of goods and services	5.167	7.92	6.636	8.328	9.508	13,475
Imports of goods and services	-3.109	-3.04	-3.179	-3.76	-5.48	-5,832
Commercial balance	2.048	4.88	3.457	4.568	4.028	7,643
Net income	-1.372	-1.681	-1.561	-1.635	-1.726	-2,484
Net current transfers	56	28	91	32	99	7
Current account balance	-1,71	795	-1.329	-150	-720	686
Conversion rate (Kw:Usd)	2.79	10.04	22.057	43.704	74.606	83,439

Source: International Monetary Fund 2005

Trade Annual Variation (in percentage)

	2000	2001	2002	2003	2004
Exports	56.60%	-17.50%	27.40%	14.20%	41.70%
Imports	-2.20%	4.60%	18.30%	45.70%	6.40%
Oil	58.60%	-18.50%	31.70%	13.60%	45.30%
Other	20.30%	-8.70%	-6.50%	20.50%	3.80%

Source: Banco Nacional de Angola

87

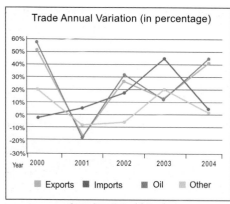

Trade Annual Variation (in percentage)

■ Exports   ■ Imports   ■ Oil   ■ Other

Source: Banco Nacional de Angola

FOREIGN TRADE

Angola's foreign trade mirrors the structure of the economy. Exports are dominated by oil and diamonds, as referred to in the table below.

EXPORTS

Oil products represent over 90% of Angola's exports, followed by diamonds at 6%.

Angola's imports are mainly dominated by imports of consumables (57%), which is explained by the low development of the Angolan productive sector, namely agriculture and manufacturing. The growth of capital goods imports is explained by the growth of investment in the oil sector.

TRADE-RELATED INDICATORS (AS A PERCENTAGE OF GDP)

	2000	2001	2002	2003	2004
Trade Balance	55.1%	34%	40.8%	29.1%	39.4%
Exports	89.4%	66.1%	74.3%	68.8%	69.4%
Imports	-34.3%	32.2%	33.6%	39.6%	30.0%
Current Account	9.%	-14.5%	-1.3%	-5.2%	3.5%
Financial and Capital Account	1.4%	15.5%	33.1%	8.7%	-1.7%
Foreign Direct Investiment	9.9%	21.7%	14.7%	25.2%	7.3%
Total External Debt	100.6%	82.7%	68.7%	61.2%	45.8%
Overall Balance	3.3%	-8.5%	-6.9%	0.7%	3.5%

Exports (million Usd)

	2000	2001	2002	2003	2004
Crude Oil	6,951	5,690	7,539	8,530	12,442
Refined Oil	132	93	96	139	148
Gas	37	20	10	16	30
Diamonds	739	689	638	788	790
Others	61	42	45	35	65
Total	7,921	6,534	8,328	9,508	13,475

■ Trade Balance   ■ Financial and Capital Account
■ Exports   ■ Foreign Direct Investiment
■ Imports   ■ Total External Debt
■ Current Account   ■ Overall Balance

Source: Banco Nacional de Angola

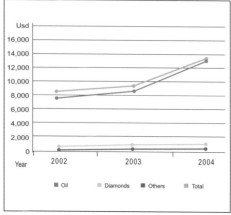

■ Oil   ■ Diamonds   ■ Others   ■ Total

Source: Banco Nacional de Angola

IMPORTS

Numerous agreements between the Angolan government and other countries have been signed, namely with China, Portugal, Russia, Germany, Brazil and Israel, amongst others, to encourage investors to come to Angola.

For example, China is financing projects for the Angolan government. These credit facilities are estimated at US $2 billion, up to the end of 2006. These resources are being used to rebuild roads, bridges and railways, construction of Luanda's new airport (in Viana), buying trucks and agricultural machinery and in building schools, hospitals and informal markets. Chinese companies guarantee the execution of the works and are required to subcontract 30% of the total to private companies in Angola.

State credit facilities with other countries are estimated to total US $500 million. For example, the second phase of Capanda Hydro Electric Dam is being constructed with funds from Russia and Brazil. The Lobito oil refinery will be constructed with funds from foreign oil companies

Imports (million Usd)

	2000	2001	2002	2003	2004
Consumables	1,950	2,174	2,193	2,928	3,305
Semi-processed goods	245	304	437	671	856
Capital goods	844	702	1,131	1,881	1,671
Total	3,040	3,179	3,760	5,480	5,832

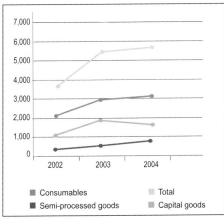

Source: Banco Nacional de Angola

that are operating in Angola. The rebuilding of the national roads system is benefiting from funds from Portugal and Germany.

PRIVATIZATION PROCESS

According to the Angolan government, the privatization process is one of its top priorities.

Law 10/94 establishes the general rules governing the privatization of state-owned small, medium and large companies, and other state properties. An exception is housing owned by the state, which is regulated by Law 19/91.

Under Law 10/94, privatization can be either total or partial. It encompasses both the transfer of ownership and divestment of operations, assets or capital stock of the companies to be privatized. Before privatization takes place, an appraisal is performed by a duly accredited entity.

Privatizations are controlled by a negotiating committee appointed for each case, composed of a representative of each of the following:

- Ministry of Finance (coordinator);
- entity overseeing company management;
- Office Managing the Government's Entrepreneurial Restructuring Programme (GARE);
- Institute of Foreign Investment (whenever foreign investment is potentially available);
- the company.

The Minister of Finance is responsible for ratification of the valuation, as well as of the results approved by the negotiating committee. Final approval for the privatization operation has to be given by the Cabinet in the case of large enterprises or by the Minister of Finance in the case of small and medium-sized companies.

The privatization process in Angola started in 1989 and since then, to the end of 2005, US $124 million were generated from the privatization of 324 companies. Only 10% of the privatized companies made new investments.

Privatization Results (1990–2000)

Government profits	100 million USD
Investments	100 million USD
Privatized companies	409
Privatized production units	1,533
Angolan shareholders	19,920
Employees transferred from the public sector to the private sector	35.40%
Business (USD) from the public sector to the private sector	29.50%
Coffee companies closed	33
Privatized coffee lands	203,660 ha (81% of the total area)

10% of the companies were responsible for the additional 90% of investments.
90% of the investments were made by private funds owned by the investors.
60% did not invest in the privatized companies.

Source: "Africa Hoje" magazine (2003–2004)

The sectors with the biggest privatization activity were manufacturing, agriculture and fishing, and on a smaller scale public works.

The privatization process in Angola has passed through two phases: Phase 1 – period between 1989 and 2000; Phase II – period between 2001 and 2005. In the first phase 202 companies were privatized. Of the total US $103 million earned, there is still a debt of US $14 million (being negotiated between the parties). In the second phase 33 companies were privatized for a value of US $21 million, but with a total subsequent investment of US $150–200 million.

The government's policies in the second phase were changed mainly because of the poor results achieved in the first phase (in this phase significant investments were not made post-privatization). Now (in phase II) the government prefers to raise the capital of the companies and find strategic partners who are prepared to commit to implementing the investments necessary to rehabilitate the enterprises.

According to the Angolan government, the privatization process is top priority.

Under the new policies, the privatization process has achieved better results, and many privatized companies have achieved positive results, such as: Vidrul (with investments of US $14 million), Cimangola (privatized for US $17 million, but now with over US $100 million of investment), Encime (privatized for US $11 million, but now with over US $60 million invested), Nocal and N'gola (with additional investments of US $20 million).

Under the new privatization policies, the Angolan government does not receive as much money but attracts other advantages. The government continues to own part of the companies' capital and the (generally foreign) strategic partner undertakes all the investment and the company becomes functional and profitable. In a subsequent phase, the government may sell its shares to Angolan investors (for example, through the proposed Angolan Stock Exchange).

Recently, the government privatized four large brewers, namely Cuca, Nocal, Eka and N'gola. In Cuca the investment necessary is US $40–50 million; in Nocal and N'gola the investment will be US $20 million.

The government has decided to create a Privatization Agency. This agency will have better human and financial resources to operate. With the creation of this agency the government intends to improve the effectiveness and credibility of the privatization process.

The government has granted to investors some acquisition benefits, such as:

• 10% off if the investment is a way to pay state debts;
• 50% off if the investment is in the provinces of Moxico, Cuando Cubango or Bié;
• 40% off if the investment is in the province of Malanje, Lunda Norte, Lunda Sul (except diamond companies), Huambo, Uíge or Cuanza Norte;
• 30% off if the investment is in the province of Bengo, Huíla, Cunene, Cuanza Sul, Zaire, Cabinda, Benguela or Namibe;
• 10% off if the investment is in the province of Luanda;
• 30% off if the investment is made by managers or employees of the company.

THE STOCK EXCHANGE

Privatization Process of Beer companies - Post-Privatization Shareholders

CUCA		NOCAL	
BIH (prior BGI)	13%	BIH (prior BGI)	26.4%
SOBA	50%	Private investors	23.6%
Private Angolan Investors	36%	Private Angolan investors	50%
Government	1%		
EKA		**N'OGLA**	
BIH (prior BGI)	46%	SAB-Miller	45%
Private investors	50%	Private Angolan investors	54%
Government	4%	Government	1%

Source: Jornal de Angola

Angola is one of the few countries in the SADC region (including the DRC and Tanzania) that still does not have an exchange in place. However, work is in progress for the launching of the first Stock Exchange, the Bolsa de Valores e Derivativos de Angola (BVDA), which was expected to take place towards the end of 2007.

The stock exchange company has already been incorporated as a public company and has indirect state participation through shareholding by state-owned companies. Amongst its main shareholders are companies such as Sonangol, Endiama, ENSA, all state companies, and the following banks BFA, BAI, BIC and Banco Millennium.

In order to ensure the adequate functioning of the stock exchange, a number of laws have been promulgated including the New Law on Financial Institutions and the Law of Securities and Exchanges, both enacted in September 2005. These laws created the Comissão de Mercado de Capitais (CMC), the body responsible for

Aerial view of Luanda

regulating the stock exchange and other non-banking financial institutions.

The CMC will function under the Ministry of Finance and will act as the supervisor of the stock exchange and associated members. It will be responsible for ensuring that members abide by the legislation regulating the industry, certification of brokerage firms and stockbrokers etc. A Financial Markets Institute has also been created and will be responsible for the training of stockbrokers and other market participants.

According to the CMC, the initial forecasts point to the listing of about 10 companies in the first year.

The stock exchange is expected to become a much-needed alternative source of equity and debt finance for Angolan companies. It is also expected to be a catalyst for the privatization process.

The Angolan exchange comes at a time when most African exchanges are experiencing new highs on returns, with South Africa leading the race, followed by Egypt. Apart from South Africa and Egypt, the majority of

92

exchanges in Africa experience low market capitalization, low liquidity, and weak regulatory systems and technology. A major challenge facing Angolan companies, and hence the performance of the Angolan exchange, will reside in achieving international standards in compliance with financial reporting, auditing and other listing requirements.

Other challenges to the successful implementation of the Angolan stock exchange and the companies to be listed include the following;

• Development of a corporate governance culture.
• Development of a clear distinction between ownership and management.
• Training of client liaison personnel devoted to the establishment and maintenance of relationships with investors.
• Compliance with international listing requirements with particular emphasis on the auditing and reporting standards.

SOME REASONS TO INVEST IN ANGOLA

Potentially one of Africa's richest countries, Angola offers great opportunities for investment in various sectors. Angola is blessed with large naturally rich agricultural regions in the Luanda, Bengo, Benguela, Huíla, Cabinda and Cuanza Sul areas. Also in place is a young and dynamic emerging entrepreneurial sector that owns underdeveloped property and resources, eager for partnerships that will give them access to additional capital, new technology and know-how. Likewise, significant public sector interests exist in banking, transportation, energy and water, which are in the process of privatization.

EXAMPLES:

• Petroleum – Greater production and greater source of foreign currency. Recent industry using advanced technology achieving high levels of profitability.
• Diamonds – Large reserves and high production, and a source of foreign currency. New technology is playing a role in this sector.
• Forests – Rich forests of tropical wood.
• Cattle-raising – Significant natural resources.
• Fishing – Angola has a long coast rich in crustaceans and valuable varieties of fish. It has a dynamic industry with developing infrastructure.
• Building construction/public works – An entire country to rebuild and de-mine.
• Agriculture – Thanks to a good hydrographic distribution and a varied ecology, Angola has a large potential for production of tropical and subtropical crops.
• Commerce and industry – Big gaps in many sectors of activity.

Each day Angola becomes more important in the global market

"A bone is not thrown away with meat on it, a person is not buried with life in them"

Angolan proverb

OVERVIEW

Before independence and the civil war, Angola was large-ly self-sufficient in all crops except wheat. The country has since come to rely heavily on imports of food and food aid. Recovery in the agricultural sector has begun but is being hampered by the presence of millions of landmines.

Angola's climate allows for the production of both tropi-cal and semi-tropical crops, providing it with a compara-tive advantage.

The Agricultural Sector accounts for only 8.8% of Angola's GDP

Angolan farmers produce a wide array of food and cash crops, albeit at low levels of output per hectare. Among cereals, maize, millet, sorghum and rice are the main crops. Cassava and Irish and sweet potatoes are the main roots and tubers. These crops make up the basic food diet of the majority of the population. Legumes, notably the common and kidney beans as well as peanuts and soybeans, also make an important contribution to the diet and incomes of small farmers. Oil crops (palm oil and sunflower oil), vegetables and fruits and some coffee pro-duction are the main cash crops.

Fruit and vegetable processing is done today mostly by craft units. The quality of locally processed vegetables and fruits for export is low, based on the applied tradi-tional (sometimes inappropriate) conditions of harvest. Prior to the civil war, Angola was the world's fourth largest coffee producer, with an annual output of 200,000 tonnes. A modest recovery in the coffee sector is under way. The government has submitted a plan to the International Coffee Organization to overhaul the sector. Under its privatization programme, the govern-ment plans to liquidate all 33 state-owned coffee compa-nies and to invite international investors to bid for the largest plantations. Assistance has been provided to the coffee sector by the World Food Programme and by the European Union, the latter having assisted in the form of seeds and farming equipment.

The agricultural sector accounts for only 8.8% of Angola's gross domestic product (GDP) and receives less than 1% of public expenditure. Nevertheless, it is a fun-damental economic activity in a country with a large rural population and small industrial sector (excluding oil). It is the main source of employment and food supply and therefore is key to poverty alleviation and food security. The agricultural sector employs two-thirds of the working population and subsistence agriculture provides the main source of livelihood for 85% of the population.

The Angolan government and Czech Republic have strengthened bilateral cooperation in the agricultural sec-tor. Bié province has benefited since 2003 from coopera-tion with the Prague Agrarian University, which has pro-vided training in agriculture at secondary school level in Kuito through the secondment of six Czech teachers spe-cializing in agriculture. Bié is now exploring, with its Czech colleagues, the possibility of running bilateral exchange programmes and raising the training pro-gramme to include a higher level technical and profes-sional course in agriculture.

The United Nations Food and Agriculture Organization, together with other international institutions, is helping Angola to obtain contributions to enable it to put into

Angola Harvest 2004/2005
(quantity in tonnes)

Utilization	Maize	Rice	Beans	Cassava	Irish Potato	Sweet Potato
Area Cultivated (ha)	1,094,964	12,397	352,700	748,969	124,161	144,591
Production	734,372	8,650	109,284	8,815,009	308,876	663,787
Lost after harvest	51,406	173	4,371	1,322,251	24,710	53,103
Total other use	80,649	1,041	22,006	2,203,752	102,234	86,292
Seeds	21,899	868	17,635	0	62,080	0
Rations	7,344	0	0	881,501	15,444	33,189
Human Consumption	653,723	7,610	87,278	6,611,257	206,642	577,494

Source: Angola Ministry of Agriculture and Rural Development

Women working in the rice fields. Agriculture's importance in the national economy is growing.

effect a medium-term plan of action in order to produce sufficient cereals to make up for an anticipated food deficit.

The family farm system and smallholder agriculture are the dominant systems in the Angolan agriculture sector. Main staple crops produced in the family system and communal farming are maize, cassava, beans, Irish and sweet potatoes as well as bananas, mangos and avocados.

MAIZE

Maize is the major cereal crop grown and normally accounts for over 80% of total cereal production in Angola. The 2005 maize harvest yielded 768,000 tonnes, which represented maize self-sufficiency and a major

improvement in food production. In 2005 monthly average retail maize prices have been substantially lower compared to the corresponding prices in 2004.

Farmers in Angola experience significant difficulties in marketing surplus production as a result of the poor state of the nation's roads.

FORESTRY

Natural forests, which have yet to be exploited, as well as plantations of eucalyptus, cypress and pine, which once formed the basis of a small export industry, add to a rich agricultural potential.

Since 1975 timber production has fallen dramatically and there are now nearly 150,000 hectares of plantations requiring rehabilitation. Valuable tree species, including rosewood, ebony and African sandalwood, as well as mahogany, tola and mulberry, are found in the northern forests, which have remained largely untapped since independence. Angolan wood production in 2004 reached 38,715 m^3, and 54,865 tonnes of charcoal was produced in the same year.

The absence of cattle herds around Luanda means that the only dairy company of any significance in Angola, Lactiangol, has to use imported milk powder for its products.

Production of cattle hides and leather has reached 536 tonnes in 2005.

LIVESTOCK

Angola has an estimated three million plus cattle, mainly located in Huíla province (with 1.3 million cattle) and Cunene province (with approximately 1.1 million cattle). These two provinces are the main centres of livestock activity. Traditional livestock owners hold the majority of cattle and make use of natural grass for feed.

Meat production declined from 36,500 tonnes slaughtered in 1973 to only 5,000 tonnes in the early 1980s, but in 2005 the production increased to 7,240 tonnes. Although cattle are plentiful in several of Angola's provinces, regular supplies of fresh milk are only available to those living in areas safe enough to keep dairy herds, such as Namibe, Benguela and Cunene. The war affected Angola's livestock as much as its people. Rebels and government troops alike have depleted stocks by slaughtering cattle for food.

Average Livestock in Angola 2004

Province	Cattle	Pigs	Goats	Sheep
Huíla	1,380,000	246,100	827,100	21,700
Cuando Cubango	257,000	157,500	438,600	6,580
Cunene	1,170,000	246,100	727,100	18,900
Namibe	350,000	67,300	506,600	32,000
Cuanza Sul	100,000	197,200	198,200	38,306
Benguela	270,200	332,400	207,000	21,000
Huambo	50,000	597,000	420,900	24,000
Bié	40,000	245,600	150,000	13,000
Moxico	33,000	30,000	38,900	12,450
Cabinda	3,800	7,700	8,700	1,000
Zaire	700	1,200	130,000	500
Uíge	1,700	89,000	156,300	17,000
Bengo	7,600	4,200	205,000	15,300
Luanda	8,000	7,100	16,000	16,000
Cuanza Norte	2,000	99,580	93,600	16,000
Malange	1,500	150,400	167,300	23,000
Lunda Norte	2,000	34,500	33,000	9,000
Lunda Sul	3,000	34,500	35,000	11,000
Total	3,680,500	2,547,380	4,359,300	296,736

Source: MINADER - Veterinarian services

FISHERIES

Angola has 1,650 km of coastline. The fishing sector has attracted significant foreign investment in spite of the civil war. However, the annual catch was significantly affected by the war. Despite recent developments post-war, the full potential of the fishing sector has not yet been realized.

The Angolan government has taken steps towards the liberalization of this sector and fish prices are no longer regulated. The government, in collaboration with the World Bank, also established the Angolan Support Fund for Fisheries Development in order to aid the sector in its growth and development.

In 2005 136,042 tonnes of fish were produced, which was only 50% of what was forecast. Industrial production of dry fish only reached 9% of forecasted production, while fish oil and fish flour exceeded forecasts by 24%.

Around 97% of the fishing companies in Angola are private. Only five companies are owned by the government and these are: Edipesca-Namibe, Fropesca and Empromar-Curoca based in Namibe province; Peskwanza based in Kwanza Sul (Porto Amboim) province; and Edipesca based in Luanda.

The government established an Institute for the Development of Artisanal Fishing and Aquaculture (IPA), which aims to promote and develop artisanal, marine and continental fishing. The IPA will promote campaigns for the purpose of creating and developing artisanal fishing communities.

Fishing boats in Luanda

Over 700 fishermen living in communities on the banks of the Zaire River are to benefit from a fishing programme that includes the distribution of boats and canoes and provides training for the fishermen. The programme is the result of an initiative by Pesnorte and the Fund for Support of the Development of Artisanal Fishing, and the intention is to extend it to other provinces in Angola.

The Angolan parliament has ratified seven international accords designed to establish mechanisms for the management and operation of fishing. The accords are as follows:

• Accord on the statutes of the Fishing Committee of the Center-East Atlantic aimed at supporting the sustainable exploitation of fishing resources through regulation of fishing and fisheries operations.

• Accord related to the protocol of the amendment to the International Convention for Conservation of Atlantic Tunas.

• Convention related to cooperation among African states along the Atlantic seaboard in developing fisheries in the region.

• Protocol on ways of applying the United Nations Convention on the Law of the Sea 1982 with regard to transzone fishing stocks and migrant fish.

Subsistence Fishing 2000 - 2004								
				Province				
Years	Unit	Cabinda	Zaire	Luanda	Bengo	Cuanza.S	Benguela	Namibe	Total
2000	Ton	1,466	2,169	8,939	2,188	2,918	11,933	10,278	39,891
2001	Ton	4,813	2,238	9,768	7,048	6,573	9,113	10,863	50,416
2002	Ton	3,691	5,707	25,125	2,032	6,843	46,560	36,619	126,577
2003	Ton	3,807	6,286	7,996	931	12,747	29,354	29,607	90,728
2004	Ton	8,997	15,811	14,377	2,079	12,407	23,925	27,364	104,960

Source: IPA – Ministry of Fishing

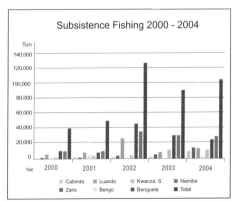

• Accord relating to the maintenance and management of fisheries in the south-east Atlantic in such a way as to preserve the sustainable use of fishing resources.

• Accord regarding the creation of an inter-governmental organization to support information and cooperation on the trading of fisheries products in Africa.

• Agreement to promote the fulfilment of international measures regarding maintenance of fishing boats operating on the high seas.

The Angolan fishing fleet is being rebuilt through donor assistance. Refrigeration facilities at the southern ports of Tombwa and Namibe have been overhauled and a new production line at the Tombwa canning factory has been installed with European Union assistance. Fish prices have been deregulated to encourage development, and the government, with assistance from the World Bank, has set up the Angolan Support Fund for Fisheries Development.

NEW DEVELOPMENT

A project costing US $1,189,378 has been approved by the UN High Commissioner for Refugees. The project will be run by FAO with the main aim of multiplication of seeds in areas of resettlement to facilitate the agricultural reintegration (self-sufficiency) of refugees returning to Angola.

The Institute for Agrarian Development (IDA, Instituto de Desenvolvimento Agrário) will distribute cattle in six different regions of the country to empower local farmers.

The Ministry of Fishing will build 48 industrial refrigerators in the provincial capitals and main municipalities. The refrigerators will be placed with private fishing companies.

The Agriculture Industry is becoming more advanced every day

MAIN COMPANIES

CAMPOTEC LDA

Mr Susantha Silva
General Manager

Mr Francisco Lourenço
Personnel Director

Board of Directors: Mr Emil M. Kumar / Mr Carlos Jaime / Mr Susantha Silva

Rua António Saldanha, nº 117, Ingombotas, Luanda

Tel: +244-222-395021 / 390331

Mobile: +244-923-922179 / 912-518760 / 912-641281

Fax: +244-222-390331

Email: campotec@limje.org.uk

Activity: Agricultural tractors and implements, construction equipment and transport vehicles

Limje Industrial Ltd from the United Kingdom (the major shareholder of Campotec Lda) has been involved in Angola in trade and investment finance, management consultancy, procurement and technical services, representation and distribution of internationally recognized agricultural equipment, construction machinery and equipment and transport vehicles. The group is also involved in the agricultural and financial sectors of the economy.

Empresa Nacional de Mecanização Agricola, (MECANAGRO-EP) is the Angolan shareholder of Campotec and is a state company that has well-equipped workshops in most of the provinces in Angola, handling machinery and equipment for the Ministry of Agriculture.

Campotec has well-equipped workshops, warehouses and office facilities in Luanda, Viana and in the provinces. Campotec represents Case IH (agricultural tractors and implements), Mahindra & Mahindra (agricultural tractors and implements), JCB (construction machinery and equipment), Tata International (buses, trucks, pickups and jeep-type vehicles) and Mahindra & Mahindra (jeep-type vehicles).

Campotec focuses on the rehabilitation of machinery and vehicles and also deals in motorcycles, cycles and spare parts.

"Our mission is the provision of top-quality products and technical support."
Mr Susantha Silva, General Manager

INSTITUTO NACIONAL DO CAFÉ – INCA

Mr Manuel Dias
Chairman

Avenida 4 de Fevereiro, nº 107–108, Luanda

Tel/Fax: +244-222-338678

Activity: Coffee

Date of Creation: 1982

Prior to independence, Angola was the fourth largest coffee producer in the world. The coffee industry has been severely hurt by war, but with an improvement in the security situation, coffee production is on the rise. Currently coffee is being cultivated in six provinces: Cuanza Norte, Cuanza Sul, Bengo, Uíge, Benguela and Cabinda.

The INCA was created in 1982 by the MINADER and it is a key institution for the health of the Angolan coffee sector. Its objectives include increasing the income of the participating families through the development and marketing of high-quality coffee for niche markets and the facilitation of the resettlement of displaced families, as well as the development of the technical capacity of the personnel and institutions involved in the project for future sustainability. The INCA is focused on those provinces which used to be the main coffee-producing area of Angola before the devastating civil war: Cabinda, Uíge, Cuanza Norte, Cuanza Sul and Bengo.

In addition to increasing the amount of land dedicated to coffee cultivation, Angola is planning to increase per acre yields. Angola has recently submitted a plan to the International Coffee Organization that would overhaul the sector over the next two years. The government has also put in place technical support teams to assist coffee producers through the INCA.

The INCA is predicting that Angola will export 22,000 tonnes per year of coffee within 10 years, a big but not an unreachable challenge as the current coffee production is just 5,000 tonnes per year.

"As foreign investors are also helping to revitalize the coffee industry, Angola facilitates the entry of those companies that are determined to open new plantations and improve the technical capacity of the sector. Foreign companies are needed to produce and transform the coffee into soluble and lyophilized product."
Mr Manuel Dias, Chairman

INSTITUTO DOS CEREAIS – INCER

Mr Estevão Miguel de Carvalho
Avenida 4 de Fevereiro, n° 101,
PO Box 1105, Luanda
Tel/Fax: +244-222-331611 / 334048

Activity: Cereals and grain

INCER – Instituto dos Cereais – was created in 1995 but did not start obtaining its first results until 1999. The mission of INCER is to increase the Angolan agricultural production so that it can cover its current shortfall of over 800,000 tonnes of grain.

The Angolan government is getting help from former soldiers to relaunch its farming activities via the distribution of plots of land for cultivation and farming tools.

As part of a national programme to encourage increased production and price stability, the National Grain Institute – INCER – is going to invest 90 million Kwanza (US $1.01 million) by the beginning of 2007 on 3,000 tonnes of grain to be put on reserve. The rise in agricultural production will increase economic security and help develop the country.

The Institute works to promote soil fertility management in order to improve Angolan food security, including:

• The use of locally available soil improvers, such as animal manures and crop residues, to make organic fertilizer use more economically attractive.
• Combining technology with an enabling environment for farmers to invest in their soils and for the private sector to invest in agricultural input and output market

Farm workers selling their produce at the side of the road

Cattle farm in Saurimo, Catoca Project

development, which further improves the economic feasibility of using fertilizer.

• Strategies that support farmers' organizations and private sector associations, and their effective cooperation with the public sector, which can help create this enabling environment.

INCER has shown that it is committed to promote the revitalization of the agricultural sector.

The Institute gives special importance to the rehabilitation and construction of basic infrastructure to support production; to agriculture expansion and rural extension; to seed spreading, production and multiplication; to conducting basic and applied research on agriculture and livestock; and to encouraging agriculture, livestock and forestry production, without jeopardising technical and professional training.

INSTITUTO NACIONAL DE DESENVOLVIMENTO AGRARIO – INDA

Mr Alfonso Pedro Canga
President
Largo Antonio Jacinto / Predio da Agricultura, 3rd Floor, Luanda
Tel: +244-222-323651 / 3322

Activity: Agriculture development
Date of Creation: 1989

The Institute for Agricultural Development (IDA) was created in 1989. This public institution is a legal entity and it has financial and administrative independence. Its main area of activity is agricultural and rural development.

INSTITUTE FOR AGRICULTURAL DEVELOPMENT

IDA's main duties:

- To coordinate and execute the policies and strategies designed to encourage the agricultural and rural development.

- To initiate the actions aimed at rehabilitating and developing rural communities.

PEDR (Rural Extension and Development Program)

Who benefits from PEDR?

- PEDR is designed for rural population (agriculture sector) which comprises the production units consisting of family units using mainly their own workforce and the natural resources at their hands.
- 802.730 families approximately will benefit from PEDR during the first year, a number to be increased to 1,197,000 in five years.

Targets of PEDR

- To guarantee food supply to the population, to reduce poverty and to encourage the integration of communities in the economic and social development of the country.
- To increase the production and productivity of family businesses involved in agriculture activities.
- To improve the life conditions of the communities involved.
- To organise the production of rural communities

ua Comandante Gika - Largo António Jacinto 3.º andar
el: 244 222 32 36 51 - Telex: 3322 MINADER
x. Postal 2109 E-mail: ida.canga@netangola.com Luanda - Angola

The general objectives of IDA are the following:

• To provide technical assistance on a constant basis to small farmers and peasants.

• To help small farmers and peasants to sell their products.

• To ensure that policies and strategies for rural development are encouraged, coordinated and executed.

• To initiate actions towards the rehabilitation and development of rural communities.

• To support those small farmers and peasants encountering difficulties with production.

• To give advice and support and work closely with other institutions devoted to help the agricultural sector.

• To draft, encourage and support development projects for small farmers and peasants and their organizations.

• To establish agreements, coordinate and be in contact with other public and private bodies and institutions, whether local, national or international, when deemed necessary.

• To support rural communities in their projects of local production capacity reinforcement.

• To increase the production and productivity of family agricultural businesses.

IDA is currently present in all 18 provinces of the country and in a large number of towns, and it maintains good relations with international institutions such as FAO, IFAD, AfDB, WB, SADEC, and bilateral cooperation agreements with the EU and some American and Asian countries.

Despite the great potential of Angolan agriculture, which is rich in cereal, cassava, sweet potato, banana and a wide range of fish and vegetables, it is nowadays a weak economy sector. Therefore IDA has an essential role for the development of agriculture in Angola, since we will only be able to fight hunger and poverty by encouraging this sector and assuring access to food for the whole population. For this purpose, IDA works closely with ANIP and AFDB, with a focus on both the technical training of farmers as well as good human resources management, in order to improve agricultural products in Angola and increase their competitiveness.

INSTITUTO NACIONAL DE DESENVOLVIMENTO FLORESTAL – IDF

Mr Tomás Pedro Caetano
Managing Director
Tel: +244-222-323934 / 222-323581
Fax: +244-222-323934
Email: idf@netangola.com

Activity: Forest development

IDF – the Instituto de Desenvolvimento Florestal – is a public body supported by the Ministry of Agriculture and Rural Development. It is a legal entity and it enjoys administrative and financial independence. Its main area of activity is executing and monitoring the application of legal rules and orders regulating the development, exploration, sustainable use, protection and conservation of both the fauna and the flora of Angola.

IDF grants permits and certificates necessary for CITES – the Convention on International Trade of wild fauna and flora species threatened with extinction, in close collaboration with the Faculty of Science of Agostinho Neto University, which has the scientific authority.

IDF carries out research that is essential to governmental policy and provides scientific support for conservation, development, management and sustainable use of biodiversity and its environment.

Its activities include: data collection and processing; preparation of expert documents for nature protection; specialized supervision and cooperation with public institutions for nature protection; specialized activities with respect to preparation of environmental assessments for individual developments; organization and implementation of educational and promotional nature protection activities; participation in execution of international nature protection agreements to which Angola is a party; implementation of nature protection projects and programmes; and also cooperation in implementation of nature protection projects.

Spectacular forests and landscape

The Institute is responsible for:

• Nature protection information system.

• Preparation of adequate databases on plant, fungi and animal species, habitats, ecosystems and landscapes.

• Monitoring the degree of conservation and threats to all components of the biological and landscape diversity and proposing protection measures.

• Preparation of a list of landscape types, evaluation of landscape types and monitoring the state of significant and characteristic features of landscapes.

• Establishment and maintenance of a register of speleological formations.

• Making nature protection data publicly available.

Forest resources that are relevant to the economy of Angola are: fisheries, medicinal plants, fruits and leaves, mushrooms, papyrus, palm oil, game, honey, wax and resin, among others.

The Institute's main mission is to guarantee the sustainable production of forest resources and assure the conservation and protection of ecosystems in order to fulfil society's basic needs.

INSTITUTO NACIONAL DE INVESTIGAÇÃO PESQUEIRA – INIP (NATIONAL INSTITUTE OF FISHING RESEARCH)

Mrs Francisca Delgado
General Director
Rua Mortala Mohamed, Ilha do Cabo,
PO Box 260, Luanda
Tel: +244-228-741465
Fax: +244-222-309330
Email: bclme.behp@nexus.ao
Website: www.angola-minpescas.com

Activity: Fishing research and development

INIP – Instituto Nacional de Investigação Pesqueira (National Fishing Research Institute) – is a government body in charge of writing technical and scientific reports and surveys about Angola's aquatic biological resources and about the marine ecosystems and continental waters, while controlling the quality of Angolan marine biodiversity.

The government supports the development and coordination of regional centres of fishing research and the training of INIP specialists and support staff, in order to enlarge the analysis capacity of the national aquatic ecosystem.

Other activities aim to reinforce the programme of biological sampling of commercial fishing, to improve laboratory equipment for quality control, as well as to develop action lines for research into continental waters resources, which definitely has an important role in the reduction of poverty.

The Ceremony of the Sea, a ritual performed to ask for a good fishing season

Moreover, in 2007 a new oceanographic investigation vessel will be acquired, and this will place Angola among the four most important countries in the world in terms of capacity for marine research.

Even in more developed countries, fishing and oil resources research is an issue. For this reason, the government created a national commission composed of all the sea-related sectors, and an oil pollution control laboratory has been set up in Luanda.

In order to increase the capacity for analysis of the national aquatic ecosystem, the government is also investing in the development and coordination of regional fishing research centres and in the training of 50 INIP scientists and support staff.

These activities complement the Angolan aquatic research development project, which also aims to intensify and extend cooperation with Norway, Portugal and Spain, as well as international institutions such as the European Union, the FAO and the International Atomic Energy Agency.

In 2007 Angola will have seven multifunction scientific research vessels to control the quality of products and by-products of the national fisheries, and which will be used for Angola's fishing and marine research.

Angola has impressive fishing resources and 1,650 kilometres of coastline.

NOVA SOTECMA

Mr Helder Morais
General Manager
Avenida 1° Congresso do MPLA, n° 24–26, Luanda
Tel: +244-222-330342 / 332327
Fax: +244-222-335378
Email: ns@novasotecma.com
Website: www.novasotecma.com

Activity: Commercialization of agricultural and industrial materials and equipment

Established in 1995 as Sociedade de Direito Angolano, the company integrates the heritage, experience and staff from the previous Sotecma established in 1952.

Until 1995 this firm was involved in water pumping, coffee machines, palm oil and corn and manioc mills.

Nova-Sotecma led the rollers distribution market with the brand SKF.

As before, the company continues in the same market with the same well-respected brand and is still a major player in the Angolan market for coffee machines, corn mills and palm oil presses.

Nova-Sotecma stands out in the commercialization of industrial protection materials, hand and electric tools, electrical pumps, power pumps, workshop equipment and handling equipment.

The company has been linking its image of quality to worldwide brands which are leaders in their fields such as:

• SKF – one of the biggest worldwide roller manufacturers
• Grundfos – electric pumps
• 3M – respiratory protection
• Legrand – electrical accessories
• Lister – diesel engines
• Slavi – welding electrodes
• Gloria, Jallate, Auda, Drager, Protector, Uvex – industrial security
• Italcom, Mega, Stahlwille, Dewalt – tools and workshop and garage equipment.

At present the company employs more than 100 people. The headquarters is in Luanda, as well as the factory and warehouse, but there are also offices in Lobito and Sumbe.

ENERGY & OIL

"Human flesh characterizes people, animals have a different name"
Angolan proverb

OVERVIEW AND TRADITIONAL SOURCES

Angola possesses rich and diversified energy resources. However, electricity generation for the country during 2003 (the most recent available statistics) was 1.9 billion kilowatt hours (Bkwh), reaching only 15% of Angola's population. Blackouts occur frequently, for those who do have access to electric power.

Angola had proven oil reserves of 5.4 billion barrels and natural gas reserves of 1.6 trillion cubic feet (TCF) as of January 2006; Angola has tripled its oil reserves in the last seven years. Angola is sub-Saharan Africa's second largest oil producer behind Nigeria. In 2005 Angolan oil consumption averaged 60,000 barrels per day (bpd). However, oil consumption is expected to increase as Angola's infrastructure is refurbished and expanded. Approximately 90% of Angola's government revenue is derived from the sale of crude oil.

ELECTRICITY

The Empresa Nacional de Electricidade (ENE), the state-owned electric utility, is the only significant power generator. ENE intends to restore its generation capacity by rehabilitating its hydropower stations.

ELECTRICITY GENERATION

Angola's electricity generating capacity as of 2003 was 0.7 gigawatts. Electricity generation for the country during 2003 was 1.9 billion kilowatt hours (Bkwh), while consumption was 1.8 Bkwh. Only 15% of Angola's population has access to electric power.

Three separate distribution networks are used to supply electricity throughout Angola: the North System supplies the provinces of Luanda, Bengo, Cuanza Norte, Malange and Cuanza Sul. The Central System provides for the provinces of Benguela, Huambo and parts of Bié. The Southern System supplies to Huíla and Namibe provinces. The government aims to link these networks to create a national grid through the Southern Africa Power Pool (SAPP).

HYDROPOWER

Hydroelectric facilities generate more than two-thirds of Angola's electricity.

The Matala dam (51 MW), situated on the Cunene River, is the main source of electricity in south-west Angola. The Cambambe dam (180 MW) on the Cuanza River and the Mabubas dam (17.8 MW) on the Dande River are the main sources of electricity in northern Angola.

The Gove dam is expected to be rebuilt as per an agreement with Namibia to jointly rehabilitate the dam. The Lumaun dam is not operational, as a result of severe damage during the war.

Odebrecht, a Brazilian construction company, has completed phase one of the construction of a hydroelectric facility at Capanda on the Cuanza River. Work on the 520-MW plant began in the mid-1980s but was suspended due to the civil war. Two of the four planned turbines began generating electricity (290 MW) in January 2004. Russian firm Technopromexport has begun installation of turbines to be operational in 2007. The completed Capanda projects will nearly double Angola's electricity capacity. Capanda-generated electricity is already supplying Luanda.

GAS

Angola has proven natural gas reserves of 1.6 trillion cubic feet (TCF) as of January 2006. The majority (approximately 85%) of natural gas produced in Angola is flared; the remainder is re-injected to aid in oil recovery. The Angolan government has plans to reduce natural gas flaring by ending flaring at fields north of the Congo River mouth in Cabinda. CABGOC has initiated two zero-flare fields, Nemba and Lomba, with plans to make Kuito the third. Future plans include converting flared gas to liquefied natural gas (LNG), natural gas liquids (NGLs) and LPG.

Chevron Texaco and Sonangol are developing a project to convert natural gas from several offshore oil fields into LNG for export. The facility will process flared gas from Blocks 1, 2, 3, 4, 15, 16, 17 and 18. The facility will have a capacity of 750 million cubic feet per day (Mmcf/d) and will be located near the city of Soyo, in Zaire province in the north of Angola. Total cost of the LNG project is estimated at US $5 billion and the LNG facility is not expected to come online before 2010. Chevron Texaco and Sonangol are the principal stakeholders in the LNG project, with Norsk Hydro, BP, Total and Exxon Mobil.

Chevron Texaco has awarded a contract to Paragon Engineering Services to lessen natural gas flaring at its Tukula, Wamba, Numbi and Malongo fields. Paragon plans to build several new gas processing platforms and modify existing platforms to recover gas that is currently flared.

PETROLEUM

Prospecting for hydrocarbons in Angola began in 1910 when Canha & Formigal was granted the oil lease of an area of 114,000 km^2 in the Congo Offshore and the Cuanza Basin. The first well was drilled in 1915. In 1973 oil became Angola's principal export. By 1974 production reached 172,000 bpd, which was the maximum output during the pre-independence period.

Angola has proven oil reserves of 5.4 billion barrels as of January 2006. The majority of the reserves are located in Angola's offshore blocks. Proven reserves are also located onshore near the city of Soyo. The majority of Angolan oil is medium to light crude (30 degrees–40 degrees API) with low sulphur content (0.12%–0.14%).

Angola is sub-Saharan Africa's second largest oil producer behind Nigeria. Angola's crude oil production has

more than quadrupled over the past two decades. In 1986 crude oil production averaged 280,000 bpd, while production in 2005 averaged 1,250,000 bpd.

Oil production is predicted to reach 2,000,000 bpd by 2008, based on new deepwater production sites. Angola's oil consumption is relatively small. In 2005 Angolan oil consumption averaged 60,000 bpd.

OIL SECTOR ORGANIZATION

Angola's national oil company, Sociedade Nacional de Combustiveis de Angola (Sonangol), was established in 1976 and was made the sole concessionaire for exploration and production in 1978. Sonangol works with foreign companies through joint ventures (JVs) and production sharing agreements (PSAs), funding its share of production with oil-backed borrowing. The most significant foreign oil companies operating in Angola are Chevron Texaco, ExxonMobil, Total and BP.

The production for January and February was 1,680,000 bpd each month. Oil production in Angola is predicted to reach two million bpd in 2008, after new deepwater production sites are expected to come online.

Crude Oil Production 1980-2005

Year	Average Quantity Produced (bpd)
1980	150,000
1982	122,000
1984	208,000
1986	282,000
1988	452,000
1990	475,000
1992	526,000
1994	536,000
1996	709,000
1998	735,000
2000	746,000
2002	896,000
2004	1,052,000
2005	1,257,000

Source: http://www.eia.doe.gov/emeu/international/angola.htm

Oil production has quadrupled since 1980 and currently stands at over 810,000 barrels per day

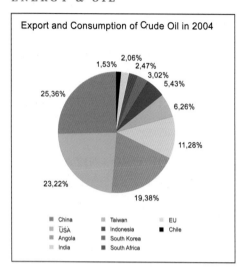

Export and Consumption of Crude Oil in 2004

2,06%
1,53%   2,47%
        3,02%
            5,43%
25,36%
            6,26%

            11,28%

23,22%
    19,38%

■ China   ■ Taiwan   ■ EU
■ USA   ■ Indonesia   ■ Chile
■ Angola   ■ South Korea
■ India   ■ South Africa

Source: Sonangol

Luanda Refinery Production

Luanda Refinery Units	Capacity (bpd)
Crude unit	35,000
Vacuum unit	2,500
Catalytic reformer	1,900
Catalytic hydro desulphuriser	2,800
Pre kero / distillate hydrotreater	3,500
Asphalt (t/d)	950

Source: Fina Refinery

Angolan crude is also exported to markets in Europe, Latin America and Asia. As an example, South Korean crude imports from Angola have grown from US $97m in 1998 to US $588m in 1999.

REFINING AND DOWNSTREAM

The Fina Petroleos de Angola refinery in Luanda, a joint venture between Sonangol and TotalFinaElf, has a crude oil processing capacity of 39,000 bpd. The refinery produces almost all of Angola's domestic requirements of petrol, kerosene and jet fuel, as well as a small amount of product for export.

Planning for a new 200,000-bpd refinery to be located in the coastal city of Lobito is in progress. A total of 50% of the products produced at the new refinery will be consumed domestically; the remaining 50% will be for export. Sonangol has linked building the refinery to ownership in Blocks 15, 17 and 18. The refinery is expected to be operating by 2009.

Oil production in Angola is concentrated in numerous offshore blocks. The offshore blocks are divided into three bands: (band A) shallow water blocks 0–13; (band B) deepwater blocks 14–30; and (band C) ultra-deepwater blocks 31–40. Block Zero is located offshore of the Cabinda province and accounts for approximately 370,000 bpd of Angola's oil production, or one-third of Angola's total crude oil production.

Sonangol estimates that Angolan demand for oil products will grow by 500% within 10 to 20 years. From 2004, Sonangol has imported fuel from abroad to ease domestic shortages as the Luanda refinery is unable to meet increasing demand.

OIL EXPORTS

Angola's largest oil export partners are China and the United States.

The United States has made Angola eligible for tariff preference under the African Growth and Opportunity Act (AGOA) and Angola has become the second largest non-OPEC supplier of oil to the US outside the western hemisphere.

Angolan exports to Asian countries have grown rapidly in recent years. Recent trade figures suggest that China's oil imports from Angola have grown more than 400%. Chinese demand for Angolan crude is primarily a result of its enormous expansion and its adoption of stricter environmental standards that will place a premium on lower-sulphur West African crude.

In March 2004 Angola committed itself to ending fuel subsidies to encourage downstream investment. As at 2006 these subsidiaries are still in place.

RETAIL SECTOR

Angola's retail sector, which once boasted over 450 filling stations, has shrunk to 100 outlets. Construction of 120 additional service stations is planned over the next few years, at an expected cost of more than US $300 million. Portugal's Galp Energia has announced its intention to build a chain of stations in Angola. Sonangol and Galp Energia currently provide product distribution and marketing in Angola.

NEW DEVELOPMENTS

Solar Turbines is developing a project in Sumbe, in Cuanza Sul province, together with INP (Instituto Nacional de Petróleos/National Institute of Petroleum). Solar Turbines is training INP staff with the objective of producing Angolan experts in gas turbine technology.

Angola is developing plans for a new 200,000-bpd oil refinery in the coastal city of Lobito. A total of 50% of the products produced at the new refinery will be consumed domestically; the remaining 50% will be for export.

Chevron Texaco and Sonangol are developing a project to convert natural gas from several offshore oil fields to LNG for export. The facility will process flared gas from Blocks 1, 2, 3, 4, 15, 16, 17 and 18. The facility will have a capacity of 750 million cubic feet per day (Mmcf/d) and will be located near the city of Soyo, in Zaire province in the north of Angola.

MAIN COMPANIES

ENERGY

ANGASES – SOCIEDADE ANGOLANA DE GASES COMPRIMIDOS

Mr Julio A. de Melo Araújo
Director General
Travessa da Boavista, nº 31–32, Luanda
Tel: +244-222-335682 / 222-392401

Activity: Gas

Date of Creation: 1954

Angases was founded in 1954 and its main activity is the production and marketing of industrial and medical gases (oxygen, dissolved acetylene, carbon dioxide, argon, etc.). It markets materials for the welding industry (autogenic, oxyacetylene and electricity) and it is also involved in the production of fire extinguishers.

As one of the main producers of this type of product in the country, Angases has industrial complexes in various provinces. It is also one of the main producers of respiratory oxygen, and thus it plays a key role in Angola as it supplies oxygen to the hospitals.

Adding value to the Angolan economy, Angases is fulfilling local market demand for gas, as well as export commitments and long-term strategic requirements.

It operates according to the prevailing laws and regulations, conducts techno-economic studies for gas projects, manages sales, gas transmission and distribution systems and coordinates all related activities in collaboration with local and international partners. It also studies and determines optimum locations for gas projects, trying to attain the best outcomes for people as well as for the environment.

As the country has opened itself to the international market, Angases is ready to combat the entrance of new competition into Angola from neighbouring countries.

EDEL – LUANDA ELECTRICITY SUPPLY COMPANY

Mr Rui Gourgel

Managing Director

Rua Cónego Manuel das Neves, n° 234, Luanda

Tel: +244-222-448130

Fax: +244-222-440268

Activity: National electricity supplier

Edel, the Luanda Electricity Supply Company, is currently facing difficulties in supplying power to the Luanda pop-ulation due to the emergence of unlawful use. Of the nearly four million inhabitants of Luanda, only 132,126 are authorized customers.

A total of US $15 million has been spent since 2003 on the installation of 60 new electricity transformation stations in the Luanda districts of Kazenga, Adriano Moreira, Hoji-ya-Henda, Petrangol, Sambizanga, Prenda, Rocha Pinto, Samba, Sagrada Esperança, Corimba, Golfe, Neves Bendinha, Kinanga and Palanca.

This was carried out by the Luanda Electricity Supplying Firm (EDEL) as part of the first phase of the project of improvement to the capital city's power network.

In order to improve the situation of electricity in Angola, technical assistance will be provided to EDEL to establish a business model based on cost recovery, management information systems and better customer relations to improve financial viability. The municipal government will also be involved in the role of planning and facilitating an improved infrastructure and a safer environment for residents. Technical assistance will be provided as well to the municipal government to increase its planning and implementation capacity to meet community needs.

ELECNOR

Mr Rodrigo López-Lax Rivera

Delegate Manager

Estrada de Catete, Campo INE, (Maristas), Luanda

Tel: +244-222-324579

Fax: +244-222-324580

Email: rlopezlax.dtf@elecnor.es

Website: www.elecnor.com

Activity: Electricity market operator

Date of Creation: June 1958

Turnover: EUR 657m (2004 in Spain))

Employees: 6,000

Elecnor, a privately owned Spanish company that is listed in the Interconnected Stock Exchange System, was established in June 1958 as an electricity market operator. Since then this Madrid-based Spanish company has pro-

116

gressively established itself in the power generation, gas, telecommunications, transport, water and environment sectors, providing integrated services for each of its activities within the framework of Total Quality required by the AENOR and ISO 14001 certificates that the company holds, thus ensuring that Elecnor's activities conform to environmental standards and criteria.

As a result of this diversification process, Elecnor currently engages in project development, design, construction, management, maintenance and operation in all aforementioned fields. It is furthermore one of the Spain's top independent project development groups and a leader in integrated project management and infrastructure development.

Elecnor, with a team of over 6,000 highly qualified professionals and a consolidated revenue of over EUR 657 million in 2004, of which foreign markets account for EUR 144 million, is present in over 20 countries.

Locally, Elecnor has been working in Angola since 1990, including during the hard years of war. Its main activity has been in the area of construction of high-voltage energy transport lines and transformer substations with clients such as ENE and EDEL, and more recently with the GPL installing the entire lighting system of the Coqueiros football stadium.

Nowadays, the company's experience and positioning in the country has enabled it to create Elecnor Sucursal of Angola, a local company that allows it to tackle new projects conceived for local companies.

Fidelity to clients is paramount in order to provide the best after-sales service in case of any problems. Local personnel are trained by highly experienced employees in order to maintain a high level of efficiency for all the various tasks.

ENE – EMPRESA NACIONAL DE ELECTRICIDADE

Mr Edoardo Nelumba
Managing Director
Edifício Geominas, nº 6–7, Luanda
Tel: +244-222-321529
Fax: +244-222-323382
Website: www.ene.co.ao

Activity: Angolan national electricity supplier

The state-owned Empresa Nacional de Electricidade (ENE) is primarily responsible for the generation and supply of electricity in Angola, in addition to which there are several privately owned generating companies.

ENE wants to consolidate and to lead the national electric market and to become one of the most competitive companies on a regional level. Its mission is to produce, carry, distribute and commercialize electric energy within the international standards of quality and reliability, and always following technical, social and ecological principles to improve the satisfaction and interest of its customers and shareholders.

The company owns and manages the Angolan electricity distribution network and it operates coal-fired and gas-fired power stations and CHP plants.

The company is involved in the rehabilitation of the thermal power stations at Lobito and Chitoto, and in many other projects, not only technical but also of social responsibility, such as the creation of the installations for a medical centre in Luanda.

The main functions of ENE are:

• Electricity generation and transmission throughout the country.
• Electrical energy supply to customers connected to the national network.
• Maintenance and construction of power generation and transmission facilities.
• Centralized purchase and sale of electrical energy.

• Import and export of electrical energy.

• Introduction and promotion of energy efficiency in the generation and transmission of electrical energy.

ENE not only provides low-cost electricity but also offers a good customer service. The company is committed to providing a safe and responsive service. It considers that electricity is essential to keep life running smoothly, safely and efficiently. If for some reason service is interrupted, it will answer complaints or arrange repairs as soon as possible.

EPAL – EMPRESA PÚBLICA DE AGUAS DE LUANDA

Mr Lucrécio da Costa

Managing Director

Rua Fredrich Engels, nº 3, Luanda

Tel: +244-222-335001

Fax: +244-222-330380

Activity: National water supplier

The water production and distribution system in Luanda is managed by EPAL (Empresa Pública de Aguas de Luanda), which currently operates under a cost-recovery system. System I (built in 1953) and System II (built in 1971/81) obtain water from the Bengo River, and System III (built in 1998–2000) and Kikuxi (1985) get water from the Cuanza River.

EPAL is responsible for planning and developing water infrastructure and it is committed to providing the highest levels of customer service and water quality by investing in improvements and operating efficiently. It is part of its strategy to provide a full support and information service for customers. EPAL provides a broad range of water and environmental services throughout Angola, from taking care of water quality standards through to protecting onsite water and wastewater assets.

At the same time, the company treats wastewater and sewage each day, from communities and businesses across the region. By cleaning it and returning it safely to

Capanda Project, Malange

rivers and streams, it helps protect the health of the environment. EPAL is always looking forward to new techniques and technologies to provide good quality water and better water treatment.

As Luanda has some problems with water distribution, the water trucks business is quite extensive in the country. There are seven points where water trucks can collect water in Luanda. The main one is Kifangondo, near the Bengo River, which fills around 450 tanker loads per day (5,000,000 litres). Kikuxi is the second largest collection point and the raw water is drawn from the Cuanza River, with an average capacity of 150 fills per day. The other five are smaller and draw already treated water from EPAL. These points see considerably less traffic as the whole process is slower. It is currently estimated that there are around 330 tanker trucks in Luanda, of which the great majority are privately owned.

GAMEK – GABINETE DE APROVEITAMENTO DO MÉDIO KWANZA

Mrs Emanuela Bernardette Alfonso V. Lopes
Managing Director
Rua do Massangano, s/n, Luanda
Tel: +244-222-445072 / 222-675801
Fax: +244-222-447973
Email: afonsoe@gamek.com
Website: www.gamek.com

Activity: Hydroelectric energy generating power
Date of Creation: 1986
Employees: 2,500

Gamek is a state-owned company in charge of the largest civil construction project undertaken in Angola. Lying in Middle River Cuanza, on the border between Cuanza Norte and the province of Malange, is the Capanda dam. The works of the dam were started in 1986 with a state investment of US $750 million paid in oil supplies to foreign companies. To date an estimated US $4 billion has been invested in the project. However, the dam has yet to produce any hydroelectric power.

According to Gamek's original schedule, Capanda was supposed to start generating power in December 1993. But the dam suffered multiple attacks during the last years of the war and the production could not start before 2000.

There are two phases to the Capanda project, the first involving the construction of two 130-MW turbines. The second phase will bring the total power-generating capacity of the dam to 520 MW. This will surpass the whole of Angola's current hydroelectric capacity. The first phase was completed in May 2003.

The Capanda project currently has 2,500 employees, most of them Angolans. However, the majority of the experts are Brazilian and Russian, and Gamek considers this crucial.

OIL

AKER KVAERNER ANGOLA LTD

Mr Kjell Valdal
General Manager
Base da Sonils OSC, Rua 6 – IL Boavista, Luanda, Angola
Tel: +244-222-310808
Mobile: +244-912-641000
Email: kjell.staale.valdal@akerkvaerner.com
Website: www.akerkvaerner.com

Activity: Aker Kvaerner Angola provides a complete range of surface and subsea solutions for the oil and gas industry.
Date of Creation: Aker Kvaerner was incorporated in Angola in 2000. The Aker Kvaerner Angola Base at Sonils opened in February 2005.
Employees: 150

Aker Kvaerner group has had representation in Angola since 2000. The Aker Kvaerner Angola Base at Sonils was opened in February 2005.

The company has since grown to over 150 employees with its main activities currently related to the Total E&P Angola Dalia Subsea Production System.

Aker Kvaerner Angola is a part of Aker Kvaerner Subsea. Aker Kvaerner Subsea is a global company with US $650 million annual turnover and over 2,700 employees. Aker Kvaerner Subsea is part of the Subsea Business Area within the Aker Kvaerner group. Aker Kvaerner Subsea is a leading provider of subsea systems for oil and gas production supporting all aspects of subsea field development.

Aker Kvaerner Subsea is a fully integrated company that provides a complete range of surface and subsea solutions for the oil and gas industry from concept screening and design through manufacturing, fabrication and commissioning. Worldwide activities are led by six business streams and supported by five regions.

BP

Mr José Patricio
President
Av. Rainha Ginga, n° 87, Luanda
Tel: +244-222-637272
Fax: +244-222-637470
Website: www.bp.com

Activity: Oil and gas

BP has been involved in Angola for almost 40 years. After BP merged with Amoco in 1998, its joint portfolio gave it substantial deepwater offshore interests – making Angola an important new profit centre for BP's exploration and production portfolio.

Angola produces over 1.3 million barrels of oil equivalent (bboe) a day, and over time, this could rise to 2 million bboe a day. By the end of the decade BP Angola will have invested in excess of US $8 billion in its Angolan business, placing it among the largest foreign investors in the country.

BP Angola has partners in all four of Angola's principal deepwater blocks – 15, 17, 18 and 31 – where a number of discoveries have been made. Deepwater operations are both complex and challenging. BP Angola drills in water depths ranging between 1,200 m and 2,700 m

across blocks and in areas where the subsurface geology tests its drilling and completions capabilities. It has the expertise and technology to make even the most remote resources accessible and viable.

BP Angola employs over 600 people. This number is increasing rapidly and is expected to double by 2012. The company's aim is to recruit Angolans and develop their skills to enable them to fill most of the jobs in the business, including many senior posts. It works in partnership with both national and foreign companies.

BP is very conscious of the need to maintain a focused corporate responsibility agenda, to bring real benefits to Angola and be part of the community at every level. That means listening to its stakeholders – the government, community leaders, church leaders, academics, local and international NGOs and others – to find out how it can be mutually beneficial in the communities where BP works. Its sustainable development and community investment programme focuses on enterprise development, access to energy and education.

CHEVRON ANGOLA

Mr Jim Blackwell
Managing Director
Av. Lenine, n° 77, Ingombotas, Luanda
Tel: +244-222-392646 / 393093
Website: www.chevron.com

Activity: Oil and gas
Date of Creation: 1950

Chevron Angola was the first oil company to work deep water in Angola, where it landed more than half a century ago. In this time it has gained and consolidated an image of being not only one of the most important oil companies – the first in Angola and the fourth on an international scale – with good relations with both public and private companies, but also one with a huge impact on society. Chevron is present in 182 countries and employs more than 3,000 people.

The beginning of a new era.

With the right partners, even the most ambitious goal is within reach. As a leader in Angola's oil industry, Chevron is paving the way to progress; we were the first to produce oil from a deepwater well and are the second largest employer of Angolan nationals. We're working today for a better tomorrow.

Chevron

As a business and as a member of the world community, it is committed to creating superior value for its stockholders, customers, partners, employees and the countries in which it operates. It aims to be the global energy company most admired for its people, partnership and performance. Chevron helps people, communities and nations build human capacity, strengthen local economies and improve health and education.

Chevron Angola pursues profitable growth through new business opportunities, expert management of existing assets and world-class capital stewardship. It operates safely, reliably and efficiently and routinely handles the petroleum industry's toughest logistical and environmental challenges. It also manages technology to achieve the best, most cost-effective results: sophisticated seismic analysis, high-angle and horizontal drilling, floating and subsurface production systems, and flooding and reservoir simulation.

However, Chevron is, above all things, a socially concerned company, which has had a huge impact on the local community for years, especially in the province of Cabinda, where the company's main platforms are. The staff is 80% Angolan, who receive regular training, and the aim is to increase this figure to 90% by 2010. Chevron invests, among others, in agricultural programmes, because it believes that Angola's potential does not only lie in oil production but in other sectors as well.

It is the proud creator of a social responsibility programme, which funds among other things a number of scholarships for young talented Angolans to study in well-known universities abroad so they can then return home and contribute with their knowledge to the growth of Angola. At present 75 Angolans benefit from Chevron scholarships in the USA.

Chevron's challenge for the future is to be the leading big oil company working with local communities.

"If you are planning to come to Angola, do so now: the sooner you come, the better the opportunities you will grab."
Mr Jim Blackwell, Managing Director

ENI

Mr Luigi Tiro
Managing Director
Rua Nicolau Gomes Spencer, n° 140, Luanda
Tel: +244-222-391844
Fax: +244-222-394133

Activity: Oil and gas

Eni is a major integrated energy company, committed to growth in the activities of finding, producing, transporting, transforming and marketing oil and gas. In recent years Eni has experienced an unprecedented period of growth and today it is one of the world's leading oil companies.

This oil company has been one of the first to develop deepwater exploration and production technologies. Eni has acquired considerable know-how and has adopted state-of-the-art technologies and methodologies in this sector. A number of deepwater exploration projects have been launched in seas around the world, Angola being one of them.

A world leader in the development of natural gas transmission infrastructure, Eni is involved in a number of highly technological initiatives both in terms of characteristics and capacity. It is also one of the most important operators in design and construction of large-scale onshore plants in the following sectors: oil and gas production and processing, refining, natural gas processing and economic exploitation, chemical compounds, networks for gathering and transporting hydrocarbons via pipeline, electricity, environmental operations and infrastructure.

Corporate responsibility is an integral part of Eni's culture and working practices. The company pursues a growth model that combines profit, innovation and sustainable development with the aim of favouring a culture of sustainability and reinforcing the trust of its stakeholders. Among other social projects, the company gives support to the Global Fund to fight AIDS, Tuberculosis and Malaria and to the Global Business Coalition on HIV/AIDS.

GALP ENERGIA

Mr Ferreira Rodrigues
Managing Director
Largo 4 de Fevereiro, n° 3, 1st Floor, Luanda
Tel: +244-217-241024
Fax: +244-210-039011

Activity: Oil and gas

In Angola, Galp Energia Group operates through three main companies: Petrogal Angola Lda, Agran Lda and Sonangalp Lda.

Petrogal Angola is held by Petrogal SA (88.7%) and Galp Exploração SA (11.3%). It manages the stakes held in the other companies and sells lubricants. Agran was set up in 1960 and is held at 98.7% by Petrogal Angola. The company manufactures and sells insecticides, fungicides and similar products. Sonangalp is held by Petrogal Angola (49%) and Sonangol (51%). The company distributes and sells liquid fuels and lubricants and operates gas and service stations.

Galp is concentrating its investments on countries where the official language was Portuguese, where Portuguese companies showed some comparative advantages. Investments in Angola showed the first significant results, with sales of 1,904,000 barrels produced in the Kuíto field in Angola, and stabilized average daily production levels in excess of 5,000 barrels were achieved. Research was also successful in Angola with the discovery of a further two oil fields at Tamboco and Lobito.

HALLIBURTON

Mr Bob Dodantedgrast
Managing Director
Base Sonils, PO Box 3736, Porto de Luanda, Luanda
Tel: +244-222-310925 / 311763 / 310926
Fax: +244-222-310363
Website: www.halliburton.com

Activity: Providers of products and services to the oil and gas industries

Founded in 1919, Halliburton is one of the world's largest providers of products and services to the oil and gas industries. The company adds value through the entire lifecycle of oil and gas reservoirs and provides and integrates products and services, starting with exploration and development, moving through production, operations, maintenance, conversion and refining, to infrastructure and abandonment.

Halliburton employs more than 100,000 people in over 120 countries working in four major operating groups: drilling and formation evaluation, fluid systems, production optimization, and digital and consulting solutions. These segments offer a broad array of products and services to upstream oil and gas customers worldwide, ranging from the manufacturing of drill bits and other downhole and completion tools to pressure pumping services.

Halliburton's philosophy statement aims to lead the world in integrated energy services, energy equipment, engineering, construction and maintenance, all supported by four key goals, described as technological leadership, operational excellence, innovative business relationships and a dynamic workforce.

Halliburton Angola contributes to the strong performance in global engineering and international project management through recently awarded liquefied natural gas (LNG) and gas-to-liquids (GTL) projects. Halliburton was recently awarded a US $20 million contract to develop oil services in Cabinda province which will benefit all oil companies operating there.

US Export-Import Bank guaranteed US $86.6 million in loans for this contract. The further development of the Cabinda concession area will benefit all oil companies operating there.

HYDRO ANGOLA

Mr Svein Breivik
Managing Director
Rua Major Kanhangulo, n° 86, Luanda
Tel: +244-222-398798
Fax: +244-222-398797
Website: www.hydro.com

Activity: Oil, energy and aluminium

Hydro is a Fortune 500 energy and aluminium supplier founded in 1905, with 33,000 employees in nearly 40 countries worldwide, having an increasing presence in Angola. Hydro has the Norwegian continental shelf as its base, but is producing oil and gas in Angola, Canada, Russia and Libya, with activities in the Gulf of Mexico, Iran and Denmark.

In the sector of oil and energy, Hydro is a leading international offshore producer of oil and gas, based on a strong position in the development of the Norwegian petroleum industry during the past 40 years. Its world-class project execution skills and expertise in deep waters and rough seas help it realize maximum results from its operations all around the world. Hydro is also at the forefront of wind and hydrogen energy production. Hydro is also the third-largest integrated aluminium supplier in the world, with a presence on every continent.

Hydro is an integrated European energy company and a main producer of hydropower and wind power and has a prime role in transport and trading of energy across Europe. As a leading European oil and energy company, it has a key role in meeting multi-branch wells, smart wells technology, deepwater and subsea installations; its presence in Angola helps to broaden new horizons in the oil market.

The company has been present in Angola for more than 15 years and is participating in projects within the oil and gas sector. It is also considering the possibility of producing aluminium in Angola, as part of its strategy to position itself in countries with favourable conditions for future energy supply.

The company is operating 13 oil and gas installations and its own production in 2005 averaged 563,000 barrels of oil equivalent, placing it among the largest offshore companies in the world. It is a partner in blocks 4, 17 and 34 offshore in Angola, with a 10% interest in the producing field Girassol on block 17.

OCTOMAR SERVIÇOS MARÍTIMOS

Mr Ricardo Amaral
General Manager
Rua Engenheiro Costa Serrão, n° 13, Luanda
Tel: +244-222-390417 / 390713 / 390279
Email: octomar@snet.co.ao

Activity: Oil and maritime services, oilfield support
Date of Creation: 1998

Octomar Serviços Marítimos Lda was established on 2nd February 1998 through a joint venture agreement between SMIT Terminals (formerly Octo Marine) operating out of South Africa, and Marsub – Trabalhos Submarinos, an Angolan diving services company.

The specific intention of Octomar's formation was to provide integrated marine services to oilfield clients within the Angolan region by combining the proven skills, resources and assets of its shareholders and associates. The agreement was further motivated by the success of contracts undertaken jointly between SMIT Terminals and Marsub over the previous three years within the Angolan region.

It is Octomar's policy to develop local infrastructure and train local people, thus assuring a high local content in its operations. Octomar provides a variety of multi-disciplinary turnkey services relating to:

• Oilfield support – anchor handling, multi-purpose and field support vessels
• Operation and maintenance of offshore tanker terminals
• Underwater operations and IRM
• Marine contracting support
• ROVs (remotely operated vehicles)
• Dive support vessels.

124

To supplement Octomar's own resources, its teams draw from appropriate group resources and capabilities for any of the following: design and project engineering, specialist vessels, oceaneering, tankers for FPSOs and ocean transportation.

PARAGON ANGOLA

Ms Paula F. Johnson
Managing Director
Largo do Pescador, n° 7 Ilha do Cabo, Luanda
Tel: +244-222-335688
Fax: +244-222-338770
Website: www.paragonangola.com

Activity: Oil and gas support services

Combining the local expertise of Angola's Prodoil Exploração e Produção de Hidrocarbonetos SARL with the global capabilities of Houston-based AMEC Paragon Inc., Paragon Angola Engenharia e Serviços provides a complete package of project management, engineering, design/drafting, procurement, construction management, inspection, and start-up/commissioning support services for Angola's rapidly expanding oil and gas industry. Paragon Angola is dedicated to enhancing local infrastructure, maximizing in-country content and contributing to Angola's long-term economic growth and stability.

Paragon Angola provides a solid foundation for responsible and cost-effective local project execution: local knowledge after years of successful work in Angola, state-of-the-art technology and automated project work processes, programmes designed to enhance local skills of its workers, and a targeted plan to continually increase local content, resulting in long-term growth of Angolan capability.

PETROBRAS

Mr Hércules Tadeu Ferreira da Silva
Managing Director
Rua Pedro Félix Machado, n° 51, 2nd Floor, Luanda
Tel: +244-222-390330 / 334722 / 390780
Fax: +244-222-390480
Website: www.petrobras.com

Activity: Oil and gas
Date of Creation: 1979

Petrobras began operating in Angola almost 30 years ago in 1979, and it continues to be involved in the development of the country with ongoing exploration and production contracts by participating in shallow-water oil extraction in block 2 in the Lower Congo Basin and its share in shallow-water exploration in block 34.

Since 1979 Petrobras has held exploration rights in block 2 for oil exploration and production in the Lower Congo Basin in shallow water (to 50 metres deep) off the Angolan coast. In this project it is in partnership with both Angolan and international companies. It has a 15% share in block 34. The 5,930-sq. km block is situated in deepwater and ultra-deepwater between 1,500 and 2,500 metres. Two wildcat wells have already been drilled, and at the moment alternative exploration models are being sought to carry on the work. This block is close to areas with significant oil discoveries, which encourages the continuing exploratory search.

Petrobras is a long-standing partner of the Angolan government and population, operating with social responsibility in humanitarian and social work and in professional and management training of skilled labour for the country's oil industry, such as its Proquadros programme. It has also implemented a programme of humanitarian work that includes a number of communities. The beneficiaries are schools, day care centres, hospitals and rural communities. Its contribution also extends to supporting Angolan sociocultural entities, such as the National Historic Archives, Agostinho Neto University and the Alpha–Omega dance group.

Petrobras wishes to be present during this stage of the country's reconstruction, analysing business opportunities and looking to provide solutions for the Angolan population on its road to development and social justice.

Petrobras can be found in every corner of the world.
Even if this corner is in the middle of the ocean.

Petrobras, a Brazilian enterprise and one of the largest energy companies in the world, is the technological reference in oil exploration and production, operating in 23 countries and several points of the ocean, at a depth of nearly 3,000 meters. In Angola since 1979, Petrobras believes in the country's growth potential and continues to invest in business undertakings and social actions, confirming its commitment to local development.

BR PETROBRAS

PETROMAR

Mr Alain Jannot
Managing Director
Rua Georgi Dimitrov, n° 5–7, Ingombotas, Luanda
Tel: +244-222-332424 / 332264
Fax: +244-222-330339
Website: www.petromar.co.ao

Activity: Oil and gas
Date of Creation: 1984

Petromar, an Angolan-registered company formed by Delong Hersent Lda (a wholly owned subsidiary of Saipem) and Sonangol EP, was created in 1984. With its wide range of activities and numerous worksites, Petromar is Angola's largest oil and gas contractor. Operating continuously for over 17 years, it has attained a leading position on the Angolan market in:

• Construction and installation of offshore platforms and subsea structures
• Offshore hook up
• Construction of deepwater equipment and structures
• Oil and gas facilities construction
• Onshore and offshore oil and gas maintenance.

Its central office and facilities are located in Luanda, including a head office and three workshops: Soyo, a mechanical and maintenance workshop; Ambriz, a workshop and fabrication yard dedicated to deepwater facilities (bundles, riser towers, manifolds, jumpers, subsea structures, etc.) and Malongo, a fabrication yard where over 25 jackets and 16 decks have been built, as well as a piping and structural prefabrication yard.

SCHLUMBERGER

Mrs Magali Anderson
Oilfield Services Manager, Angola
Schlumberger Technical Services Inc., Sonils Oil Service Center, Base, Luanda Port, Luanda
Tel: +244-222-310050/509/913/340
Fax: +244-222-311745 / 310079
Email: manderson@luanda.oilfield.slb.com
Website: www.slb.com

Activity: Oilfield services provider

Schlumberger is the leading oilfield services provider, trusted to deliver superior results and improved E&P performance for oil and gas companies around the world. Through its well site operations and its research and engineering facilities, it is working to develop products, services and solutions that optimize customer performance in a safe and environmentally sound manner.

Schlumberger is an international and multicultural company providing technical services and products to the oil industry in more than 104 countries. Its global workforce of about 66,000 people includes more than 140 nationalities.

It has been in Angola since the 1950s working for Petrangol in the Cuanza land fields. During 1998 Schlumberger companies were reorganized and put together under the Oilfield Services (OFS) umbrella.

The Schlumberger West & South Africa headquarters and the Angola operations are based in Sonils Oil Center in Luanda. Schlumberger's operations in Angola currently include more than 500 people. Of these, the large majority are Angolans.

Since 1998 Schlumberger has been engaged with local business initiatives and technology transfer projects in Angola. This has included cooperation agreements with Sonangol for the provision of some services in relation to the oil sector. These cooperation agreements are established today for the following services: seismic data processing, fluids and core analysis, data centre, secure connectivity.

www.sonangol.co.ao

SONANGOL E.P
Holding

Manuel Domingos Vicente, Chairman of the Board
Syanga Abilio, Administrator
Mateus Morais de Brito, Administrator
Fernando Roberto Joaquim, Administrator
Anabela de Brito Fonseca, Administrator

Created in 1976, Sonangol E.P. is the exclusive concessionaire for the prospecting, the research and the production of liquid and gaseous hydrocarbons, in the Angolan subsoil and continental platform. Its activities include the prospecting, the research, the development, the commercialization, the production, the transport and the refining of hydrocarbons and its by-products and these activities can be performed autonomously or in association with foreign companies.

Currently Sonangol has 14 Subsidiaries and has a stake in 25 companies.

The company aims to become an integrated and competitive company, it strives to be able to fulfil its responsibilities with the government, its commercial partners and with the society in general as well as to gain a position of prominence in the world market.

With a work force estimated at around 7.500 employees, Sonangl E.P. and its subsidiaries produce to transform oil into jobs, resources and development, thus contributing for a better future for all Angolans.

1º Congresso do MPLA Street, 8/16
PO BOX 1316
Luanda – Angola
Tel: +244 222 632339 / 632339 / 636999
E-mail: secretaria.geral@sonangol.co.ao
www.sonangol.co.ao

Internationalization

Sonangol is currently present in all continents through its subsidiaries, and essentially their mission is to get the best deal possible for the Angolan government's quota of oil. These are considered Trading Units.

- **Sonangol Limited (London)**

- **Sonangol USA or SonUsa (Houston, USA)**

- **Sonangol Asia or SonAsia (Singapore)**

- **Sonangol Cape Verde**

- **Sonangol Sao Tome**

Sonangol Pesquisa & Produção

Research and Production

Sebastião Gaspar Martins, Chairman of the Board
Sector: Research and production of oil
Founded: 1991
Start of activities: 1994

With a vocation for the prospecting, the research and the production of liquid and gaseous hydrocarbons.

It is the only national operator and it has continuously contributed to the strengthening of the Sonangol Group in the national petroleum industry guaranteeing the supply of energy for the country, its technical, financial and social development, the inclusion of national companies and the development of the Angolan workforce.

It currently produces over 90.000 barrels of oil per day. It holds a stake in several blocks in shallow, deep and ultra-deep water. It is present in the Cabinda onshore blocks (C/N/S) and offshore in Angola, in Gabon and in Nigeria.

Comandante Dack Doy Street, 2
PO BOX 5997
Luanda – Angola
Tel: +244 222 633261 / 633285 /633300
Fax: +244 222 353037
E-mail: sonpp@ebonet.net
www.sonangolpp.com

Antonio Santos Domingos, Chairman of the Board
Sector: Aviation
Founded: 1998

It supports the Oil Industry and the various governmental institutions in the internal, regional and international markets and the transport of passengers, cargo and non-regular mail. Its fleet is composed of 17 helicopters and 26 airplanes.

Within the country it flies regularly to Benguela, Cabinda, Catumbela, Huambo, Lubango, Soyo and Ondjiva and it has an international connection, Luanda – Houston – Luanda, with three weekly flights, the "Houston Express", destined for the members of the energy association United States – Africa (USAEA).

4 de Fevereiro
International Airport
PO BOX 2675
Luanda – Angola
Tel: +244 222 633 631

Reservations: +244 222 633 567
(National flights and
the freight of National
and Regional executive flights)
Fax: (+244) 222 321 995
222 321 572
222 325 855

SonAir Benguela
Tel: +244 272233118
Lobito
Tel: 244 272225725
Fax: + 244 272221645
SonAir Soyo
Tel: +244 232 36457

E-mail: comercial@sonairsarl.com
www.sonairsarl.com

Sonangol Logística, Lda
Logistics

Maria Filomena Rosa, Chairman of Management Council
Sector: Logistics
Founded: 2003

It provides primary transport and storage services (pipelines and cistern-wagons) of gas and liquid fuels. It has an approximate storage capacity of 200.000 m3 (gasoline, Jet-A1, Jet-.B, Kerosene, Fuel). Its infrastructure includes 10 terminals and 7 installations located in Luanda, Lobito, Cabinda, Namibe, Huambo, Malange, Soyo, Bie, Porto Amboim and Kwanza Norte.

Secil Building
4 de Fevereiro Avenue, 42 - 4th and 10th floors
PO BOX 2436
Luanda – Angola
Tel: 244 222 634736 / 634724
Fax: +244 222 310967
www.snl-logistica.com

Sonangol Distribuidora, S.A

Distribution and Commercialization

Fernando Joaquim Roberto, Chairman of the Board
Sector: Distribution and commercialization of oil by-products
Founded:

It has the ability to perform in the area of distribution and commercialization of oil by-products, it is divided into territorial units of management: North (Luanda, Zaire, Kwanza Norte and Uige), Northeast (Malange, Moxico, Lunda-Norte, Lunda-Sul), Cabinda, West (Benguela and Kwanza-Sul), Centre-East (Huambo, Bie and Kuando Kubango) and South (Huila, Huambo and Cunene).

It has over 200 Filling Stations, 80 Service Stations, and it services 25 private Filling Stations.

It possesses the line of lubricants NGOL with products for the automobile, the industrial and the marine sectors.

Amilcar Cabral Street, 110
PO BOX 1316
Luanda – Angola
Tel.: +244 222 632777
Fax: +244 222 6322841 / 392190

Office
Boavista I Installation
Tel: +244 222 634504

ESSA
Empresa de Sondagens e Serviços de Angola, S.A

Bento Lourenco, Chairman of the Board
Sector: Professional Training
Founded: 1995

It offers training to enable the upstream and the downstream sectors of the Petroleum Industry. Courses such as Helicopter Underwater Escape Training and Personal Survival Techniques are internationally certified (ISO 9001/2000).

It has trained over 37.700 students and it holds as its clients the Sonangol Group, BP Angola, Chevron, ESSO, De Beers, DNV, Pride Foramer, Schlumberger and Total E&P Angola.

Some of the courses offered:
Category: Fire fighting and prevention
Basic Fire Fighting (BFF)
STCW95 Advanced Fire fighting
Fire fighting and rescue in helicopters
Category: Petroleum Industry
Heliport Assistant
Dangerous goods by air
Well control and blow-out prevention
Helicopter Underwater Escape Training (HUET)

ESSA Training Center
Cacuaco Road, Km 9
Luanda – Angola
Tel: +244 222 511187
Fax: +244 222 511059
E-mail: essa.formacao@sonangol.co.ao
www.snl-essa.com

SonaShip
Maritime Transportation

Fernando Vieira Martins, Chairman of Management Council
Sector: Maritime transportation
Founded:

It guarantees the maritime transportation of oil by-products (gasoline, diesel oil, Jet A1) and liquid gas (LPG). It has a fleet of 11 ships with a capacity for the transportation of 66.430 m3 of oil by-products and 3.300m3 of liquid gas (LPG) and also the storage capacity of 196.079m3 of oil by-products.

Sonanship vessels operate in the East and West coasts of Africa and in Europe.

João de Barros Street, 64
Luanda – Republic of Angola
Tel: +244 222 310449 / 310590
Fax: +244-222 310-310 / 310870
E-mail: sonanship@netangola.com
www.snl-sonanship.com

MSTelcom
Telecommunications

Alberto Serafim Araujo, Chairman of the Board
Sector: Telecommunications
Founded: 1999

Operator of the Angola Telecommunications fixed-services network, it offers data transmission services by satellite, satellite and wireless Internet, the renting of circuits and radio, microwaves, fixed telephone services IP. It has 30 antennas spread all over the country and it holds amongst its over 250 company and residential clients the Group Sonangol, Unitel, Enana, Tropico Hotel, Alvalade Hotel, TAAG, ESSO and Kwanda Base. It has recently purchased Nexus to respond in a more dynamic way to the demands of the market.

Help Desk
Tel: +244 222 635005 / 635006
Mobile: +244 923 341094
Fax: +244 222 633899
E-mail: helpdesk@sonangol.co.ao
www.snl-mstelcom.com

Sonangol Gás Natural
Natural Gas

António Orfão, Chairman of Management Council
Sector: Natural gas
Founded: 2004

It aims to research, evaluate, produce, process, store, transport and commercialize the by-products resulting from the transformation of natural gas.

The project Angola LNG, of which Sonangas is a partner, constitutes an important part of the Sonangol Strategy for the development of a gas industry in Angola as well as for the growth of the oil industry without the burning of gas.

Lenin Avenue, 58 – 6th floor
AAA Building
Luanda – Angola
Tel: +244 222 635738

Sonangol SGPS, Lda
The Strength of Partnerships

António Sabalo, Chairman of Management Council
Sector: Business partnerships
Founded: 2004

Sonangol SGPS manages the financial holdings of Sonangol in other companies. It currently has 25 holdings in companies spread throughout the 3 main sectors of activity (upstream, downstream and non-core business).

1º Congresso do MPLA Street, 8/16
PO BOX 1316
Tel: +244 222 632118

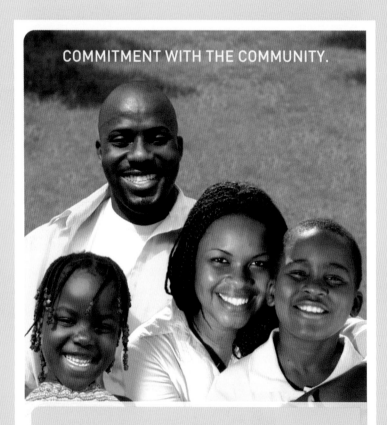

COMMITMENT WITH THE COMMUNITY.

We produce to transform solidarity
into sustainable development.

Sonangol

PRODUCING TO TRANSFORM

www.sonangol.co.ao

Social Responsibility
To transform resources into social well-being

Sonangol uses, on a daily basis, a code of ethics that values the human being, society and the environment. In tune with the new dynamics affecting society and the business world it is socially responsible and it extends its activities well beyond its legal obligations.

Sonangol's commitment towards the sustained development and the stabilization of the Angolan nation is expressed in its philosophy, and its annual budgets hold a provision for social, cultural, sports, scientific and environmental investments.

SOMOIL – SOCIEDADE PETROLÍFERA ANGOLANA SA

Mr Alberto A. Sousa
President
Rua dos Coqueiros n° 6, Ingombotas, Luanda
Tel: +244-222-397917 / 339065
Fax: +244-222-338213
Email: somoil@snet.co.ao

Activity: Oil and gas
Date of Creation: 2003
Capital: Kz 7,800,000,00 (US $100,000,00)
Turnover: 890,000 barrels of petrol, US $71.5 million (2005–2006).
Employees: 126

Somoil started providing consulting services in April 2003 to the Angola–Congo interstate body that coordinates exploration and production activities in the Unitization Zone 14K/A-IMI.

It has also carried out a technical study on geological and geophysical data, in cooperation with a Brazilian private company acquired by Sonangol. This project led to an appraisal of the main old oil fields of the Cuanza Basin (onshore).

In February 2004 Somoil entered into the domestic market for fuel distribution through the operation of a service station in Luanda. More recently, from November 2005, a second service station in Luanda has been operated by Somoil. In mid-July 2005 Somoil was awarded rights to participate, under Production Sharing Agreements, in offshore blocks 3-05, 3-05A and 4-05 in which it holds as a non-operator associate respectively 10%, 10% and 15% of participating interest. Somoil is also doing business in the field of renewable sources of energy. While awaiting the opportunity to enter into oil exploration and production activities, Somoil has decided to diversify its activities to providing equipment, materials and services, including maintenance, for producing solar and aeolian (wind) energy.

Somoil has been one of the four foreign companies qualified to participate in the second round bid of inactive areas with marginal oil and gas accumulation in oilfields of the Brazilian states of Maranhão, Rio Grande do Norte and Espírito Santo in June 2006. Somoil delivered bids for three of these four areas and was placed second. Somoil offered the highest premium for the concessions but the winning companies offered better local content proposals. However, for Somoil this has been a good opportunity to show its capabilities to potential partners in the Brazilian market. Somoil participated in the 18th World Congress of Petroleum, which took place in Johannesburg, South Africa, between 25th and 29th September 2005. In Angola, Somoil participated for the third time in the Industrial Fair of Angola (FILDA), holding its own stand in the Oil Pavilion in July 2006.

STATOIL ANGOLA

Mr Holger Boge
Country Manager
Rua de Benguela, n° 17 r/c, Patrice Lumumba, Luanda
Tel: +244-222-640900
Fax: +244-222-640999
Website: www.statoil.com

Activity: Oil and gas

Statoil is a Norwegian integrated oil and gas company with considerable international activities. Represented in 33 countries, it is engaged in exploration and production in 15 of these and has more than 25,000 employees. One of the major suppliers of natural gas to the European market, Statoil is also one of the world's biggest sellers of crude oil.

Statoil is one of the world's most environmentally efficient producers and transporters of oil and gas. It aims to conduct business without causing harm to people or the environment. With this value base as a starting point, it aims to create value for its stakeholders and the communities in which it works through profitable and safe operations.

The company's current asset portfolio in Angola comprises a 13.33% owner interest in the deepwater blocks 15,

17 and 31 operated by ExxonMobil, Total and BP respectively. These three blocks rank among the most prolific in Angola in terms of exploration success and production volumes, hence enabling Angola to become a major world oil producer.

At present, Angola is by far Statoil's largest producing asset internationally. The group has so far invested around US $2.4 billion in the country. Statoil's equity production from blocks 15 and 17 currently amounts to about 110,000 barrels of oil equivalent per day, and is expected to continue to increase over the years to come.

It is of key importance to Statoil to act as a good corporate citizen wherever the company is active. In Angola it supports a variety of social investment projects through the three block partner groups. In addition, it invests around US $1 million directly through its NGO partner projects country-wide. These projects include mine clearing activities, programmes to fight HIV/AIDS, basic education for refugees, drilling of water wells, and development of education infrastructure, as well as teacher training programmes.

TOTAL E&P ANGOLA

Ms Amélia Santana
External Communications Manager
Av. 4 de Fevereiro, n° 37, PO Box 2610, Luanda
Tel: +244-222-672000

Fax: +244-222-674166
Email: amelia.santana@total.com
Website: www.total.com

Activity: Oil and gas
Date of Creation: 2003 (from the merger between TotalFina and Elf)
Employees: 1,200

Total is a leading multinational energy company committed to leveraging innovation and initiative to provide a sustainable response to humankind's energy requirements. It is the fourth largest publicly traded integrated oil and gas company and a world-class chemicals manufacturer. Total operates in more than 130 countries and has over 95,000 employees, together with its subsidiaries and affiliates. Its businesses cover the entire oil and gas chain, from crude oil and natural gas exploration and production to the gas downstream (including power generation), transportation, refining, petroleum product marketing, and international crude oil and product trading. Total is also a world-class chemicals manufacturer.

From the first hydrocarbon strikes in the Cuanza Basin in the mid-twentieth century to the discovery of Angola's deep and ultra-deep offshore resources, Total's operations there attest an enduring industrial commitment. In addition to its pioneering role in developing Angola's onshore reservoirs and its determined efforts to extend the life of mature fields in classic offshore, Total E&P

Sonangol, service station

Angola has combined technological excellence with a capacity for managing large-scale projects to optimize the ambitious deep offshore developments of block 17 and to look at the future with the new discoveries in block 32.

It is by setting its initiatives within the framework of a long-term partnership that Total now intends to pursue its decisive role in helping the country capitalize on the value of its human geological resources. Innovation, expertise and responsibility: three strengths already demonstrated on the Girassol field, and soon to be deployed on Dalia and Rosa as well, will also benefit future ultra-deepwater developments and the monetization of Angolan gas, two drivers of the country's future economic growth. Building the qualifications of the local workforce in the oil industry vital to the country is a priority of the Angolan authorities and one of the pillars of Total's strategy in Angola.

W.A.P.O.
ANGOLA GESTÃO E SERVIÇOS LDA

Mr Gilles Bernard
Sales Manager
Rua Domingos Tchekahanga, nº 18, Luanda
Tel: +244-222-396995 / 390837 / 397342

Activity: Provision of logistics services and operational assistance for companies in the oil and gas industry in Angola
Date of Creation: 1998
Capital: US $250,000
Turnover: US $13.4m (2004)
Employees: 380

Wapo Angola Gestão e Serviços Lda has been present in Angola since 1998 and provides a wide range of services to petroleum and petrol-related companies based in the country. The company took over from WAPO, which already offered the same type of services. Wapo Angola provides a wide range of logistics services to companies in the oil and gas sector, as well as their suppliers. It has a solid infrastructure and the capability to respond to the outsourcing needs of clients, helping them to realize economies of scale.

Through a relationship with Universal Sodexho, a remote site specialist, Wapo Angola has benefited for over a year from the technical assistance necessary to improve the level of its service delivery and conformity to HSE standards.

Wapo Angola is involved in the provision of the following services:

• Ground-based logistics: rental of light vehicles (in collaboration with Europcar), management of public transportation, vehicle maintenance, management of a service/gas station, personnel transportation and fuel provision.
• Travel assistance: pick-up and airport greeting, transfer to/from the airport, hotel reservations and visa services.
• Location management: rental of offices and rooms, maintenance and supervision of building construction.
• Training of Angolan employees working in the oil and gas industry in a fully-equipped training centre situated in the heart of Luanda. This is equipped with an IT centre, a language laboratory, a conference room and a number of specialized laboratories for technical training in mechanics, electricity, instrumentation, soldering and industrial refrigeration, among others. It has single and double rooms and a company restaurant.
• Provision of personnel: A provision of personnel permit allows Wapo to make Angolan or foreign workers available to its clients in the context of petroleum-related operations. This activity goes hand-in-hand with the training described in the section above.
• Wapo Angola is a socially concerned organization. It collaborates with an orphanage, to which it gives administrative support and provides a day care centre. Wapo also provides teaching staff and takes care of the maintenance of the premises.

Wapo Angola has a good reputation among its clients as well as the companies, both public and private, with which it has collaborated in the past.

We provide all the different services for companies operating in the oil industry in order for them to offer the best service. In our formation centre, we train personnel to multiple tasks related to petroleum activities: mechanicians, electricians, welders and plumbers. We also provide all transportation necessary, and technical assistance.

World Assistance Petroleum Operations

W.A.P.O

WE SUPPORT YOU EVERY STEP OF THE WAY

18 Rua D. Tchekahanga,
Luanda/Angola
Tel.: +244(222)396995/ 397342.
Fax: +244(222)394080

MALANJE - PROJECTO CAPANDA © Henrique

"Skin covers the human body, responsibility covers the human heart"

Angolan proverb

151

BANKING

Prior to independence there were eight banks operating in Angola. On independence in 1975 and the adoption of a planned economic system, the banking sector became a state monopoly operated by the central bank, which simultaneously executed monetary policy and acted as a commercial bank.

In 1976 Banco Popular de Angola (BPA) was established as a department of the central bank with the exclusive purpose of capturing personal savings.

From 1991 the promulgation of new banking industry laws made way for additional government-owned banks to be established, namely Banco de Poupança e Crédito (BPC) and Banco de Comércio e Industria (BCI).

In 1992 private banks were allowed to enter the market, the first being Banco Totta & Açores, Banco de Fomento e Exterior and Banco Português do Atlantico, all three of Portuguese origin.

From 1997 BNA ceased to operate as a commercial bank, restricting its activities from there on to those of a traditional central bank.

More recent approvals of new laws and amendments of existing banking legislation have had a significant impact in revolutionizing the banking sector, which has become one of the most dynamic of the Angolan economy.

As at December 2005 BNA had registered 12 banking institutions, namely: Banco Africano do Investimento (BAI), Banco Comercial de Angola (BCA), Banco de Fomento Angola (BFA), Banco Internacional de Credito (BIC), Banco Espírito Santo (BESA), Millennium BCP, Banco Sol, Banco Regional do Keve (BRK), Novo Banco, Banco Totta & Açores (BTA), Banco de Comercio e Industria (BCI) and Banco de Poupança e Credito (BPC). According to the central bank, as at December 2005 there were about 165 ATMs (automatic teller machines) operating throughout the country and 172 bank branches operating countrywide.

As at December 2005 the total volume activity of the banking industry in Angola was estimated at US $5,340 million in deposits (US $3,049.34m in 2004) and US $2,972 million in credit (US $1,668.99m in 2004). Credit issued represented 56% of total deposits against 55% in 2004. When compared to the 22% it represented in 2002, this ratio reflects the dynamic nature of this growing industry.

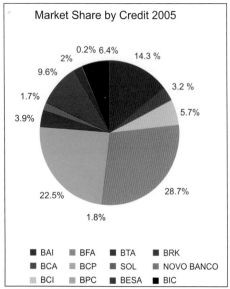

Source: BNA

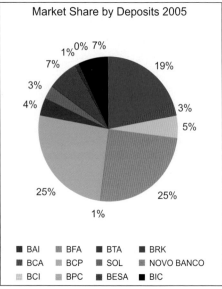

Source: BNA

Although the local currency is the Kwanza, the high level of dollarization of the economy is reflected in the structure of deposits. Deposits in foreign currency, USD in particular, have generally outweighed deposits in local currency, despite efforts to promote the Kwanza. At December 2005, of the total deposits in the banking system, 48% were in local currency against 52% in foreign currency.

Total credit available was estimated at US $2,972 million of which US $1,655m represented credit in local currency and US $1,317m credits in foreign currency. Whilst in 1998 state-owned banks were responsible for the bulk of credit issued, today private banks are responsible for 71% of total credit issued.

Of the total amount of credit available, 56% was granted to the private sector. The following graph shows the allocation of credit by sector at December 2005.

The range of services offered by the banking sector in Angola is still limited. The main source of revenue is foreign exchange services and short-term trade financing (generally backed by sustainable contracts in foreign currencies). The contribution of loans is relatively low due to the lack of reliable credit rating analysis. The fact that treasury bills and central bank bonds offer higher returns than the interest charged by banks on loans leads commercial banks to invest in monetary instruments rather

than expanding the availability of credit. Other factors negatively impacting on the application for loans by small enterprises include the demand for collateral and the absence of an effective judicial system. The new land law is expected to clarify the issue of property rights and thus expand the available collateral. Interest rates charged by the banks are considered relatively high compared to SADC standards, currently standing at 8% per annum (for loans denominated in foreign currency).

In terms of risk exposure, changes in exchange rates constitute the major source of risk affecting Angolan banks as the sector maintains most of its assets in foreign currencies.

In terms of foreign investment in the banking industry, there are at least five banks with shareholdings by Portuguese private banks, namely BFA, BTA, BCP, BESA and Novo Banco, and one bank (BCA) with shareholdings by a South African bank.

Foreign banks with representative offices in Angola include Equator Bank (US), Citibank (US) and Banco Paribas (French).

In April 2001 Angola signed a Staff Monitored Program with the International Monetary Fund under which the central bank of Angola is expected to implement an independent monetary policy targeting inflation and

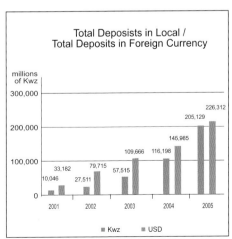

Source: BNA

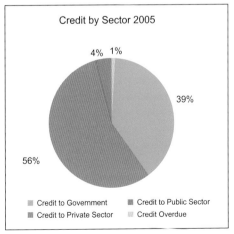

Source: BNA

exchange rate stability. This agreement also included clauses addressing the privatization of the remaining state-owned banks (BPC and BCI). In 2004 new regulations were introduced with the aim of promoting competition and efficiency within the sector. Amongst these measures were the compulsory display of a list of fees and charges by banks and the introduction of mechanisms to promote the effectiveness of central bank supervision. The new regulations have also reduced the minimum capital amounts required for the establishment of foreign exchange agencies and have thus contributed to the expansion of this segment of the market.

Generally speaking, the banking sector in Angola is very oligopolistic in structure, with the top three banks (BPC, BFA and BAI) holding about 70% of all deposits. The industry is currently very dynamic and there are significant prospects for growth. Additional new banks are expected to enter the market in the foreseeable future. A state-owned development bank has also recently been created by the government.

CAPITAL AND FINANCIAL MARKETS

Angola's capital markets are still in their incipient stage. There is currently no stock exchange and no company bonds available. Capital markets are currently limited to short-term public debt.

The interbank money market does not exist as a formal market and transactions between banks are limited.

For many years the development of capital markets was adversely impacted by macroeconomic instability and hyperinflation. The progress accomplished by the monetary authorities with regard to controlling inflation and improving exchange rate stability has effectively eliminated these impediments.

The successful issue of treasury bills, government and central bank bonds in 2004 was considered to be a major breakthrough. Of these, treasury bills and central bank bonds with longer maturities registered a higher demand and offered higher returns. This was only possible due to the excess liquidity in the banking sector resulting from enhanced exchange rate stability and reduced inflation.

The new law on financial institutions promulgated in September 2005 constitutes a milestone for the Angolan financial sector, and in particular for the country's incipient capital markets. This legislation divides the financial system into two main categories:

1. Banking institutions – regulated by the central bank
2. Non-banking financial institutions – regulated by the Insurance Institute or by the Capital Market Commission, as appropriate.

An important provision of the new law is the recognition and regulation of financial institutions and financial instruments not previously considered by Angolan law such as stock exchanges, stock brokering firms, private investment funds, leasing and factoring institutions.

Other recent major developments in the financial markets include new legislation governing the insurance industry, the creation of the Comissão de Mercado de Capitais, the body responsible for the supervision of non-banking financial institutions and which will act as the market's watchdog once the exchange is launched.

INSURANCE

Until 2000 the insurance industry in Angola was restricted to the state monopoly held by ENSA (Empresa Nacional de Seguros de Angola).

Between 1998 and 2001, a number of amendments and new dispositions were introduced to the insurance law that revolutionized the industry. Amongst the most important were the following:

• Termination of the monopoly of the state insurance company.

• New decrees on pension funds allowing companies to create their own pension funds.

The newly opened branch of the BAI in Kwanza Sul - Sumbe

• New labour laws that institutionalized the need for industrial accident and professional illness insurance.

• New decrees on reinsurance and co-insurance.

The industry is also regulated by the new law of financial institutions of September 2005. The insurance regulator is the Instituto de Supervisão de Seguros de Angola.

There are currently four companies operating in the market, each providing services ranging from personal insurance to transport, property and natural hazard insurance. The main players in the market are ENSA, AAA, Global Seguros and A Nossa Seguros, the first two being the main competitors.

ENSA is the state-owned insurance company, which still dominates the market in which it exercised absolute monopoly for many years. It is currently the only insurance company providing a broad range of insurance services across different industries, including aviation.

AAA was the first private insurance company to be registered in 2000 and currently holds second place in the market. It currently insures assets for the oil industry estimated at US $18 billion. It also manages pension funds for Sonangol, Sonils, British Petroleum and the Ministry of Petroleum of Angola, the Luanda Port and Banco Africano de Investimentos. Until very recently the global perception was that AAA was created mainly to serve the oil industry. However, the company has been extending its range of services to the general public.

Global Seguros and A Nossa are the remaining new players in the industry, with less significance than the other two mentioned above.

In terms of insurance brokerage, there are currently about five firms operating in the market.

Overall the industry remains very limited in terms of diversification of the services on offer.

VENTURE CAPITALISM

Until 2005 the Angolan legal system made no provision for specialized financial institutions, including venture capital firms. The scenario has, however, changed with the advent of the law on financial institutions of September 2005.

In 2005 the first venture capital fund FIPA (Fundo de Investimento Privado Angola) was created in a partnership between Banco Africano de Investimento, Sonangol and the Norwegian Fund for Developing Countries (NORFUND). Nevertheless, due to the absence of specific industry legislation and regulations, this fund is still not licensed and is consequently not operating.

FIPA will invest primarily in privatization and restructuring projects across different industries.

NEW DEVELOPMENTS

In terms of new developments, the new law on financial institutions of September 2005 and the law on securities and exchanges remain the key features in the promotion of the financial system in Angola.

These new laws make for the first time provisions for specialized financial institutions and instruments such as leasing, factoring, venture capital and clearing houses, which were not recognized by the system in the past.

A branch of the BES - Banco Espírito Santo in Angola

As a result, considerable activity is currently in progress in planning for the establishment of such entities as well as pension funds, pension fund management companies, and real estate and investment funds.

MAIN COMPANIES

AAA SEGUROS & AAA PENSÕES SA

Mrs Neusa Silva
Communication Manager
Rua Lenine, n° 58
PO Box 505, Luanda
Tel: +244-222-69282 / 691200
Fax: +244-222-691342
Email: nesilva@aaa.co.ao
Website: www.aaa.ao

Activity: Insurance group
Date of Creation: 2000
Employees: AAA Seguros: 76, and AAA Pensões: 29

The Angolan Group AAA, specialists in the financial services of risk management, brokerage, insurance and reinsurance, has in the last two years invested more than US $117 million in the capitalization of its 10 societies and in the acquisition of shares from Africa Reinsurance Corporation and Starfish Oil & Gas SA.

AAA originated from a private–public partnership whose purpose was to provide the services the national oil society – Sonangol – needs for the execution of its strategy of managing risk in oil operations.

In Angola AAA is organized as an entrepreneurial group coordinated by a holding company, AAA Financial Services, which integrates AAA Insurance SARL, AAA Pensions, AAA Broker and Insurance, and AAA Services and Risk.

With these five companies, AAA provides services needed for management of risks, financing and transfer of these risks, as well as providing products and services for the development of Angola, thus contributing to a viable and modern insurance and pension market.

As a result of the increase of petroleum investments, oil industry assets under AAA management will reach, in the next years, a value higher than the Gross Domestic Product (GDP) of Angola.

BANCO BAI – BANCO AFRICANO DE INVESTIMENTO

Carlos A. Bessa Victor Chaves
Director
Rua Major Kanhangulo, nº 34,
PO Box 6022, Luanda
Tel: +244-222-693800 / 693899
Fax: +244-222-335486
Email: BVictor@bancobai.co.ao
Website: www.bancobai.co.ao

Activity: Banking
Date of Creation: 1996

Banco Africano de Investimentos – Banco BAI – was established as a universal bank in November 1996 and was the first privately owned bank to operate in Angola. The major shareholders of BAI are Sonangol (17.5%) and three international banks: Caixa de Crédito Agrícola Mútuo, Portugal (10.0%), Investec, South Africa (10.0%) and Banco Comercial Português, Portugal (5.0%).

As of December 2002, BAI was the largest bank in Angola with total assets of US $586.4 million and equity of US $59.0 million.

BAI's network is composed of 35 branches in Angola, 14 in Luanda and the other 21 spread over 13 provinces, giving this bank one of the best banking networks in the country.

The bank is planning to expand its geographical base by increasing its branch network to more than 35 in the next years. BAI employs more than 300 people. Internationally BAI has opened a subsidiary in Lisbon and is planning to open branches in Cape Verde, Sao Tome and Principe, Brazil and South Africa.

With its leadership in the banking market solidly established, BAI is looking to relaunch in the investment market, with particular focus on the oil and mining sectors. To this end, the bank is training staff to the highest technical standards.

BAI's commitment to new technology has led it to introduce many useful systems such as ATMs, cash points, and credit and debit cards. These encourage people to deposit their savings in banks, which in turn allows the banks to build up their resources and offer more loans.

Micro-credit is also an excellent way of encouraging growth. BAI remains committed to encouraging small and medium-sized businesses to flourish in Angola.

BANCO BCI – BANCO DE COMÉRCIO E INDÚSTRIA

Mr Generoso Hermenegildo Gaspar de Almeida
President of the Board
Rua Rainha Ginga, nº 73–83, PO Box 1395, Luanda
Tel: +244-222-333684 / 331637
Fax: +244-222-333823 / 331498
Email: galmeida@bci.ebonet.net

Activity: Bank services, Western Union offices
Date of Creation: 1991

Banco de Comércio e Indústria – Bank of Commercial and Industrial Commerce – is a semi-private bank, occasionally restricted to government financing. The government owns about 40% of the BCI's shares.

BCI was Angola's online banking pioneer and plans to expand deeper into that area. As new economic centres developed throughout the country, BCI followed that trend by creating other national entities. The relaunching of economic life embraced the nation as a whole, especially where the most favourable conditions lay.

The oil-rich province of Cabinda quickly became an attractive market. BCI played an important role in developing that area. In 1992 the bank opened a branch in Cabinda, reinforcing local business expectations and goals, followed three years later by the inauguration of another branch in the Maculusso Quarter and in Lubango, part of Huíla province. It subsequently began offering Huíllian entrepreneurs a vital instrument for development in the area. The establishment of the Huíla branch also served as a boost to development in Namibe province.

The Benguela regional office, with a brand new two-storey structure, and the Lobito and Porto-Amboim branches were expected to open in 2006 . A main focus of 2007 will be the completion of the Soyo Branch in Zaire province. Over the course of the years, BCI is preparing to open branches at the customs area in Luanda harbour, Luanda airport, and at the tax collecting central office. Thus BCI is poised to enter several new and promising business areas in the immediate future.

"Our goal is to have an universal bank, one that will play a key role in developing the country, and to that end, we welcome the help of strategic partners."
Mr Generoso Hermenegildo Gaspar de Almeida
President of the Board

BANCO ESPIRITO SANTO ANGOLA – BESA

Mr Álvaro Sobrinho
President
Rua Guilherme Pereira Inglês, n° 43, 2nd Floor, Largo das Ingombotas, Luanda
Tel: +244-222-333758 / 333652
Fax: +244-222-337654 / 333645
Website: www.besa.ao
Email: besangola@angola.bes.pt

Activity: Banking

BESA's international expansion strategy is to concentrate on countries with cultural and economic affinities with Portugal, such as Portuguese-speaking countries or countries with sizeable Portuguese immigrant communities.

Headquartered in Angola, BESA is a financial institution that began operations in 2001.

The bank is undergoing a phase of strong expansion and investment, for example in its geographical coverage, which has been significantly extended in the last few years.

BESA has a 99.96% interest in the institution, while various individual shareholders hold the remaining capital.

Banco Espirito Santo offers a complete range of products and services, from the more traditional transactional services to sophisticated and complex trade finance structures.

BESA has widespread presence across the globe, in over 50 cities in 17 countries, which makes it the most international of Portuguese banks and, most importantly, allows its customers – individuals, corporate, institutional etc. – to fully rely on its capability to serve their banking requirements in different locations.

BANCO BIC SA

Mr Fernando Leitão
Commercial Director
Rua Cerqueira Lukoki, n° 78–80
Tel: +244-222-391816 / 391526
Fax: +244-222-391274
Email: Fernando.morgado.leitao@bancobic.ao / bancobic@bancobic.ao
Website: www.bancobic.ao

Activity: Banking
Date of Creation: 26th May 2005
Capital: US $10,000,000,00 / Kz 807,941,050,00
Employees: 550

Banco BIC SA started its activity on 26th May 2005. BIC is an Angolan Bank with private capital held by national investors (65%) and foreign investors (35%).

The BIC brand, even if young, is already well respected in the Angolan banking system. It is a modern and dynamic bank that implements the newest and most sophisticated technologies.

BIC pays special attention to providing efficient personalized services and aims to be known as a main strategic partner for business. It has a strong network of agencies spread throughout Angola, including Luanda, Benguela, Cabinda, Cafunfo, Catumbela, Huambo, Uíge, Lobito, Malange, Namibe and Nzagi provinces, and aims to cover the whole country by the end of 2007. BIC's Angolan network has 34 branches, namely 20 in Luanda, 4 corporate centres and 1 private banking office. So far it has over 60,000 clients.

BIC is a financial institution that wants to cover the Angolan national market, but also aims to become an excellent partner in Angolan business abroad. BIC is able to support large entrepreneurial groups as well as small and medium-sized companies.

The know-how of BIC's employees is one of its key features, with most staff having more than 30 years of experience in the private banking sector, providing an excellent professional team specialized in resolving business problems, not only in the national market, but also in the international arena.

"Crescemos Juntos" – "We Grow Together".
Mr Fernando Leitão, Commercial Director

BANCO DE FOMENTO ANGOLA – BFA

Mr Pedro Alexandre Amorim
Marketing Director
Rua Amílcar Cabral, n° 58, Maianga, Luanda
Tel: +244-222-638900
Fax: +244-222-638911
Email: pedro.alexandre.amorim@bfa.ao
Website: www.bfa.ao

Activity: Banking
Date of Creation: 9th July 1993
Capital: 2,800,000,000,000 Kz
Turnover: US $224.28 million
Employees: 900

The Banco de Fomento SARL, which also uses the trade name of Banco de Fomento Angola (BFA), has been operating in Angola since 1990.

The main pillar of BFA's segmented and sustained growth strategy rests on expanding the network of branches, investment centres and corporate centres, reorganizing and consolidating its operational infrastructure and integrating new distribution channels.

To accomplish all that, BFA is heavily investing on its expansion. By the end of 2005, BFA had a 20% share of the Angolan banking system's total branch network. Today BFA has 50 branches all over the country, 24 of which are in Luanda. By the end of 2006, BFA will have about 70 branches, 7 corporate centres and 3 investment centres, all fully connected online. With the exception of Cuanza Norte, BFA has a presence in all other provinces, with at least one branch located at each province's capital.

Corporate centres were conceived for greater segmentation and specialization with corporate clients, and consequently an increase in commercial capacity and an improvement in efficiency and operations.

BFA is a universal bank with a segmented approach that has a complete array of typical financial solutions both for individual and corporate consumers.

The bank has been responsible for some of the major product and service innovations in the Angolan financial market (for example, the launch of the first debit card and credit card and the introduction of the home banking service expressly designed for corporate consumers).

BANCO MILLENNIUM ANGOLA

Mr Gonçalo Moreira
Manager
Rua Rainha Ginga, n° 83, Luanda
Tel: +244-222-397946
Email: goncalo.moreira@millenniumbcp.pt
Website: www.millenniumbcp.pt

Activity: Banking

- BANCO DE ANGOLA © Henrique Santos

In 1994 the Banco Português do Atlântico opened a Branch in Angola. In 2000 the BPA was bought by BCP – Banco Comercial Português – and since April 2006 this branch in Angola has functioned as a local bank, named Banco Millennium Angola.

Millennium BCP carries out the development of autonomous operations in diversified geographic markets either with strong historical relations with Portugal or in ethnic markets with relevant presence of Portuguese communities, namely through BCM (Macao), Millennium Angola, Millennium bim (Mozambique), Banque BCP (France and Luxembourg) and BCP bank (USA and Canada).

Currently, the Millennium Group BCP is present in Europe, Africa, Asia and America and employs over 19,000 people, with more than four million customers and nearly 1,500 branches and 189,000 shareholders worldwide.

BANCO NACIONAL DE ANGOLA – BNA

Mr Amadeu Mauricio
President
Avenida 4 de Fevereiro, nº 151, Luanda
Tel: +244-222-370563
Fax: +244-222-370563
Website: www.bna.ao

Activity: National bank

Being the central banker for the country, the bank has big responsibilities. In May 1999 the bank implemented a set of measures with a view to stabilizing the economy and increasing competition among domestic banks.

The bank's functions extend well beyond preserving the value of the national currency. The bank not only acts as the banker to the government, but also advises it on the financial and monetary fronts, acts as an intermediary in the monetary relations of the state, guards the stability of the national financial system and acts as the financer of last resort.

Other functions of BNA:

• To establish the rules of conducting banking transactions, accounting and reporting, protection of information, funds and property for banks and other financial and credit institutions.
• To organize, and to provide the methodological support to, the system of monetary, credit and banking statistical information and the statistics on the balance of payments.
• To exercise the banking regulations and supervision.
• To keep a register of banks, their branches and representative offices, currency exchanges and financial and credit institutions, to license banking business and transactions, if provided for by law.
• To compile, analyse and forecast the balance of payments.
• To analyse the status of monetary, credit, financial, pricing and currency relations.

Headquartered in Luanda, the bank has 1,845 workers on its roll. The bank has a presence in the provinces of Benguela, Cabinda and Huíla and is opening branches in other provinces.

BANCO DE POUPANÇA E CRÉDITO – BPC

RECOMMENDED PARTNER

Mr Paixão Antonio Junior
Managing Director
Largo Saidy Mingas, Predio da BPC/BPC Building
Tel: +244-222-390241 / 390841
Fax: +244-222-391580
Email: etmonteiro@bpc.ao
Website: www.bpc.ao

Activity: Banking
Date of Creation: 1956

The BPC, Banco de Poupanca e Crédito, is the biggest commercial bank in Angola. It was founded in 1956 as Banco Comercial de Angola. Its headquarters are located in Luanda and it currently has 55 branches distributed among the 18 provinces of Angola.

It has a modern structure based on new market tendencies. As the bank of reference in Angola, its strategy relies on three elements:

• Continuous improvement of the services offered, by supporting both public and private initiatives of investment, always respecting and understanding the customers' needs.
• Development of its information system, with an excellent network all over the country, which allows BPC to fulfil its operations to a high quality standard.
• Motivation and training of its employees, preserving the health and safety of all its installations.

It has three organizational bodies, the general assembly, the administrative council and the fiscal council.

The bank offers four types of loans to companies, namely loans for the agricultural, industrial, commercial and services sectors.

Banco de Poupança e Crédito

B P C

History

Originally established in 1956 under the name of Banco Comercial de Angola,(BCA) chan
to BPA BANCO POPULAR DE ANGOLA firstly operating as a department of BNA with
exclusive function of capturing private savings in 1975.

Later on BPC (Banco de Poupança e Crédito) was founded in 1991, in sequence of the finar
sector reform performed by the Angolan government, splitting the commercial banking activi
the National Bank. In the same year ,the new organic law of the National Bank of Angola
financial institution law were published ending the single bank system allowing the new entry
the market of the financial institutions. BPC's capital is totally held by the Angolan Governm
being one of the most important banks in Angola, and market leader by credit issued.

In 1975,on Angola´s independence,banking system comprised 8 operating banks and over
branches,covering the national territory and BPC was among those banks.

 In more   than a decade BPC has been part of the national economic revolution and adop
various strategic plans with clear and achievable objectives..associated with clear managen
style.

Number of Branches

Present all over the country,currently with 71 branches corresponding to30% of the total ban
sector,comprised with a total of 12 banks at the moment

Indicators

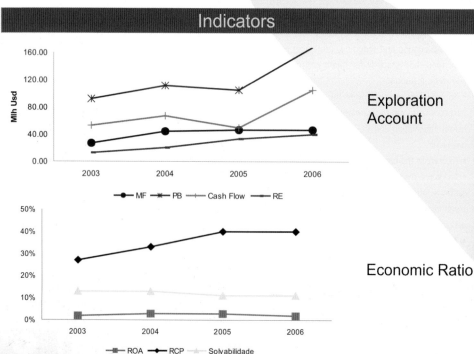

BPC economic evolution, since 2003 is described in the following figures.

Summary of Key Indicators

			UM: Thousand Usd	
	2003	2004	2005	2006 (Estimated)
Assets	594,149	915,979	1,631,704	2,366,663
Customer Deposits	461,536	748,140	1,296,210	2,014,932
Loans	235,469	324,808	519,531	881,142
Financial Margin	26,775	44,324	46,229	46,647
Banking Revenue	92,344	110,904	105,309	167,152
Net Profit	12,770	20,911	33,882	40,447
Cash Flow	53,029	67,144	49,265	105,030
Equity / Share Capital	42,936	72,269	105,340	146,146
Solvency Ratio	13%	13%	11%	12%
Return on Equity	27%	33%	40%	40%
Number of Branches	52	53	56	70
Employees	1,332	1,366	1,404	1,506

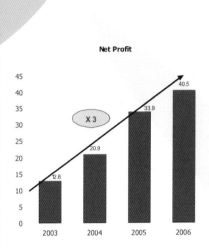

Net Profit

Balance Evolution

2003

Active 594,148 — Passive 551,396

42,752

2004

Active 915,979 — Passive 805,685

110,294

2005

Active 1,631,704 — Passive 1,472,075

159,629

2006

Active 2,366,663 — Passive 2,234,078

132,585

BPC also offers financial products and services that are key in the development of the Angolan economy and it is also planning to provide more than US $10,000,000 in micro-loans in the immediate future.

BIVAC INTERNATIONAL

Mrs Françoise Grimbert
Managing Director
Rua João Barros, n° 56–58, Luanda
Tel: +244-222-310451/730
Fax: +244-222-311105/110
Website: www.bivacangola.com

Activity: Consultancy

Since it was founded, Bivac International has pursued a strategy of helping facilitate trade among all the countries of the world.

The company has focused efforts on providing assistance to customs authorities and implementing international trade facilitation programmes for governments. Conformity, compliance, valuation, risk management and cutting the time and cost expended on import customs formalities: these are the core concerns of Bivac International.

Bivac, which is a wholly-owned subsidiary of Bureau Veritas, was contracted by the Angolan Ministry of Finance in 2002, and since then Bivac has provided pre-shipment inspection (PSI) services to Angola.

Concerning the PSI services and supervision of imports in Angola, Bivac is carrying out the following activities:

• Import eligibility
• Quantity, quality
• Price verification
• Customs classification
• Value for customs purposes
• Assessment of customs duties and taxes
• Supporting customs investigations
• Risk management
• Valuation database
• Reconciliation of data
• Container sealing.

Bivac is contributing to safeguard the Angolan financial interests (by preventing the flight of capital and commercial fraud, as well as customs duty evasion, among other things), and to modernize and reform customs procedures in Angola.

DELOITTE

Mr Diamantino Silva de Carvalho
Senior Partner
Rua Engenheiro Costa Serrão, n° 13, 1st Floor, Luanda
Tel: +244-222-39167
Fax: +244-222-391972
Email: dicarvalho@deloitte.pt
Website: www.deloitte.com/pt

Activity: Consultancy
Turnover: US $2,000,000

With over 5,000 Deloitte people working in more than 28 African countries, Deloitte is well positioned to meet business needs and assist in this market.

The size and diversity of continental African markets present unique challenges for local, national and international business.

Following the return of democracy to South Africa, the global Deloitte firm appointed the Southern African firm in 1993 to implement its global operational protocols and strategies in its African member firms. The regional coordination function included the formulation of policies, followed by plans and implementation programmes. As part of this initiative, new practices were established in Angola and Mozambique, which today are leading professional services firms in their respective countries. The group has therefore been in Angola for more than 10 years and is providing services to both private and public institutions.

Main activities include outsourcing, accountancy, and corporate and administrative services.

Deloitte aims for quality, and is always looking to obtain new clients.

"If someone wants to start running a company in Angola, Deloitte has legal experts to assist."
Mr Diamantino Silva de Carvalho, Senior Partner

DNV – DET NORSKE VERITAS

Mr Bror A. Berge
Country Manager
Monumental Building, Rua Major Kanhangulo, n° 290, 2nd Floor, Luanda
Tel: +244-222-391631 / 391735 / 391862
Fax: +244-222-392373
Email: bror.berge@dnv.com
Website: www.dnv.com

Activity: Leading international provider of services for risk management

Established in 1864, DNV is an independent foundation with the objective of safeguarding life, property and the environment and is a leading international provider of services for risk management. DNV is a knowledge-based organization. Its prime assets are the creativity, knowledge and expertise of its employees. Most of its worldwide 6,100 employees are highly qualified engineers and technical personnel. DNV is an international company with about 300 offices in 100 different countries. Headquartered in Oslo (Høvik), Norway, DNV's global network is linked by efficient information technology enabling DNV to create value for customers in a coherent and consistent manner all over the world.

DNV operates in multiple industries internationally, but has a strong market presence and a large customer base in four industries: maritime, oil and gas, process and transportation. DNV is one of the world's leading classification societies, and helps the maritime industry manage risk in all phases of a ship's life, through ship classification, statutory certification, fuel testing and a range of technical, business risk, financial and competency-related services.

The firm is a leading supplier of risk management services to the international oil and gas industry. Its aim is to work proactively with customers to optimize asset safety, availability and productivity. DNV offers a wide range of services to the transportation industry, from classification services, safety management and fuel testing to consulting services and environmental assessment.

DNV Angola Serviços Lda started its local operation in Luanda in January 2003, with a workforce of four people. As at July 2004 it employed 52 people, 80% of which were Angolans, and the aim is to increase the workforce, with 90% being Angolan.

ERNST & YOUNG

Mr Mario Barber
Managing Director
Avenida 4 de Fevereiro, n° 95, 2nd Floor, Luanda
Tel: +244-222-336295 / 371390 / 371461
Fax: +244-222-336295
Email: ernst.young-angola@netangola.com
Website: www.ernst-young.com

Activity: Auditing and consultancy
Date of Creation: 1954
Employees: 10

The members of the Ernst & Young global organization help companies and businesses across all industries – from emerging growth companies to global powerhouses – deal with a broad range of business issues. The 106,000 people in 140 countries around the globe pursue the highest levels of integrity, quality and professionalism to provide clients with a broad array of services relating to audit and risk-related services, tax and transactions.

Ernst & Young Angola was created in 1954. A wide range of services is provided, including auditing (the core business), tax advisory, tax reporting and financial consulting.

With clients in different sectors of the economy, such as petroleum, financial, communications, real estate and construction, Ernst & Young Angola is involved with the most important companies in the country and has a strong tradition of contributing to the world's leading corporations' understanding of fraud and risks of emerging markets.

Although Ernst & Young Angola is smaller than other Ernst & Young delegations in African countries, it works directly and also linked with Ernst & Young Lisbon, with whom it shares formation programmes and exchanges of staff. Ernst & Young Angola wants to base its growth strategy for the next years on building young professional teams with an open mind, able to share their know-how with the entire Ernst & Young company.

"Ernst & Young Angola provides high-quality services."
Mr Mario Barber, Managing Director

GLOBAL ALLIANCE – G+A

Mr Robert Lewis
General Manager
Avenida 4 de Fevereiro, nº 79, 1st Floor, Luanda
Tel: +244-2-330368/0425/0512/0623
Fax: +244-2-398815
Email: rlewis@globalalliance.co.ao
Website: www.globalalliance.co.za/angola.htm

Activity: Insurance company

G+A Angola Insurance was formed by the Global Alliance Group in response to the group's multinational client base requiring a superior standard of insurance in Angola. In 2003 Global Alliance's directors undertook a detailed study of the Angolan market and the decision was taken to apply for an insurance licence in the territory.

Although the process took over two years and was fraught with many frustrations, Global Alliance is proud that it is the first non-government-owned insurance company to have received a licence in Angola.

The company's management is made up of highly qualified and experienced insurance technicians. It is a requisite that all staff speak English and Portuguese; however, various members of staff also speak French and Afrikaans.

G+A Angola clients can expect the same level of service as clients of the Global Alliance Group have grown accustomed to. The group has committed vast resources to its operation. Kindle Insurance Technologies has provided the insurance software, which is without doubt the most advanced system in Angola, Africa and quite possibly the world. The management team has been put through stringent training exercises, which prepared them for the unique skills set that working in Angola requires. The team is committed to both the company and the country. Global Alliance's Chief Training Officer Margi Wilkinson, who has over 35 years' experience in the insurance industry, will be conducting and coordinating the training of personnel.

INSTITUTO NACIONAL DE ESTATÍSTICA – INE

Mrs Maria Ferreira dos Santos Oliveira
Co-General Director
Rua Ho-Chi Min,
PO Box 1215, Luanda
Tel: +244-222-322757 / 322730 / 320430
Fax: +244-222-320430
Email: M-Ferreira.Oliveira@ine.gv.ao

Activity: Preparation, analysis, distribution and coordination of Angolan statistics
Employees: 122

The INE – Instituto Nacional de Estatística – is a subdivision of the Ministry of Planning. There is a great lack of statistics in Angola due to the long civil war suffered by the country. However, since the civil war ended, the national statistics system is involved in a process of modernization in which the INE has an important role to play.

The National Council of Angola is the institution that coordinates the INE and the local bodies of the Angolan statistics system.

The Institute is responsible for the preparation, analysis, distribution and coordination of Angolan statistics and works in partnership with the World Bank, the EU, FNUAP, UNICEF, and SADEC and countries like Norway, Brazil and Portugal.

Angola celebrates its National Week of Statistics every November. The country has not published a census since 1970 but INE is about to launch a new one.

The Institute is growing every year. It currently has 122 employees and has offices in Bengola, Cabinda, Huíla and Cuanza Sul, with plans to open new branches in all the provinces of the country.

"We challenge the present, we trust the future!"
Mr Sebastião A. Mixinge, General Manager

KPMG

 Paul de Sousa
Senior Partner
Edificio Presidente, Largo 4 de Fevereiro,
nº 3, 1st Floor
PO Box 2021, Luanda

Tel: +244-222-310825/6/7/8
Mobile: +244-924-175130
Fax: +244-222-310549
Email: pdsousa@kpmg.com / igserrao@kpmg.com / kpmg@kpmg.co.ao
Website: www.kpmg.co.ao

Activity: Audit, tax, advisory services
Date of Creation: 1996
Employees: Approximately 120

In June 1996 KPMG International signed a foreign investment agreement with the Republic of Angola and established KPMG – Auditores e Consultores SARL in Angola as a fully accredited member firm of KPMG International. As the first international firm of its type to invest in Angola, KPMG has demonstrated its continuing commitment to meeting its clients' needs wherever in the world they choose to do business.

Luanda is continually growing

Doing business in Angola

Incredible opportunities

Significant risks and hurdles

Let our professionals advise you

Angola is amongst the world's fastest growing economies. Opportunities abound and investors are crowding in. Some have lost their way in regulatory, bureaucratic corporate governance and risk issues characteristic of a developing economy. KPMG has been in Angola for 10 years, where we are the leading advisory firm. We combine local know how with global vision.

For more information contact Paul de Sousa +244 924 175 130, pdsousa@kpmg.com or Isabel Serrão +244 222 310 825/6/7, igserrao@kpmg.com

www.kpmg.co.ao

AUDIT ▪ TAX ▪ ADVISORY

KPMG

KPMG in Angola offers a wide range of professional services to foreign, national and international companies and organizations in Angola. In addition to its core audit, tax and advisory services, KPMG offers specialist services in the following areas:

- Foreign investment advisory services
- Tax and legal consulting
- Financial advisory services (corporate finance, corporate
- recovery, forensic accounting)
- Integrated information systems
- Strategy and marketing advisory services
- Human resources advisory services
- Risk advisory services.

KPMG's core services are structured through multidisciplinary industry units. The industry teams serving the Angolan market are:

- Financial Services
- Industrial Markets
- Commercial Markets
- Infrastructure, Government and Healthcare
- Information, Communication and Entertainment
- Energy and natural resources.

NOSSA SEGUROS

Mr Licínio Cruz
Sales Director
Avenida 4 de Fevereiro, n° 111, Luanda
Tel: +244-222-399909 / 399929
Fax: +244-222-399153
Email: licinio.cruz@nossaseguros.com
Website: www.nossaseguros.com

Activity: Insurance

Nossa Seguros – Nova Sociedade de Seguros de Angola SA – is an Angolan insurance company whose activities are divided into two main lines of work: insurance plans and management of pension schemes. Insurance plans cover both life insurance and property insurance such as cars, equipment and machinery, work accidents and travel insurance. Aircraft and ship insurance are also available.

Among its shareholders are REAL Seguros SA (a Portuguese insurance company), IFC – International Finance Corporation (World Bank investment company specialized in private sector funding) and BAI – Banco Africano de Investimentos SA.

Financial insurance services offered by Nossa Seguros are provided by renowned insurance companies such as Swiss Re, Hanover Re, Munich Re and Africa Re.

With its range of products and services, Nosssa Seguros aims to contribute to the improvement of the quality of life of its clients, shareholders and partners. Its key values are quality, innovation, development and profitability, which it always employs to offer the best of services.

PRICEWATERHOUSECOOPERS – PWC ANGOLA

Mr Fernando Barros
Manager Director
Largo Saydi Mingas, BPC Building, n° 16, Luanda
Tel: +244-222-395004
Fax: +244-222-395677
Email: fernando.barros@ao.pwc.com
Website: www.pwcglobal.com

Activity: Consultancy, auditing
Date of Creation: 1998
Employees: 50

The work PricewaterhouseCoopers does in the Africa Central region provides examples of practical solutions to development problems. It works with governments and the private sector to help make the continent a truly Emerging Africa.

PricewaterhouseCoopers publishes comprehensive guides on conducting business and investing in approximately 46 countries worldwide based on the most current information available. These publications provide a valuable overview of the country's economic climate and business opportunities as well as legal and tax environments.

PricewaterhouseCoopers provides industry-focused services for public and private clients in order to build public trust and enhance value through the application of what it calls Connected Thinking.

Its core businesses in Angola are:

- Auditing
- Fiscal consultancy
- International tax structuring
- Various services for investors.

"The Angolan economy is going to increase dramatically in the next five years, like any other country in the world. Never again in our lives will we witness such a boom in the economy. Although doing business is sometimes difficult in Angola, you have to invest time and resources and it is really worth it in the end due to the competitive advantages it offers right now."
Mr Fernando Barros, Manager Director

QUANTUM CAPITAL SA

RECOMMENDED PARTNER

Mr Jean-Claude de Morais Bastos
Chairman and CEO
Rua Rainha Ginga n° 37, 1st Floor,
Mutamba, Luanda
Tel: +244-222-330501 / 330263 / 334597
Fax: +244-222-394388
Email: info@quantum-capital.net
Website: www.quantum-capital.net

Activity: Financial solutions (finance, investments, partnerships, projects, advice)
Creation Date of: 2004

Quantum Capital is an independent Angolan firm providing investment banking services, operating together with a network of international partners. Quantum Capital primarily focuses on emerging growth companies acting in Angola, to whom the firm offers the full range of investment banking and investment management services.

Clients come to see Quantum Capital when they need professional support related to financial issues and solutions tailored to their individual and personal needs. Such clients include among others entrepreneurs, high net worth individuals, private venture-backed enterprises, corporations, listed and state-owned companies, banks and other financial consultants, private equity firms and public market institutions that finance them.

Quantum Capital provides its clients with high-quality professional services such as planning, structuring and execution of finance transactions, lead/assist merger and acquisition transactions, including setting up joint ventures and partnerships in Angola.

Quantum Capital provides investment banking services such as corporate finance advisory services; mergers and acquisitions; debt and structured finance; venture and development capital sourcing; management buyouts and buyins.

Quantum Capital's target markets are oil and gas; real estate; mining and commodities; industry and infrastructure; and capital markets.

What makes Quantum Capital unique in the Angolan market is its strong local and international network combined with highly skilled management and staff, its commitment to establishing long-term relationships with its clients, and its dedication to the local market and its local market expertise.

"Angola is in a post-war/early-stage market phase and is one of the fastest growing economies in the world, caused by a major oil boom and a national reconstruction boom. GDP growth forecasts are 26% for 2006 and 21% for 2007. Inflation reached 17.7% at the end of 2005 and will reach 10% by the end of 2006. The recently modified civil law system based on European law with significant foreign investor protection, the large amount of untapped mineral resources and the launch of the Angolan Stock Exchange at the end of 2006 makes Angola a very unique place to do business."
Mr Jean-Claude de Morais Bastos, Chairman and CEO

RIDGE SOLUTIONS

Mr Jannie Breed
General Manager
Rua Marqués das Minas, Luanda
Rua Robert Schields nº 25, 1st Floor, Luanda
Tel: +244-222-392153 / 390745
Fax: +244-222-396027
Email: info@ridgesolutions.biz
Website: www.ridgesolutions.biz

Activity: Consultancy

Ridge Solutions Angola Lda is an Angolan-constituted company that forms part of the Ridge Solutions International group of companies.

The firm is an international management and operations company that specializes in advanced, innovative and practical solutions for problems in virtually all the sectors of the economy.

To ensure the very best solutions, RS has formed a network of strategic partnerships with various individuals and organizations to allow RS to respond to specific opportunities. It also assists with implementation, management and progress monitoring. Its clients include corporations, private companies, governments and institutions.

After decades of isolation and war, Angolan people are optimistic and have a strong belief in their own self-worth. It is necessary for outside investors to go into business with local partners. This can be a great asset if properly managed.

Ridge Solutions serves the needs of the Angolan economy and provides real answers, particularly with a view to becoming a vital part in the global economy. It combines intimate knowledge of the local political scene and the Angolans' belief in their self-worth with the best practices available worldwide.

In 1992 private banks were allowed to enter the market

INDUSTRY & TRADE

"To punch with a strong fist, you need to turn over your hand"
Angolan proverb

OVERVIEW

The industrial sector in Angola was devastated by the departure of the Portuguese on independence in 1975 and the subsequent civil war (1975–2002). The sector has now begun wholesale restructuring and modernization. There are significant industrial business opportunities for investors in many areas of activity. Existing industries include manufacture of consumer goods, the processing of local agricultural raw materials, oil refining, metal-working, cement production, textiles and pharmaceutical production.

There is significant potential to expand food processing and light industry with an infusion of capital, technology and training. The government plans to privatize many of the state-run industrial enterprises.

Under Portuguese colonial rule (before 1975), the manufacturing sector was dominated by light industries that produced consumer goods, especially the food processing industry, which accounted for 46% of the value of manufactured output in 1973. In contrast, heavy industries accounted for only 22% of output. By 1976 only 284 out of 692 manufacturing businesses were operating under their old management. In March 1976 the MPLA government nationalized all of the abandoned businesses. In 1985 industrial production was only 54% of its real value in 1973.

By 1986 only approximately 180 companies were operating in the manufacturing sector, and their output was equal to about 13% of GDP. Of that amount, state-run companies accounted for 56%.

Currently the Angolan economy is booming, mainly due to the increase in oil output and oil prices. Other sectors of the economy, including manufacturing, are also benefiting.

The strategy of the Angolan government to relaunch its industrial sector is based on a series of measures that include reinforcing the banking sector and the creation of new laws and incentives for private investment, new incentives granted to productive sectors and changes in import duties.

INDUSTRY

The industrial sector is currently growing from a low base. Industrial production growth in 2004 was 13,5%. Industry in Angola accounts for 65,8% of GDP, although most of this is oil production or oil-related (approximately 50% of GDP).

GDP growth rate (%)

Real GDP
Oil
Non-Oil

Source: IMF and own estimates

Gross Domestic Product by Sector (% of GDP unless otherwise indicated)				
	1999	2000	2001	2002
Agriculture, forestry, fishing	6.5	5.8	8	7.8
Oil and gas	58.8	60	53.6	55.3
Diamonds	8.2	6.4	5.8	5.5
Manufacturing	3.5	2.9	3.8	3.7
Construction	2.9	2.8	3.5	3.4
Trade and commerce	15.3	14.6	15.6	8.8
Non-tradable services	4.7	6.9	9.6	8.8
GDP at market prices (Kz m)	17	88.9	208.9	489.6

Source: IMF

Angola offers enough water resources to supply different industry sectors

The main industrial sectors are petroleum, diamonds, cement, basic metal products, fish processing, food processing, brewing, tobacco products, sugar, textiles and ship repair.

Major investments are planned for the next few years in key industrial sectors, such as cement, oil refining, sugar production, construction materials, oil-related industries (chemicals and steel works), beverages, food processing and mining.

TRADE

Because of the weakness of its manufacturing sector, Angola imports the majority of its finished goods requirements and primarily exports natural raw materials.

Main imports are machinery and electrical equipment, vehicles and spare parts, medicines, food, textiles and military goods (according to the CIA web page).

According to the CIA, Angola's main import partners in 2005 were:

Number of major plants per industry in 2006

Breweries	5
Cement plants	2
Wheat mills	2
Sugar refineries	1
Milk processing	1
Steel mills	1
Oil refineries	1

Source: IMF

- South Korea (28.3%)
- Portugal (13.1%)
- US (9.3%)

175

• South Africa (7.4%)
• Brazil (5.6%)
• Japan (4.8%)
• France (4.4%).

Total imports for 2005 were US $8.2 billion.

Main exports are crude oil, diamonds, refined petroleum products, gas, coffee, sisal, fish and fish products, timber and cotton.

The main export partners in 2005 were:

• US (37.7%)
• China (35.6%)
• Taiwan (6.7%)
• France (6.4%).

Total exports for 2005 were US $26.8 billion.

In March 2003, Angola agreed to adhere to the SADC Free Trade Protocol that seeks to harmonize and reduce tariffs by establishing regional policies on trade and customs duties. In September 2004 the government announced reduced customs duties on imported goods and in December exempted entities in the enclave of Cabinda from all customs duties. These reductions and exemptions do not apply to the oil industry.

Angola has signed customs cooperation agreements with Portugal and Sao Tome and Principe, and is expected to sign others with South Africa and members of the

Community of Portuguese Speaking States (CPLP). Angola is also currently negotiating with Namibia, Zambia and the Democratic Republic of Congo, all fellow SADC members, to implement customs agreements.

According to the UN Conference on Trade and Development (UNCTAD), Angola was the second-largest recipient of FDI in sub-Saharan Africa in 2003 and the largest overall between 1999 and 2003. The World Bank estimates inward flows of US $1.55 billion or about 9% of GDP in 2004, up from US $1.42 billion in 2003, and projects US $1.5 billion for 2005. The bulk of this investment was in the petroleum sector. There are no significant direct investment outflows from Angola.

NEW DEVELOPMENTS

The Angolan government approved in 2004 a new law granting significant tax incentives to foreign and national investments, which will contribute to the development of manufacturing industry and other priority sectors.

Many major economic players (such as China, Brazil, the EU and others) are opening or extending lines of credit to Angola. China recently agreed to an oil-backed US $2 billion loan to be used largely for infrastructure projects. During President Dos Santos's visit to Brazil in May 2005, a credit line of US $580 million, also tied to oil, was negotiated.

New industrial development projects include:

• Construction of three pharmaceutical plants in Luanda, Benguela and Dondo.
• Rehabilitation of a fish-processing factory in Namibe.
• Installation of a television assembly line.
• Expansion of the Luanda steel complex.
• Construction of a shipyard and seaport in Cabinda province.
• Installation of a local assembly line for military trucks.
• Construction of a new cement plant in Lobito.
• Construction of a diamond-polishing unit.
• Car assembly unit.
• New brewery.

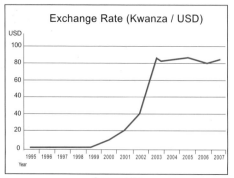

Exchange Rate (Kwanza / USD)

Source: BNA

MAIN COMPANIES

ÁGUAS DO BOM JESUS – MITC INVESTIMENTOS SARL

Mr Joffre Van Dúnem Jr.
President
Rua Rei Katyavala, nº 103, Luanda
Tel: +244-222-448611/16
Fax: +244-222-448622
Email: abj@multitel.co.ao / angola.office@mitc-invest.com

Date of Creation: 2001

Águas BomJesus belongs to Group MITC Investimentos SARL, which is an Angolan conglomerate with ventures in agro-industry, farming and cattle raising, trading, communications and marketing, construction, property development, industry and information technology and telecommunications. Águas BomJesus is produced using the most modern water treatment and purification techniques. This large project starts in a modern production plant producing a quality product targeted at Angolan families.

A close and rigorous quality control means that each litre of Águas BomJesus complies with all the international purity requirements.

The technological advancement of the equipment means that the company can treat 30,000 litres of water per hour, and bottle an average of 96,000 litres per day in 1.5 L bottles. BomJesus also produces 33 cl and 5 L bottles in accordance with market demand.

In addition to the coordination of the treatment and bottling processes it also has a distribution team, which ensures the transport of Águas BomJesus from the point of production to the table.

MITC Investimentos SARL's main objectives are to identify, promote, develop and coordinate business activities in Angola where MITC already has a consolidated operational infrastructure. Angola's rapid growth and excellent

The industrial sector is daily adapting to new technologies

development potential allow MITC Investimentos SARL to offer important investment opportunities to its partners with attractive returns, while contributing to create new jobs, training and better living conditions in Angola.

MITC's associates include important companies, both Angolan and international, such as Águas do BomJesus, Multipack, Agrinvest and Doxa.

ANGOLAN INDUSTRIAL ASSOCIATION– AIA

Mr José Severino
Rua Manuel Fernando Caldeira, n° 6,
PO Box 6127, Luanda
Tel: +244-923-600420 / 222-350441
Fax: +244-222-392241
Email: secretariado@aiaangola.com
Website: www.aiaangola.com

Date of Creation: 1930

AIA – Associação Industrial de Angola (Angolan Industrial Association) – was established in 1930 and had an interregnum between 1976 and 1992 during the civil war, resuming its activity in 1992.

It is an important association for Angola's private enterprises in several branches of activity such as the manufacturing, technological and services sectors.

AIA has a national spread with nearly 60 branches of business, with special focus on the manufacturing industry, agriculture and cattle breeding, building construction, fishing, transport, telecommunications, informatics, building materials, chemistry and services, etc.

The managing members are elected every three years to the Board, the Council of Auditors and Board of Directors.

AIA has 1,300 members and activities in the provinces of Luanda, Benguela, Cabinda, Huíla, Huambo, Namibe, Bié, Uíge, Cuanza Sul and Cuanza Norte.

It has overseas representation in South Africa, Belgium, China, Congo (Brazzaville), DRC Congo (Kinshasa), Netherlands, India, Mozambique, Namibia, Portugal and Zimbabwe.

The association owns the Filda Complex, which covers 24 hectares of land and has 19,000 m^2 of covered area with nine pavilions for exhibitions, which are in need of new investment. It is managed by the consortium Expo Angola and led by AIA, in partnership with associations and state bodies involved with shows and exhibitions, such as FILDA and Fenapro.

AGÊNCIA NACIONAL PARA O INVESTIMENTO PRIVADO - ANIP

ANIP
Agência Nacional para o Investimento Privado

Mr Ari Carvalho
Board Member
Rua Cerqueira Lukoki, n° 25, 9th Floor, Luanda
Tel: +244-222-391434
Fax: +244-222-332956
Email: aricarvalho@investinangola.org
Website: www.investinangola.org

The Agência Nacional para o Investimento Privado (National Agency for Private Investment – ANIP) is a government agency created to reduce red tape and facilitate and encourage private investments in Angola. It is charged with implementing the national tax incentive policy and providing a direct channel of communication with investors.

ANIP will also be responsible for detecting investment opportunities in Angola, as well as the complete administrative handling of processes, including applications for tax and financial incentives, licensing and start-up processes, and the negotiation of administrative investment agreements.

The National Agency for Private Investment will take on a special significance that will, on the one hand, actively contribute to fostering policies and practices that may help lower public administration-related costs. On the other hand, it will constitute an exclusive entity that will concentrate all national and foreign instruments included within the objective and subjective scope of the private investment law in Angola, thereby acting as a well-identified interlocutor for any investor.

Through ANIP, the periods for evaluating investment proposals have been reduced to 15 days for investments of US $50,000 to US $5 million, and 30 days for projects worth more than US $5 million, which must be approved by the Cabinet of Ministers. It is mandatory for all potential investors in Angola to have their file approved by ANIP.

ANGONABEIRO

Mr Rui Melo
Manager
Estrada do Cacuaco Km 5,
PO Box 5727, Luanda
Tel: +244-222-840161 / 62
Fax: +244-222-840630
Email: anabeiro@snet.co.ao

Angonabeiro – Comércio de Cafés Lda – was formed when an old coffee factory was renovated in 2000 by Nova Delta – Comércio e Industria de Cafés SA, which started managing it with the main aim of launching Café Ginga, a 100% Angolan coffee brand.

The steady evolution of Café Ginga is the result of the active participation of the brand in the market, making the most of opportunities and implementing changes. This, together with Nova Delta's support and know-how, helped consolidate Angonabeiro's production structure, and since then it is a leader in the national market.

Factory of Bom Jesus In Viana

As well as these business plans, the company wants to implement projects to continue improving the coffee's quality in order to increase the standing of Café Ginga in both the national and international markets.

To this end, Angonabeiro is working with producing communities with the aim of training and qualifying the producers, encouraging and awarding the production of high-quality coffees, and enabling producers to keep sustainable businesses, making them responsible towards both the population and the environment.

Angonabeiro has a range of both ground coffee and coffee beans sold to both the general public and restaurants. It is also responsible for the sale and technical maintenance of coffee-related machinery and appliances.

AROSFRAM

Mr Mohammed Tajideen
Vice President
Avenida 4 de Fevereiro, n° 13 r/c,
PO Box 6172, Luanda
Tel: +244-222-311919
Fax: +244-222-311211
Email: mtadijeen@golfrateangola.com
Website: www.golfrateangola.com

Date of Creation: 1992
Employees: 3,000

Arosfram is a widely diversified group established in 1992. Group Arosfram currently operates a network of supermarkets. It also owns and operates a plastic products manufacturing plant and in addition operates a number of warehouses with capacity for wholesale and retail sales. Arosfram Group also has interests in private security services, civil construction and public works projects. Its main core business is food imports. It produces world-known products locally (such as OMO), as well as its own brands of soaps, spaghetti and biscuits. With a market share of almost 50%, the group owns more than seven factories nationwide and is the biggest food distributor in Angola.

Arosfram is the holding company of other important subsidiaries, such as Golfrate and Afri-Belg, and participates in other firms such as Mae-Mena, which offers rent-a-car services.

Golfrate is in charge of all the trade and distribution of the foods. This Angolan company, which was formed in 1995, today touches the lives of people across the length and breadth of Angola by meeting their daily needs for food and household and personal care products. Golfrate offers an ever-developing infrastructure; proven processes and a strong trading heritage have given rise to exclusive relationships with multinationals like Unilever, Nestlé and Kraft. Afri-Belg is a supermarket chain selling all the various imported products of Arosfram and Golfrate.

Arosfram also produces for other actors on the market on average 70 to 80 tonnes of plastic a day and PVC thanks to imported machines. So far the group Arosfram is answering local demand and hasn't contemplated exporting elsewhere in the subregion. Arosfram is also starting the construction of four buildings in Luanda for home and office space. The group employs over 3,000 people.

These relationships are testimony to Arosfram's credentials and ability on the ground to drive the penetration and consumption levels of its brands. This has in turn provided a strong foundation for Arosfram to commit significant investment to local manufacture and the marketing of its own brands.

"Arosfram's vision is to be the leading producer and distributor of quality essential consumer products, making them accessible and affordable to the people of Angola."
Mr Mohammed Tajideen, Vice President

BRITISH AMERICAN TOBACCO – BAT ANGOLA

Mr Luis Ribeiro
Managing Director
Rua Deolinda Rodrigues n° 535–539,
PO Box 1263, Luanda
Tel: +244-222-260158

Fax: +244-222-262138

Email: luis.ribeiro@bat.com

Website: www.bat.com

Activity: Tobacco industry

British American Tobacco sells its brands in 180 markets around the world. It makes high-quality tobacco products for the diverse preferences of millions of consumers, spans the business 'from seed to smoke', and is committed to embedding the principles of corporate social responsibility group-wide. Through more than 100 years of operations, it has built a strong international reputation for high-quality tobacco brands to meet consumers' diverse preferences.

BAT has been one of the FTSE 100's most successful companies – delivering an average total shareholder return over the past five years of 26.7% per year compared to 1.4% for the FTSE 100 overall.

In the early 1990s BAT decided to grow its business by focusing solely on tobacco – a decision that regalvanized and transformed the group. In 1995 BAT set itself the credible, if challenging, vision of regaining leadership of the global tobacco industry and established a strategy to get there. Over the last decade or so, its market share has increased by nearly 50%. It is now the second-largest international tobacco group, accounting for some 17% of the global market.

BAT is the world's second-largest quoted tobacco group by global market share, with more than 300 brands sold in 180 markets. It holds robust market positions in each of its regions and has leadership in more than 50 markets.

The group's subsidiary companies have 64 cigarette factories in 54 countries producing some 678 billion cigarettes (including the make-your-own cigarette 'stix', and seven factories in six countries manufacturing cigars, roll-your-own and pipe tobacco. The group's associate companies have 14 cigarette factories in seven countries producing some 232 billion cigarettes. The companies, including associates, employ almost 97,000 people worldwide.

BAT has a significant interest in tobacco leaf growing, working with some 250,000 farmers worldwide. Its companies run leaf programmes in 23 countries providing direct agronomy support to farmers, if it is not otherwise available, covering all aspects of crop production and environmental best practice.

COCA-COLA BOTTLING

Mr Samuel Jerónimo

Managing Director

Estrada de Cacuaco, Km 55, Luanda

Tel: +244-222-380353 / 382044

Email: elizabeth.esmeraldo@sabmiller.co.ao

Website: www.coca-cola.com

Coca-Cola Company has returned to Angola 26 years after civil war forced it to leave, and it has already invested more than US $40 million in the country, a big sum by African standards. Coca-Cola's experience shows that a single large investment often has only modest benefits in a country like Angola, and the challenges facing Coca-Cola show how hard it will be to persuade other investors that risk is worthwhile. Although the oil and diamond sectors have remained buoyant throughout the long years of civil war and general decline, the rest of Angola's industry has been at a virtual standstill for decades. One of the major indications that things are moving forward again is the fact that Coca-Cola has opened not just one, but two bottling plants in the country.

Coca-Cola opened the first plant in 2000 just outside Luanda at Bom Jesus in Bengo province. This represented the first significant foreign investment in Angola outside oil and diamonds for many years. Production at the Bom Jesus plant reached 14 million cases per year in the first 12 months of operations. Coca-Cola has now opened a second plant in the southern city of Lubango.

The US Coca-Cola Company will invest US $50 million in the forthcoming five years in Angola to increase its projects. This investment will be focused on the improvement of infrastructure and material in different areas of the industry of non-alcoholic and soft drink products, as well as in social projects.

Coca-Cola's investments will also fund microeconomics, where it employs a high number of people. In the social field, Coca-Cola intends to invest in programmes for fighting against HIV/AIDS, environmental initiatives, education and improvement of water quality. It intends to provide material for some schools, particularly those located in the communities where the firm develops its businesses. Coca-Cola is also trying to implement a programme of can picking for recycling.

CUCA BGI & EKA

Mr João Luis Vanhaecht
Managing Director
Rua N'Gola Kiluanje, Estrada de Cazenga, Km 8
PO Box 1281, Luanda
Tel: +244-222-380044 / 380379
Fax: +244-222-380379 / 380743
Email: cuca.luanda@cuca.snet.co.ao

Cuca BGI in Angola belongs to the French Castel Group, which has more than 50 years of history. The group specializes in wine, water, beer and soft drinks.

Cuca BGI is the first beer producer in Angola. It also produces Coca-Cola soft drinks. BGI assumes the management of the brewery. Cuca BGI is building another plant in Benguela.

Cuca BGI produces 100,000 crates of beer per day. The product has approximately five million customers in the country. The product has a national market share of 60%.

The Angolan brewery of Cuca BGI is also in charge of the production of the Portuguese beer Sagres, which has a yearly production of almost 60 million litres. Angola is the second-largest market for this label after Portugal. Angola is the first country worldwide authorized to produce Sagres.

In Angola Sagres is the second-most-consumed drink (45%) preceded by Cuca BGI. Sales for Sagres reached 200 million litres worldwide, with 60 million in Angola.

The government has approved the privatization of the Cuca BGI and Nocal breweries, located in Luanda.

EAL – EDIÇÕES DE ANGOLA LDA

Mr Carlos Alberto Arques Santos
Director General
Rua Vereador Prazeres, nº 41–43, Bairro São Paulo, Luanda
Tel: +244-222-442899 / 442109
Email: edicoesdeangola@yahoo.com

Activity: Artworks, printing, binding, stationery, corporate image products
Date of Creation: 1965
Employees: 100

Edições de Angola Lda set up business in 1965 with less than 20 employees. More than 40 years have passed by and the family-owned company has not stopped growing and adapting to modern times. It combines the latest state-of-the-art, most sophisticated technology with know-how and attention to detail that can only be achieved through years of operation. Quality and experience define this business. Its wide range of services includes anything a company may need in terms of stationery and editing and publishing material: books, calendars, diaries, envelopes, folders, invoice books, magazines, maps, notebooks, notepads, posters, stamps, templates, among others. Edições de Angola is a one-stop shop that satisfies all the needs businesses may have.

The company also has a creative department where qualified and experienced staff are devoted to taking care of and enhancing the corporate image of clients. They not only create artworks and graphic designs for their customers, but also fulfil the different stages of the creation process: editing, printing, finishing, binding. Corporate products include among others banners, brochures, business bags, business cards, flyers, headed notepaper, leaflets and posters and customized gift items.

Edições de Angola not only supplies the needs of business but also personal needs, since it can also deal with invitation cards and souvenir gifts for personal celebrations: wedding stationery and favours, birthday parties, graduation parties, among others.

Edições de Angola has been working for years for some of the most reputable companies in Angola and it has also collaborated in government campaigns and with local and international institutions. Its chairman, Mr Carlos Alberto Arques Santos, believes people are the lifeblood of the business and hires and trains staff personally in the company premises. Edições de Angola is a company that cares about its staff and strongly believes Angolan people are the key to the development of the country. It is socially responsible and actively contributes to the benefit and growth of the country.

"Peace is a value we all learn to respect. It makes us an extraordinary, humble people, incredibly dedicated and willing to learn. If we add to this human element the fact that in this huge country everything, from the smallest thing to the most complicated, is left to be done, here we have the two basic ingredients for any enterprise destined for success."

Mr Carlos Alberto Arques Santos, Director General

EMPRESA NACIONAL DE ESPUMAS E PLÁSTICOS DE ANGOLA – ENEPA

Mr Francisco C. Cabral de Sousa
Manager
Rua Ngola Kiluange, nº 440, 1st Floor, Luanda
Tel: +244-222-381330 / 381339
Fax: +244-222-381338
Email: enepa@ebonet.net

Activity: Plastic products manufacture
Date of Creation: 4th June 1983

Enepa is a public company created on 4th June 1983 by the Angolan government as part of its nationalization plan of the country's economy. Enepa is a holding company with 10 factories in the Luanda, Benguela, Huambo and Lubango provinces.

Enepa, as a state-run producer of both plastics and packaging, manufactures a wide range of products including plastic foam, expanded polystyrene and thermal insula-

tion for refrigeration units, packaging materials, PVC profiles and polythene pipes and fittings. Although Enepa still has a monopoly in areas such as packaging for the food and drink industry, it recognizes the need for change in this business. Market development is a key element of any attempt to expand the economy. Enepa manufactures a wide range of products:

• Household plastic products, HDPE pipe, soft PVC hoses and profiles, rigid PVC extrusion profiles, industrial products such as crates, boxes, bottles for detergent, lubricants and vegetable oil.
• Mattresses and polyurethane flexible foam products.
• Furniture and sport boats made of reinforced polyester resin fibreglass. EPS boxes and isolation products.
• Plastisol toys, dolls and balls.
• Electrical appliances.
• Plastic film, plastic bags and industrial plastic bags with capacity of up to 50 kg.
• PVC shoes.

EXECUTIVE CENTER

Mr Nuno Fernandes
Administrator
Rua Emilio Mbidi, n° 120 r/c,
PO Box 1348, Luanda
Tel: +244-222-323292 / 323708
Email: executiveang@ebonet.net

The Executive Center Ltd was founded in 1992 and specializes in communications, marketing and brand image. Its client portfolio demonstrates the service the company has been providing in the Angolan market, and the dedication and professionalism that has been its hallmark since the start.

The day-to-day activity of the Executive Center focuses on maintaining client loyalty through rapid response at the level of quality shown by its team of professionals, on reaching its objectives and on turning clients into friends.

Many ongoing studies of advertising show that technological change has been exponential but that people, deep down, do not want to change. The mission of the Executive Center is to get to know people and to be in the right place at the right time, doing the right thing in the right way.

The Executive Center is responsible among other things for the publication of *Austral*, the in-flight magazine of Taag, Linhas Aéreas de Angola, and for the magazine *Economia & Mercado*, which focuses on the country's economic and financial affairs and is a powerful vehicle for business advertising.

It holds the exclusive concession for advertising in the airports of Angola and on the Luanda public transport system. It can therefore offer its clients yet another way to promote their products and services by means of cover across a wide array of impact points.

In its day-to-day affairs, the Executive Center puts together integrated advertising campaigns where strategies are moulded as an integrated whole, from photographs and graphics, including indoors and outdoors, through audio and video productions, with the best digital processing systems and allied quality of picture and sound.

Customer service goes hand in hand with the campaigns, thus providing a seamless operation covering planning, placement and readability.

FATA – FABRICA DE TUBOS DE ANGOLA

Mr Mário Almeida Ribeiro
Managing Director
Av. Deolinda Rodrigues, Km 18, Zona Industrial de Viana, Viana
Tel: +244-222-290029 / 290054
Fax: +244-222-290955
Email: fatametin@nexus.ao

Activity: Metal industry
Date of Creation: 10th May 1964
Capital: US $100,000,00
Turnover: (+/-) US $9,000,000,00 /year
Employees: 178

Eminpack Machinery

Fata has an important standing in the Angolan metal industry, and until August 2006 it was the only one in the sector. Its main target is enlarging its range of products, putting an emphasis on the manufacture of metal furniture for hospitals and schools. It relies on the quality of its products and professional training. Fata also aims to produce inexpensive building materials that all Angolan people will be able to afford.

Fata is a 100% public company that needs technological innovation. Fata has two lines of production of pipes, Italian and Japanese, and its facilities extend to 117,000 sq. m. Currently, it only has capacity to manufacture 12,000 tonnes per year, since the equipment is quite old.

Fata's main primary goods are cold- and hot-rolled bobbins from South Africa and India and the target market of the finished products is Angola. This uses 40% of Fata's current capacity due to the lack of primary goods and the irregular electricity supply. As well as renovating the facilities, Fata needs to attract more investment and medium- and long-term credit lines.

FEPEL COMMERCE & INDUSTRY LTD

Mr Estevão Cauanda
General Manager
Rua Gil da Liberdade, nº 7D, Comandate Valódia, Luanda
Tel: +244-222-442190 / 449324
Fax: +244-222-448640
Email: fepel@nexus.ao / fepel@fepel.net

Date of Creation: 2002

Fepel Commerce & Industry Ltd is a young Angolan company with private capital established on 11th September 2002, mainly directed to serving small and medium enterprises, but also larger companies. It has devoted its efforts to graphic design and serigraphy (screen printing) as well as developing other segments of the graphics market including manufacturing of graphical and marketing materials, such as stamping of t-shirts and caps, making pens, key chains and other promotional merchandise.

The company is equipped with highly skilled personnel with a vast experience in the field of graphics and serigraphy design, which ensures excellent quality of service.

It aims to provide quick and inspirational solutions in order to help solve graphic and marketing problems.

The company is aware of the fact that the huge key to success in today's business environment is time management. Each day must be very structured and organized, using every moment with a good purpose. Fepel can fulfil all a client's editorial needs, keeping creativity always at a high level. Fepel guarantees the highest standard of quality and trust to satisfy customers' needs, focusing on the ethics and legality of services provided.

Fepel Lda has expanded its business and has recently opened Fepel Travel Agency, which also offers car hire services together with the latest advances in travel agency services.

Fepel hopes to develop other paths of commerce as well, specifically retail and wholesale products. Lastly, the firm has participated with other partners in mining exploration. Fepel has its main office in Luanda and will soon open an office in Lobito, Benguela province, for mining exploration.

"Our main aim is to work within a social perspective, so that we create a company to help the government in social and human development."
Mr Estevão Cauanda, General Manager

GRUPO BARTOLOMEU DIAS

Mr Bartolomeu Dias
General Manager
Rua 21 de Janeiro, Morro Bento,
PO Box 6546, Luanda
Tel: +244-222-469074 / 469069
Fax: +244-222-469080
Email: grupobd@grupobd.com
Website: www.grupobd.com

Activity: Diverse industry and trade
Date of Creation: 1992

Grupo BD is a group of six independent companies. It was established in 1992, and with almost 13 years of experience, the group has experienced good growth and is today a main player in the economy of the country. The group has several activities in the fields of industry, commerce, import and export, transport, hotels and tourism, research and mine exploration.

In the industrial sector the group is represented by Nova Rede Industrial. It is an Angolan company that belongs to Grupo BD and was created in 1996. Among its main activities it produces and distributes vegetable oil and soaps for cosmetic use. It also imports and exports engines, raw materials and other industrial products.

In the transport sector the group also has the company Diexim – Divisão de transporte Lda, which was created in 1997. Diexim provides services to companies specializing in baked and confectionery products and transport services. Diexim has 60 trucks, 43 platforms, 30 tankers and 10 refrigerated trucks, which makes possible transportation of solid and liquid goods. The company deals with the transportation of merchandise in several locations in Angola.

The group also has the company Boa Viagem, which has two Embraer 120 RT planes and one Kinger 350 for passenger transportation and VIP services. Boa Viagem has a staff of 60 workers specialized in technical, administrative and auxiliary fields.

In the tourism sector the group has Internacional Travel Lda Agência de Viagens and Rent a Car. The company was created in 2001. It has a staff of 15 people including operators, drivers, tourist guides, etc. It offers a wide range of tourist services for groups and individuals and car rental possibilities. The company provides reliable services regarding visa procedures, baggage control, etc. Internacional Travel offers quality service and has competitive prices.

In the agricultural sector the group has three companies: Angoinform Lda, Angoinform DS and Angoinform Construtora, which were created in 1992.

GRUPO CHICOIL

Mr Elias Piedoso Chimuco
President – CEO
Av. Hoji Ya Henda, n° 40, Apts. 1 & 2, Luanda
Tel: +244-923-471664
Fax: +244-222-448152
Email: chicoil@ebonet.net

Activity: Diverse industry and trade

Chicoil Group was founded in 1992 and it is now one of the most important companies in Angola. The group works in the areas of industry, commerce, transport, hotels and tourism and is represented in the provinces of Cuando Cubango, Benguela, Huíla, Cabinda, Cunene, Lunda Norte, Bié, Huambo and Cuanza Sul as well as in other countries such as South Africa, Portugal and Namibia.

Chicoil Group has recently invested about US $5 million for the expansion of its activities in the areas of commerce and sports in central Benguela province and is also planning to build a shopping centre in the surroundings of Benguela city. It is expected to serve over 1,000 customers per day and provide 70 jobs.

The group is growing rapidly and is composed of six companies involved in a large range of activities such as public works, health, tourism, transport, import and export and general trade. Chicoil Group is a very good example of expansion and business development and also provides a model for social development as its projects are an expression of solidarity.

An important target of the group is to facilitate the development of industry and commerce services in the Angolan regions, both by preparing community groups to develop their local businesses and by offering the opportunity to improve quality of life in those areas, while expanding their brand into the whole Angolan territory.

Chicoil can be considered one of the largest intermediary goods suppliers in Angola. It has established a strong base of long-term relations with major worldwide producers in the product range it is handling, with high efficiency and capability to supply competitive prices and high quality to its consumers.

GRUPO SOGEC – SOCIEDADE GERAL DE COMÉRCIO E INDÚSTRIA

Mr Antonio Alberto Briffel Neto
Chairman of the Board
Rua Dr Américo Boavida, n° 131, 133, 137,
PO Box 12042, Luanda
Tel: +244-222-395145 / 394830 / 394543
Fax: +244-222-394826
Email: sogec@snet.co.ao

Activity: Diverse industry and trade

Sogec is a major Angolan holding involved in various parts of the economy. The company's main area of focus is importation of general consumer goods, especially foods. Sogec acts as a wholesaler for imports of rice, sugar, oil, milk, corn, flour and noodles among others. The company has its own distribution network through the supermarket Jumbo, but also sells its products nationwide to all retail stores. Sogec also imports medicines to be distributed in pharmacies all over the country.

Apart from this activity, the group is involved in hotels. It currently owns the Hotel Tivoli and the Hotel Central. Sogec is currently undertaking two projects, one to build a new five-star hotel in the Luanda Sul area, with 25 presidential suites, a casino, reception rooms and all other features of this standard. The hotel is planned to open in 2008. The other project is the rehabilitation of the Hotel Tivoli to make it more modern, to add a façade and build underground parking.

Finally Sogec is involved in the transportation industry. It operates a transport network of trucks to dispatch any types of goods throughout the country. Sogec has a rich portfolio of high-quality brands, the collective success of which has been responsible for the company's growth, strength and enduring achievements. Sogec is also the proprietor of the AVIS franchise in Angola.

Although very diversified, the activities of Sogec are complementary to each other, creating a positive synergy to better satisfy its customers.

"Come to Angola to invest. All the sectors are opening, from agriculture to civil engineering. There is a big opening for foreign investors to come."
Mr Antonio Alberto Briffel Neto, Chairman of the Board

GUE – GUICHÊ ÚNICO DE EMPRESAS

Largo Antonio Correia de Freitas,
Av. Marginal, nº 120, Luanda
Tel: +244-222-372328 / 372829

GUE – Guichê Único de Empresa – is a new public service whose objective is to facilitate the processes of constitution, alteration and extinction of companies and similar.

In August 2003 the Angolan government established the Guichê Único, or one-stop shop, to simplify the process and reduce the time required to register a company by unifying procedures required by various government ministries under one roof. However, the Guichê Único lacks authority over other government ministries, which must approve licences, permits and other requirements, and thus has encountered great difficulty in expediting company registration. Nonetheless, the Guichê Único succeeded in issuing 320 new business licences in 2005, more than double the 151 issued in 2004.

In 2006 it established a website that will permit online registration. GUE has delegations in all the public administration bodies and services responsible for this activity, namely: Ministry of Justice; National Directorate of Registrars and Notaries; Ministry of Finance; National Directorate of Taxes; Ministry of Planning; National Institute of Statistics; Ministry of Commerce; Legal Cabinet; Office of the Cabinet of Ministers; the national press.

Available services include: granting of the admission certificate; granting of the public writing; statistical registration of the company or firm; registration in the commercial register; publication in the press; collection of the fees due; attribution of the contributor number.

Philosophy/purpose of the service:

• Stimulate entrepreneurship with a view to the development of the entrepreneurial community, the creation of jobs and wealth.
• Monitor social and economic development.
• Provide a technical specialized service to advise and aid compliance with the legal requirements and provide other services and information about entrepreneurial activity.

By concentrating all of its services in a single physical space, GUE achieves the reduction of bureaucracy and a streamlined process, thus promoting the economic development of the country

ICELAR – RÉPLICA – EMPREENDIMENTOS COMERCIAIS E INDUSTRIAIS SARL

Mr Octavio Baptista
Administrator
Zona Industrial de Viana, Luanda
Tel: +244-222-262458 / 263490
Fax: +244-222-263491 / 262235
Email: replica@snet.co.ao; info@icelar.info
Website: http: icelar.info

Date of Creation: 1992
Turnover: US $12,000,000
Employees: 140

Icelar SARL opened its doors in June 1999. Its main activities are: production of fridges (petrol, electric and gas); technical assistance and selling of fabrication materials.

The years during the war were a difficult period for the company, when 25 people assembled 30 refrigerator units daily. Six months after the end of the war, the first factory started working and now the company is a great example of industry development in Angola. Between the end of 1999 and 2000 it invested in training its staff of 35 people. The company moved to an industrial pavilion, previously occupied by Replica. In 2000 it started negotiations with Group Zuid and Casa Holandesa, and Replica shareholders bought the company Zuid Industrial, which

HOLDING

GRUPO CHICOIL S.A.R.L.

Grupo Chicoil started its activities fourteen years ago.

● **Grupo Chicoil** - Comércio e Agro-Pecuário, S.A.R.L., is a limited company based in Luanda, whose activities are the following: coordinate the management of the companies of the Group, managing their social programs, creation and management of industrial projects, consulting services in the financial and economic fields, promoting and managing businesses, commercial representations and export/import of goods, among others. Our Board of Directors are always open to approuve other businesses and economic activities under the applicable Laws.

Grupo Chicoil, S.A.R.L. is composed of the following companies:

Chimuco Comercial e Industrial, Lda., whose social purpose consists of carrying out trade activities, hotel industry, fisheries and agriculture activities and import/export.

Constrói-Angola, Lda., building, public works and sale of building materials and equipment.

Chik-Chik, Agência de Viagens e Comércio Geral, Lda., travel, tourism and hotels agents, aerial transportation, rent-a-car, private security services, education and training programs, clothing, trade activities and import/export..

Chico-Car, Lda., sale of first and second hand vehicles, car rental, spare parts sale, service station, transport of goods.

Chico-Clínica, Lda., general medicine services and chemists.

Dabrinchi, Comércio Geral, Lda., general trade, fisheries, and agriculture, civil building works, cabotaje, import and services.

Grupo Chicoil, S.A.R.L. has branches in South Africa, Portugal and Namibia.

a vision of the future

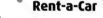

SOCIEDADE GERAL DE COMERCIO E INDÚSTRIA, LDA

Rua Dr. Américo Boavida 131, 133, 137
C.P.: 12042
Luanda,   Angola

Tel: + 244 2 39 51 45 / 39 48 30 / 39 45 43
Fax: + 244 2 39 48 26
Telex: 2513

SOCIEDADE GERAL DE COMERCIO E INDÚSTRIA, LDA

SOGEC
Sociedade Geral de Comercio e Indústria, Lda.

"Come to Angola to invest, all the sectors

are open - from agriculture to civil engineering.

There is a big opening for foreign investors to come her

António Alberto Briffel Net
Chairman of the Boar
SOGE

SOCIEDADE GERAL DE COMERCIO E INDÚSTRIA, LDA

Rua Dr. Américo Boavida 131, 133, 13
Luanda, Angola

Tel: + 244-2-395145 / 394830 / 394543
Fax: + 244 2 394 826

SOGEC is a major Angolan holding company involved in various sectors of the economy. Although very diversified, the activities of SOGEC are complementary to each other, creating a positive synergy to better satisfy their customers.

IMPORTS

The Company's main area of focus is the importing of general consumer goods,especially foodstuffs. SOGEC acts as a wholesaler for imports of: Rice, Sugar, Oil, Milk, Corn, Flour, Noodles and much more!

DISTRIBUTION

The company owns its own distribution network through the JUMBO supermarkets, however they also sell their products nationwide to many retail stores.

SOGEC also imports medicines to be distributed in pharmacies all over the country.

TRANSPORTATION

Finally SOGEC is involved in the transportation industry. It operates a transport network of trucks, which can dispatch all goods throughout the country.

SOGEC is also the proprietor of the AVIS franchise in Angola.

TOURISM

The group is actively involved in tourism and business travel, and currently owns the Hotel Tivoli and the Hotel Central.

In this field, SOGEC is currently undertaking two new projects:

1. To build a new 5-Star hotel in the Luanda Sul area. It will boast 25 presidential suites, a casino, receptions rooms and much more. The hotel is predicted to open in 2008.

2. The other project is the refurbishment of the Hotel Tivoli, to make it more modern,to add a façade and to build an underground parking lot.

set up in the industrial park of Viana in 2001. With a total area of 40,000 m^2, the industrial park offers 5,000 m^2 dedicated to manufacturing, 1,000 m^2 dedicated to the social sector (clinic, dining hall, social sector) and 400 m^2 dedicated to the administrative sector.

The company now employs more than 150 people and produces approximately 4,000 freezers a month, as well as many other products such as fridges and cookers, which are official national products of Angola and also registered brands known as Icelar and Cetron.

"You have to come and see for yourself the Angolan reality; difficulties will disappear with hard work. Industry has a place in this serious and wonderful country that is worth visiting."
Mr Octavio Baptista, Administrator

IDIA – INSTITUTO DE DESENVOLVIMENTO INDUSTRIAL DE ANGOLA (INDUSTRIAL DEVELOPMENT INSTITUTE OF ANGOLA)

Mr Gabriel Kiala Ngone
PManaging Director
Rua Cerqueira Lukoki, n° 25, 8th Floor,
PO Box 780, Luanda
Tel: +24-222-338492 / 395296
Fax: +244-222-338492
Email: idiadg@yahoo.com / idia.dg@netangola.com
Website: www.idia.gov.ao

The Industrial Development Institute of Angola (IDIA) is a public body with an autonomous administration and financial structure. This organization is responsible for the management of reindustrialization and is subject to scrutiny by the Ministry of Industries.

The main duties of the Institute are to:

• Instigate industrial development that will enable the creation of national economic integration and equilibrium between diverse regions of the country.
• Promote the construction of infrastructure needed for industrial operations and initiate the creation and appropriate operation of the policies of industrial development.

• Promote the formation of industrial development societies (IDSs).
• Act as a driving force in regional development in the industrial sector.
• Initiate and encourage actions aimed at improving the competitiveness of companies or industries.
• Cooperate with business associations, trade unions and other organizations by urging them to participate actively in the identification of strategies and plans that will allow the reconstruction of industrial activities and enhance the country's reindustrialization process.
• Collaborate with government ministries and other government bodies in the collection of tax and customs duty, which is important for industrial development.
• Coordinate with provincial administrations with a view to encouraging industrial development in every province.
• Organize technical courses to help in the fields of business management and economics.
• Help in the organization of trade fairs and commercial shows to promote the industrial sector.

LACTIANGOL

Mr Antonio Russo
Director
Av. Deolinda Rodrigues, Km 5, Luanda
Tel: +244-222-265217/18
Fax: +244-222-63379
Email: lactiangol@ebonet.net

Lactiangol produces a wide range of dairy products including milk (pasteurized and ultra-pasteurized), solid and liquid yogurt, butter and ice cream and also produces a variety of juices. The company employs around 200 people, but is still operating at a fraction of its capacity. The Portuguese consortium Agropromotora holds 49.5% of the capital.

Lactiangol envisages that greater demand for its products will come as people's nutritional habits change. In Angola the most common morning beverages are coffee and tea, even for children; the company is actively trying to encourage the consumption of milk. The potential market remains small – 100,000 consumers of dairy products have been identified in Luanda – but this market growing. As 60% of

Institute of Industrial Development of Angola

e Industrial Development which will make possible the creation of a
l economic integration and equilibrium between diverse regions of the

e the construction of infrastructure for the basis of industrial operations and
he creation and appropriate operation of the Poles of Industrial
oment.

e the creation of Industrial Development Societies (IDSs).

driving force in regional development in the Industrial Sector.

or encourage actions and tendencies aimed at improving the
itiveness of companies or Industries.

Rua Cerqueira Lukoki, n° 25, 8th Floor, Luanda
Tel. +24.222.395296,Fax. +244.222.338492 P.B: 780
E-mail: idiadg@yahoo.com / idia.dg@netangola.com
Web: www.idia.gov.ao

the capital's population lives on less than US $1 per day, they cannot afford Lactiangol products until salaries rise.

During the 1970s, Angola was a major dairy producer. Today Lactiangol could be producing 2 million litres of fresh milk a day, but produces none. This is because it lacks the security, investment and technology to keep large herds of dairy cattle. The absence of cattle herds around Luanda means that the only dairy company of any significance in Angola, Lactiangol, has to use imported milk powder for its products, as there is no large-scale milk production locally and so there is no choice but to import dried milk powder.

Lactiangol will start producing packed powdered milk with an initial investment of around US $0.5 million, with the aim of making the packed milk powder more accessible to consumers. Lactiangol has invested in the last decade around US $9.5 million in equipment used for production and distribution. These investments have enabled the company – for the first time in its history – to raise the value of milk products sold to over US $10 million.

In May 2001 Lactiangol signed a major contract with the government to supply its products to schoolchildren in Luanda. As a result, the company raised its production levels to 50% capacity, instead of its former 30%. This so-called *merenda escolar* (school-snack) has been purchased by the Angolan Education Authorities in some Angolan provinces in order to be distributed in primary schools. Composed of bread, a little portion of butter and a pack of milk with chocolate flavour, it has significantly changed the life of many children.

PINTO BASTO ANGOLA

Mr Bernado Pedra Soares
Director General
Rainha Ginga, n° 187 r/c, Suites E & F, Luanda
Tel: +244-222-330439 / 331285/98
Fax: +244-222-338868
Email: bsoares@pintobasto-angola.com
Website: www.pintobasto-angola.co

Date of Creation: 1771

The Pinto Basto Company was set up in Portugal in 1771 when Domingos Pinto Basto founded an import and export firm in Porto. In the first half of the nineteenth century, Pinto Basto also set up a company in the capital, Lisbon. With a historical background of more than two centuries, Pinto Basto's pioneer spirit, experience and professionalism have contributed to making it a model organization in the sector of freight transportation.

Pinto Basto now aims to place all its experience and professionalism at the service of Angola, where the company has set up an office recently. It will thus contribute to the progress and development of the country, which has the greatest potential for economic growth in all of Western Africa.

Today the Pinto Basto Group comprises several enterprises in the areas of maritime, terrestrial and aerial transportation, namely shipping agents, express transportation, P&I clubs, forwarding agents, air cargo, expert inspections, and inspection services. These are independent companies that rely on excellent teams of professionals and enjoy the advantages of belonging to a solid and prestigious holding company.

The most important reason for the success of the Pinto Basto Group is the experience gathered in working with some of the world's biggest and oldest companies. In Angola these include the MSC Mediterranean Shipping Company, the world's second-largest container line.

Pinto Basto is prepared to offer in Angola, as much as it does in Portugal, the global solutions that best fit its clients' needs, taking care of all operations as well as all logistical and legal procedures.

"By sea, land or air, we have the solution that serves you best. Tell us what you need, we work out the best transportation strategy for you and put all our energy into achieving that goal. Work with the best, work with Pinto Basto."
Mr Bernado Pedra Soares, Director General

REFRIANGO

Mr Carlos Rodrigues
Managing Director
Rua de Porto Santo, nº 24 B, Luanda
Tel: +244-222-310365 / 392791 / 382615
Fax: +244-222-311496
Date of Creation: 2002

Refriango is an Angolan company founded with Portuguese and Angolan capital. It specializes in soft drinks and its production plant was set up in 2002. With a production capacity of 200 million litres per year and employing 428 Angolan, Portuguese and Brazilian workers, Refriango's production capacity is above average in the African continent. Refriango has recently launched two soft drinks, one under its own brand name and another through a concession from a North American company:

• Blue: a carbonated soft drink launched in February 2005 in seven flavours.
• American Cola: in October 2004 Refriango began producing, packaging and selling a cola licensed by The Monarch Beverage Company, USA.

Refriango's sister company, Abastango-Industria e Comércio Lda, is a beverage plant that produces wines, sangria (Dom Cacho, Gaivota, Tropicana), brandies (Vento do Norte) and dry gin (Ginsky).

Activities related to importing, distribution, financing, administration, marketing and human resources of Refriango and Abastango are performed by Luanday-Distribução e Servicios Internacionais Lda.

Because of Angola's fast-paced economic development and the company's leading position, thanks to its quality and well-known products, in the medium term Refriango plans to invest in technology, innovation, communication and personnel training and to form new partnerships with other players in the sector.

"A passion for Angola."
Mr Carlos Rodrigues, Managing Director

SAGRES BEER

Mr Bernado Pedra Soares

Director General

Rainha Ginga, nº 187 r/c, Lojas E & F, Luanda

Tel: +244-222-330439 / 331285/98

Fax: +244-222-338868

Website: www.cerveja-sagres.pt

Date of Creation: 1934

The Sagres brand of beers are brewed by the Sociedade Central de Cervejas e Bebidas and were introduced at the 1940 Exposição do Mundo Português (Portuguese World Exhibition). More commonly known as Central de Cervejas (literally Beers Central), the Sociedade Central de Cervejas e Bebidas, SA is owned by Edinburgh-based Scottish & Newcastle Breweries Plc. Sagres is the name of the south-westernmost tip of Portugal, and Sagres is considered the 'Lisbon beer', as opposed to the Porto-based Super Bock, which is more popular in the north of Portugal.

In Angola the brand already has a 15% market share, according to the company's figures. Angolan soft drinks factory Refriango will begin producing Sagres beer under the terms of an agreement with Portuguese company Central de Cervejas. With the start of production in Angola, Central de Cervejas expects to increase market share to 40%.

Sales in Angola already account for around 5% of the company's total turnover, or the equivalent of EUR €20 million per year.

Print machinery

SILNOR

Mr Carlos Alberto Arques Santos

Chairman

Rua Francisco das Necessidades C. Branco, nº 51–51A,

PO Box 6691, Luanda

Tel: +244-222-331868

Silnor is a family-owned company but it delivers the demanding quality standards and management structures of large businesses. Its main aim is to satisfy customers' demands and needs. This entire process is fulfilled by trained professionals, who use their expertise and care in offering the best results. This quality process is applied to all the services offered: notepads, books, diaries, boxes, stickers, leaflets, magazines, among others. Its promotional gifts section has been a high-quality supplier of customized printed promotional products for many years. Silnor's customers range from multinational corporations and public services to small and medium enterprises and individuals, worldwide.

Silnor offers a wide range of products, at all price levels, sourced from around the world and chosen for being useful, well priced, of good quality and suitable for being effectively personalized or customized. Its professional skill and expertise lies in placing the customer's crest, logo, message, drawing, picture or badge on the product of their choice, which will help promote their project, business, service, product or event. Prices include design, screens, dies and printing.

The design studio of the firm is equipped with the very latest colour graphic computer technology and the design team have many years' experience designing print for adding to a wide range of products.

Silnor's state-of-the-art product print machinery includes multicolour pad and screen printing, foil stamping, laser engraving, embroidery, full colour printing on clothing, laminating and shrink wrapping.

"Nor pain nor pleasure endures"
Angolan proverb

MINING

Angola has numerous mineral deposits, including diamonds, iron, gold, phosphates, manganese, copper, lead, zinc, tin, wolfram, tungsten/vanadium, titanium, chrome, beryllium, kaolin, quartz, gypsum, marble, granite and uranium. The full extent of these resources has yet to be fully evaluated. Since independence mining activity has been limited to diamonds and, on a smaller scale, to the extraction of marble and granite.

The supply industry for mining activity is thus not well developed at all and, as with many other activities, companies that are now beginning to operate in Angola are sourcing equipment from South Africa. It is expected that, as the sector matures, companies will establish in-country distribution networks.

In Angola all minerals belong to the state. The Ministry of Geology and Mines manages mineral exploration and development activities through the granting of relevant prospecting and mining titles. According to the law, any mineral prospect is transferred to a state company for further development. The Mining Law of 1992 reflects a change in policy aimed at reducing the dominance of the state by eliminating monopoly mineral rights and providing opportunities for private sector investment in the mining sector.

Endiama (state diamond mining company) was formed in 1981 and started operating in 1987. Ferrangol is a state-owned company responsible for mining iron ore and manganese. Roremina is a state company responsible for mining ornamental stone. Minaquartz is responsible for mining quartz and Fosfang for mining rock phosphate.

PRECIOUS METALS

Gold

The Maiombe region of Cabinda province accounts for 90% of gold production in Angola. It has been reported that approximately 500 kg of gold have been removed from this region, mainly from small tributaries of the Luali River in central Cabinda. The alluvial gold was associated with vein quartz in granite. The average recovered grade varied between 1 and 2 g/m^3; however, a number of higher grade 'pockets' were recorded. Most high-grade material has been removed, leaving only lower grade gold occurrences. There are other alluvial gold deposits in Cuanza Norte, Huíla and Cunene provinces.

The Mpopo Deposit is the largest primary gold deposit in Angola, some 36 km south-west of Cassinga. This deposit comprises auriferous quartz veins, and has an estimated possible mineral resource of 700,000 t at 8 g/t. It is thought that 23,300 t of ore at 6 g/t gold (a total of 140 kg gold) have already been removed from this deposit. Alluvial placer deposits also occur nearby, and have been mined in the past.

No industrial gold mining operations exist in Angola. Approximately 90% of the country's production has been mined by artisan miners. Both Huíla and Cunene provinces have been prospected by companies such as Ashanti Gold Company Limited and Anglo American plc in the past.

Platinum

Platinum has been reported in association with norite complexes in the Cunene Complex in south-western Angola.

BASE METALS

Copper production has largely been from the high-grade ore of the Tetelo-Mavoio Bembe region. Lead and zinc have also been recorded in this region. Copper deposits of potential economic value occur in the coastal plain (e.g. the Cachoeiras and Loeto deposits) and copper of volcanic origin has been identified in the Menongue district of south-east Angola. Vanadium has been mined at Lueca and Kinzo.

Prior to 1963 Angola's copper production ranked second to that of diamonds in terms of value, producing an estimated 200,000 t of high-grade copper ore of between 2–23% copper. Limited work has been carried out at the Tetelo copper and Cachoeiras copper-gold deposits that appear to have potential.

FERROUS METALS

DIAMONDS

Iron

Most iron mined in the past in Angola has been from the Cassinga Mine in Huíla province, where the high-grade portion of the reserve has been largely depleted. A slump in global iron ore prices, coupled with the onset of the war when the rail link connecting the mine at Cassinga to the port of Mocamedes (now Namibe) was destroyed, saw production end. The Cassinga Mine produced 40 Mt of high-grade iron ore (graded 50–60% Fe) between 1957 and 1975, with 6.1 Mt having been produced in 1974. Rehabilitation of the Cassinga Mine by state-owned iron company Companhia de Ferro de Angola (Ferrangol) was completed in 1986, but production never recommenced.

Since then several attempts to revive production have failed. A Japanese consortium, comprising Kobe Steel and Nissho Iwai, and Odebrecht Mining Services carried out a feasibility study for the development of a direct-reduction iron plant utilizing domestic iron ore resources. From 1998 the government has transferred all iron ore mining rights from Ferrangol to a new company, Sociedade Miniera de Kassinga, which plans to reopen Cassinga. Cassinga has remaining reserves estimated at 34.2 Mt (44%Fe) and 1,000 Mt at 30% Fe. At other deposits at Cassala-Kitungo, a proven reserve of 194 Mt (23–33% Fe) iron has been identified, of which only 84 Mt are amenable to open-pit mining.

Manganese

Numerous small manganese deposits occur scattered throughout Angola. The most economically viable of them is known as the Lucala manganese triangle, which is situated in Cuanza Norte and Malanje provinces. Numerous small manganese deposits occur in this region, concentrated in alluvial or near-surface deposits.

In Angola both kimberlite and alluvial diamonds occur. Some 700 known kimberlites occur in Angola and are aligned in a north-east–south-west direction across the country. The kimberlites vary in shape from rounded to elongate and diamond grade increases with depth. The Camafuca and Catoca kimberlites are the best known. A number of kimberlite pipes occur in Lunda Norte province. These include the economically interesting Camafuca, Camatchia and Camagico and Camatue pipes.

Most alluvial diamonds in Angola originate from erosion of kimberlites. The Lunda Norte and Lunda Sul areas of north-eastern Angola host rich alluvial diamond fields.

Diamonds were first found in the north-eastern parts of Angola in 1912 following discoveries in the neighbouring Belgian Congo (now the DRC). Diamang was established in 1917 with operations commencing in the 1920s. Prior to independence, production peaked in 1971 when 2.1 Mct were produced. However, with the war, production fell, reaching a low of 350,000 ct in 1977. In the temporary stability after the signing of the Lusaka Protocol in 1994, a mini-mining rush occurred, with several foreign consortia teaming up with Endiama to evaluate potential alluvial and kimberlite diamond resources. This led to production of 1.5 Mct in 1997 and to over 5 Mct in 2001.

Angola is currently the world's fourth-largest diamond producer, with alluvial resources alone estimated at containing 110–185 Mct. Some 70% of Angola's diamonds are considered to be gem quality, with 20% being near-gem and 10% industrial quality. Angola's diamonds are thus rated second only in quality to those of Namibia.

Endiama, a state company, controls industrial diamond mining. It has several joint ventures, including with companies from Brazil, Israel, Russia, South Africa, Australia and Canada. Angola's formal diamond production is dominated by one kimberlite operation, Catoca, and several medium- to large-scale alluvial operations.

Diamond exploration can be carried out in two ways: alluvial exploration (in rivers); exploration of kimberlites.

• A concession for alluvial exploration is issued for an area covering up to 10,000 hectares.
• A concession for the exploration of kimberlites (zones where diamonds are formed) is issued for an area of up to 30,000 hectares.

Obtaining Authorization for a Concession

• For alluvial exploration, a fee of US $15–20 million has to be paid to the state.
• For the exploration of kimberlites, a fee of US $80–100 million has to be paid.

Surveying

The cost of surveying is borne by the applicant. The state will take up a stake of between 15% and 20% in a com-

pany for alluvial explorations, and 51% in the case of kimberlites.

Acquiring an area with the prospect of the existence of diamonds is really difficult at the moment, and the only option is to go into partnership with people who already possess demarcated areas.

INDUSTRIAL MINERALS

Decorative Stone

Good quality red and black granites are exported from Angola. These rocks occur in Namibe and Huíla provinces in south-eastern Angola. These provinces are also known for deposits of crystalline quartz and marble.

After diamonds, the development of Angola's stone industry is a priority for the Angolan Ministry of Mines. This sector has recently experienced rapid growth with exports of black granite nearly doubling over the last few

Opening of the diamond polishing factory

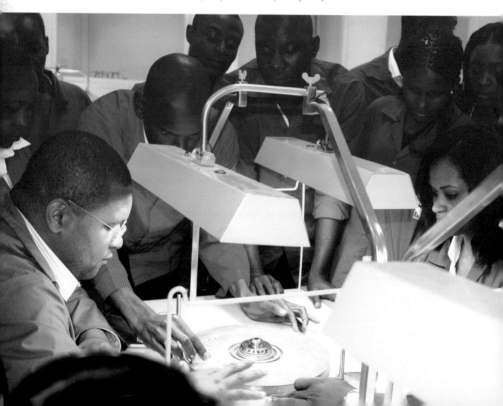

years. Exports in 2000 totalled 7,200 m^3, worth around US $2.2 billion. Angola's south-eastern Namibe and Huíla provinces have a variety of stone deposits, including marble, crystalline quartz and the highly sought-after red and black granites.

At present, Angostone Lda produces most of Angola's stone, although Metarocha Lda is evaluating a US $3 million project to produce an initial 1,000 m^3 of granite per year. State-owned companies produced limited quantities of marble and granite from Namibe and Huíla provinces in 1983. Studies suggest that the region can sustain an annual output of 5,000 m^3 of marble over a period of 20 years.

Phosphates

Substantial phosphate resources have been found in Cabinda and Zaire provinces. The Angolan government established a company to exploit the known phosphate resources located in these areas, where resources were estimated to exceed 200 Mt. Although studies were carried out by Yugoslav and Bulgarian companies, the deposits were never fully exploited, with only 30,000 t being produced by Fosfang/Bulgargeomin between 1982 and 1984.

Kaolin

Kaolin has been found in Bengo, Huíla, Bié and Uíge provinces. It was produced on a small scale between 1972 and 1973 when 140 t was produced for the domestic market. There are plans to develop the Quihita deposits located in Huíla province.

Cement and Raw Materials

Although large volumes of limestone, sands, sandstone and clays occur, production has not been substantial.

MAIN COMPANIES

ALROSA

Mr Alexander Nichiporuk
Alrosa Chief Executive Angola
Rua Coronel Aires de Ornelas, n° 1 r/c, Luanda
Tel: +244-222-443900
Fax: +244-222-443900
Website: www.alrosa.ru

Activity: Diamond mining company

Ten years ago, the first diamonds were found at Catoca Project, created by the Angolan government and Alrosa among others.

Nowadays, this bilateral cooperation in diamond exploitation contributes not only to the development of the country but also means more employment, professional training and health care to thousands of Angolan citizens.

In 2005 Catoca's second phase was launched, and in 2007 5.4 million carats will be recovered thanks to the two treatment plants at this field.

Since 2005 Alrosa not only extracts diamonds but also trades diamonds extracted by Catoca Mining Company. Alrosa's Russian experts contribute to enhance efficiency in the sale of diamonds and therefore to increase the benefits to the Angolan government.

Alrosa is also involved in the construction of a water power plant on the Chicapa River, sharing 55% of the stock. The power plant will considerably boost the mining company Catoca, another Alrosa business partner that has been working on the project for 10 years. Alrosa is ready to invest US $85m in the project. The 2006 completion of the Rio Chicapa Hydroelectric Power Station means that new projects will open in Lunda Sul province, improving the social and economic situation in this region.

The Russian diamond group Alrosa has two subsidiary companies in Angola. The first one will develop two major diamond veins – Camatchia and Camagico. The company's 45% stock share belongs to the joint venture Escom-Alrosa, founded by Alrosa and its Portuguese partner Espirito Santo.

Alrosa carries out a number of social programmes as part of the Catoca and Camatchia-Camagico projects, such as grants, training programmes, and creation of basic education programmes for the local population, as well as different aid programmes in Lunda Sul and Lunda Norte provinces.

ASCORP – ANGOLA SELLING CORPORATION SARL

Mr Firmino Valeriano

Chairman of the Board

Rua Guilherme Pereira Inglês, n° 43, 7th Floor, Luanda

Tel: +244-222-396465 / 370530 / 370682

Fax: +244-222-397615 / 394724

Email: ascorpadmin@ebonet.net

Activity: Diamond trading

Strict mining regulations aimed at controlling the proliferation of the so-called conflict diamonds have whittled down the sector to a handful of respectable companies, the most successful being the Angolan Selling Corporation, or Ascorp, jointly owned by the government and private players.

According to Angolan law, all diamond trading must be undertaken through Endiama or a proxy company appointed by Endiama, a role that Ascorp has filled since it was created in February 2000 with state and private financing. Ascorp also assists the government programme aimed at registering illegal diamond miners. In early 2000 Angola created a single channel of distribution to control production in the mining sector. A new company, Angola Selling Corp. (or Ascorp), was formed to market rough diamonds bought from small- to large-scale mining operations and independent miners. Ascorp's three main objectives are to fight illicit diamond traffic, as set down by United Nations resolutions,

increase revenues to the state budget, and reinvest the profits into other areas of industry, because diamonds are a non-renewable resource. Ascorp's private funding comes from one of Angola's most respected businessmen, Uzbek-born Lev Leviev, who in 1997 helped rescue the Catoca diamond project with a US $70 million investment and turned it into one of the world's most prosperous mining operations.

Ascorp is a joint venture by Angola – which owns half – and Leviev and Omega Diamonds of Antwerp, Belgium, who each control about a quarter. Leviev, who reportedly sold the concept of Ascorp to Angola, oversees the job of marketing Angolan diamonds.

Today all legal buying inside Angola goes exclusively through a company called Sodiam, in which Leviev also owns a stake. Then the diamonds are channelled through Ascorp to reach the wider market. The agreement between Leviev and Angola seems to be working, despite grumbling by sellers required to market their diamonds through Ascorp. Ascorp, the only legal diamond rough marketer in the country, holds Angola's production in the palm of its hand.

"We feel that if we register the illegal miners and qualify them to work with a company that has an agreement with the state then we can crack down on the dealers of these illicit minerals and assist the government in terms of revenues and the flow of diamonds."
Mr Firmino Valeriano, Chairman of the Board

CATOCA – SOCIEDADE MINEIRA DE CATOCA LDA

Mr José Manuel Augusto Ganga Junior

CEO

Rua Major Kanhangulo, n° 100, 4th Floor, Endiama Building, Luanda

Tel: +244-222-390239 / 502530/31

Fax: +244-222-394378

Email: catoca@catoca.com

Website: www.catoca.com

Activity: Diamond mining industry

Located in Angola's Lunda Sul province, Catoca was officially established on 16th September 1993 and has the following shareholders: the national diamond company of Angola, Endiama (Angolan firm of public capital), Almazzi Rossi-Sakha SA, Alrosa (Russian public firm), Daumonty Financing Company, Grupo BV, Lev Leviev (Israeli private firm), and Odebrecht Mining Services Inc (Brazilian private firm).

The Catoca diamond mining project operates Angola's largest diamond mine, accounting for 65% of the country's total production. Producing more than four million carats of rough diamonds annually, the project is expected to generate US $11 billion over the next 40 years. Catoca expects to double its production in the upcoming years.

Unlike most mining projects in Angola, Catoca's operations have never fallen into rebel hands. The joint geological studies in the Catoca Chimney up to a depth of 600 metres show a potential of 271 million tonnes of diamonds and 189 million carats being mined, corresponding to a profit of US $11 billion in 40 years. Until recently, Catoca had a workforce of 2,600 workers. At the moment it has 2,900 Angolans and 300 expatriates, making a total of 3,200 workers. The new investment has enabled it to create 600 work posts, of which 90% are mainly in Lunda Sul. Catoca might be considered as an example to be followed in terms of Angolanization of its workforce, as it mainly employs Angolans, and most of its directors are also Angolans.

The company's management quality and efficiency has been recognized in Angola as well as internationally, having been awarded gold medals and diplomas by organizations such as Global Rating (London, 2003), Foundation for Excellence in Business Practice (Geneva, 2003) and The Arch of Europe (Frankfurt, 2005).

The objectives of Catoca are prospecting, mining, treatment and trading of diamonds of the kimberlite deposits of the Catoca Chimney. The Catoca Chimney, which occupies 639,000 square metres, is made up of a complex geological structure: its mineralized body is subdivid-

A diamond treatment plant, part of the Catoca mining project.

ed into porphyritical kimberlites, tufistical kimberlites and autolytic kimberlite deposits.

"Angola has very high diamond-producing potential, so much so that it cannot even be properly quantified, but what Angola needs is partners whose interests also include the social development of the country. The diamond industry needs financing, not only to conduct detailed geological studies of the potential, but also to get the sector up and running. The business opportunities in the industry here are endless."

Mr José Manuel Augusto Ganga Junior, CEO

DE BEERS

Mr Gaspar Dos Santos Cardoso
CEO
Rua Rainha Ginga, n° 87, 5th Floor, De Beers Building, Luanda
Tel: +224-222-638888
Fax: +224-222-336382
Email: gcardoso@debeers.co.za
Website: www.debeers.com

Activity: Diamond mining
Date of Creation: 1888

De Beers is steeped in diamond tradition and heritage spanning over 100 years – a heritage unparalleled anywhere in the world.

Its cut diamonds and diamond jewellery are exclusive and only available from the De Beers boutiques around the world (New York, London, Paris, Tokyo, Beverly Hills and Osaka).

The four most popular factors used to measure diamond quality – cut, colour, carat and clarity – commonly known as the 4Cs, were introduced by Mr De Beers in 1939 in order to provide a benchmark standard for evaluating the 'quality' of diamonds.

The company is present worldwide, with its major centres being in Johannesburg and London. It is one of Angola's leading diamond companies. In May 2005 the Angolan Council of Ministers approved the first prospecting con-

tract for De Beers since the company filed arbitration proceedings against the government in 2001. This agreement will allow De Beers to exercise the mineral rights for prospecting, evaluation and research of kimberlite deposits in the Lunda Norte concession area. De Beers will explore a 3,000-sq. km concession in the Lunda Norte province, which may hold up to 60 kimberlite deposits. The company has committed to making a minimum investment of US $10 million.

De Beers is confident that this agreement will set the framework for a mutually beneficial and lasting partnership that will contribute positively towards the future growth and stability of the Angolan diamond sector and the Angolan economy.

ENDIAMA EP – EMPRESA NACIONAL DE DIAMANTES DE ANGOLA

Mr Manuel Arnaldo de Sousa Calado
President – Chairman of ENDIAMA Group
Rua Major Kanhangulo, n° 100
PO Box 1247, Luanda
Tel: +244-222-333018 / 337276 / 332718
Fax: +244-222-337216 / 332718
Email: pca@endiama.net
Website: www.endiama.co.ao

The Angolan National Diamond Company, Endiama EP, is a public-funded company constituted in 1981. It has two functions: state and entrepreneurial.

In the first, the public company was created under decree n° 6/81 by the Commission of the Council of Defence and Security with a fund of 667,897,000,00 Kwanza to function as the national concessionary of mining rights in the diamonds sector.

As a company, the objectives of Endiama EP are prospecting, research, recognition, mining, transforming, polishing and diamond trading. During the last decades, Endiama EP has structured itself as an organization with the characteristics of a holding company, already possessing many branches and participating as a shareholder in other companies.

One of these branches is Endiama Prospecting and Production (Endiama P&P), which has both alluvial deposits and at least 18 kimberlites to mine in the coming years and a polishing factory, Angola Polishing Diamonds SA, created through its trading company Sodiam SARL.

Endiama EP also extends its activities beyond the diamond sector: it has an air company (SAL), a logistics branch (Enditrade), a Foundation (Fundação Brilhante), a security company (ALFA 5), a health care centre (Clínica Sagrada Esperança) and a sports soccer team (Clube Desportivo Sagrada Esperança).

At the international level, through its trading company Sodiam SARL, Endiama EP holds diamond-trading centres in Israel and Belgium.

The company also has interests in Asia where it constituted, in Hong Kong (China), Endiama China International Holding Limited.

Endiama EP is due to expand to Dubai, the United States and India.

Endiama, the state diamond concessionaire, announced two new diamond projects in early 2005, both located in the province of Lunda Norte. The Muanga diamond project foresees investments of US $15–20 million in the coming year to begin exploration operations for alluvial deposits. The Cucuilo project involves a US $6 million initial investment. In November 2005 Endiama signed eight prospecting contracts for primary and secondary diamond deposits with BHP Billiton Escom Diamond Ltd, a joint venture between the Portuguese group Espirito Santo and Canadian company BHP Billiton. The concessions are located in the provinces of Lunda Norte, Lunda Sul, Bié and Malange.

ENDIAMA P&P

Mr José Chimupi
Board Member
Rua Rainha Ginga, nº 87, 5th Floor, Endiama/De Beers Building, Luanda
Tel: +244-222-397938 / 397982
Fax: +244-222-398112
Website: www.endiama.co.ao

Endiama Prospecting & Production SARL (Endiama P&P) is a subsidiary company of Endiama EP and was set up in 2003 under decree n° 39/03 of 27 June of the Cabinet.

Endiama P&P has shareholders such as Endiama EP, with 99% of shares, and Sodiam SARL, with 1%.

The objectives of Endiama P&P are prospecting, research, recognition and mining of diamonds, and it is also specialized in other industrial and trade activities, by itself or in association with other companies or societies.

In its main field, Endiama P&P has already undertaken the following projects:

• Start of the main production phase of the Camuanzanza Project.
• Beginning of the assessment of primary deposits.
• Execution of topographic survey of regions corresponding to the IGM projects of Cuango International.
• Technical-geological studies, work programmes of prospecting, research, recognition and technical-economic feasibility studies of the firm's projects.
• Mining operations in the projects of the company.

ENDIAMA – FUNDAÇÃO BRILHANTE

Mr Bruno dos Santos
Executive Director
Rua Rainha Ginga, Endiama Building
PO Box 1247, Luanda
Tel: +244-222-392778
Fax: +244-222-392778
Website: www.endiama.co.ao

Fundação Brilhante is an institution set up in 2004 by Endiama EP, in charge of both social and cultural aid, and helping to promote special programmes for communities in the mining regions.

Due to decades of war in Angola, which impoverished its population, managers of Endiama EP were forced to create conditions to address these problems.

Today, along with the creation of the Fundação Brilhante, the Endiama group focuses on the execution of the core business of its companies, namely prospecting, production, polishing and trading of diamonds.

Fundação Brilhante is a collaborative venture: all companies that act in the diamond mining sector in Angola can be part of it, most of them as trustee members, which gives them the right to influence the managing policies of the Foundation.

Since its institution, Fundação Brilhante has consolidated itself as the social and cultural face of the Endiama group.

The institution carries out systematic actions with a view to helping local populations, and the various community organizations, to overcome the poverty barriers when carrying out their tasks for the social, cultural, economical and political growth of the country.

Founded as a united channel of sociocultural aid on the part of its members, Fundação Brilhante coordinates the efforts and profits of all companies in the diamond sector to benefit communities.

ENDIAMA SODIAM – SOCIEDADE DE COMERCIALIZAÇÃO DE DIAMANTES DE ANGOLA SARL

Mr Manuel Arnaldo de Sousa Calado
Chairman of the Board
Rua Rainha Ginga, n° 87, 7th Floor, Endiama/De Beers Building,
PO Box 1072, Luanda
Tel: +244-222-370311 / 370217
Fax: +244-222-370423
Email: sodiamadmin@ebonet.net
Website: www.endiama.co.ao

The Diamond Trade Society of Angola (Sodiam SARL) was founded in 1999, under the decree 33/99 of 31st December 1999 of the Cabinet.

Sodiam SARL was created with the following objectives:

- Trading all rough diamonds produced in Angola through a single channel.
- Entry of Sodiam SARL into the international diamond market.
- Creation of added value to rough diamonds produced in Angola.
- Contributing to the increase in fiscal revenues.
- Collaborating in the fight against the illegal trafficking of diamonds.

From August 2003, under the Resolution 21/03 of 8th July 2003 of the Cabinet of the Council of Ministers, Sodiam SARL started the direct trading of diamonds from both the formal market (mining companies in Angola) and also the artisan market.

Meanwhile, a new decision of the Cabinet of the Council of Ministers issued in May 2006 turned the Society into the Diamond Purchasing and Sale Centre (Sodiam Central de Compra de Diamantes) through the New Diamond Trading Policy.

As a purchase centre, Sodiam SARL will define the goals to be achieved annually, based on data relating to demand and supply of rough and polished diamonds both nationwide and worldwide. Sodiam SARL will also be in charge of organizing and supervising the trading process. The trading of rough diamonds will be based on a system of models that will include:

- The purchasing and sale of diamonds in Luanda through the Purchase and Sales Room of Sodiam SARL.
- The sale of diamonds overseas through the Sodiam Trading Centres (STCs).

The governmental initiative on diamond trading introduces other models of selling diamonds, namely sights, auctions and supervised quotas.

ITM MINING LTD

Mr Naïm Martins Cardoso – Managing Director
Mr Rodrigo Filgueiras – Administration Manager
Rua Joaquim Capango, nº 19A r/c, Luanda
Tel: +244-222-337751 / 393915
Fax: +244-222-335275 / 336098
Email: rodrigo@itmmining.com
Website: www.itmmining.com

Activity: Mining operations
Date of Creation: 1993

In Angola since 1993, ITM started its mining operations as a joint company between ITM International (51%) and KNR (49%). In February 1995 KNR acquired the shares of ITM International and became the sole corporate owner of ITM Mining Ltd.

ITM is currently one of the leading companies in the management, operation and development of alluvial diamond mining projects in the country.

ITM uses the most appropriate modern technologies, has a constant appreciation of its employees both personally and professionally and plays a key role in the social and economic development of the communities in its mining areas. ITM's competitive advantage stems from an experienced and skilled workforce combined with the dynamism of a younger team. By this means, it secures a balanced symbiosis between mining technology – operating management – and the functional management of technology – administration, logistics and finance.

ITM Mining Ltd operates as a cost-effective company yielding profitable results from a financial, economic and social perspective, thereby ensuring corporate sustainable development and customer satisfaction at all times.

At present ITM is involved as mining operator in the projects of Calonda, Chitotolo, Cuango and Mufuto, actively contributing to the development of the regions where these projects are taking place.

Its corporate business philosophy draws attention to many social initiatives. This commitment derives from its ethical conduct of accountability and reciprocity towards human capital. ITM recognizes the importance of corporate social action to the company's prosperity and so is keen to contribute to key societal value. More details are at: www.culturalunda-tchokwe.com.

"We are the longest-operating mining company in Angola, contributing to the national development and progress of the country."
Mr Naïm Martins Cardoso – Managing Director,
Mr Rodrigo Filgueiras – Administration Manager

SDM – SOCIEDADE DE DESENVOLVIMENTO MINEIRO DE ANGOLA SARL (MINING DEVELOPMENT SOCIETY)

Mr Pinto
Managing Director
Estrada do Futungo – Av. Pedro de Castro Van-Dúnem 'Loy', s/n, bloco D. Luanda Sul
Tel: +244-226-676772 / 676782
Fax: +244-226-676729
Website: www.sdm.net

Activity: Mining

Sociedade de Desenvolvimento Mineiro de Angola SARL – SDM – is a mixed Angolan public mining company and holds the mining rights in an area of concession of 2,950 km^2, located in the hydrological basin of Cuango River, Lunda Norte province.

As a joint venture, its board of shareholders includes the following companies: Endiama (National Diamond Company of Angola), an Angolan public company and OMSI (Odebrecht Mining Services Inc), a Brazilian private company.

Its main goals are prospecting, developing, mining and trading diamonds from primary and secondary deposits, identified in the region of Cuango River, in the northeastern region of Angola that produces good quality stones. Bulk sampling of river terrace gravels in the vicin-

ity of the Ganzo, Tázua and Ginge river diversions have revealed economic diamond grades.

SDM is a successful company with active profitable operations, which has established key strategic relationships within Angola and has long been well known as a major primary quality diamond producer. Although SDM uses the most up-to-date technology to carry out its business, it is the people it employs and the skills they bring that make the company a successful operation.

This corporation generates positive cash flow from its tailings operations, and it now plans to use portions of those cash flows to fund an extensive initial exploration project on key properties adjacent to its current facilities for which it currently holds the ownership and surface rights. It is considering several other significant opportunities for further expansion, and will continue to do so with the aim of further increasing revenues and shareholder value for its investors.

SDM is one of the world's leading diamond producers by value and has played a significant role in the transformation of Angola's economy and business development.

SOCIEDADE MINEIRA DO CHITOTOLO LDA

Mr Alexandre Rocha
Rua Eduardo Mondlane, n° 168, Luanda
Tel: +244-222-337075 / 398687
Fax: +244-222-391288
Email: chitotolo@ebonet.net / projectochitotolo@chitotolo.com
Website: www.chitotolo.com

Activity: Diamond mining industry

The Chitotolo Project is based in the N'Zagi region in Lunda Norte. The project began functioning in 1996 and soon after the start of its activities, started focusing on establishing a communication channel with workers as a tool to better understand their needs. It immediately founded a social department to reinforce mutual communication and began funding some social needs of its collaborators.

Chitotolo is the largest contributor to the government's development plans excluding Catoca, which mines kimberlite sites where the production level is far greater. Chitotolo has three partners – Endiama (35% and the exploration licence holder), ITM Mining (50%) and Lumanhe (15%). The company has recently authorized investments of more than US $5 million to procure new equipment and step up production at its mining area in Lunda Norte.

Sociedade Mineira do Chitotolo Lda is the alluvial diamond mining project in north-east Angola, where diamonds have been mined in the region for 70 years and are still achieving high production levels. Chitotolo's production averages some 12,000 carats a month. Chitotolo is a leading diamond producer that is committed to high standards and leadership in the areas of environmental management and health and safety for its employees and neighbouring communities.

The company's excellent exploration prospects, operating expertise, minimal debt and good cash position make it an excellent precious diamond investment vehicle. Chitotolo prides itself on the dedication, professionalism and skill of its exploration teams. The company today has one of the most impressive portfolios of diamond exploration projects, with advanced projects under way in Angola. All projects are located in high-potential diamond-rich areas with mineral analyses taking place in the company's laboratories.

Along with its future development vision, the project strongly invests in the education, health and wellbeing of its workers. Already established is the Projecto Educar (education project), which has two schools, primary and secondary, that were totally rehabilitated and accommodate around 2,300 students of all ages. The project also has a health centre in N'Zagi, where around 30 diseases are treated, and the service also covers workers' dependants.

"The potential is so great that we are investing a great deal into prospecting and plan to expand mining."
Mr Alexandre Rocha

Nowadays security standards have improved according to International Regulations

SML – SOCIEDADE MINEIRA DO LUCAPA LDA

Mr Silchy de Almeida
Chairman of the Board
Rua Eng°, Armindo de Andrade, n° 103 r/c, Miramar,
Luanda
Tel: +244-222-445984
Fax: +244-222-446209
Email: silchyal@yahoo.com.br

Activity: Diamond extraction
Employees: 2,500

The Sociedade Mineira de Lucapa Ltd is a company involved in exploration, prospecting and extraction of diamonds. Its capital is held 51% by Endiama and 49% by the Sociedade Portuguesa de Empreendimentos (SPE SA).

The concession of the company is located in the Lunda Norte province. SML employs over 2,600 people overall. It has contributed significantly to the social development of the region by supplying electricity and water and by repairing all the access roads to the operating site.

Although partnerships with foreign companies have existed on various occasions, SML is currently working more for Angolan clients. SML is looking for foreign investors that have the financial capacity and technical know-how in geology needed for a partnership on one of the projects of the current concession.

Good corporate governance is of fundamental importance to the board of directors and the management team. Transparency and adherence to best principles guide the company in all jurisdictions in which it does business. SML has been ranked highly by independent monitors for its achievements. SML is also contemplating opportunities to operate outside of Angola in the future.

The Catoca Diamond Mining Project in Lunda Sul

PUBLIC SERVICES

"Scolding woman has self to blame when husband who liked her puts her away"
Angolan proverb

EDUCATION

In Education, as far as human resources are concerned, the pupil/teacher ratio is somewhat high. For example, in Luanda there is one teacher for 70 pupils. Despite the government's efforts, most teachers still have no teaching qualification.

The increase of classroom numbers was not followed by an increase of school infrastructure. As a result, there is a deterioration of the pupil/classroom ratio from 81 per classroom in the 2000 school year to 108 in 2003 in level I, while in levels II and III the ratio went from 79 to 108. This situation is more problematic in Luanda and the main urban centres, where the rooms have to be used for three repeated sessions each day.

The school results clearly reflect these conditions. The rates of repeating a year and leaving school early are very high. This means a real waste of time and resources that could be profitably used by others. Only 15.7% of the pupils who attend class 1 finish class 4, and for the pupils who complete the first level education, 4.75 times more resources are invested than would be necessary if they completed after the four years provided for by the law. In levels II and III the results are also very poor.

In 2001 for the over 15 population in Angola, the illiteracy rate was 58%, far higher than for other sub-Saharan Africa countries where it is about 38%. There is a clear sex inequality in access to education, with the illiteracy rates of the female population reaching substantially higher levels than the national average. *(Source: general programme of the government for the two-year period 2005–2006.)*

Education Indicators

Pupil/teacher ratio (primary)	42
Percentage of repeaters, primary (%)	29
Public expenditure on education:	
% of GDP	2.6
% of total government expenditure	6.4

Source: UNESCO Statistics Institute

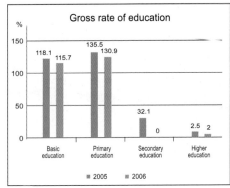

Gross rate of education

	Basic education	Primary education	Secondary education	Higher education
2005	118.1	135.5	32.1	2.5
2006	115.7	130.9	0	2

*Results of the global value of people of regular and non-regular school age

Source: general programme of the government for the two-year period 2005–2006

GOVERNMENT EDUCATION PROGRAMME

The actions programmed for the Education sector aim to continue expanding and equipping the school network, improving the quality of education and improving school management. The pursuit of these general targets assumes that the following more specific targets should be in place:

- Preparation of the primary education school charter.
- Reduction of the geographic disparities of gender and access to education.
- Reduction of adult illiteracy.
- The reform and expansion of professional technical education.
- Integration of those children with special educational needs into the normal system of education.
- Improvement of the internal efficiency of the system.
- Improvement of pupil learning.
- Improvement of the scientific and teaching quality of the teaching staff.
- Strengthening school inspection.
- Improvement of the information system for the running of the Ministry of Education.
- Training school administrators.
- Strengthening the capacity of the administration.

Over 2 million Angolan children are registered in primary education

These targets will be followed by:

• Restoration, construction and equipping of infrastructure, dependent on low-cost infrastructure construction using local origin materials and above all participation of the community in primary education.

• Distribution of school manuals and teaching material in primary education.

• Boosting adult literacy programmes by privileging those zones with higher of illiteracy, women and those demobilized and displaced by war.

• Development of the informal education programme and integration with the post-literacy phase, with involvement of civil society.

• Provision of continuity in the teacher training process to meet the growing demand for education, paying particular attention to primary education and reducing illiteracy.

• Strengthening the institutional capacity of the different levels of educational administration and the management capacity of the school institutions.

• Exclusive use by the Agostinho Neto University of the Universitário do Golfe campus, with a capacity for 17,500 students.

• Allocation of the current assets of the Agostinho Neto University to new public higher education institutions that offer other courses – not necessarily university courses – and within the scope of the Agostinho Neto University.

• Transformation of the current university centres of Huíla, Benguela, Huambo and Cabinda into public universities.

• Drafting a study to create the conditions for opening a university in the east of the country.

NEW CHALLENGES

The Ministry of Education has reformulated the Framework Plan for Reconstitution of the Educational System, defining new targets to reach before 2015.

The challenges remain enormous: to reach the intended numbers of registrations and completions of primary education, and at the same time to follow the rapid growth of the population of school age, the number of pupils enrolled in primary education has to grow from the estimated 1.2 million in 2002 to 5 million in 2015. The results of the recent efforts have seen a mass increase in the number of registrations, with 2 million children in primary school in the 2004 school year.

Moreover, in order to improve the availability and the quality of primary education, the Ministry of Education and UNICEF recently outlined a development plan for the national capacity. To this end, and aiming at improving teaching abilities, some of the 30,000 newly registered teachers will work with the most recent education models.

Education Sector Infrastructure (2005-2006)

Intervention	No. of achievements	Provinces
Restoration	6	
School of II level Cdte Bula (2nd phase)	1	Huambo
School of II level of Saurimo (2nd phase)	1	Lunda Sul
School of II and III levels of Uíge	1	Uíge
Intermediate level industrial teaching institute	1	Huambo
Intermediate level agrarian institute	1	Malange
Intermediate level institute of Caxito	1	Bengo
Restoration	2	
School of level III, Dundo	1	Lunda Sul
School of levels II and III, Kuito	1	Bié
Extension	1	
School of levels II and III, Kuito	1	Bengo
Education project	2	
BAD/FAD	1	National
The retraining of professional technical teaching	1	National
Construction	1	
Sports fields of the Ngola Kiluanje school	1	Luanda (Ingombota)
Construction and restoration	40	
School of level II	8	Luanda, Huambo, Benguela, Malange, Huíla
School of level III	10	Huíla, Namibe, Luanda, Huambo, Benguela, Uíge, Malange
Polytechnic institute	14	Luanda, Benguela, Huambo, Namibe, Cabinda, Uíge, Lunda Norte, Cuanza Sul, Bié, Lunda Sul, Malange
- Intermediate level agrarian institutes	6	Bengo, Uíge, Huambo, Bié, Cuanza Norte, Cuanza Sul

PROFESSIONAL TRAINING

Training Actions

One of the reasons for the low productivity indices in Angola is the low level of education/training of the workforce, and improvement is dependent on the quality of the reorganization and reforms of the national education policies that can be implemented. This means that the majority of the Angolan human capital structure remains the same and that results will take time.

Years	Enrolled	Desisting	Apt	Not Apt
2004	19,080	1,538	16,273	1,369
2005	20,246	878	14,146	811
Total	39,326	2,416	30,419	2,180

Source: Economic report on Angola 2005

The INEFOP (National Institute of Employment and Professional Training) is the body responsible for executing the policies of training defined and approved by the government, and it is responsible for the organization, administration and supervision of the national system of professional training.

Two new structures are currently the target of analysis and evaluation, namely the Centres of Technological Development and the Agricultural Schools of Arts and Crafts that are to be proposed in the short term. Professional training is developed by the INEFOP and partners and includes all citizens, mainly those that are:

- Candidates for their first job (young with schooling or not)
- Unemployed
- Disabled
- Demobilized
- Others

Professional training integrates initial professional training, initial training for adults, initial training for young people and the ongoing training process.

The network of professional training institutions in the country is composed of public and private entities, based on an elementary principle of participation of the private sector in the improvement of the productivity conditions of the national workforce. The public network of the professional training centres and professional rehabilitation is managed by some ministries, which also deal with the running of courses.

The INEFOP and partners promote courses of professional training by speciality, at the end of which a certificate is given that qualifies the trainee to exercise that particular activity. For the time being, there are not many professional training centres available in the country, but the new post-war dynamism will result in a more interventionist attitude by the state in the preparation and enhancement of professional profiles in the workforce.

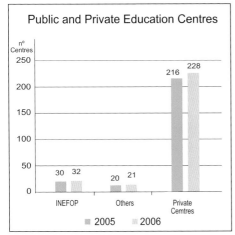

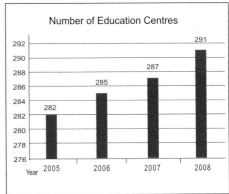

Source: Economic report on Angola 2006

HIGHER EDUCATION

In Angola today there are no BA programmes yet (*bacharelatos*), only MA programmes (*licenciaturas*), which last four to five years. The structure also provides for *mestrados*, or post-MA programmes leading to an academic degree (*mestre*) in its own right, which is at the same time a step towards the PhD (MD, etc.) degree. However, several projects in post-MA programmes are already planned for development in Angola.

The Angolan Ministry of Education recently informed all students applying for university places in 2005–06 that there are only seven – two public and five private – government-recognized institutions in the country. It also warned prospective students against enrolling at private institutions not recognized by the government.

Agostinho Neto University and the Institute of International Relations are the two public institutions authorized to offer university degrees. The private recognized institutions are:

• Universidade Católica de Angola
• Universidade Lusíada de Angola
• Universidade Independente de Angola
• Universidade Jean Piaget de Angola
• Instituto Superior Privado de Angola.

Agostinho Neto University

The Agostinho Neto University (UAN) is the only public higher education institution in Angola. Under the terms of its statutes (approved by executive order 60/01 of 5th October), it is a legal entity in public law, endowed with scientific, pedagogical, administrative and financial autonomy and tuition status, in the various branches of learning intended for the training of top management.

The UAN guarantees the freedom of scientific, cultural and technological creation, in a perspective of respect and promotion of the human person, the community and the environment. Moreover, it assures the plurality of opinions and freedom of expression. It promotes the par-

ticipation of all the university bodies in the common academic life and assures methods of democratic management, through the exercise of the direct election of representatives of the distinct bodies with its agencies. There are 30,000 students and 1,243 teachers, of whom 79 are teachers at the top of their career, 89 are associates, 273 probationary assistants, 376 assistants and 340 assistants who are due to start. The university has difficulties with some issues. There are few teachers and the educational resources are insufficient. This is the reason why there are 200 foreign teachers from various countries, such as Portugal, Brazil, Cuba and Spain.

The following university centres exist:

• Faculty of Engineering
• Faculty of Medicine
• Higher Institute of Nursing
• Faculty of Law
• Faculty of Science
• Faculty of Economy
• Faculty of Arts
• Higher Institute of the Science of Education.

In 2003 the office in charge of the Agostinho Neto University inaugurated a new stage in public higher education in Angola with the introduction of post-graduate courses in its programmes, staffed currently by a total of 259 teachers, 116 of whom are teachers of the UAN.

Responding to the 'race for lessons', the universities and higher education private institutions have been established in the country for a little more than 10 years. Besides the previous lack of institutions for higher education protected by the state and the poor facilities, candidates first had to pass entry tests, which excluded thousands of potential students. It was difficult to sustain the idea that a dozen faculties could accommodate the country's student population, so the private universities were formed:

• ISPRA – Private Higher Institute of Angola
• Jean Piaget University
• Catholic University
• Lusíada University
• Independent University

W.A.P.O. - Training Centre

Today, five years after the appearance of the private universities, these institutions are important providers in the education sector.

ISPRA

The University Campus of the Private Higher Institute of Angola is located adjacent to the Filda Complex in Luanda. It has been functioning since 17th April 2000 and is in a growth phase. It has teaching and research agreements with Paulista University of São Paulo, University of São Paulo, UNICAMP, Federal University of Pernambuco, Unibratec Brazil, Polytechnic and D. Alfonso III Institutes, University of Coimbra of Portugal, Higher Institute of Accounting and Administration Lisbon, University of Braga, European Institute of Business Management Training Portugal, and the Polytechnic University of Madrid in Spain.

The courses are:

- Pharmaceutical sciences (Degree)
  - Pharmacy
  - Clinical analysis
- Physiotherapy (Degree)
- Dentistry (Degree)
- Nursing (Degree)
- Psychology (Degree)
- Management and Accounting (Bachelorship/Degree)
  - Company Management
  - Accounting and Auditing
- Computer Science (Bachelorship/Degree)
  - Business Computer Science
  - Computer Systems
- Architecture and Town Planning (Degree)
- Social Communication (Degree)
- International Relations (Degree)
- Tourism (Degree)
- Civil Engineering.

Jean Piaget University

Functioning since June 2000 and inaugurated officially in December of that year, the Jean Piaget University of Angola, in Viana on the outskirts of Luanda, represents a further step in the realization of one of the great dreams of the Piaget Institute.

223

The courses given are:

• Law
• Computer Science
• Economics and Management
• Civil Engineering
• Nursing
• Sociology.

Catholic University

The Catholic University of Angola (UCAN) was created in 1999 while the war was still going on. Seven years later, it already has four faculties (Humanities, Law, Economics and Management, Engineering) and others are on the way. It has four research centres: The Centre of Studies and Scientific Research (CEIC), the Centre of European Documentation (CDE), the Centre of Research, Information-gathering and Opinion Studies (CENSOP), the Centre of Christian Reflection 'Faith and Culture'. It has a computerized library with thousands of works and thousands of readers and researchers. It continues to construct buildings. It has a Centre of Computer Science and its Social Support service also gives poor students access to an academic training.

Basic options are available in Science and Technology.

Lusíada University

The Lusíada University is a small Portuguese private university. It was founded in Lisbon, Portugal in 1986. It later opened branches in the Portuguese cities of Oporto and Vila Nova de Famalicão, and abroad in Angola at Luanda, Benguela and Cabinda. It is one of seven recognized universities, both private and public, in Angola.

The Lusíada University of Angola initiated activities with pre-course studies in 1999 in economics, legal studies and engineering. In its six years of existence, the Lusíada University of Angola has expanded its areas of activity. Today it offers degrees in Psychology, Computer Science, Architecture, Economics, Accounting, Company Management, Human Resource Management, Law, International Relations, as well as maintaining the struc-

ture of the pre-course year. Student numbers have risen from a total of 370 to a total of 2,800. The first graduates completed in 2004 in economics.

The university's motto is "*Sol lucet omnibus*" (The sun shines equally over everyone).

Independent University Of Angola

The Independent University of Angola (UnIA) is a private Angolan university aiming to create an institutional environment that promotes the intellectual development of the students, imparting social responsibility and the sense of citizenship. Through such initiatives as research, the intention is to create a healthy and solid relationship between students and teaching staff, stimulating the exchange of knowledge as a progressive method of learning. It started activity in the 2004–05 academic year in the province of Luanda with the pre-course year. Its facilities are located in the Samba zone.

The current degrees (with pre-course and year 1) are:
• Natural Resources and Environment Engineering (Natural Resources; Environment)
• Computer Science Engineering
• Civil Engineering (Works and Infrastructure, Hydraulics; Stability and Calculation of Structures)
• Communication Sciences (Journalism; Television).

Three new degrees (pre-course year) were introduced in 2005–06, namely:

• Law
• Electrical Engineering and Telecommunications
• Management and Marketing.

Raising the qualification levels of the country's human resources has been characterized by the government as a great challenge. This means a clear, intense confidence in education and professional training at every level.

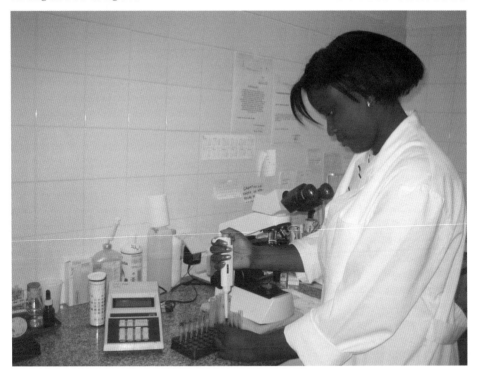

Clinica Clidopa, a well-equipped healthcare facility

HEALTH

In relation to the state of the health of the population, the infant and youth mortality rates are high. The mortality rate of those under five years of age is 250/1,000. Among the illnesses of greatest incidence are malaria, acute respiratory and acute diarrheic illnesses. Of major concern and worthy of a special campaign is HIV/AIDS. According to UN estimates this affected about 350,000 adult Angolans in 2001, and corresponds to an incidence rate of 5.5% of adults. According to other studies, the rate among sex workers in Luanda is 33%.

Human resource availablity in health is extremely limited. The latest data lists about 53,000 workers in this sector, of whom only 811 are doctors. About 17,000 are classified as nurses, but only 163 have higher training. To these figures must also be added 3,670 technicians of diagnosis and therapy. The war affected the geographic distribution of health professionals, concentrating a great number of these professionals in Luanda.

In the field of health equipment and infrastructure, the network is insufficient to cover the needs of the population. The health centres are scarce and concentrated in urban areas. Only 30–40% of the population are considered to have access to health systems. There is a serious lack of basic diagnosis equipment, and a significant number of health centres and units are not operational.

As for essential medical supplies, the severe shortage is abundantly clear, and access for the population is still very limited. According to WHO (World Health Organization), only 20% of the Angolan population had access to medicine in 2001.

(Source: General programme of the government for the two-year period 2005–06.)

GOVERNMENT TARGETS FOR THE 2005–2006 TWO-YEAR PERIOD

The government has defined a general principle for this sector that consists of improving the situation of the health of the Angolan population, without discrimination and on the basis of the assumption of fairness. The targets are the following:

• To improve the access to primary health care, with special emphasis on mother and infant care.
• To extend preventive activities and the correct diagnosis and standardized treatment of ITS/HIV and AIDS.
• To improve the quality of the diagnosis and treatment of major epidemics.
• To improve the quality of the existing services, granting a special emphasis to training, supervision and the availability of medicines.
• To strengthen the capacity of management at the global, provincial and municipal levels.
• To improve the system of information, monitoring and evaluation of health.

These targets are pursued according to these action lines:

• To promote the access to primary health care through increasing the number of health units and the provision of a set of services at primary and secondary levels.
• To improve the provision of maternal and infant health services and the prevention and treatment of the most current illnesses.
• To improve the quality of the health services, increasing the activities of continuous training and by timely, regular and adequate supply of essential medicines and other indispensable material.
• To fight the proliferation and spread of HIV/AIDS by recourse to diverse structures, from the improvement of the knowledge of those professionals who work with the illness to the reinforcement of safety, for example in transfusions.
• To increase the technical capacity of the health professionals through appropriate training and retraining in knowledge and practices.
• To empower the institutions, strengthening the management power at the different decision levels.
• To assure the continuous availability of vaccines and essential medicines as well as other material indispensable for providing health services.
• To promote community-based health activities, aiming at the participation of families in health care and demand for it.

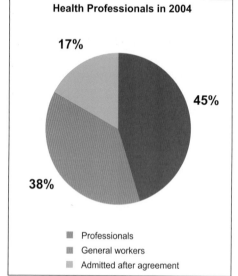

Health Professionals in 2004

17%
45%
38%

■ Professionals
■ General workers
■ Admitted after agreement

Source: MINSA 2004

Estimate of the HIV / AIDS Epidemic in Angola 2004

	Estimate
Incidence in adults (%)	3.9
People living with HIV	240,000
Children (0–14 years)	23,000
Women (2003)	130,000
Deaths (adult and children)	21,000
AIDS orphans (0–17)	110,000
Pregnant women (%)	2.8
Pregnant women (15–24 years) (%)	2.5
Prostitutes (%) (Luanda 2001)	32.8

Source: UNAIDS, 2004 Report on the Global HIV/AIDS Epidemic

THE HIV EPIDEMIC IN ANGOLA

Angola has a seroincidence for HIV that is comparatively lower than that in the other countries of Southern Africa. Recent data of the HIV monitoring system in pregnant women in antenatal consultations in the 18 provinces of the country (2004) showed a seroincidence of 2.8% and 2.7% in 2005. These results reflect the exceptional situation of the epidemic in Angola with regard to the other countries of sub-Saharan Africa where the incidence is always over 10%.

CHALLENGES: KEY PROBLEMS OF THE HEALTH POLICY AND CURRENT OUTLOOK

The capacity of the health sector to satisfy the needs of and to respond to the request for services has been very limited. Many factors limit the capacity of the government to formulate health policies that can be implemented, adapted to the deficiencies of the system and be compatible with the available resources. The competition

Targets: Infrastructure of the Health Sector 2005-2006

Intervention	No. of Achievements	Provinces
Restoration of hospitals:		
General hospitals	11	Luanda, Cunene, Huambo, Bié, Malange, Moxico, Lubango
Paediatric hospitals	1	Luanda
Psychiatric hospitals	1	Luanda
Sanatoriums	2	Luanda and Huambo
Construction and municipal equipping of hospitals with 60 beds	28	Bié, Cunene, Huambo, Huíla, Cuanza Norte Cuanza Sul, Lunda Norte, Lunda Sul, Namibe, Zaire
Restoration of the Centre of Physical Medicine and Rehabilitation	1	Luanda
Restoration/equipping of orthopaedic centres	1	Luanda
Restoration/expansion of the National Oncology Centre	1	Luanda
Restoration of maternity centres	2	Benguela and Namibe
Permanent health centres	15	Huambo, Huíla, Cuando Cubango, Cuanza Norte, Malange, Moxico, Namibe, Zaire
Restoration of the Professional Health Technician School	1	Luanda
Construction of the National Blood Centre	1	Luanda
Construction of the AIDS Counselling Centre	1	Luanda
Construction and equipping of provincial public health laboratories	2	Benguela and Namibe
Construction and equipping of the Quality Control Laboratory	1	Luanda
Construction and equipping of a national medicine deposit	1	Luanda
Construction and equipping of a provincial medicine depot	1	Benguela
Acquisition of ambulances for all the cities of the country	162	All country

with other sectors, mainly defence, has left insufficient resources for health. The limited resources of external aid, the disintegration of the system and the lack of coordination mechanisms are also responsible.

The political and military instability, the destruction of health units, the inadequate capacity of management (above all at peripheral level) and the concentration of the health professionals in the main provincial capitals (especially in Luanda) are formidable decisive factors, responsible for the frailty of the health system. Low wages and high cost of living discourage health professionals, and this is reflected in the lack of staff at peripheral level and in the poor quality of the health services given there. On the other hand, a very small percentage of the population with better financial conditions can access health care in private clinics in the main urban areas. Some private clinics have quickly sprung up in suburban areas, giving questionable quality of care, and that have never been appraised. This results in limited access to care for a great majority of the population.

Leaving the above factors to one side, it is possible to identify the main challenges and the new opportunities for the health sector in the context of peace. These factors require an immediate expansion of health care services, so as to respond to the needs of the people who have started to have better access to them.

EXTERNAL AID FOR THE HEALTH SECTOR

A study of the flow of donor aid from the European Union, European Commission, Norway and USA revealed that health, with 14% of the total of the AOD (official aid for development), was the most important segment financed by the donors, with a total of US $43.8 million.

A more detailed analysis, at provincial level, reveals that the contribution of the donors exceeded 50% in seven provinces: Bengo, Bié, Huambo, Cuando Cubango, Cuanza Norte, Malange and Uíge. In reality, half of the provinces received more than 40% from external financing for the health sector.

Targets / Results in the Health Sector

Indicators	Target 2006
Rate of detection of cases of tuberculosis	60%
Rate of cure of people with tuberculosis	75%
Family that has impregnated mosquito netting	60%
No. services for the treatment of AIDS	4
Peripheral health units that give antenatal care	65%
Peripheral health units with rooms for childbirth	50
To increase the current number of childbirths in the health units	24%
To reduce the rate of mortality of children under 5 years old (%)	20
To reduce the rate of malnutrition of children under 5 years old (%)	15
To reduce mortality of women with obstetric complications (%)	24

Source: General programme of the government for the 2005–06 two-year period

For the period 2005-06 in the field of health, the government declared its general target for the country to be: "To improve the situation of the health of the Angolan population, without discrimination and on the basis of the assumption of fairness."

SECURITY

The security situation in Angola has improved markedly since the end of the civil war; however, visitors should still exercise caution. Although the war has ended, ground travel throughout Angola is occasionally problematic due to land mines, which were used extensively during the war. Frequent checkpoints and poor infrastructure contribute to unsafe travel on roads outside of the city of Luanda. The authority of police and military officials should not be challenged. Travel in many parts of Luanda is relatively safe by day, but car doors should be locked, windows rolled up, and packages stored out of sight. Visitors should avoid travel after dark, and no travel should be undertaken on roads outside of cities after nightfall.

The civil war between the National Union for the Total Independence of Angola (UNITA) and the government of Angola has ended and Angola has become a peaceful and friendly country. The insurgency pursued by the

Front for the Liberation of the Enclave of Cabinda (FLEC) has virtually ended, although the government of Angola continues to pursue the remnants of FLEC forces.

Throughout Angola, taking photographs of sites and installations of military or security interest, including government buildings, may result in arrest or fines and should be avoided.

MAIN COMPANIES

EDUCATION

AGOSTINHO NETO UNIVERSITY

Dr Prof. João Teta
Dean of the University
Avenida 4 de Fevereiro, n° 7, 2nd Floor
PO Box 116, Luanda
Tel: +244-222-310887
Fax: +244-222-387945
Email: jteta@uan.ao

Activity: Higher education – university
Date of Creation: 1979

The University of Agostinho Neto – Universidade Agostinho Neto – is a large public Angolan university based in the capital, Luanda, and Huambo. The university functions only as a graduate school because there are no Bachelor of Arts (BA) programmes (*bacharelatos*), only Master of Arts (MA) programmes (*licenciaturas*), which last four to five years. It is one of seven recognized universities, both private and public, in Angola.

It was founded as the Universidade de Angola (University of Angola) in 1979 to replace the limited institutions created by the Portuguese colonial administration. It became known by its current title in 1985 to honour the first president of Angola, Agostinho Neto. It essentially was founded to produce secondary school teachers as part of a goal of the government's to reduce illiteracy in Angola, although it has expanded significantly since that time to include faculties of: natural sciences, law, agricultural sciences, economics, engineering, medicine, education, and

nursing. These faculties are based on various campuses of the university across the country; for example, the faculty of agricultural sciences is based in the central Angolan town of Huambo.

The university depends overwhelmingly on the state budget. The university has fee-based evening study programmes for workers. The university and some private universities have benefited from contributions by sponsors operating within the country, such as the oil and diamond companies as well as a range of international entities.

Agostinho Neto University recognizes the importance of its location in Luanda and seeks to link its research and teaching to the vast resources of a great city. It seeks to attract a diverse and international faculty and student body, to support research and teaching on global issues, and to create academic relationships with many countries and regions. It expects all areas of the university to advance knowledge and learning at the highest level and to convey the products of its efforts to the world.

CATHOLIC UNIVERSITY OF ANGOLA

Mr Ibamba
Secretary General
Rua N. Sra da Muxima, n° 29,
PO Box 2064, Luanda
Tel: +244-222-331973
Fax: +244-222-398759 / 398765
Email: josei@ucan.edu / info@ucan.edu

Activity: Higher education – university
Date of Creation: 1992–1999

Additional Information: The Catholic University of Angola is a small private university located in Angola's capital of Luanda. It was founded by the government of Angola on 7th August 1992 and established on 22nd February 1999. It is one of seven recognized universities, both private and public, in Angola.

It currently has about 1,000 enrolled students. The language of classes is Portuguese, although English as a second language is also offered. Currently, three departments have been founded: Economics, Law and Computer Engineering. Despite its name, the university does not receive funds from the Catholic Church, nor are the students organized by their religious beliefs. In fact, the school does not even offer any religious instruction. The university's location in Luanda is at the former Colegio St. Josè de Cluny. This remodelled building is in front of the Museum of History, one block from the Kinaxixi Market, and will house the first two faculties of the university in its first years of existence. The final complex of the Catholic University will be built on a selected site and will host additional faculties. Also, subsidiaries are being considered in other important Angolan cities.

Many nations have contributed to the establishment of the university, most prominently the United States, but also Portugal, South Africa, Norway, Spain and Italy, in the form of private business assistance and non-governmental agencies. The university receives all of its government funds because of decree 20/82 in 1982 that required petroleum companies operating in Angola to invest in educational and training programmes the amount of US \$0.15 per barrel of oil produced. These funds are commonly known as Training Levy Funds. The Angola Educational Assistance Fund AEAF, a Boston-based non-profit organization, has been working with the Catholic University of Angola (UCAN) and has participated in the establishment of a computer and Internet access centre. The Council of Ministers of the Republic of Angola approved on 11th July 1997 the decree no. 51/97 in an effort to provide a funding mechanism for higher education institutions in the country. The decree states that a portion of the Training Levy Funds, in the amount of 1¢ per oil barrel, will be used to finance the Catholic University. With Angola currently as one of the main producers of barrels of oil in the world, this amounted to a large majority of the funding for the university.

IL – INSTITUTE OF LANGUAGES

Mr Alberto Paulo
Director
Rua Amílcar Cabral, Bairro Maianga
Tel: +244-222-394887

Fax: +244-222-394484
Email: ilinguas@snet.co.ao

Activity: Language courses
Date of Creation: 1994
Employees: 20

Since colonial times, education in Angola has always served to create and preserve social differences, and to consolidate social relations of domination. This is particularly evident for higher education and languages courses. Until independence, the vast majority of the students in higher education were Portuguese or their descendants; in 1974 only an estimated 5% were of other origins. Happily the situation has changed. Soon after the transition to the Second Republic, the decision was taken to replace this system by permitting and even fostering the establishment of private institutions of education, directly or indirectly funded by the state. One example is the iL – Instituto de Lenguas.

The iL – Instituto de Lenguas was founded in 1994 by the Ministry of Education as a project to teach English as a foreign language and to better educate the people. Currently it is partly dependent on the Ministry.

There are 18 professors working five days a week in order to ensure the best quality of teaching. The Institute has about 500 students of all ages and provides flexible schedules. Classes are open to everybody from 0830 to 20.00. Course prices are US \$200 per month for an hour and a half five days a week.

All levels are welcomed since the Institute of Languages has continuous courses based on different phases of learning.

UNIVERSITY JEAN PIAGET OF ANGOLA

Mr Rochas
Administrator
Av. Norton de Matos
PO Box 2915, Bairro Capalanga, Viana
Tel: +244-222-290259
Fax: +244-222-337317

Email: lpaget@netangola.com
Website: www.netangola.com/piaget/

Activity: Higher education – university
Date of Creation: 8th July 1998

The Jean Piaget University of Angola is a private universi-ty created via a cooperation agreement signed on the 8th of July 1998 between the Ministry of Education and Culture of Angola and the Institute Piaget of Portugal. Functioning since 2000, Jean Piaget University of Angola is a reliable institution in Angola, with campuses in the capital of Luanda and in the Benguela province of Angola. It currently has around 1,000 students enrolled and is one of seven recognized universities, both private and public, in Angola. It currently offers the following faculties: law, economics and management, computer sciences, sociology, civil engineering and nursing.

An estimated US $8 million are planned to be spent in an upcoming university expansion project that will add four buildings with three floors each, in an area of 35 hectares, to accommodate 2,500 students. The universi-ty was founded in 1998 as part of the reintegration of Angola into the global capitalist order.

Jean Piaget University is one of the world's most impor-tant centres of research and at the same time a distinc-tive and distinguished learning environment for under-graduates and graduate students in many scholarly and professional fields. Its academic environment attracts outstanding students and scholars from around the world.

Jean Piaget in Angola has grown into a great university with a mission to advance knowledge, promote teaching and research, and help society discover new ways to overcome its most pressing problems. At this institution, education is limited neither by time nor space. It is an ongoing and restless search, one to which this university is dedicated.

"Quality Today, Security in the Future."
Mr Rochas, Administrator

HEALT.

CLÍNICA BIODEN

Mr Jorge L. Velho
Director
Largo Che Guevara, n° 4, Luai
Tel: +24-222-396095
Fax: +24-222-391201

Activity: Dental services
Date of Creation: 1998

Biodente is a well-reputed dental clinic that was founded in 1998. It believes in excellent hygiene conditions and has both Angolan and foreign specialists offering the lat-est technologies and medical methods.

Biodente offers a full range of specialist and family den-tal treatment, with dental implants, cosmetic, and home-opathic dentistry being the cornerstones of the practice. The clinic provides dental surgery and other services including dental implants, tooth whitening, dental X-rays, crowns and bridges, root canal treatment and cavi-ty fillings, always giving a personal treatment to its clients.

The clinic provides the highest quality dental care in a high-tech and friendly environment. Concentrating on the provision of the latest dental treatment in a pain-free manner, the team undertake frequent postgraduate training to enable the most appropriate care to be used. Prevention is the philosophy at the heart of the clinic Biodente.

Biodente specializes in the following areas of dentistry: homeopathy and mercury-free dentistry, dental implants and mini-implants, cosmetic dentistry, Cerec – allowing the dentist to assess, design and prepare perfectly fitted ceramic (porcelain) restorations in one visit, anxiety-free treatment, preventive dentistry, and a dental hygienist.

A bigger clinic with new equipment is planned for 2007, which will consolidate Biodente as one of the leading medico-dental practices in Angola.

...sta

Manager

...da Rainha Ginga, n° 98–106, Luanda

Tel: +244-222-391488 / 587

Fax: +244-222-332933

Email: clidopa@snet.co.ao

Activity: Medical services

Date of Creation: 1995

Employees: 200

Created in 1995, Clidopa is considered one of the best clinics in Angola. Indeed, in 2005 it was awarded the Gold certificate for Global Quality of Geneva, and the Global Medal for Excellence in Business Practice, and it is linked to SOS International.

It is located in Luanda and Soyo, and provides its services to local and international companies, mainly related to the oil industry, as well as international embassies.

Its success relies on the wide range of specialities of its well-trained staff and its modern equipment. Opening 24 hours a day, 7 days a week, 365 days a year, Clidopa is involved in all the existing medical activities, and is well reputed for the following specialities: ophthalmology, paediatric services, gynaecology, cardiology, surgery, stomach otology, urology, neurology, psychology and psychiatry, dermatology, physiotherapy, neurology, esthetical surgery, orthopaedics, intensive care unit, X-ray, angiology.

During office hours the clinic's policy is to see patients with dental emergencies on the same day, wherever possible. After hours, there is a mobile telephone number on the practice answer-phone to allow access to a dentist when the clinic is closed.

Recently Clidopa has started offering pharmacology, clinical analysis, blood transfusions, check-ups and midwifery services. Its specialized child care services are very well known and well considered, as are the antenatal, postnatal care and birthing suite.

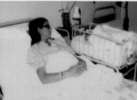

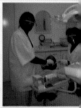

Another excellent service to improve patient care is the pharmacy, located just inside the clinic building, completing the range of medical services. Clidopa pharmacy is operated by licensed pharmacists who offer a friendly, professional and efficient health care service. It provides comprehensive prescription medicines and a large range of natural health products including vitamins, supplements and homeopathic remedies.

Quality and service at Clidopa clinic can also be measured in other ways such as the amount of time spent with each patient; making sure each patient is treated with respect, kindness and dignity by every member of the Clidopa team; making sure appointments are on time and that all test results and other patient information are available to every doctor whenever it is needed.

CLÍNICA SAGRADA ESPERANÇA

Dr Mr Rui José Veiga Pinto
Director of Finance and Administration
Rua Murtalha da Ilha, CP 484/13, Luanda

Tel: +224-222-309361
Fax: +224-222-309033
Email: sagradaesp@ebonet.net

Activity: Medical clinic
Date of Creation: 1992
Employees: 500 total and 150 doctors

CSE – Clínica Sagrada Esperança – is an independent organization set up by Endiama (Angola's national diamond company) in 1992. It was established to provide medical services to Endiama staff but has subsequently taken on other corporate, as well as individual, clients. Its major clients include many of the international institutions and staff from the large national and international companies in Angola. The clinic's objectives are to deliver quality medical care at affordable prices.

Its success is mostly due to its highly trained staff, many of whom have trained abroad, as well as its well-equipped facilities.

CLÍNICA SAGRADA ESPERANÇA

...n for consultations, 24/7 (including holidays)
...n standards of personalised treatment and care
...our ambulance service and.home visits
...ite operating theatres and intensive care unit
...e-natal and post-natal care and birthing suite.

··· Onsite pharmacy
··· Specialised laboratory for clinical testing and analysis
··· International vaccines.
··· Physiotherapy and Hydrotherapy
··· Radiology, TAC, Scans, Electro/Cardiograms, Brain Scans, Endoscopes

...CA SAGRADA ESPERANÇA - ILHA DE LUANDA
Phone: 00244 (222) 309361/034/360
Fax: 00244 (222) 309033
C.P. :484/13
E-mail: sagraesp@ebonet.net

CLÍNICA SAGRADA ESPERANÇA
PRESTAÇÃO DE SERVIÇOS DE SAÚDE

CSE offers services of European standard, and has available (amongst others): intensive care unit, private ambulance, X-ray and CT scanner, hydrotherapy, physiotherapy and a very good and modern operating suite. The dental department is also highly recommended and offers the latest technologies.

The quality of services at CSE is assured by a continuous upgrading of facilities and equipment, as well as ongoing training of medical staff by outside specialists. In addition, outside consultants are employed periodically to audit the quality of services being provided at CSE.

Clinica Sagrada Esperança works in association with SOS International, offers a MedEvac (medical evacuation) service to South Africa or any other appropriate country should it be unable to treat a patient locally. The fleet of fully equipped air ambulances together with doctors and nurses on board includes a Falcon 10, Falcon 200 and a Learjet.

In the near future CSE will be opening a new clinical analysis laboratory as well as a traumatology unit, whilst continuing to stay abreast of new developments in technology, treatment and services.

The clinic's motto is to strive to deliver medical services that compare favourably to the services provided by leading overseas facilities.

"When coming to Angola, follow the recommended health regulations: have all the necessary vaccines and prepare food carefully. However, should you fall ill, Clínica Sagrada Esperança is open 24 hours a day, 7 days a week, 365 days a year."
Dr Mr Rui José Veiga Pinto, Director of Finance and Administration

CLÍNICA SOCLIMEDIC

Dr Mr Armando
General Director
Largo Marquês das Minas, nº 9, Luanda
Tel: +244-222-338498

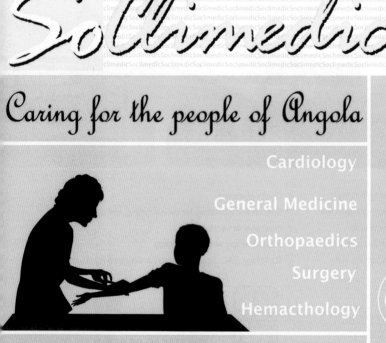

Soclimedic

Caring for the people of Angola

Cardiology

General Medicine

Orthopaedics

Surgery

Hemacthology

Largo Marquês das Minas, B.º Maculusso, Tel.:+244.222.338 498

Activity: Medical clinic

Soclimedic is a private clinic belonging to Gemini Group. It offers services of both general medicine as well as a number of specialities, these being orthopaedics, surgery, cardiology and haematology, which are available to the Group's staff. It also has a service of general medicine for external patients. Among the facilities are an X-ray ward, an analysis laboratory, a pharmacy and a number of bedrooms.

Soclimedic has expansion plans with the aim of attending a greater number of patients. For this purpose, it will expand its facilities and will offer other specialities in the future, to both Gemini Group's staff and external patients.

Soclimedic is a socially concerned centre. Some of the doctors have taken part in campaigns organized by the Ministry of Health and NGOs aimed at raising social awareness about a number of issues such as AIDS.

INSTITUTO NACIONAL DE SEGURANÇA SOCIAL

Sr. Sebastiao Mixinge
Managing Director
Rua Cirilo da Conceiçao e Silva, 42
Tel: +244-222-330426
Fax: +244-222-330426

Activity: Social Security
Date of Creation: 1990

The Social Security National Institute is a public organization which, on the basis of the Code for the Obligatory Public Insurance, guarantees the citizens' right to pensions and benefits. The Institute provides for quality service and its aim is to manage the funds of the state social security in an effective way.

The INSS falls under the ministry of Public Administration, and is in charge of the repartition of all tax collected for Social Security. The amount of this tax is mandatory for

REPUBLICA DE ANGOLA

SOCIAL SECURITY NATIONAL INSTITUTE

INSS

BUILDING A SOCIAL SECURITY FOR EVERY CITIZEN

Rua Cirilo da Conceição e Silva, 42, 1.° -C.P. 3822
Telefax: +244 222 33 77 36   Email: inss@netangola.com
Luanda
REPRESENTATION OFFICES ALL OVER THE COUNTRY
Instituto Nacional de Segurança Social

both employees (3% of their monthly revenue) and companies (8% of the monthly benefits). The Social Security policy was enforced in 1990 with the backing of the international labour organization.

The institute redistributes its money in pensions for funerals, maternity leave, invalidity, work injuries and certain medical operations. As the black market is still very important, the main challenge clearly remains trying to identify all the money transfers done between employers and workers. All money given to citizens is made via bank transfer.

But with representation offices all over the country, the INSS is more and more becoming a warranty of stability in a country that wasn't all that much used to such a redistribution of wealth.

Today the INSS is trying to build a social security for every citizen.

"We challenge the present, we trust the future."
Sr. Sebastiao Mixinge, Managing Director

today belongs to the Endiama Group.

Since 1993 it has diversified between the different branches of the security sector in Angola. Nowadays one of the services it more exclusively offers is integrated security, (combining human security and electronic systems). Alfa-5 works only with the latest security technologies.

The services provided are as follows: industrial security, transport of valuables, integrated systems (alarms, armoured doors, safety deposit boxes), demining, information centre.

The meaning of the name Alfa-5 is the link between the five Portuguese-speaking countries in Africa where Alfa-5 would like to develop its services in the future.

"Visit Angola – you are going to be in a very friendly country which needs the help and contribution of foreigners and friends to stabilize. Alfa-5 will do its best to guarantee your safety."
Mr Francisco Borges Guerra, Managing Director

SECURITY

ALFA-5

Mr Francisco Borges Guerra
Managing Director
Rua da Missão, n° 74, Kinaxixi, Luanda
Tel: +224-222-3333588 / 334922 / 3338022
Fax: +244-222-371556
Email: da@alfa.ebonet.net / alfa5dg@ebonet.net
Website: www.ebonet.net/alfa5

Activity: Security services
Date of Creation: 1993
Turnover: US $18 million
Employees: 1,000

Alfa-5 started in 1993 with the purpose of giving stability to the diamond exploitations. At the beginning it only offered services within Endiama or industrial security but later on developed into a firm in its own right, which

ANGO-ATENTA

Mr Arnaldo de Albergaria e Faro
Managing Director
Rua Martin Luther King, n° 25,
Luanda
Tel: +244-222-443725
Fax: +244-222-448177
Email: adealbergaria@hotmail.com

Activity: Security services
Date of Creation: 1998

Ango-Atenta Lda is dedicated to providing electronic and human security services to its clients. In these areas of activity, it possesses a proven experience in arranging technical solutions adapted to modern life. Ango-Atenta is able to coordinate and install high-quality products.

Ango-Atenta not only recommends the best security solutions, but also installs and maintains systems. In order

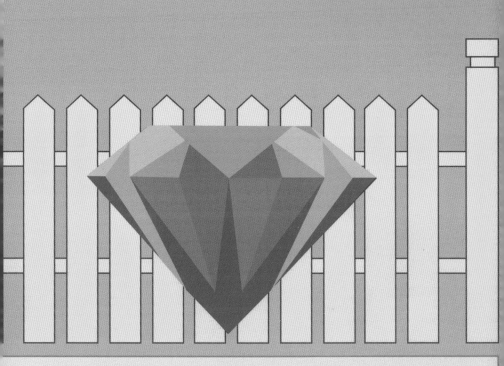

to implement this high-quality service, Ango-Atenta works with all the principal organizations in this sector all over the world.

The company is currently undertaking the development of projects in the following sectors:

- Electronic protection of files
- Access control and alarm monitoring
- Identification and electronic control of people, objects and vehicles
- CCTV, fire detection, radio alarm systems
- Safes, armoured doors, fireproof doors, specialized locks GPS monitoring of vehicles.

The alarm operation room operates on a 24/7 basis and is permanently connected with all clients. Ango-Atenta also operates an innovative system in Angola, which is the GPS detection, localization and control of vehicles, boats and aircrafts.

ANGO PATRULHA

Mr Manuel Costa Vunge
Managing Director
Travessa da Maianga, nº 12, Luanda
Tel: +244-222-396370 / 396978
Fax: +244-222-394166

Activity: Security services
Date of Creation: 1995

Private security is one of the most important sources of economic recovery in Angola since it retrains former army soldiers and combatants.

Ango Patrulha, one of Angola's leading security companies, employs former combatants and offers them excellent employment opportunities. It makes its employees aware of the importance of security and trains them to be the best security guards.

ANGO-PATRULHA
SERVIÇOS DE SEGURANÇA

SECURITY SERVICES

TRAVESSA DA MAIANGA Nº 12
Tel:+244 222 39 63 70 +244 222 39 69 78 Fax:+244 222 39 41 6

LUANDA, ANGOLA

Ango Patrulha was set up in 1995 by five partners. Their work philosophy and a number of projects have been taken on by the management team, which has made Ango Patrulha one of the most reputed companies in the security sector. Among its services are goods, valuables and personal protection. Its clients include a number of banks in Angola, well-known international companies and the Luanda provincial government. Its bodyguards are trained for protocol acts and fulfil the needs of any client, either from the public or the private arena.

Ango Patrulha is currently present in Luanda and Cuando Cubango and it plans to open up offices all over the country. It aims to continue growing, expanding its facilities and increasing the range of security services and related products.

The high quality of its staff will satisfy the most demanding client. It has a training centre, and staff training and professional and personal growth is a key element of its success.

Staff training, professionalism, quality of services and fair remuneration for its employees are key pillars in the human resources area. The low turnover of staff reflects the quality of internal services, as well as external services.

Ango Patrulha is open to receive new investment and is looking forward to obtaining new opportunities to collaborate with national and especially international partners. Ango Patrulha is committed to protect goods, valuables and people.

"Encourage people to come and invest in Angola. As soon as you come, you can breathe the air of peace and prosperity."
Mr Manuel Costa Vunge, Managing Director

AP SERVICES

RECOMMENDED PARTNER

Mr Fernando Manuel
Managing Director
Rua Antonio Feijó, nº 5, Vila Alice, Luanda
Tel: +244-222-320986

Mobile: 923-345156 / 912-500232
Fax: +244-222-326284
Email: ap.services@multitel.co.ao
Website: www.apservices-online.com

Activity: Security services
Date of Creation: 2000
Employees: 1600

Angolan Petroleum Services (AP Services) is a company registered under Angolan law with private capital and was formed in November 2000. It was first created as a security company for companies operating in the oil industry, diamond industry, inland transport, civil engineering and any other type of businesses that might require its services.

The company is based in Luanda but operates in 15 provinces nationwide. Since it was created, AP Services has diversified its activities from its core business of security. The company is also involved in mining, construction, transport, agriculture and communication. Its main project currently is the exploitation of copper mines in the north and of diamond mines in the west. In order to have this project carried out, AP Services will build all the infrastructure (such as roads, electricity network and water pipes among others) required for the implementation of such a task.

AP Services is working closely with international partners (Chinese among others) for the exploitation of natural resources in various parts of the country. AP Services is also setting up a department of geological studies to help public and private companies in geology, geophysics and other related activities.

"We are pioneers in every sector of our activities and try to provide all services to the people. Now is the time to come to Angola; otherwise it could be too late."
Mr Fernando Manuel, Managing Director

COPEBE

"Angola is working very hard to improve the country situation and show to the rest of the world that it is a country with good prospects for the future. In a short time Angola will be a new country and everyone in their own field will help to achieve this aim."

Mr Venâncio Quilola, PManager Director

Mr Venâncio Quilola
Manager Director
Rua N'dunduma, n° 38–44, Miramar, Luanda
Tel: +244-222-448814 / 912-513849
Fax: +244-222-448814
Email: copebe-security@netangola.com

Activity: Security services
Date of Creation: 1995
Turnover: US $7–8 million
Employees: 975

Copebe Security Services Angola Lda was involved in a joint venture with Coin Security International (Pty) until it sold its share to the local shareholders. The company was established in 1995 but only reached maturity in July 1998. Copebe Security Services has retained the skills and technology transferred from the Republic of South Africa during the course of the joint venture.

Copebe Security Services offers a world-class service to any client in Angola, making use of the skills and know-how of its experienced expatriate operations managers. When clients need specialized training, Copebe will outsource to private companies specialized in that specific field to ensure that the high standard required is met.

Copebe Security Services provides the following services: guarding (residences, offices, warehouses and breweries), bodyguards, electronic security (access control systems, alarm systems, CCTV, etc.), quick reaction force, drivers, protocol service and specialized training.

Copebe is backed by a very distinguished board of directors and its clients include some of the most important companies and embassies in Angola.

DSL – DIVISÃO DE SEGURANÇA LUANDA

Mr José Alexandre F. dos Santos
Managing Director
R. Marquês das Minas, n° 15–17, Luanda
Tel: +244-222-396680 / 396598
Fax: +244-222-294749
Email: dsl@snet.co.ao

Activity: Security services

DSL Lda is a company dedicated to protection of people and goods. The main activities of the company are home security and industrial security (at work, in case of fire, of loss, and first aid security). But DSL is also widely diversified in consulting (related to security issues), cash in transit monitoring, quick reaction force, fires, VIP security, diplomatic security, protocol services, security in the mining industry, in ports and airports. DSL can also provide its clients with the installation and maintenance of alarm systems.

All personnel working for DSL are highly trained by national and international specialists in security matters. Three daily shifts ensure an around-the-clock presence, 24/7. For any emergency an armed quick reaction force will be dispatched to the premises within minutes of the radio alarm call.

DSL can also provide its clients with a complete line of electronic systems including radios, alarm buttons and smoke detectors.

Through its seriousness and professionalism, DSL has managed to build a portfolio of clients including the most prestigious national and international companies in the country.

LINCE SERVIÇOS SARL

Mr José Baptista de Sá Junior and Mr Andre Rossouw
General Manager / Regional Manager
Antunes, nº 66, Zona 5, Barrio da Maianga - Luanda
Tel: +244-222-356809 / 355608 / 356708
Fax: +244-2222-358911
Email: lince.dirt@nexus.ao / lince.dg@netangola.com

Activity: Security Services and Rent-a-Car
Date of Creation: 2001
Employees: 850 people (including Specialized Expatriate Managers)

Lince is registered in Angola as an independent security risk management entity. Lince offers customers the distinct advantage of a nationally founded company that thoroughly understands local risk management requirements. Being in a dynamic and competitive market, it has distinguished itself from competitors by rendering above average quality service and also adding value for its customers.

The key product range within Lince is focused on four main areas:

• Guarding and Response
Lince's security operations include physical measures conducted by the security teams on a specific site to achieve physical security, loss prevention and special operations.

• Technology and Monitoring
Technology has become an integral part of operations. This would include planning and management of systems to suit the needs of customers.

• Vehicle Rental, Travel and Protocol
The provision of a professional managed transport service on a long- or a short-term rental base with the option of trained bilingual drivers.

• Humanitarian Landmine Clearance
Lince is accredited by CNIDAH and follows the highest international mine action standards from impact and technical surveys, quality assurance to clearance procedures, which may be manual or mechanical.

LINCE
SERVICES
S.A.R.L.

INTELLIGENT SOLUTIONS
FOR INTEGRATED SAFETY

- Personal and Technical Safety
- Rent-a-car
- Demining

Tel.: + 244 (222) 356809/355608/356708
Fax: + 244 (222) 358911
Control Room: + 244 (222) 353105
E-mail: lince.dg@netangola.com
        lince.dirt@nexus.ao

Antunes, nº 66, Zona 5,
Barrio da Maianga. - Luanda
Angolazz

"Before you come here you have to know the country and the ways things are done here. Lince will be here to help and protect all the new people interested in Angola."

Mr José Baptista de Sá Junior and Mr Andre Rossouw,
General Manager / Regional Manager

MAMBOJI

Mr José Napoleão
Managing Director
Rua Hélder Neto, nº 42, Maianga, Luanda
Tel: +244-222-322048 / 321841
Fax: +244-222-322048
Email: mamboj@netangola.com

Activity: Security services
Employees: 1,500

Mamboji is a company registered under Angolan law with private capital and was formed in November 1999. It was first created as a security company for companies operating in the oil industry, diamond industry, inland transport, civil engineering and any other types of businesses that might require its services.

Mamboji has been involved in various activities since its inception: instruction and training of all personnel linked to private security businesses; private security and transport of all valuable goods; protection of residential areas; protection of industrial sites (ports, airports, railways); protection of mineral exploration areas; and protection of oil companies.

Mamboji currently employs 1,500 people, including former military troops, in protecting over 10 mining exploration fields nationwide for both local and international companies.

For developing its staff, Mamboji owns a training facility with state-of-the-art technology. The security services are also equipped with advanced technology and equipment for the best quality service at a cheaper price. Electronic security, radio systems, CCTV and alarms are all part of the services provided.

Regarding support and protection of demining compa-nies, Mamboji provides safe machines (Bozena 4), allowing the manipulation and lifting of mines in security. Mamboji is working closely with international companies in this area.

Mamboji SARL is currently involved in projects in the provinces of Luanda, Cabinda, Lunda Norte, Lunda Sul, Bié, Moxico, Huambo, Benguela and also in Congo Brazzaville.

PROTECTOR

Mrs Alice Carvalho
Managing Director
Rua Mozambique n° 2, Bairro Cruzeiro, Luanda
Tel: +244-222-449919
Fax: +244-222-447741
Email: protector@snet.co.ao

Activity: Security services
Date of Creation: 1991

Employees: 1,100

Established in 1991, Protector Lda is specialized in a wide variety of industrial and commercial security services and it is registered with the Angolan National Police.

Protector is self-contained in the fields of administration and operations recruitment and training and logistics. It owns a fleet of 51 vehicles.

In Luanda some 90 premises are protected, from govern-ment buildings to private residences and industrial premises.

Outside Luanda the company was involved in the protec-tion of the Capanda Hydroelectric Project. It is also charged with the protection of diamond projects across Angola.

Its services include a sophisticated control room, numerous guards and supervisors, all of whom have received substantial training and have been trained with the company's dog unit. The logistics department offers

SECURITAS DE ANGOLA LD.

SURVEILLANCE AND SECURITY

- Integrated Security and Surveillance
- Vehicle and foot patrol

ELECTRONIC SURVEILLANCE AND SECURITY

- CCTV
- Intrusion Unit
- Fire Unit
- Access-Control Unit
- Frequency patrols
- Alarm control centre
- Sales and Fitting of Technical Equipment
- Major Projects Special Unit

CASH IN TRANSIT

ARMED EMERGENCY UNIT

CANINE UNIT

Tel: + (244) 222 39 51 96/33 05 17

Fax: + (244) 222 33 95 75

info@securitas-angola.com

www.securitas-angola.com

Rua Dr. António Agostinho Neto

nº67/68 Praia do Bispo

Bairro da Kinanga

Luanda, Angola

such services as cash in transit and convoy escorts. The company is also well known in Angola for its VIP protection programme.

"Everyone who has the chance to better know Angola should do it."
Mrs Alice Carvalho, Managing Director

SECURITAS OF ANGOLA

Mr Seiça Neto
Commercial Director
Head Office: Dr António Agostinho Neto, nº 67–68, Bairro da Kinanga, Luanda
Tel: +244-222-395196
Fax: +244-222-339575
Email: info@securitas-angola.com
Website: www.securitas-angola.com

Activity: Private security
Employees: 1,300

As a private company, Securitas of Angola offers a wide range of security services and products for both specialized and general companies. Using the most up-to-date technologies, it offers services to improve security together with surveillance. For a number of years Securitas has been able to install CCTV, anti-intrusion, access control and fire detection systems for any project, regardless of its size.

Securitas of Angola can also provide special and emergency units, as well as canine security.

Securitas of Angola has its head office in the capital, Luanda, together with branches in Lobito, Benguela, Lubango and Odjiva.

Angolan Government is also investing in the modernization of the Police Forces

TSERVICE
TELESERVICE
Telecomunication, Security and Services

Teleservice is one
of Angola´s leading
security providers in

⊙ Patrimonial protection

⊙ Telecomunication

⊙ Residential protection

⊙ Demining

*Teleservice, our intelligence
at your service.*

TSERVICE
TELESERVICE
Avenida 4 de Fevereiro 208-1ª Esq,
Tel.: +244-222-390765/332396
Fax: +244-222339237,
E-mail: teleservice@netangola.com

Although it is a recently formed company – founded in 1998 – it is already a market leader for cash in transit. Banco Espírito Santo of Angola (BESA), Banco Comercial Português (BCP) and the National Bank of Angola are some its most important customers in this particular business area.

The selection and training of its personnel is an important part of its work. It has already installed two different training centres in Angola, one in Luanda and another in Benguela.

Securitas of Angola maintains business relationships with partners from different parts of Europe, but mainly from Portugal, Spain, Germany and England. Securitas of Angola is always investing in new technologies because it truly believes that security, together with electronic surveillance, will be the future.

"Look at Angola with different eyes, with eyes of peace. All reliable investment projects are always welcome, but we need people who are willing to come and build up things, not just to sell."
Mr Silvio Madaleno, General Manager

TELESERVICES

Mr Mario Nelson Mendes Ramalho
Managing Director
Av. 4 de Fevereiro, n° 208, 1st Floor, Luanda
Tel: +244-222-390765 / 332396
Fax: +244-222-339237
Email: teleservice.dg@netangola.com /
teleservice@netangola.com

Activity: Security services and demining
Date of Creation: 1992
Employees: 3,840

Until the end of the 1980s in Angola, the concept of private security did not exist. There was a general idea of using the military forces to protect both private and public investments until the first foreign private companies started working in the country.

Teleservices started in 1992 during the war; initially it supplied security to the mining sector and later on in 1998 it approached the oil sector.

Nowadays Teleservices has developed and diversified its products and services and the firm is able to provide its clients with vehicle protection, personal and residential protection, and commercial demining. The company has succeeded into becoming one of Angola's main security providers in all the different fields it is involved in.

In order to efficiently train its staff, Teleservices owns training centres in both England and South Africa (OMEGA). The company is going to pursue expanding its activities to reinforce its businesses.

Teleservices is the biggest company providing security and related services in Angola, especially to multinational corporations operating in the country. The company is therefore able to offer outstanding security guards, alarm systems, emergency protection and security audits. Its highly trained security staff enable Teleservices to accomplish two important goals: first, deter incidents before they happen; and second, have a fast, professional response when necessary.

Teleservices is a well-known leader in the Angolan market and it is constantly setting the standard for training and quality in security services, thanks to:

• Reliable people
• High standard of training
• Consistent management support
• Solid technology infrastructure.

"You have to visit Angola and see the possibilities it offers for the future."
Mr Mario Nelson Mendes Ramalho, Managing Director

WORKS & HOUSING

"When the source of the river is dry, people move"
Angolan proverb

OVERVIEW

Since peace in 2002 Angola has entered a phase of intense infrastructure rehabilitation under the direction of the Ministry of Public Works. The president of Angola, José Eduardo Dos Santos, is on record as having stated that his government intends to convert Angola into a vast construction site, to reconstruct the infrastructure (including hospitals, schools, roads and bridges etc.) destroyed during the war.

By taking advantage of credit lines, especially from China (US $2 billion), and smaller facilities from Brazil, Germany and Portugal, the government has begun this vast reconstruction project throughout the country.

The Government Budget (OGE – Orçamento Geral do Estado) states the government's general programme for 2005/06 consists of a plan of public investments destined to consolidate the peace and national reconciliation, to construct the basis for the constitution of an integrated and self-sustaining national economy.

The Minister of Public Works, Higino Carneiro, continually encourages the private sector to invest seriously in the construction sector, given the importance of public works and private construction for the growth of the gross domestic product of Angola (GDP) and to generate employment.

ROADS

One of the key goals of the government is the complete rehabilitation and asphalting of the national road network, including the paving of 1,200 km of highways by the end of 2006.

CONSTRUCTION OF THE HIGHWAYS IN LUANDA

In 2006 construction of a new 54-km highway in Luanda, with three lines in each direction, was planned. The Angolan Roads Institute (INEA – Instituto de Estradas de Angola) is the owner of the project, and the work has been contracted to two Brazilian construction companies. This highway will be a regional highway, linking provinces adjacent to Luanda with the capital city and several residential and non-residential areas, including the Camama project

Government Plans for Public Investment in Basic Infrastructure

Sectors	Projects / Goals	Cost (millions USD)		
		2005	2006	Total
Public works	-Transport infrastructure; -Public administration infrastructure; -Erosion control; -Improvement of basic sanitation for Luanda.	441	297	738
Electricity	-Enlargement of the Kapanda Hydroelectric Dam and the associated energy transport networks; -Installation of additional thermal energy to Benguela, Lobito and Huambo; -Recovery and enlargement of the energy distribution channels in Luanda, N'dalatando, Caxito and Malanje; -Other rehabilitation and enlargement of electric power facilities.	303	106	409
Water	-Luanda south-east water project construction of stage III, with prominence for the enlargement of the distribution channel; -Construction of the new system of integrated provisioning of Benguela, Lobito, Catumbela and Baia Farta; -Recovery and enlargement of the water system of Malanje, N'dalatando, Huambo, Cuito, Caxito, Uíge.	168	96	264

Source: Ministry of Finance

and the new university Centre. It will also facilitate access to the new Luanda International airport, as well as the access from the Port of Luanda to the dry port at Viana.

The cost of the new highway is estimated at more than US $30 million.

BICHEQUETE MASSABI ROAD

In 2005 the government began the work of rehabilitation of the highway that links the locality of Bichequete (Cacongo) to Massabi (territory of Congo Brazzaville), appraised at US $16.7 million. After having built the highway, the government will work on the only commercial port in Cabinda. The highway to be rehabilitated is 41 km long.

HIGHWAY LUANDA / SUMBE / LOBITO

The rehabilitation works will complete the highway between Luanda, Sumbe and Lobito, in an extension of 497.5 km. The works are estimated at US $25 million and are detailed in a proposal from Cabinet of National Reconstruction. Initially, it will rehabilitate the 150 km of the highway from Sumbe to Lobito, which is considered the most critical part along the highway.

HOUSING

Throughout the country numerous residential and non-residential constructions are in progress, financed by both public and private sector initiatives. Under the aegis of the Ministry of Public Works, 800 houses and 1,680 apartments were built in 2005, in the course of the first phase of the New Life Project in Luanda Sul (south Luanda). In the second phase 1,862 residences will be built and 20% of these homes are destined for public officers.

Many offices and hotels are being built with public and private capital. For instance, a consortium between the state company Emproe and MKP of Malaysia will build 2,500 houses in Luanda (Camama), Bengo, Uíge and North Cuanza; Uniprev plans to build up to 32,000 houses throughout the country over seven years from 2006. The Belas Shopping Centre, covering 28,000 m^2, is under construction in Luanda Sul and will be the first large-scale shopping centre in Angola.

The road to Sumbe

PUBLIC WORKS

Taking into consideration the key contribution to economic growth that improved circulation of people and goods will bring to Angola, the national highways are considered to be the principal priority for national reconstruction.

Examples of work already undertaken in 2005 include:

• Basic recovery work was accomplished on 500 km of national highways (filling pot holes, earth-moving, clearing forest from roads, cleaning of the verges and stabilization of the road platform).
• Construction of the bridge on the Cavaco River (172 metres in length) in Benguela.
• Assembly of five steel bridges (total length of 407 metres).
• Rehabilitation of the bridge on the Dande River, and the assembly of three more steel bridges.
• Rehabilitation of the Saurimo and Kuito aerodromes.

• Erosion control work.
• Coastal protection at Chicala (Luanda).
• Dredging and maintenance of Mussulo Bay.
• Flood control in the Bero River in Namibe.

In 2005 the number of children attending schools increased by 21%, (4,022,970 in 2004 and 4,879,811 in 2005) as a result of the rehabilitation and re-equipping of 17 primary schools in Lunda Sul, Huíla, Huambo, Cabinda, Lunda Norte, Uíge, Luanda, Bié and Moxico province and of 17 secondary schools in the provinces of Huambo, Cuanza Norte and Lunda Norte, as well as the building of five rural schools in Cunene province.

In the health sector, to extend the capacity to combat endemics and sexually transmitted diseases including HIV, seven health centres were built in the provinces of Huambo, Bié, Cabinda, Lunda Sul and Uíge as well as one hospital and eight health posts. In Luanda the Boavista health centre was completed.

New buildings are being constructed in Marginal

MULTISECTOR EMERGENCY AND REHABILI-TATION PROJECT (PMER-PROJECTO MULTISECTORIAL DE EMER-GENCIA E REHABILITAÇÃO)

The World Bank (WB) will finance US $102 million in Angola for the execution of the second phase of the Multisector Emergency and Rehabilitation Project (PMER). Angola will receive the amount following an agreement that it signed with the WB at the end of the first quarter of 2006, for the execution of the programme from July 2006 to June 2010.

The project is designed to meet basic social objectives for the low-income population, such as rural development, social services and highway rehabilitation in Bié and Malanje, reconstruction of infrastructure destroyed by the war (particularly the highway and the bridge that join the locality of Lucala (Malanje) to Negage in the northern province of Uíje), rehabilitation of the distribution channel of electric energy to the capital of Luanda and the provinces of Cuanza Norte, Uíje, Malanje (north), Moxico (east) and Bié (centre).

NEW DEVELOPMENTS

LUANDA BAY PROJECT

Valued at US $113 million, this private development will clean up pollution and silt from Luanda Bay, including the dredging of channels to allow a better circulation of water and the prevention of future pollution.

The reclamation of land from the sea through the extension of the waterfront, enlarging of the marginal (waterfront) avenue and the creation of new public leisure spaces plans to attract private capital estimated at US $2,000 million, and will last 13 years.

NEW CITY IN CABINDA

Cabinda will have, within 30 months, a new city, with 44 buildings of 15 floors each, giving a total of 5,000 apartments, in an area of one million square metres 18 km to the south of the provincial capital.

SONILS BASE

A significant contract is in progress to enlarge the oil-production logistics base (Sonils) that serves as a base for several oilfield services companies.

The construction of a number of office towers is in progress, based on public and private finance, such as the new Sonangol building, Esso Tower, Import Africa Towers and the new headquarters of BESA (Banco Espírito Santo Angola).

MAIN COMPANIES

EMPRESA DE DESENVOLVIMENTO URBANO LDA – EDURB

Mr Miguel Antonio Nogueira
General Manager
Rua Engº Pedro de Castro Van Dunem 'Loy', s/n, CS-02
Sector B, Talatona, Samba, Luanda
Tel: +244-222-678371
Fax: +244-222-503561
Email: batalha@edurb.net
Website: ww.edurb-luandasul.com

EDURB is an urban development partnership between the government of Angola and Prado Valadares, which is currently involved in the development of the Luanda-Sul Self-financed Urban Infrastructure Programme.

Initiated in 1995 through a self-financing process to improve living conditions in the city and to meet the immense unmet needs of low-income and displaced communities, the programme operates through an Achievement and Management Fund.

The process involved the identification of suitable land for urban development, the acquisition of the land from landowners by the state, legalization of the status of the land according to a land-use plan and the mobilization of capital investment from the private sector.

The programme involved an initial investment of US $30 million and a subsequent investment of US $14 million. The infrastructure development included community facilities, schools, commercial establishments, an industrial estate and a hospital.

The programme has so far: resettled 2,700 families displaced by the war; managed to service 8 million sq. m with 121 km of power lines, 70 km of piped water and three sewerage treatment plants; generated and invested US $96 million, mostly in social services; and created 4,000 jobs.

MOTA-ENGIL

Mr Heitor Ferro
Director Comercial
Rua Narciso Espirito Santo, n° 54, Luanda
Tel: +244-222-350263 / 350592
Fax: +244-222-350299
Email: heitor.ferro@mota-engil.pt
Website: www.mota-engil.pt

The two contractors Mota and Engil were founded in 1946 and 1952 respectively. Mota-Engil, however, is a relatively new name and dates back to 2000 when the Mota family acquired the Engil group and formed what is today known as Mota-Engil. With a turnover of EUR 1 billion and some 12,000 employees, the company is a major industrial group in Portugal.

The core business lies in construction with diversification into services, environment, real estate, logistics and transport infrastructure concessions. Mota-Engil is Portugal's biggest construction company and operates a string of 12 quarries in Portugal itself, but is also engaged in Africa (Angola, Mozambique, Ghana, Benin, Malawi and Chad), in South America (Argentina and Peru), in Eastern Europe (Poland, Hungary and the Czech Republic) and in the US.

The construction of the Luanda International Airport was awarded in 1952, which was to be the first major contract to be realized in the country and became the benchmark for the company's activity in subsequent years.

In 1980 Mota & Companhia maintained and expanded its operations in the Republic of Angola. During the year it set up a company called Paviterra UEM, in association with the government of Angola, engaged in earthmoving. For many years the two companies were the only corporate structures engaged in public works in Angola .

Mota-Engil Engenharia is currently building the Torres Atlântico undertaking in Luanda. Over and above its volume, the complex is outstanding for its high safety indices, unmatched in Angola

NOVA CIMANGOLA SA

Mr Manuel Correia Victor
President
Av 4 de Fevereiro, n° 42, 2nd Floor
PO Box 2532, Luanda
Tel: +244-222-334941 / 310190
Fax: +244-222-334940 / 840016
Email: cfrancisco@novacimangola.com

Activity: Cement production, clinker and paper bags

The National Cement Factory – Nova Cimangola – is an Angolan firm with a total of 800 workers and reaches a production capacity of 4,000 tonnes of cement per day.

With the war now over, reconstruction, including increasing the woefully inadequate housing stock, is the highest priority on the government's agenda. There is an urgent need for construction or rehabilitation of roads, houses, schools and industry. Shortage of housing is a chronic problem that has led to widespread slum development, particularly in and around the capital, Luanda, a city built to sustain a population of 700,000 and now home to around 4 million people.

The Portuguese group Cimpor – Cementos de Portugal – has recently sold its participation in the Angolan company Nova Cimangola for approximately EUR 74 million. The Angolan Nova Cimangola has already started new developments in order to renovate the factory and improve its products and services.

The firm has just launched in Luanda a new product called Tunga I, Tunga II and Tunga III, designed for small, medium and big civil engineering and public works.

Tunga I is used for the construction of concrete houses of medium resistance, whilst Tunga II is for pre-reinforced works that require greater consistence (small buildings and bridges), with Tunga III manufactured for reinforced concrete used in buildings and other infrastructure that demand a great initial and final effort in its use. A 50-kg sack of Tunga I will cost Kw 539, Tunga II Kw 588. Tunga III, due to its limited use, will only be produced and sold to order.

Nova Cimangola believes that this product is part of the company's modernization policy, which aims at better serving the clients and in accordance with their particular needs.

The firm will invest more than US $100 million from 2007 in order to increase the production of the company to over 2 million tonnes from the 1.2 million tonnes produced in 2006.

This improvement, along with many others, will be made in order to try to cover the whole national demand, as well as to offer a better product with more quality and a lower price. The first priority is to meet the need for cement in Angola.

ODEBRECHT

Mr Genésio Lemos Couto
Administrative and Planning Director
Parque Empresarial Odebrecht, Rua Engº Pedro de Castro Van-Dumen 'Loy', s/n, Luanda Sul, Luanda
Tel: +244-222-678000
Fax: +244-222-678015
Email: genesio@odebrecht.com
Website: www.odebrecht.com.br

Date of Creation: 1944

Odebrecht is a Brazilian business conglomerate with international standards of quality. Founded in 1944, the group is present in South America, Central America and the Caribbean, North America, Africa, Europe and the Middle East. Odebrecht is mainly involved in construction works, real estate and social works.

On a more local aspect, Odebrecht Angola was established in 1984 during the years of the war and has become the major construction company on the market. Its first contract still remains Angola's biggest construction project: the Capanda dam. This dam is 110 metres high and 1,470 metres long and forms a 170-square kilometre lake. For this project Odebrecht trained more than 10,000 workers over the years of construction.

Since it first started, the group has widely diversified its projects to different provinces in order to contribute to the decentralization of the country's economic activities. Besides providing engineering and construction services, Odebrecht has invested in its own ventures (Atlantico Sul Condominium, Belas Shopping mall, etc.) and has interests in oil prospecting projects and diamond-mining complexes (Sociedade Mineira de Catoca, Sociedade de Desenvolvimento Mineiro de Angola).

But what singles out Odebrecht among other construction companies is its will and effort to undertake social works. Some of its current projects are: the treatment of water in Luanda (benefiting about 1.6 million persons); the sanitation programme in the Luanda, Samba and airport regions (drainage ditches, sewages, public lighting and telephone systems); and the treatment of water in Benguela, Lobito, Catumba and Baïa.

Odebrecht has confidence in Angola, its people and its future and it is contributing to the development of the infrastructure of Angola. The company also strongly believes that the education and training of its people is key to achieving development. That is precisely why the company has developed many patronage and corporate social responsibility programmes. These programmes consist of leadership training, professional courses in universities, engineering prizes, scholarships, courses for illiterate people, fighting HIV, and building/renovating schools.

The company is therefore helping to rebuild the country, installing infrastructure that will improve the lives of millions of Angolans, generating wealth, job opportunities and taxes, and training people for work, enabling Angola to grow.

PAGENA – PARTICIPAÇÃO GERAL AFRICANA

Complexo Industrial e Comercial, Rua 6 L, Kima Kienda, Boa Vista, Luanda
Tel: +244-222-310489 / 310956 / 311856 / 310991
Email: direction@pagena.net

Pagena is one of the biggest steel suppliers in Angola, participating actively in the development of the Angolan economy. The company meets the increasing demands of the civil construction and industry sectors, offering its customers products of the highest quality and economic viability.

The company has 250 workers, most of them Angolans, and offers products of proven quality approved by the CEE and other international institutions.

With eight years of experience acquired in the Angolan market, and with foreign cooperation, the company is a key player in the Angolan economy and has contributed with the construction of Agostinho Neto University, Dos Coqueiros Stadium, Sonangol Clinic and Sonils, among others.

The firm currently specializes in the importation and sale of all kinds of steel products and iron pipes for civil construction and public works such as roads and bridges.

Pagena owns extensive logistics facilities and has strategic plans to continue increasing its efficiency and competitiveness in the future.

SOARES DA COSTA

Mr Roberto Pisoeiro
General Manager
Rua Cónego Manuel da Neves, nº 19, Kinaxixe
PO Box 2726, Luanda

Tel: +244-222-447360
Fax: +244-222-447236
Email: dtc.scosta@netangola.com
Website: www.soaresdacosta.pt

The origins of the Soares da Costa SGPS Group go back to 1918. At that time, only 10 workers were part of this small company, which was founded in Porto by José Soares da Costa and carried out high-quality finishing and paint works in fine gold.

In the nearly 90 years since the start of operations, the world has changed greatly, and the company has managed to develop with this change:

• From the small company registered under a sole proprietorship system, it became a major economic group listed on the stock exchange.
• It went from 10 workers to over 2,500.
• From a company that carried out finishing work, it became multidisciplinary as it branched out to every area associated with the construction business.
• With completed works on four continents, what started out as a regional company became an international one.

The group's current structure was drawn up in 2002, implemented in late December of that year, and is based on an overall management company, Grupo Soares da Costa SGPS SA, with a capital stock of EUR 160,000,000, allocated to the various areas in four other companies, whose capital stock is held by the parent company:

• Soares da Costa Construção SGPS SA with a capital stock of EUR 90,000,000, involved in general contracting work;
• Soares da Costa Indústria SGPS SA with a capital stock of EUR 40,000,000, which is involved in the industrial spheres of construction, namely in the fields of carpentry, steel erection and machinery, electrical and mechanical installations, hydraulic installations and railway infrastructure;
• Soares da Costa Concessões SGPS SA with a capital stock of EUR 20,000,000, with activities in the field of concessions of services and public infrastructure;

When Odebrecht came to Angola we brought our experience and technology with us. But it was here that we found the talent

...ebrecht, always at the forefront of great projects, stands out as a company that ...ieves, and invests, in the development and reconstruction of Angola. This ...mmitment entails above all the creation of employment and training opportunities ...those Angolans who wish to become qualified professionals. Over the last twenty ...rs, Odebrecht Angola has created more than 40,000 positions, in different ...vinces of the country, and more than 20,000 professionals have benefited from ...training programs. It is by investing in talent, and in the abilities of our employees, ...t we have created a well-based company, ready for the challenges that the future ...l bring.

...jects include: Capanda, Águas de Luanda, Casas Económicas do Zango, Águas de ...guela, Luanda Sul, Catoca, SDM.

ODEBRECHT

THEY ARE NOT MADE OF CONCRETE NOR IRON, BUT OUR SOCIAL PROGRAMS ARE SOLID AS ROCK

ODEBRECHT SOCIAL ACTION

FIGHT AGAINST AIDS CAMPAIGN
- More than 100,000 people have already benefited from it.
- 350,000 condoms distributed.
- More than 300 educators have been trained and qualified.
- 900 voluntary tests.

VACCINATIONS CAMPAIGN
- Odebrecht has taken part in the poliomyelitis eradication program for the last six years.
- Staff and logistic support provision to the teams.
- Creation of incentives to encourage children's participation.

SUPPORT TO AGOSTINHO NETO UNIVERSITY
- Training programs.
- Specialisation complimentary courses.
- Technical visits to Odebrecht works.
- Support to the libraries of the different faculties.

LUANDA PAEDIATRIC HOSPITAL
- Improvement of hospital conditions.
- Building of radiology section.
- Building of annexe for mothers.

LITERACY PROGRAM FOR ADULTS
- Literacy courses for builders working in Odebrecht building projects.
- Partnership with St. John Bosco Salesian Centre.

PROFESSIONAL TRAINING COURSES
- 6,000 Angolans have benefited from professional training programs.
- Courses taught by specialists from the National Industrial Training Service (SENAI) and the Industrial Social Service (SESI).

AGRICULTURAL PROGRAMS
- Capanda agricultural program aimed to guarantee self-sufficiency of 22 products.
- 210 hectars of cultivated land.
- Teaching of sowing and growing techniques.

WORK OPPORTUNITIES FOR THE CRIPPLED
- 100 disabled veterans work now in Capanda.
- Integration of these individuals into qualification programs.

SUPPORT TO CULTURE
- "Casa de Angola" in Brazil.
- Support to "Brazil-Africa – Similitudes" photography display in Luanda.
- Support to "Arts and Crafts in Brazil" photography display in Luanda.
- Publication of "Angola and the expression of its Arts Culture", an art book.

ODEBRECHT
Odebrecht Angola, Lda.

• Soares da Costa Imobiliária SGPS SA with a capital stock of EUR 80,000,000, and with activities in the field of real estate development and management.

Over the course of its long history, the Soares da Costa Group has shown that it is able to adapt to the signs of the times and respond to them with suitable changes, based on its high-quality staff, who are willing to take on challenges involving diversification and innovation.

In the next 90 years, the world will keep on changing. And in the next 90 years, the Soares da Costa Group will keep on being successful, because it will be able to change too.

TEIXEIRA DUARTE

Mr Waldemar Marqués
Managing Director
Rua Amílcar Cabral n° 27 r/c, Maianga, Luanda
Tel: +244-222-330236 / 393933
Fax: +244-222-393927
Email: val@tduarte.co.ao
Website: www.teixeiraduarte.pt

Activity: Engineering and construction

The principal activities of Teixeira Duarte – Engenharia e Construções SA – are construction, civil engineering and public works. Construction activities include car parks, offices, a swimming pool, a cinema hall and warehouses. Civil engineering and public works include roadways, airports, tunnels and bridges.

The group also has activities in real estate development, hotel management, vehicle sales, fuel distribution, the food industry, investment management and other activities. The group operates at national and international level.

It has branches in Luanda, Cabinda, Soyo, Benguela, Lubango, Huambo and Namíbe. TD has exclusive dealership for three of the biggest worldwide manufacturers of vehicles (Nissan, Peugeot and General Motors) and offers 20% of the hotel capacity in Luanda, with two hotels of note, the Tropical Hotel and the Alvalade Hotel.

Moreover, the firm participates in the sector of food distribution through the cash and carry MAXI, serving Angolan companies from four locations in Luanda, Viana, Sumbe and Porto Amboim, and contributing to the stabilization of prices and the improvement of supply circuits. Teixeira Duarte currently employs 2,395 workers in Angola, of which only 6% are expatriates.

The strong construction sector - rapidly evolving - gives a cosmopolitan air to Luanda

TOURISM

"The one throwing the stone forgets, the one receiving it remembers it forever"
Angolan proverb

MESSAGE FROM HIS EXCELLENCE
THE MINISTER OF TOURISM

DYNAMISING THE HOTEL AND TOURISM INDUSTRY

Angola is gaining more and more recognition as a major tourist destination thanks to new climate of peace and development. Its natural resources and beauty more than fulfill the expectations of westeners' imagination, who throughout the years have developed a conception of Africa as a universe of surprises to discover.

An endless number of natural marvels turn Angola into one of the most interesting African countries for tourism: wide tropical forests, lakes, mountains, rocky formations, caves, grottos, deserts, exotic beaches, together with its amazingly rich fauna and warm and cheerful people.

In this sense, one of our main priorities nowadays is building and repairing facilities.

Tourism is a sector that so far has not received much private investment, but now that we speak about specific figures, about how small companies can get support and how to create employment, this is starting to change. We need to implement a campaign to show the resources available, our richness, to the rest of the world as well as Angola itself, since many Angolans do not know what their country has to offer, and only discover its natural beauty when travelling to the provinces.

In my opinion, our most urgent need is accommodation. Between 10 and 20 hotels would be needed, to cover for the 3,500 hotel beds that Angola is lacking now, 2,500 in Luanda and 1,000 in the rest of the country. A new airport is needed as well to respond to the changes of the airlines that operate in Angola. We are working on this matter to assure that by 2009 all those international visitors that come for business or pleasure find accommodation available. In that respect, we are considering the possibility of hosting the Coupe d'Afrique des nations 2010 (CAN-2010), which would imply making a large investment in hotels.

H.E. EDUARDO JONATÃO CHINGUNJI
Minister of Tourism

OVERVIEW

Angola is not regarded as one of the main African tourist destinations yet, but in 2004 the number of tourists crossing the borders reached a total of 194,300, of whom 82% (159,300) were men and 18% (34,900) women. This figure, compared to 2003 when there were 106,600, meant an increase of 82%. The main source countries were Portugal, South Africa, France, Brazil, United Kingdom and USA, and the travelling purposes were mainly services 69%, visits to relatives 11.3% and business 11%. These visitors travelled by plane 74%, train 24% and ship 2%. At the time of the study, Angola had 737 accommodation units: 130 hotels, 547 hostels and 60 units which fall under different types of premises categories. There were a total of 5,691 establishments where food is served, among which 949 were restaurants and 1,500 snack bars. There were 158 licensed travel and tourism agents, whose turnover reached US $29 million.

On an international level, tourism increased 5.5% from 2004 to 2005, despite elements such as terrorism, natural disasters, diseases, oil price rises and political and economic instability. International tourism surpassed all expectations and achieved US $808 million, this being a historical record. This meant an increase of US $42 million, comprising Europe US $18 million, Asia and Pacific zone US $11 million, America US $7 million, Africa US $3 million and Middle East US $2 million.

Africa was the only region that improved in 2005 compared to 2004. There was an increase of 10% compared to 8% in 2004. This growth was especially high in sub-Saharan Africa (13% in 2005 compared to 5% in 2004). Tourism in Angola, in spite of the fact that it does not have a important position in comparison to its African neighbours, is steadily increasing year after year, especially after the peace agreements were signed. This change is shown by the 209,900 tourists received in 2005, most of them from Portugal, South Africa, France, Brazil, China, United Kingdom and USA.

In 2005 the main travelling purposes were 69% services, 13% business, 9% visits to relatives, 6% holidays and 3% were passing trade. The hotel and tourism sector employed 49,500 workers.

The government has established the following targets to encourage the growth of tourism for 2005/2006:

• Diversify the tourist market by supporting private projects such as the creation of new tourist resorts as well as

Welwitschia Mirabilis, unique plants of Angola that are unusual for their large, straplike leaves that grow continuously along the ground

restoration of infrastructure and facilities, which will create employment at the same time.

• Qualification of people working in the tourist sector and certification of premises.

• Revision and assessment of natural, cultural tourist resources.

In order to achieve these targets, a number of new policies will be passed so as to attract more public and private investment, to increase the tourism and hotel facilities, to increase human resources training, to review the tourist resources available, to build a website for the Ministry of Tourism, and to plan a tourism and hotel network.

MAIN COMPANIES

AAVOTA – ASSOCIAÇÃO DAS AGÊNCIAS DE VIAGENS E OPERADORES TURÍSTICOS DE ANGOLA

Mrs Ana María Grión and Mr José Veiga
President and Secretary General
Rua da Missão, nº 93, Etram Building, 1st Floor, Suite 12, Luanda
Tel: +244-222-372259
Fax: +244-222-372259
Email: presidencia@aavota.com / geral@aavota.com
Website: www.aavota.com

Activity: National travel and tour operators trade association
Date of Creation: 27th October 1992

AAVOTA – Associação das Agências de Viagens e Operadores Turisticos de Angola – is the only association of its kind in Angola and it is the oldest and most representative of national tourism. It was created on 27th October 1992 by a group of travel agents who wanted to defend their rights and interests by joining and creating an association. It comprises:

• Main members: national travel agents and tour operators;

• Collaborating members: other companies related to the tourism sector such as foreign travel agents, airlines, hotels, restaurants, car hire companies, official tourism organizations, campsites and road transport companies, among others.

The Association has a major role in the development of national tourism by initiating debates among its members, presenting proposals, forecasting how the market will change and preparing the sector for the challenges ahead.

AAVOTA's main tasks consist of implementing activities that contribute to its members' development and encourage solidarity among them. The Association also represents its members in their relations with both public and private bodies, trade unions and other associations, Angolan and foreign financial groups, its main target being the defence of its members' legal rights and the promotion and development of tourism in Angola.

AHORESIA – ASSOCIAÇÃO DE HOTÉIS, RESTAURANTES E SIMILARES DE ANGOLA

Mr João Gonçalves
Managing Director
Calçada do Município, nº 49, Ingombota, Luanda
Tel: +244-923-520197

Activity: Association of hotels, restaurants and catering bodies
Date of Creation: 2005

AHORESIA – the Association of Hotels, Restaurants and Similar Entities of Angola, is an association that seeks to strengthen its position in the tourist sector with the aim of helping this sector to contribute positively to the country's economic balance and to work to reduce poverty.

One of its main challenges is the creation of a fund able to support tourism in order to make the Association self-sustainable. Another main objective, according to the association's strategy, is to reach a high level of qualification and training. Through this it seeks to reach the whole country, and especially the staff in the tourism sector, and provide everyone with technical and systematic knowledge.

To achieve higher quality in the sector, the purpose of the training programme is to be able to compete on the same level as the best in the world. One of the most important objectives is to see national tourism getting a better return on investment. The tourism sector in Angola currently has 737 registered accommodation units (130 hotels, 547 pensions and 60 other establishments). This low number, which is still considered an exaggeration, is due to the Angolan war from 1975 to 2002. The construction and recovery of the country's infrastructure is considered a main priority for the Angolan government and necessary for attracting tourism to the country.

As its main target, AHORESIA wishes to set up and develop cooperation agreements between hotels, restaurants, similar establishments and international non-governmental organizations. It also supports companies in order to increase financial and trade cooperation on both a national and an international level. Its board of directors is composed of renowned and experienced professionals from the tourism sector. The funding is mainly private and it is very interested in attracting more investment in order to implement different development and business strategies. AHORESIA strongly believes in the strengths of the natural resources and wonders that Angola has to offer to the international public. The association is very aware of the hard work that is still left to do in order for Angola to develop all its potential and achieve the position it deserves as a major tourism destination.

AGÊNCIA DE VIAGENS ATLAS VIAGENS LDA

Mrs Filomena Lopes
Gerente
Rua Amílcar Cabral, nº 159, Luanda
Tel: +244-222-331631
Fax: +244-222-396694
Email: filomena@atlasviagens.com

Activity: Travel agency

Atlas Viagens was created in 2004. The agency has witnessed an exponential growth since its inception due to the numerous existing clients of its creator. Atlas Viagens

Rua Amilcar Cabral,159
Luanda - Angola

Tel.: 00244 - 33 16 31
Fax.: 00244 - 39 66 94

Email: reservas@atlasviagens.com

is providing services to embassies and public and private companies, as well as to the general public. The company works as much on international routes as on national destinations, with all the major airlines.

One of the numerous services the company provides its customers with is the handling of all the visa formalities for people entering or going out of Angola. In the very near future, Atlas Viagens will also implement a service offering transportation to the airport and the check-in process.

Its connection with the European agency allows more flexibility than are available to operations based only in Angola. As a result of its efficient services it has become the first choice of many companies and international companies in Angola; in fact, 70% of its business comes from corporate clients.

With partnerships in Portugal, South Africa and Brazil, Atlas Viagens is clearly expanding as one of the main travel agencies in Luanda. In the future it expects to see an increase in branch offices across the country, as Angola's infrastructure continues to improve.

"Although 99% of Angola's tourism is business tourism, there is great potential for growth in this sector. It is important that investors get the right information, rather than fearing the unknown. Angola is safe and well developed, and you can find everything here."
Mrs Filomena Lopes, Gerente

AGÊNCIA DE VIAGENS EUROSTRAL

Mr Laurent Lepetit
Managing Director
Rua Manuel Fernando Caldeira, nº 3 A-B, Bairro Coqueiros, Luanda
Tel: +224-222-398058 / 398059
Fax: +224-222-335635
Email: eurostral@snet.co.ao

Activity: Travel agency and car hire
Date of Creation: 2003
Turnover: US $800,000–1,000,000

RENT A CAR

Marechal Broz Tito nº27 1º andar direita Kinaxixi. Luanda, Angola
Tlfs: + (244) 222 44 13 46 / 95 25   + (244) 222 43 24 02   Móvel: + (244) 923 45 21 11 / 12 + (244) 923 54 99 69
Email: eurostral.rentacar@snet.co.ao Fax: + (244) 222 44 30 22

AGÊNCIA DE VIAGENS E TURISMO, LDA.

Rua Manuel F. Caldeiras 3A / B. Coqueiros. Luanda, Angola
Tlfs: + (244) 222 39 80 58 / 59 + (244) 22239 90 91 Móvel: + (244) 923 30 79 62 + (244) 923 45 68 45
Email: eurostral.rentacar@snet.co.ao Fax: + (244) 222 33 56 35

BILHETERIE
eurostral@snet.co.ao eurostral@amadeus.co.ao tourismecentre@snet.co.ao

TURISME
eurostral.tour@snet.co.ao eurostral.tour@amadeus.co.ao location Peugeot Open Europe email: peugeotTT@snet.co.ao

PEUGEOT OPEN EUROPE
HOLIDAYS BY CAR

Eurostral is an Angolan–French partnership started in 2003. It aims to offer travel agency and car hire services. At present it is operating at 70% of its sales volume and the general turnover of the company is between US $800,000 and US $1 million.

Services offered are:

- Ticketing
- Holiday packages
- Visa services
- Car hire (with or without drivers).

This company wants to differentiate from others in Luanda in the quality of the services provided. It wants to continue growing, but only if quality is maintained. For this firm, quality is always before quantity.

"Angola is a very nice country with a challenging future and great opportunities. The idea of the firm is to grow at the same time as the country does, always keeping the high quality services provided to serve any new visitors."
Mr Laurent Lepetit, Managing Director

AGÊNCIA DE VIAGENS EXPRESSO

Mr José Veiga
Managing Director
Rua Amílcar Cabral, n° 172, PO Box 1359-C, Luanda
Tel: +244-222-331719 / 331479 / 923-416431
Fax: +244-222-336755
Email: jose.veiga@expressoangola.com
Website: www.expressoangola.com

Activity: Travel agency, tour operator
Date of Creation: 22nd August 1966
Capital: US $300,000,00
Employees: 10

Expresso Viagens is the oldest travel agency in Angola, existing since 1966. It is a member of AAVOTA, IATA and ASTA and is the travel representative of American Express all over the country.

It is also the representative of STA Travel, the world's travel agency specialist for students and young travellers.

Muserra Stones

The headquarters are based in Luanda but it also has two branch offices in Lobito and Benguela.

The services provided are:

• Transfers in/out
• Airport assistance
• Hotel accommodation booking for FIT and groups
• Car hire, with or without driver
• Coach rental for tours
• City tours and local excursions
• Booking and selling of air tickets for domestic flights in all Angola for TAAG and SAL Airlines.

Currently it has the rights for and is developing a tour operator called Tour Africa. Angola is an emerging market where this new concept of tourism created with different holiday packages will be running from 2007.

"Come and visit Angola, the land of the future."
Mr José Veiga, Managing Director

AGÊNCIA DE VIAGENS HULL BLYTH ANGOLA

Mr António Matias and Mrs Zinha Carmos
Managing Directors
Rua 4 de Fevereiro n° 23–24, 1st Floor, Marginal, Luanda
Tel: +244-222-310007 / 310044 / 310301
Fax: +244-222-310879 / 310309
Email: zinha.carmo@hullblyth-angola.com
Website: www.hull-blyth.com

Activity: Travel agency
Date of Creation: 1990
Employees: 300 people directly in Angola and 2,000 more indirectly

Hull Blyth Travel Agency is looking after thousands of business people, project workers, oilfield employees and sailors each year, arranging travel to and from all around the world.

In the recent past Hull Blyth has also developed the following services:

• Visas
• Local assistance
• Reservation and ticketing
• Property services
• Property rental
• Maintenance and repair services (air conditioners, generators, water pumps, electrical systems, general building maintenance and repairs, fuel and water supply, light construction and engineering)
• Guest houses (HBA operates two guest house facilities located close to the central business district in Luanda to cater for long-term residents, visitors and transit passengers).

Hull Blyth has been operating in Africa for well over 100 years. During this time it has developed and expanded a wide range of services. Hull Blyth Angola operates in the areas of personnel supply and transportation.

Demand for reliable support services in Angola led Hull Blyth to create an organization that provides a single point of focus. This allows its customers to concentrate on their core business without the time-consuming distraction of dealing with the various logistical elements related to working in a complicated and demanding environment.

Hull Blyth is the leading supplier of semi-skilled and unskilled labour to the onshore and offshore oil industry in Angola. Its travel agency looks after thousands of people each year, arranging travel to and from all parts of the world. The ship agency division represents a range of ship owners, operators and caterers from all aspects of the shipping industry.

The success of this philosophy, combined with the continued trend for outsourcing of non-core services and the expansion of the oil and gas industry, has further increased that demand, leading Hull Blyth to upgrade its facilities, strengthen its staff and expand the product range.

"You should come to Angola to invest in good opportunities with a high return of investment in the medium run. Angola is the future."
Mr António Matias and Mrs Zinha Carmos, Managing Directors

AGÊNCIA DE VIAGENS PRISMATUR

Mr Silvio Camilo da Costa
Managing Director
Comandante Eurico nº45 r/c, Patrice Lumumba, Luanda
Tel: +244-222-445488 / 912-401440
Fax: +244-222-445336
Email: prismatur@mail.com
Website: www.prismatur.com

Activity: Travel agency
Date of Creation: 2002
Turnover: US $1.5 million
Employees: 10

Since the war ended in Angola, many businesses have been established. Prismatur is a very good example of this. Prismatur started when a group of people linked with the tourism sector decided to create their own company, and ever since Prismatur has been growing at 40% annually in equity.

Prismatur decided to create a website where all facilities and services such as air travel, hotels, check in/out, tourist packages, car hire and client registration are provided.

It will help any client find information about airline routes and many other options to plan a trip. It also offers a guide for travellers or tourists who want to visit other countries without leaving home.

Cars in excellent condition are available for hire at very reasonable prices. For the best comfort of its clients, Prismatur offers the best options in car rental. Rent a car quickly and easily with no bureaucracy. Cars are delivered to clients upon arrival at the airport.

Prismatur knows the deficit of knowledge about the things Angola has to offer; therefore, it is creating the first holiday packages in the country. It is enabling peo-

ple to discover the marvellous places that can be found not far away from Luanda, and in the near future the range of options will be extended.

"Angola is a country willing to grow. Angolan people are kind, open and want the country to develop a step further."

Mr Silvio Camilo da Costa, Managing Director

TRANSCONTINENTAL VIAGENS & TURISMO LDA

Mr Pedro Salmo Fernando
Administrador
Rua Travesa da Sorte, nº 22, Maianga, Luanda
Tel: +244-222-338003 / 339836 / 310033
Fax: +244-222-331395 / 310313
Email: tcv@snet.co.ao

Activity: Travel and tourism – travel agency and cargo services
Date of Creation: 2005

Transcontinental Viagens & Turismo Lda is a newly created travel agent conveniently located in the centre of Luanda within easy access for customers.

It is also a customs broker that is well reputed in Angola. Its administrator, Mr Pedro Salmo Fernando, has been working in the sector for a number of years and decided to use his expertise and experience to set up this modern business. As a customs broker, he has a long experience of processing goods through customs.

Transcontinental Viagens & Turismo Lda uses the latest technologies to provide its customers with an efficient, dynamic and friendly service. The company contributes with its professional work to the ever-expanding tourism sector and will develop with it.

The company offers both national and international routes and package tours. Among its clients are both public and private companies.

BAMBOO IMPERIAL

Rua General Roçadas, nº 43, Maianga, Luanda
Tel: +244-222-394716
Mobile: +244-923-962508 / 612657

Activity: Beauty and health
Date of Creation: 2003

"Come and pamper your body and achieve peace of mind."

Health, well-being, relaxation, anti-stress, beauty and pleasure define what Bamboo offers to its clients.

Bamboo's owners brought from their trips to Macao a number of Asian and eastern therapies, importing a new concept of well-being as an alternative to western medicine. Bamboo Imperial means peace of mind, happiness and joy. Once in their premises, an amazing feeling of peace and well-being invades you. Fortunately, the city of Luanda offers a place like this: this is definitively the Angolan peak of relaxation. Bamboo, as a pioneer centre, is always willing to work in partnership with international providers and to open its doors to innovative products.

Do not miss out on its cosmetic services for both men and women, which include paraffin treatments, foot spa and flawless wax hair removal. All kinds of manicures and pedicures will bring you joy. Try the wide choice of therapeutic techniques: acupuncture, ear therapy, Reiki, cromotherapy, facial and body lymphatic drainage, reflexology, shiatsu and the internationally known blackhead craniosacral therapy, which produces very good results in rebalancing nervous and glandular systems, using only soft movements and specific positions. Bamboo is also well known for its excellent reducing, relaxing and anti-stress massages. Cosmetic and medical physiotherapy are also offered, as well as hydrotherapy (aqua gym, sauna).

As for body treatments, it recommends the imperial or traditional moon bath, immersion bath, therapy bath and flowers bath. And for that special occasion, the bride bath (special programmes available for the bride and groom). And of course, do not miss out the marvellous facial treatment, which will address the specific needs of your skin. The hairdressing and make-up services are the best in town. If you have a party or special celebration, you must come to Bamboo first. You will shine like a star.

Bamboo also offers the services of nutritionists who will give you professional advice. And while you wait for your turn, you can have a healthy snack and natural fruit juice at the bar. Give your body and soul to the pleasure of pampering yourself and boosting your energies.

Opening times: weekdays and Saturdays 0800 to 2100; Sundays 1200 to 2100.

DNAT – DIRECÇÃO NACIONAL DE ACTIVIDADES TURÍSTICAS

Mr Januario Marra
Director
Largo 4 de Fevereiro, Palácio de Vidro, 3rd Floor, Luanda
Tel: +244-912-518250 / 923-523772
Fax: +244-222-310347
Email: jfmjmarra@yahoo.com

Activity: National directorate for tourism activities

Angola has a big tourist potential, but in order to make it effective, it is necessary to set up politically steered measures to assist branch operators to work and get help without any problems.

Direcção Nacional de Actividades Turísticas – DNAT – belongs to the Ministry of Tourism and its objectives are to manage research, encourage and monitor measurements and actions for the implementation of national policies in the tourism sector.

DNAT regulates the activities carried out by travel and tourism agents and other professions and activities related to the tourism sector, such as campsites, water sports, hunting and fishing as a sport, as well as the activities fulfilled by professionals working in tourist information centres and souvenir shops.

DNAT is very aware of the fact that tourism should be considered one of the main sectors of the economy, helping to create many direct and indirect jobs. In the first phase of development, DNAT is working to create mechanisms to facilitate investment in this sector of the economy.

General objectives of DNAT are, among others:

• Tourist information management including:
- Development, publication and sale of booklets, promotional materials, maps and video materials concerning the tourist potential of the country.
- Promotion of Angolan tourist resources to the world market.
- Creation of a positive image of the country as a tourist region.
• Certification of tourist and hotel services.
• High school tourism education.
• Retraining and raising the level of skill of personnel in the tourism sphere.
• Methodical support for tourism organizations.
• Sociological investigations and the audit of tourists.

Other functions include promoting Angola as a tourism destination, cataloguing the historical and tourism heritage of Angola, encouraging its protection and promotion, as well as giving guidance on, coordinating and promoting tourism on both a national and international level.

FITNESS CLUB

Mr António Nunes
Director General
Rua do Massangão, s/n, Anangola, Luanda
Tel: +244-923-416646
Fax: +244-923-404749
Email: fitness@netcabo.co.ao
Website: www.fitnessangola.com

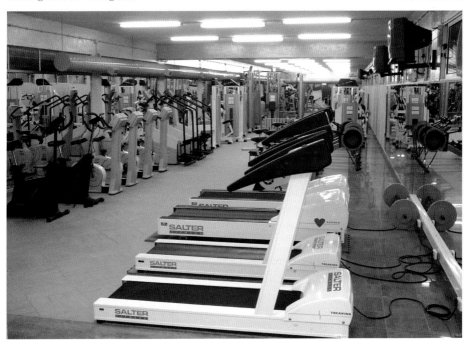

Activity: Fitness and sports, health and beauty

Date of Creation: 1995

This extremely well-equipped gym, number one in Luanda, was created in 1995 and it is located in the centre of the Angolan capital. It covers 3,500 square metres including gardens with parking, sports courts for different functions, swimming pool, sport shops and a cafeteria with a wide variety of food and drinks that is an ideal place to relax after exercising.

The facilities reflect the high quality and standard expected of a five-star establishment. This modern gym offers a good selection of ABS, aerobics, ballet, capoeira, dance courses, muscle building, spinning, step, aqua, taekwondo, and cardio. It also has a clinic and beauty salon, including depilation, sauna and massage areas, with a special space and activities for children.

The gym offers cardiovascular and strength machines which are easy to use, reliable and flexible enough to adapt to all levels of fitness. With such a variety of equipment, you can meet your goals whilst enjoying your exercise. Fully equipped for users with disabilities, with help-ful, friendly and well-trained staff on hand to assist you. Fitness also offers to its members a lifestyle evaluation, advice and support in maintaining a healthy lifestyle, through personalized programmes of 2–3 months' duration, as well as physiotherapy services.

HOTEL FORUM

Mr Tomas Borrel

Manager Director

Avenida Ho-Chi Min, s/n, Luanda

Tel: +244-222-324344 / 324346 / 324348

Fax: +244-222-322193

Email: hotelforum@netangola.com

Website: www.hotelforum.ao.com

Activity: Hotel and catering services

Nearby the International Airport of Luanda and only 15 minutes away from the famous beaches of the 'Island of Luanda', the Hotel Forum offers comfort in its 60 suites with bathroom, air conditioning and television with satellite TV, as well as minibar, telephone with direct access to external calls, Internet facilities and safety deposit box.

Business and conferences facilities that meet very exacting standards are available. Forum is a good place to hold meetings: two conference rooms and an auditorium are suitably equipped to provide the ideal setting for seminars, conferences and receptions.

At your entire disposal are also a very nice restaurant, a bar, and a private parking area with fence and security.

Besides the services mentioned above the hotel offers industrial catering for both private and public companies, and currently provides more than 4,850 daily take-away menus. It provides good food at good prices.

INFOTUR – INSTITUTO DE FOMENTO TURÍSTICO

Mr José Apolinário de Oliveira Diogo
Rua Ho-Chi Min, nº 410, Maculusso, Ingombota, Luanda
Telefax: +244-222-448787/26
Email: infotur@snet.co.ao

Website: www.minhotur.gv.ao
Activity: Angolan Institute for the Promotion and Development of Tourism

The Institute for the Promotion of Tourism in Angola, Infotur, is a public institution with financial and administrative autonomy. The institute works under decree no. 2/96 in conjunction with the Ministry of Tourism, which has the power to approve the activities carried out by Infotur.

Some of the functions of Infotur include:

• To monitor the facilities of all tourist accommodation, including the control of the licensing of exploitation of new areas that may be of interest for tourism in Angola.
• To control every aspect of the construction and planning of any tourist accommodation.
• To monitor all aspects of projects planned for tourist areas and only to approve those plans that support the tourist industry.
• To monitor farms used as tourist attractions.

Instituto de Fomento
Turístico de Angola

 Ho Chi Minh, N.º 410

ef_Fax: (+ 244) 222 448 787
ef.   (+ 244) 222 448 726
            (+ 244) 222 444 400
            (+ 244) 222 444 493
ail: infotur@snet.co.ao
w.minhotur.gv.ao   LUANDA-ANGOLA

- To contribute to develop the tourism industry in Angola, using financial contributions or assets such as concessions of public areas.
- To act as a mediator for the state in monitoring all aspects of new developments in the tourism industry.

The goals of Infotur are:

- To be responsible for the development of a successful tourism industry in Angola.
- To assist in answering any queries made by public or private bodies in relation to the tourist industry.
- To assist the national and international businesses which are setting up beneficial projects in the tourism sector.

Infotur is a comprehensive one-stop shop for all travel needs of individuals as well as tour operators. At Infotur you will find ample information regarding many travel areas: general information on Angola, Angolan places and cities, cultural and archaeological heritage, accommodation, eco-tourism, as well as unique information about the country.

Infotur is a one-stop shop for your next trip, corporate meeting or conference, or exciting thematic tour through Angola's secluded and thrilling sites.

MADIBA RESORT

Mr José Figueira Victor
President
Rua Direita de Futungo, Bairro Talatona, Luanda Sul
Tel: +244-222-460221
Fax: +244-222-460167
Email: prevel@netangola.com
Activity: Tourism resort

Date of Creation: 2000
Employees: 94

Located 10 minutes by car from the Luanda airport, Madiba resort has many facilities and services, which include a hotel (194 bungalow rooms), restaurants (two different environments), function rooms for celebrations, swimming pool (open to the public), discotheque, live music, theatre on Thursdays, special activities for children on Sundays, and its own bakery.

Apart from this, Madiba also offers on the last weekend of the month what they call Noches Danzantes where many people join in the dancing and have fun.

Madiba is only the beginning of a dream, the dream of creating a wide range of facilities for people. This project includes the construction of a new hotel called Hotel Thanza with gymnasium, swimming pool etc. It will also open ANTEC, a new shop selling technological equipment. Furthermore, a hotel in Malange will be constructed and a new university too.

"Angola is a young country rich in resources which needs the capabilities from abroad to develop its businesses. If important foreign companies come here the benefit will be for both of us."
Mr José Figueira Victor, President

MANGAIS ECO-TURISMO VARANDA DOS MANGAIS – GOLFE DA BARRA DO KWANZA

Mr Francisco Faisca
Administrator
Barra do Kwanza – Clube de Golfe, Eco-Turismo, Bengo province
Rua Major Canhangulo, 3B, Ingombota,
PO Box 1889, Luanda
Tel: +244-222-391653
Fax: +244-222-336633
Email: mangais@mangais.com
Website: www.mangais.com

Activity: Tourism resort, golf club and boutique hotel

The group Mangais is composed of two different companies. The first one, Afro-Jardin, was created in 1992 and specializes in open spaces and garden-related activities. is currently undertaking the construction of an 18-hole golf course. This golf course, designed by Jorge Santana da Silva (a Portuguese golf designer, very well known for several projects built in other countries), will be one of

nadiba

el and Touristic Complex

e perfect place
to relax
and
have fun

Bungalow rooms

estaurants

imming pool
(pen to public)

cotheque

e Music

+244(222) 460221
+244(222) 460167
ail: prevel@netangola.com
Direita de Futungo
o Talatona
da - Angola

ECOTURISMO
Mangais

Rua Major Canhangulo, nº3 B Ingombota, Luanda, Angola
Tel: (+244) 222 391653 / 222 394825 (+244) 923 408675 / 923 4086
mangais@mangais.com www.mangais.com

Communion with Nature

x: (+ 244) 222 336633

Relax at Mangais, Barra do Kwanza

the top international courses in the world. Apart from this, Afro-Jardin is also involved in interior design. It produces its own furniture from local materials and acts as a design company for major hotels, restaurants and bars in Luanda.

The company Mangais is involved in real estate construction. Current projects include the construction of condominiums along the golf course that will offer exceptional conditions of comfort. With rental and residential housing, it will offer all-included services.

Mangais is also building a five-star hotel in the Mangais area and operating a bungalow complex with a spa centre.

The company focuses on eco-tourism, that is to say ecological tourism of quality. The priority of eco-tourism is the focus on the conservation of nature and its various species.

On the company's website are a lot of pictures from the Mangais Estate and surrounding areas, such as Kissama National Park, Mussulo and Cabo Ledo beaches, Luanda city, etc., as well as fantastic images of the bungalow resort and the Veranda dos Mangais restaurant, whose view and peaceful location are breathtaking. You can eat

or simply rest and appreciate the Kwanza River, the tropical forest of mangroves and a lot of exotic birds inviting us to enjoy the beauty of African nature!

RESTAURANTE - PUB

TAMBARINO, RESTAURANT & CATERING

Mr Luis Salgado
Managing Director
Rua Amílcar Cabral n° 23, r/c, Luanda
Tel: +244-222-396884
Mobile: +244-912-240188

Activity: Restaurant and catering
Date of Creation: 1994
Employees: 32

Tambarino opened its doors in 1994 and since then it has found itself a place in the leisure life of Luanda. The basic ingredients of its success are good food, good wines and excellent service. It specializes in home-made Portuguese food, seafood and fish and takes special pride in its wide range of desserts and extensive wine list, the latter being not easily found in this town.

The restaurant also offers a complete and superb catering service, which includes not only a wide selection of food and drinks but also the services of a very well-trained staff. This is the perfect combination to make all your events and receptions look better and taste better, thanks to the professional and outstanding services. Tambarino combines earthy, tasty food with an elegant and chic style that has attracted well-known personalities from the social and political sphere of Angola's capital.

Tambarino specializes in business lunches and dinners, and its rooms can be closed to the public should your company need a relaxed and more intimate environment. The restaurant is closed on Sundays because it is the day all Angolans devote to their families. Mr Salgado contributes with this policy to the welfare of his staff.

Tambarino can also be booked for private parties, such as birthdays, business or family dinners (book in advance for large groups). There is a nice bar downstairs to enjoy if you have to wait. Relax in the Tambarino bar with good music while enjoying a wonderful Caipirinha with some snacks as you wait for your main dish.

There is a great atmosphere from the moment you walk in. The menu and the experience are both amazingly good. For many, this is the best restaurant in town.

Mr Salgado's extension plans and the new terrace will enlarge the already generous seating capacity of Tambarino.

Restaurante Veneza

OLIVEIRA & OLIVEIRA HOTELARIA E TURISMO LDA
RUA CMTE CHE-GUEVARA Nº 116 A 120
TELEFAX: 222320954
TELEMOVEIS:923 401900 / 912 200135
923 4017040 / 923 346701

RESTAURANTE VENEZA

Mr Márcio Ricardo Alves Oliveira
Managing Director
Rua Che Guevara nº 116–120, Luanda
Tel: +244-222-320954 / 328184 / 328283

Mobile: +244-923-401900 / 912-200135
Email: rest.veneza@netangola.com

Activity: Restaurant and catering

Well known in the city, Veneza Restaurant has gained many awards, such as the Golden Award for Tourism and Gastronomy Section during the New Millennium in Madrid, Spain in 2005.

Veneza is a high-quality Portuguese restaurant with a cafeteria-type atmosphere, offering good food and large portions at reasonable prices.

Whether it is a family event, an executive business lunch, a presentation, an agreement, a reception, a meeting or even an important discussion, success is guaranteed in Veneza.

Do business or chat with friends over a dish of tasty home-made *feijoada* or the delicious and unique *Bife na pedra*. Among the menu's traditional dishes, this restaurant is famous for its Steak on a Rock, a speciality at Veneza. It's a strip steak served raw, with olive oil and a little garlic, on a very hot slab of baked marble. The steak cooks on the marble, right at the diner's table. The customer decides when it's done.

Salt cod – or *Bacalhau* – is also featured prominently, as well as the generous *Paelha Valenciana*, enough to feed at least two. The saucy, slightly overcooked rice is filled with a generous amount of meat.

The menu reflects the commitment of the chef who creates the unique culinary delights inspired by Portuguese, Mediterranean, Brazilian and Angolan cuisine. The menu consists of only the freshest local meats and products.

The restaurant will also offer catering and delivery services and excellent take-away and home delivery in the near future.

"For business or pleasure, come to Veneza."
Mr Márcio Ricardo Alves Oliveira, Managing Director

TRANSPORT & COMMUNICATIONS

"A person who dies does not extinguish fire, but the living keep on playing with it"
Angolan proverb

TRANSPORT

The transport sector plays a vital role in the Angolan economy, given its crucial function of linking the country's interior to the rest of the world.

Of the four primary transport services, roads and railways are the worst affected by the 27 years of war that resulted in the wholesale destruction of highways, bridges and railways.

AIR

Angola has one international airport and 17 provincial airports, and a state-owned national air company, Angola Airlines (TAAG – Linhas aéreas de Angola), which provides domestic and international flights.

Other airlines including TAP, Air France, South African Airways, Ethiopian Airlines, Air Gabon, British Airways, Air Namibia, Sabena and Aeroflot operate international routes from Luanda Airport.

In 2005 TAAG acquired nine new Boeing aircraft (three are 777s for long haul and six are 737s for domestic flights) for US $900 million. Two of the nine aircraft were scheduled for service in the second semester of 2006 and the remainder in 2007.

TAAG International destinations

Continent	City
Africa	Johannesburg Windhoek Harare São Tomé Kinshasa Brazzaville, Ponta Negra Lusaka
Europe	Lisbon Moscow Paris
America	Rio de Janeiro Havana

Source: Gabinete de Estudos, Planeamento e Estatística

Luanda Airport is reputed to be among the 30 busiest airports in the world. In 2002 an expansion of Luanda Airport commenced, budgeted at US $300 million. In the north of the Angolan capital, Luanda, construction work for a new Angolan international airport has commenced. Also in progress are studies for the reconstruction and modernization of the Huambo province airport, to serve as an alternative to Luanda. Most of the provincial capitals have domestic airports, as well as some municipal districts.

PORTS AND RAILWAYS

Angola has three main ports connecting it to the world. The three existing railway lines connect to these three ports as follows: Luanda, Lobito and Namibe.

Port of Luanda

Located at 8° 47 'S and 13° 14 'E in Luanda Bay. Port access is easy as the entrance to the bay is about 1.5 miles wide. It is the main port in Angola, moving more than 80% of the country's imports and exports, excluding petroleum.

The port has 2,738 metres of wharf, divided into three terminals and a support platform for the oil industry. The port works 24 hours a day and it is managed by Luanda Port Company EP. It has three tugs with a capacity of between 750 and 2500 HP.

The port handles about 1.5 million tonnes a year, primarily import cargo (1.2 million tonnes), of which half is containerized. In 2004 the port handled 3,194,756 tonnes and was used by 2,645 ships. The goods handled are mainly: flour, rice, cereals, construction materials, manufactured products, vehicles and transport equipment.

The maximum depth of the ship channel is 9.5 metres. The depth along the wharf varies between 10.5 and 12.5 metres, except at the coastal traffic terminal, when the depth varies between 3.5 and 5.5 metres.

Bus station in Luanda

Port of Lobito

Located at 12° 20 'S and 13° 34 'E in Lobito bay, with the natural protection of a sandbank. Lobito Port was the main port in Angola in the past, as a result of being the oceanic terminal of the Benguela Railway. With peace in Angola and the ongoing reconstruction of the Benguela Railway line, this position will eventually be restored as this port handles mineral export traffic from the Democratic Republic of Congo and Zambia.

The port has 1,122 metres of wharf, divided into two areas, and works from 0700 to 2400. It has two tugs, 15 cranes with capacities between 5 and 22 tonnes and a floating crane with a capacity of 120 tonnes. Besides naval shipyards and fuel banks for ships, the port has the potential capacity to handle 500 tonnes per day of railway traffic.

The port handles about 600,000 tonnes per year, including the tonnages related to about 15,000 TUs that are moved annually. Commodities handled mainly include cereals for grinding, raw material for the industrial area of Catumbela, as well as flour, sugar, rice and construction materials and equipment for the cities of Lobito and Benguela.

In 2005 Lobito's port was used by 706 ships and handled 1,015,264 tonnes of diverse merchandise, 40,700 containers, 700 light vehicles and 400 heavy vehicles. In 2004 the port was used by 500 ships. The maximum depth is 10 metres.

Port of Namibe

Located at 15° 12 'S and 12° 08 'E, Namibe Port is the third-largest port in Angola.

The port has 870 metres of wharf, divided into three areas. Zone 3 is the largest area at 480 metres. The port is managed by the Namibe Port Company and has a tug, three cranes from 5 to 15 tonnes and a container lifter with a capacity of 40 tonnes.

The port handles about 200,000 tonnes per year, including 2,500 TUs that are moved annually. The goods handled are primarily manufactured products, food, materials and equipment for the neighbouring province of Huíla, as well as the export of marble and granite. This port will assume greater importance when the mining exploration of Kassinga (in Huíla province) becomes operational again. The maximum depth is 10 metres.

Rail

Due to the 27 years of war that devastated the country, the railway system that connected the coast to the interior of the country became inoperative because of the destruction of the railways, planting of mines and the destruction of rail bridges.

The Angolan rail system is composed of three lines, namely Luanda, Benguela and Namibe railways, that cross the country west to east, with a total coverage of about 2,750 km. The main network is the Benguela railway, CFB (Caminhos de Ferro de Benguela), with 1,305 km. This was one of the most important railway lines in Southern Africa, linking the centre-south of Angola to the Democratic Republic of Congo and Zambia and ending at the port of Lobito.

The second railway line is the Namibe railway of 907 km that links the port of Namibe to Menongue, in Cuando Cubango province. When it is totally rehabilitated, it will transport people and goods between the port-city of Namibe to the south of Angola and to the north of Namibia. The rehabilitation of Namibe railway is in progress and is estimated to cost US $1.2 billion. The work is due to be completed in August 2007. Once completed the line will transport two million passengers and 15 million tonnes of merchandise a year, with up to 30 trains a day.

The third railway line runs from Luanda to Malanje, known as the Luanda railway. It is 538 km long and once rebuilt will link Luanda with the agricultural areas of Cassange and Cuanza and to the diamonds fields of Lunda Norte and Lund Sul.

Aimed at increasing the capacity of the rail infrastructure, the Angoferro 2000 project is divided into four phases and is valued initially at US $4 billion. The project includes the rehabilitation of about 3,100 km of railway, 8,000 km of extensions, 36 bridges, and rehabilitation and building of 100 stations and 150 new substations.

The project is planned to extend to the construction of the Congo railway, a new line that will begin in Luanda going via Caxito, Uíge, Mbanza Congo, Cabinda and the Republic of Congo. Mobilization of potential backers for the project is in progress.

ROADS

Since the end of the colonial period, the national road network has deteriorated significantly due to the war and lack of maintenance and investment. During the rainy season, many major roads become impassable. The roads in the north of the country are in the worst state, and there is an urgent need to rebuild the numerous bridges that were damaged and destroyed during the war. By 2009 1,300 bridges out of the 6,000 existing bridges will be rebuilt.

In 1994 the road network comprised 75,000 km, which included 8,000 km of asphalted roads and 7,870 km of gravel roads. Out of this total, 16,000 km of roads are

LUANDA - KINAXIXI © Henrique Santos

administered by the Angolan National Institute of Highways (INEA – Instituto Nacional de Estradas de Angola).

Several roads are being constructed in Angola, such as the Luanda highway and the Bichequete to Massabi road. The most important road being rebuilt in 2006 is the Luanda, Sumbe and Lobito highway, with an extension of 497.5 km, estimated to cost US $25 million.

TELECOMMUNICATIONS

The war and inadequate investment over the last 27 years have resulted in extensive degradation of telecom infrastructure. Between 1992 and 1994 various provincial capitals were without telephone connections with the rest of the country and the world.

Angola is one of the bottom 30 countries in the world in the telecom sector, primarily due to the low coverage and poor quality of service.

In 1975 the number of telephone lines installed was 46,000 and by 1991 had risen to 78,000. Currently, the number of customers using fixed telephones lines is estimated to be 100,000.

In the telephony market there are currently five licensed operators, but only two are working: the state company Angola Telecom, which has more than 90,000 customers, and the privately owned Nexus, which started operations in 2003 and has more than 1,000 customers.

Mobile telephones are currently used by 1.5 million customers, representing more than 8% of the population of Angola.

The mobile telephone market consists of two service providers: the state-owned Movicel (2003), owned by Angola Telecom, and the privately owned Unitel (2001), the current market leader with more than one million customers. Currently, these two cover all 18 provinces of Angola. Movicel has about 500,000 customers.

In the last three years, the Index of Digital Access (DAI) has increased from 0.11 to 0.23, according to the Ministry of Telecommunications (figures were calculated in the second semester of 2005). The Ministry reported that there were 0.61 fixed telephones, 7.14 mobile phones and 0.87 Internet users per 100 inhabitants.

The monthly price of 20 hours of Internet access is approximately US $74. There are six operators of fixed

Telecommunications are rapidly developing, SISTEC is a clear example

Internet services and two mobile Internet suppliers. The number of cyber-cafés operating in June 2005 was 22.

POSTAL SERVICES

With the approval in 2004 of the national strategy for postal services, Angola began modernizing this service. Estimated to cost about US $24 million, the strategy will take nine years to implement, divided into three phases.

The total network of ENCTA, the national post company of Angola, comprises 126 facilities, including 103 post offices. ENCTA offers the following services: standard post, express post (national and international), parcel post, telegraphic, postal orders and registered mail.

The strategy includes the computerization of commercial operations (front office and back office) of ENCTA.

Express mail services are also offered by DHL, SAGA, UPS, JF Aguiar, TNT, FedEx, GAC and AMI.

NEW DEVELOPMENTS

• Implementation of the government's investment programme for 2005–2006.
• Rail rehabilitation (Luanda and Benguela railways).
• Construction of a new Luanda international airport.
• Construction of a dry port in Viana.
• Rehabilitation of the lighthouses and navigation aids.

MAIN COMPANIES

COMMUNICATIONS

MOVICEL

Mr Francisco Basilio
Managing Director
Rua Mãe Isabel, n° 1, Luanda
Tel: +244-222-692000 / 692007
Fax: +244-222-692090
Email: francisco.basilio@movicel.net
Website:www.movicel.com

Activity: Telecommunications company

Since its formation as a mobile operator in 2003, Movicel has been confirming its commitment of being always in the vanguard of the communications sector, consolidating its position of telecommunications leading operator for innovation and quality of service in Angola.

Present in all provinces of the country, Movicel has permanent facilities to respond to customers, with its own stores' motto being "Sempre Consigo" (Always with you), which offer customers all the services that the company provides, as well as a free 24-hour customer support centre.

To guide the day-to-day work of the team, composed of about 400 people, Movicel adopted the values of: consideration; to respect and to attend to the customer's needs; always acting with honesty and integrity in all situations; clarity in information, and being clear and perceptible the whole time; innovation, acting with intelligence and creativity with a customer-focused attitude.

The goal of Movicel is not only to be close to customers, but each Angolan citizen. In the last few years, Movicel has contributed to the inauguration and restructuring of schools countrywide, with donations of school material and furniture and the construction of libraries. Besides projects in the education area, Movicel has promoted and motivated local culture, sponsoring cultural events and local artists' shows. Social responsibility is part of its day-to-day functioning, because Movicel is genuinely an Angolan company.

ANGOLA TELECOM

Mr João Augusto Avelino Manuel
Managing Director
Angola Telecom Building, Rua das Quipacas, n° 186, Luanda
Tel: +244-222-395990
Fax: +244-222-391688
Email: Sec_CA@angolatelecom.com
Website: www.angolatelecom.com

WELCOME TO ANGGGOLA

Angola has 3G. Third-Generation Technology.

Movicel has brought to Angola the world's most advanced and complete data service and transmission network. This 3G technology provides top-quality, secure and high-speed cell phone and mobile Internet services. Once again, Movicel is living up to its commitment to staying at the cutting edge of communications and providing its customers the best service all the time.

M VICEL
Sempre consigo.

3G

3G

Welcome to the next generation.

Activity: Telecommunications company

Date of Creation: 6th March 1992

Angola Telecom is the principal telecommunications company in Angola. It is the Angolan entity with the highest national and international presence.

Angola Telecom is a public company, established in March 1992 as result of the merger of two former para-statals, Eptel and Enatel.

• Eptel: Empresa Pública de Telecomunicações was established in December 1976 and started its activities in 1977 as a public operator of international telecommunications while the then Directorate of Post and Telecommunications continued to operate the domestic services.

• Enatel: Empresa Nacional de Telecomunicações was established in February 1980 by separation from the previously mentioned Directorate of Post and Telecommunications, which also led to the establishment of the Angola Post Office.

Angola Telecom has several social responsibilities and plays an active role in the progress of the country. The company has been sponsoring public and private institutions in the areas of health, education, environment, culture and sports.

Angola Telecom has turned into a successful company by providing Angolan society with telecommunications services of international standard for its social and economic development and the welfare of the Angolan people.

ARENA DIRECT

Mr Manuel Novais

General Manager

Rua Samuel Bernardo, nº 59, 1st Floor, Luanda

Tel: +244-222-393369

Fax: +244-222-397320

Email: manuel.novais@arenaangola.com

Website: www.arenaangola.com

Activity: Communication, marketing and publicity

Date of Creation: 2003

Strong relations with both public and private enterprises underpin the good work of this company, which always receives great praise and support. Its core businesses are marketing, advertising and special events. It currently covers all the needs in the Angolan market, where it is a leader, applying the latest trends. Its services are synonymous with quality and efficiency. Its adaptability and attention to customer service reinforces its credibility.

Whilst Arena Direct organizes exhibitions, its sister company, Arena Angola, handles the marketing and promotional tasks for all types of projects. Essentially it is a publicity agency that offers the full scope of services, ranging from publicity campaigns to drawing up a company's letter of introduction, and through to the shooting of an advert. Arena also organizes seminars, conferences, workshops and events for companies and private individuals.

Arena Angola has put its stamp on the organization of many of Angola's main events. It has excellent relationships with the TV, radio and press, which further endorses its presence in the market. Similarly its protocol and translation services come highly recommended, whilst it also has the capacity to produce and print all types of marketing and promotional material.

Arena Direct organizes various fairs itself, or in partnership with Expo Angola, making it the know-how leader in the market. Amongst its key fairs are Constroi Angola (construction), which is normally held in October; Feira Alimenticia (food and drink), which is normally held in May; and Feria del Motor, which is normally held in September. In 2006 Arena planned to organize the first Angolan IT Forum. The future will also see it organizing an Interior Design Fair and a Bridal Exhibition. Its partnership with Expo Angola also includes the installation of line stands.

CITELFÓNICA

Mr José Gomes Ferreira

Managing Director

Address: Av. Portugal, n° 75A, Luanda

Tel: +244-222-336542

Fax: +244-222-339498

Email: gf@citelfonica.com

Activity: Telecommunications-related services

Employees: 30

Citelfónica was the first private company created after independence in Angola. The company first started with Telefónicas Alcatel, and pioneered with all forms of digital equipment.

In 2001 José Gomes Ferreira re-established the company and created a new product: Angola Call. With this product, it was possible and easy to call at very competitive prices. Thanks to this technology, the company differentiates itself from Sistec, Telefonica, Unitel and Movicel, who provide the same services in the Angolan market.

Citelfónica has led a substantial programme of development in telecommunications with telephone, data processing on computer, network and Internet broadband. This technology has enabled Citelfónica to receive the Golden Award for Quality in 2003.

In the future, the company plans on developing communication infrastructure with American and European partners.

In 2006 Citelfónica will be represented in the Communication Museum, which confirms its reliability as a middle-sized company.

DREADLOCKS

Mr João Chagas

Managing Director

Av. Comandante Gika, n° 199, Luanda

Tel: +244-222-320281

Fax: +244-222-320399

Email: dreadlocks@snet.co.ao

Activity: Communication, publicity and film production
Date of Creation: 1990

Dreadlocks started as an independent/alternative production house with a social communication and arts bias in 1990 and was registered as a company in 1995.

Dreadlocks has produced 100 TV programmes – single and in series – and 15 video documentaries. The experience gained in broadcasting, in both TV and radio, by Dreadlocks has led to national and international recognition. Among other prizes, Dreadlocks was awarded the Premio Nacional de Cultura e Artes in 2005.

The company has an extensive filmography ranging from documentaries like *O Grande Desafio* (The Big Challenge) and *Massacre De Kassinga* to institutional video commercials such as the Tapolio's Stories series about vaccination against polio.

"I would like the people to know Angola better; we need the support of other countries to develop sustainable growth. They have to come and see for themselves the true Angola, see to believe."
Mr João Chagas, Managing Director

JAT – JEMBAS ASSISTÊNCIA TÉCNICA

Mrs Meganne Brechê
Managing Director
Largo do Soweto, nº 88, Vila Alice, Luanda
Tel: +244-222-638200
Fax: +244-222-638304
Email: jembas@jembas.com
Website: www.jembas.com

Activity: IT technical support
Date of Creation: 1989

At the end of 1989 a small group of young Angolan entrepreneurs, with much hard-earned business and technical experience both within Angola and overseas, decided to create their own company. The company aimed to respond to perceived customer needs for premium products and service support in the key developmental and essential industrial sectors of energy and communications in Angola. Starting with the supply and maintenance of diesel generators, two-way radios and communication systems, they called their company Jembas.

The sales, installation and servicing of generators and the development in wireless communication represented much of Jembas's growth for the first successful decade. However, capitalizing on the core skills base developed within these essential industry sectors of energy and communications, Jembas has gradually expanded and also diversified its activities into other related sectors including water management, refrigeration and cooling, construction and also servicing and supply of agricultural and transport equipment.

Its head office is in Luanda, whilst the main operations facility is at Viana. There are also several retail outlets in Luanda and Viana. The company has also expanded throughout Angola and today Jembas has wholly owned provincial branches in Cabinda, Soyo, Lobito, Namibe and Lubango. New branches are planned in the near future for the cities of Huambo and Kuito.

Jembas's success is not only based on its technical reputation for knowing the premium quality products that it sells, the services provided and the high calibre of its technicians and support staff, but also on its large stocks of equipment and spare parts. This commitment allows Jembas to be a single source supplier, from the initial appraisal stage through to supply and installation of products and the essential service and maintenance support.

Today Jembas employs more than 1,200 Angolan nationals and approximately 90 expatriates in its operations in Angola.

MSTELCOM – NEXUS, TELECOMUNICAÇÕES E SERVIÇOS SARL

 Mr Mario Oliveira
General Director
Av. Lenin, nº 2/4, Luanda / Rua dos Enganos, nº 1, 1st Floor, Kinaxixi, Luanda
Tel: +224-222-740020 / 397540

Fax: +224-222-390995

Email: comercial@nexus.ao / mario.oliveira@netangola.com

Website: www.nexus.ao

Activity: Telecommunications, Internet, fixed line and database services

Date of Creation: 2002

Capital: US $1.5 million

Turnover: US $7.5 million

Employees: 85

Nexus was the result of the merger between Ebonet, Netangola, Telesel and the participation of independent shareholders. In 2005 Mercury, part of the Sonagol Group, then bought it.

Its mission is to specialize in global communications systems, guarantee client satisfaction through understanding their requirements and fulfilling their needs, whilst constantly investing in technological and human resources.

It currently provides HUB satellite services (private satellite connections to voice and data that covers the entire African continent, although this at present is concentrated in Angola) giving its clients private VSAT services, as well as providing Internet and fixed wireless access based on ADSL (asymmetric digital subscriber line).

Nexus boasts a broad network of corporate clients, including Assembleia Nacional, Ministério Relações Exteriores, Ministério da Defesa, Banco Nacional de Angola, Banco Comércio Indústria, Banco Africano Investimento, Endiama, ENSA, TAAG, Angola Airlines, Sonangol Holding, Sonangol Distribuidora, Sonangol Pesquisa & Producção, Universidade Agostinho, Neto Universidade Católica, Universidade Lusíada, PNUD, and UHCR.

Its network of agents across the country provides the public with services for telephone and Internet access. Its expansion plan is to create similar services to the ones that already exist in Luanda in the rest of the country.

SISTEC

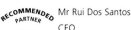

 Mr Rui Dos Santos

CEO

Av. Che Guevara, n° 138/195

PO Box 3245, Luanda

Tel: +224-222-330404 / 448700 / 325350

Fax: +224-222-332488

Email: rsantos@netangola.com

Website: www.sistec.co.ao

Activity: Diverse telecommunications-related services

Date of Creation: 1991

Capital: US $1.5 million

Turnover: US $20 million – asset value: US $50 million

Employees: 400

In 1981 Protecnica, the first private company in Angola, was formed. It consisted of three branches dealing with IT, cars and military equipment. In 1991 the company split into three independent parts, and the IT business became Sistec. Today Sistec has eight branches across Angola, and has five business divisions:

• Office Division (Minolta copiers/Riso duplicators)

• Computer Division (IBM business partner for iSeries, pSeries and xSeries, software development, printers and UPS)

• Systems Division (intelligent networks, Internet systems and services, integration of communications, PA, TV and other systems)

• Industrial Division (metalwork factory)

• Home Division (JVC, Sony and Whirlpool household appliances, and DSTV Multichoice resellers).

Each division is a separate business unit, with the Systems Division having the most growth potential in the market. In the next five years the company will be expanding its operations and creating two new divisions, Sismotel and Mampesa Village. This will see Sistec expand its activities into a hotel chain with business services for travellers. By 2007 it will have five hotels, under the Sismotel brand, with 240 rooms and 40 shops, targeting business travellers.

Mampesa Village will be formed from a 67,000-m^2 compound with a shopping mall with 60 shops, and a living area of 128 houses. This project includes the Equimina Valley, where there will be one agricultural project side by side with a lodge and beach resort.

Most important for the company in the coming years is the completion of these projects, plus sustained growth across all its divisions. Sistec is looking for serious investors for these new projects.

"When you arrive in Angola, give us preference."
Mr Rui Dos Santos, CEO

UNITEL SA

RECOMMENDED PARTNER

Mr Nicolau Jorge Netto
Managing Director
Unitel Building, Rua Kwame N'krumah, s/n, Maianga, Luanda
Tel: +244-923-199100
Fax: +244-222-371739
Website: www.unitel.co.ao

Activity: Telecommunications company
Date of Creation: 2001
Employees: 350

The telecommunications sector in Angola has achieved amazing development in the last five years, particularly since Unitel's entry into this market as the first operator to provide GSM services in Angola. According to the National Communication Institute (INACOM,) with the introduction of GSM in 2001, the telecommunications sector in Angola has undergone massive change. Today, Angola has new types of consumers and a culture with new telecommunications technology.

Over the past five years, Unitel has increased its number of clients and agents, as well as achieving expansion of the signal and improved human resources. Unitel believes that the success of its service is substantial because it has a team of young and excellent workers.

In its first year, the operator launched voice mail and SMS for 250,000 clients. Today, Unitel has over 1,500,000 clients. Unitel is in all the provinces of Angola, offering

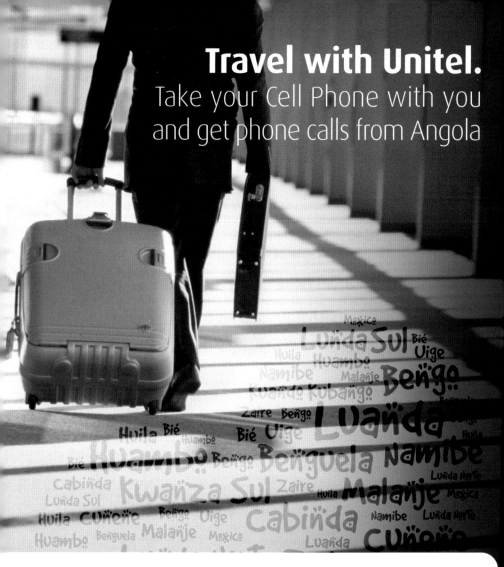

Travel with Unitel.

Take your Cell Phone with you and get phone calls from Angola

different services such as roaming, monthly contract and prepaid services. Unitel is now preparing to reach two million clients by the end of 2006.

Unitel's main goal is to work on the expansion of the GSM signal for more than 50 counties in Angola by the end of 2006, in order to increase the number of clients in the 'biggest family of Angola'.

Unitel also focuses on social programmes such as helping the Angolan community in health, education, culture and sport. The mobile company is the major sponsor of the Angolan football team, who participated admirably in the World Cup 2006 in Germany. In cultural terms, the company is supporting the Angolan Carnival in Luanda and Angolan musicians and painters (Horácio Dá Mesquita, an artist sponsored by Unitel, produced the aquarelle painting for Unitel's top-up cards).

Unitel is a company with Angolan managers, constituted as an anonymous society (SA) and includes Angolan entrepreneurs and international investors from Portugal and United Kingdom.

Unitel's intentions are to expand its signals across the country, putting all Angolans in communication, cancelling the distance between them and bringing them together.

"Unitel, the biggest family of Angola."
Mr Nicolau Jorge Netto, Managing Director

TRANSPORT

ATS

Mr Raul Gomes
Director General
Rua Amílcar Cabral, nº 13, Luanda
Tel: +244-222-398252 / 392444
Fax: +244-222-390275
Email: atslad@snet.co.ao / info@ats-angola.com

Activity: Cargo
Date of Creation: 1982
Capital: US $50,000
Turnover: US $2,500,000
Employees: 38

Infrastructure are improving

ATS (Angola) is an Angolan forwarding company with Portuguese capital providing air and maritime transportation of merchandise and goods from and to Angola and has been operating in the country since 1982.

The services offered by ATS are as follows:

• Freight forwarders
• IATA consolidators
• Sea freight
• Container transport
• Logistics
• Internal road transport
• Customs brokers

ATS is a well-reputed company in the transport sector thanks to its capacity for response, fulfilling customers' expectations in time, and treating clients, both private and company, with a high standard of quality, seriousness and respect.

The headquarters are situated in the capital, Luanda, and ATS is planning to open offices in Lobito, Namibe and Cabinda (where it is represented) in the near future as the company is expanding its activities, not only in Angola but also internationally, where it already has offices in Bissau (Guinea-Bissau), São Tomé (São Tomé and Príncipe Islands), Lisbon and Porto (Portugal) and through the GFG (Global Freight Group), an international association of forwarding companies.

"Our secret is experience, efficacy and transparency."
Mr Raul Gomes, Director General

CARGOTEAM

Ms Sonia María Gonçalves
Managing Director
Rua Amílcar Cabral, n° 23, Luanda
Tel: +244-222-394800 / 805 / 807 / 903
Fax: +244-222-394900

Activity: Cargo
Date of Creation: September 2004
Employees: 20

CargoTeam is a forwarding company providing air and maritime transportation of merchandise and goods from/to Angola. CargoTeam Angola opened its doors in September 2004.

The firm is boosting its presence in the market and has already more than 350 clients. Its success relies on the quality of its services, keeping its clients fully informed during the whole process.

It makes up to five weekly aerial shipments and weekly regular maritime loads in complete containers (20 and 40 foot) – as well as shipping vehicles and group loads every 10 days. The company also offers the following services:

• Customs forwarding
• Packing and storage
• Insurance
• Collections and deliveries.

CargoTeam Angola is a forwarding agent capable of handling all intercontinental shipments. Based on an unfailing network, it guarantees excellent service and timely deliveries. It has a direct link with customs and arranges for timely clearances and follow-up.

Although relatively recently in business, CargoTeam Angola has developed itself into a steady logistics service provider, aiming for a good product and satisfied customers.

"We treat the merchandise as if it were ours."
Ms Sonia María Gonçalves, Managing Director

DHL EXPRESS ANGOLA

Mrs Belinda Figueiredo
Sales & Marketing Manager
Rua Kwame Nkrumah, n° 274–276, Luanda
Tel: +244-222-395180
Fax: +244-222-390326
Website: www.dhl.co.ao

DHL is the global market leader in international express, overland transport and air freight. It is also the world's number one in ocean freight and contract logistics. DHL offers a full range of customized solutions – from express document shipping to supply chain management.

It transports shipments rapidly, safely and on time all over the world. The basis for this is its comprehensive network, combining air and ground transport for optimal delivery performance. On the one hand, this gives DHL worldwide reach, and on the other, a strong local presence and unique understanding of local markets and customers.

In the logistics area, globalization is creating ever more complex supply chains. Again, DHL's combination of global reach and local knowledge is a key competitive edge.

DHL Angola also offers a wide range of standard services as well as tailor-made industry solutions. This is the only way to deliver to the high standards that its global customers are demanding.

DHL's international network links more than 220 countries and territories worldwide. Around 285,000 employees are dedicated to providing fast and reliable services that exceed customers' expectations in 120,000 destinations in all continents.

DIREÇÃO NACIONAL DAS ALFANDEGAS

Mr Silvio Burity
Managing Director
Largo das Alfandegas, Luanda
Tel: +244-222-330331 / 339492
Fax: +244-222-339490
Email: alfandegasangola@hotmail.com
Website: www.alfandegas.com

Activity: Angolan customs directorate

Direcção Nacional das Alfandegas – Angolan Customs Directorate – is a part of the Ministry of Finance and has the following main objectives and duties:

DHL EXPRESS ANGOLA
222 39 51 80

Headoffice:
DHL EXPRESS ANGOLA
Rua Kwamme Nkrumah, 274 276 - Luanda
Tel.222 39 51 80 / Fax 222 39 03 26

Present in 11 provinces of Angola: Luanda, Benguela, Bié, Cabinda, Huambo, Kunene, Kwanza Sul, Lubango, Malange, Namibe, and Soyo.   www.dhl.com

Deutsche Post ❤ World Net
MAIL EXPRESS LOGISTICS FINANCE

• Implement and make effective statutes, prohibitions and restrictions under the law.

• Fight fraud and other financial crime.

• Support and give assistance to all import/export activities.

• Protect the population against goods that may be risky to public health and safety. For this purpose, the Directorate is responsible for the inspection of goods before shipment.

Its targets for the medium and long term include the following: make sure all customs duties and taxes are collected and implement all regulations, which are undergoing change in order to adapt them to the country's new demands and needs. The Directorate is trying to reduce red tape as much as possible and to simplify all procedures. Transparency and efficiency are its main goals.

An advanced business management information system is being implemented as part of a long-term organization plan under the Luanda Customs Project. This new plan tackles such topics as management, accounting organization, competition and marketing.

The main goal of the Customs National Directorate of Angola is to create conditions for exporters to bring in their goods with trust, good prices and fairness. Encouraging the emergence and strengthening of the national business as well as stimulating the reorganization of the formal market and reducing the impact of the informal trade in the economy are other objectives of the Customs National Directorate of Angola.

ENANA – EMPRESA NACIONAL DE EXPLORAÇÃO DE AEROPORTOS E NAVEGAÇÃO AÉREA

Mr Jorge de Melo
President
Rua Amílcar Cabral, n° 110, 3rd Floor, Luanda
Tel: +244-222-393744
Fax: +244-222-393626
Date of Creation: 1980

Activity: Angolan national company for airspace management and aviation development

ENANA – Empresa Nacional de Exploração de Aeroportos e Navegação Aérea – a public company created in 1980 under the auspices of the Ministry of Transportation, was able to secure Cabinet approval for a US $300 million strategic development plan to upgrade Luanda Airport.

Most of the financing will come from the development of hotels, shopping malls, a massive parking area, and a new cargo terminal on airport land. The parking business alone will generate some US $165 million over 10 years, and the cargo business another US $435 million, according to ENANA estimates.

Should everything be as planned, ENANA can finance the airport project with its own money and need not use resources from the government's budget. Foreign investors are welcome to take part in the company's concession offerings at the airport, the revenues from which will eventually help both to modernize provincial airports and to finance a long-term project for a second international airport in the capital to be up and running by 2025.

International transportation analysts recently predicted that as the conflict in Angola subsides, air traffic into the oil- and mineral-rich south-west African nation would increase at a rate higher than in any other developing country in the region. They cited Angola's huge economic potential and its key geographical location as the two main reasons.

FACAR ANGOLA LDA

Mr Nagib Farouk Farhat
Administrator
Rua Avenida 4 de Fevereiro, n° 59–60, Luanda
Tel: +244-222-333802
Fax: +244-222-311515
Email: facar.nagib@multitel.com.ao /
facar.info@multitel.co.ao

Activity: Import and trade of vehicles
Date of Creation: 1996 (in Angola)

Facar Angola is a branch of the Belgium-based company Facar. The company has been operating in Angola for 10 years and has acquired important experience in the market. In Angola its core business is selling and buying of new and second-hand vehicles. Facar trades in many brands, such as Suzuki, Santana, Mitsubishi, Toyota, Lexus and Nissan.

The company is also involved in the maritime shipping of any type of wheeled vehicles to Luanda. In order to provide this service, Facar also provides its clients with transit services such as customs clearance and door-to-door delivery. Although these activities are the main business of Facar Angola, the company also offers services of transport in Luanda and other inland provinces, as well as vehicle maintenance services.

Facar is currently undertaking the development of an 800-m^2 showroom with different facilities and car stocks. Its showrooms maintain a premium selection of quality contemporary luxury cars, as well as one of the world's most respected collections of 4X4 automobiles. Facar gives its customers an unparalleled car trading experience, with facility features, resources and amenities that reinforce its commitment to comprehensive customer

service and incomparable product selection. With a large group stock nationwide, customers can be confident that they will have the make and model they are looking for.

This company is also one of Angola's largest used car groups. Right from the beginning, its success has been based on its ability to offer the quality car people want at the right price.

In fact, people trust Facar because its combination of competitive pricing and one-stop-shop facilities makes the whole process of buying a used or new car easier for clients.

For quality, choice and genuine peace of mind at the right price, visit one of the best car dealers in Angola – Facar.

"I want to encourage people to know Angola; people here are very kind and very open for every kind of business. This country offers a very high return on investment for good partners. People should trust Angola."
Mr Nagib Farouk Farhat, Administrator

HULL BLYTH

HULL BLYTH

Mr Antonio Matias
Managing Director
Av. 4 de Fevereiro, n° 23–24,
Luanda
Tel: +244-222-310301 / 310571 / 310007
Fax: +244-222-310879 / 310309
Email: HBenquiries@hull-blyth.com

Activity: Transport

Hull Blyth Angola is a division of Hull Blyth & Company Limited (HB) based in London. With more than 150 years of experience in the Angolan market, and branches in the provinces of Luanda, Lobito, Cabinda, Soyo and Namibe, Hull Blyth is a leading company in the following areas:

Shipping: The HBA shipping department provides Angola's foremost and most comprehensive ship agency service, with a particular accent on oil field support and project cargo shipping services using an unrivalled network of offices throughout Angola.

Travel Agency: HBA looks after thousands of business people, project workers, oilfield employees and sailors each year, arranging travel to and from all around the world.

Manpower Supply: HBA is the industry leader in personnel supply in Angola. It provides a wide range of personnel to the oil industry, construction and other services industries.

Global Logistics and Freight Management: Provided in Angola through partnership with DHL, Danzas Air and Ocean, HBA's project forwarding solutions are targeted at customers in the select industries of oil and gas, engineering and construction, exploration and production, power generators and producing entities, mining and metals.

Transportation: HBA offers domestic and international transportation services at any time and to any destination around the world. The transportation capabilities include: dedicated carriage, shared-user fleet, carrier management, hazardous goods including packaged and bulk chemicals and petrochemicals, offroad services, time

specific services, fleet management, customs clearance, and document preparation.

MAERSK ANGOLA LDA

Mr Jan Sand Jørgensen
General Manager Angola
Rua Major Kanhangulo, n° 290 r/c, Luanda
Tel: +244-222-394306 / 324
Fax: +244-222-392363
Mobile: +244-923-543716
Email: angloggen@maersk.com /
anglogmng@maersk.com

Since Maersk Angola Lda was founded in 1998, it has been its primary goal to serve the Angolan import and export community with the transport solutions they require, when they require them.

Today Maersk Angola Lda is serving as agent for Maersk Line and Maersk Logistics, giving this company a unique ability to supply door-to-door services and value-added transport solutions to customers, making it the obvious choice for importers and exporters in Angola.

Maersk offers inland haulage, which includes transportation from vendors to the port of shipment, and from discharge port to the point of unloading the ocean container by truck and or rail.

The company ensure that products are moved at the right time to the right place. Whatever the need for inland transportation, you can count on Maersk to deliver an effective and cost-efficient inland haulage service.

The firm has its head office in Luanda and branch offices in Lobito, Namibe, Cabinda and Soyo, plus a dedicated Maersk Angola Lda team of operations staff in the port of Luanda.

PANALPINA

Mrs Eliane Britt
Marketing & Sales Manager
Rua Kima Kienda, n° 106, Estrada da Boavista

PO Box 3682, Luanda
Tel: +244-222-691000
Fax: +244-222-310034
Email: eliane.britt@panalpina.com
Website: www.panalpina.com

Activity: Freight forwarding company
Date of Creation: 1999
Employees: Approximately 260

Panalpina is the global market leader in providing safe and environmentally friendly integral logistics supply chain solutions to the demanding oil and gas industry. It has:

• More than 40 years of experience serving this industry. Leading offices in the industry axis – Houston / Aberdeen / Singapore.
• Operates in most of the major oil and gas exploration and production areas of the world.
• Industry focused supply chain solutions:
- Freight – air/sea/land
- Expediting – warehousing – packing
- Deepwater agency and husbandry services
• Offices in Luanda, Cabinda, Soyo and Lobito.

The Panalpina Group is one of the world's leading suppliers of forwarding and logistics services, specializing in intercontinental air freight and ocean freight shipments and associated supply chain management solutions.

Thanks to its in-depth industry know-how and state-of-the-art IT systems, Panalpina provides globally integrated door-to-door forwarding solutions tailored to its customers' individual needs. The Panalpina Group operates a close-knit network with some 500 branches in over 80 countries. In a further 60 countries, it closely cooperates with partner companies. Panalpina employs some 14,000 people worldwide.

PORTO DO LOBITO – EMPRESA PORTUÁRIA DO LOBITO

Mr Carlos Gomes
Managing Director

Av. Independência, Ed. Transportes

PO Box 16, Lobito, Benguela

Tel: +244-272-222401/410

Fax: +244-272719

Email: eplobito@netangola.com

Website: www.eplobito.com

Activity: Lobito port services

Lobito Port Authority – Porto de Lobito – is one of the most important organizations on the African west coast. It plays a key role in Angolan trade as it is located at a crucial point of the African port network.

Currently, The Republic of Congo wants to reinstate the exportation of gold through the Port of Lobito, as soon as the railways of Benguela are rehabilitated.

The Democratic Republic of Congo has more than 4 million tonnes of gold that are to be exported through the Lobitos Corridor, as it is the best way to get to the Atlantic coast.

The Port of Lobito is essential to carry out the industrial and commercial activities for the provinces of central and southern Angola and for those African countries that have no access to the sea.

The rehabilitation of the railways in Benguela, which is expected in 2007 and is being executed with Chinese capital and workforce, will boost the volume of operations and reinforce the commerce in the area.

Even though the railway system in Benguela is not yet operating, the Port of Lobito is progressing every year, with more that 1.25 million tonnes of diverse merchandise moved in 2005, against the 945,000 tonnes that were moved in the preceding year.

PORTO DE LUANDA

Mr Silvio Barrios Vinhas

Managing Director

Largo 4 de Fevereiro

PO Box 1229, Luanda

Tel: +244-222-310655 / 311201

Fax: +244-222-310355 / 311178

Email: geral@portoluanda.co.ao

Website: www.portoluanda.co.ao

Activity: Luanda port services

The natural conditions of this port, which is located on the north side of the Angolan coast, are among the best in Africa south of the equator. It is located in a large bay, whose general shape and dimensions facilitate manoeuvres, with the main axis running SW–NE and formed by a coast and the Island of Luanda. Commercial and industrial sections are located around the modern deepwater port and government and residential districts are inland on higher ground.

The port entrance canal varies between 24 and 33 metres. Apart from the oil industry, the Port of Luanda is one of the main Angolan industries. Around 80% of cargo passes through it.

There are two small places for ship repair for fishing vessels and small vessels. There is also a floating dock for emergency ship repairs up to 6,000 dwt and there is a quay available for tankers as well. The city's main exports include petroleum, diamonds, iron ore and fish products. Among its manufactures are refined petroleum, motor vehicles, textiles and processed food. Major imports include iron, steel, machinery, flour and coal.

The terminals of the port consist of a general cargo area, a multipurpose area, a container base and an oil supply base. The Port of Luanda has been certified ISPS compliant since 29th November 2004

SDV AMI ANGOLA, AGÊNCIA DE NAVEGAÇÃO E OPERAÇÕES LOGISTICAS LDA

Mr Bernard de Buor

Managing Director

Estrada de Cacuaco, Km 4, n° 288, Luanda

Tel: +244-222-841266

Fax: +244-222-840535

Email: shipping@ao.dti.bollore.com /

forwarding@ao.dti.bollore.com

Website: www.sdvoilfield.com/aang.htm

Activity: Shipping, forwarding, logistics, express courier, packing and removals

Date of Creation: 1931

Employees: 276

AMI has been in Angola since 1931 and became part of the French Bolloré Group in 1999. Now, under the name of SDV AMI Angola, it is one of the most active operators in the sector of logistics, being part of an international network covering 85 countries.

A wide range of services are provided, including air freight, sea freight, forwarding, trucking, handling, warehousing, storage, packing and removal, express courier. SDV AMI Angola acts as shipping agent for Delmas, Otal, Setramar, Hoegh Line, Lin Lines, the US Navy and the British Royal Navy among others, and is a member of the international AFRITRAMP network. It has strongly invested in Angola: a yard of 41,000 m² with spacious storage

facilities in Luanda, another yard of 39,000 m² with 4,500 m² of warehouses in Lobito, newly opened branches in Soyo and Cabinda. AMI is determined to continue to invest in the future.

AMI invests in training its staff as part of an HSE process. Quality and response are its clients' main concerns and to fulfil these demands AMI relies on its fleet of equipment, which includes cranes, forklifts, trucks, super stackers and ancillary machinery.

"We have been in Angola for more than 75 years. The experience speaks for itself."

Mr Bernard de Buor, Managing Director

TAAG – LINHAS AÉREAS DE ANGOLA

Mr Anastácio C.S. Fernandes

Communication Manager

Rua da Missão, n° 123, 11th Floor, Luanda

Tel: +244-222-633614 / 327112

Fax: +244-222-332714

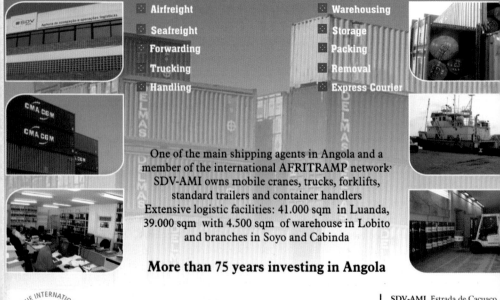

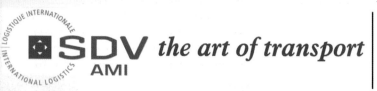

Email: anafer@taag.aero

Website: www.taag.com / www.taag.com.br

Employees: 4,000

Activity: Air transport national company

TAAG – Linhas Aéreas de Angola, UEE – was founded on 8th September 1938 under the name of DTA – Divisão dos Transportes Aéreos. Immediately after Angola gained independence in November 1975, it changed its name to TAAG and reorganization and expansion plans were implemented. In March 1976 the first Boeing 737-200 was put into service. On 9th September 1980, the Statutes of Linhas Aéreas de Angola, UEE were approved. These have been and are still today a legal instrument of great importance for the life of the company.

Currently, TAAG has a fleet of seven aircraft, which includes two Boeing 747-300 Combis for long-distance transfer of both passengers and goods, and five Boeing 737-200s, which are used for national and regional flights.

TAAG aims to continue growing, to consolidate its presence in the market and offer its customers the best of services. To achieve this, TAAG has implemented a programme for the renewal and modernization of its aircraft fleet, effective from September 2006. This programme includes the acquisition of four Boeing 737-700s (for short and medium distances) and three Boeing 777-200ERs (for long and very long distances). TAAG plans to increase the number of commercial flights.

The company offers all services: domestic, regional and international flights, for the transfer of both passengers and goods.

TAAG takes prides in the excellent relationships it maintains with its national and international partners. It believes that working together and collaborating with each other is the only way of functioning and developing as a company. It aims to achieve its customers' satisfaction and comfort.

TRANSCONTINENTAL

Mr. Pedro Salmo Fernando

Customs broker

Largo 4 Fevereiro, n° 3, Office 418/420, Luanda

Tel: +244-222-396884

Mobile: +244-923-417534 / 912-408442

Email: tcv@snet.co.ao

Activity: Import and trade

Date of Creation: 1993

Transcontinental Ltd was created in 1993 and it is a specialist in clearing customs, "*despachante & transitario*". As a dispatcher or supplier, they are one of the best intermediates in Angola and their activities as transporters are of the highest calibre.

The Ports and Customs of Angola are well known for their big transport market and large quantity of merchandise that pass by on their travels on a daily basis. A lot of merchandise arrives in Angola each day from every corner of the globe and to clear customs in a proper and quick way is not an easy task.

Customs brokers in Angola are mainly private individuals, more than partnerships, associations or corporations licensed, regulated and empowered by Angolan Customs Authority to assist importers and exporters in meeting national requirements governing imports and exports. Each day, brokers submit necessary information and appropriate payments to the Ports and Customs Authorities on behalf of their clients and charge them a fee for the service.

Brokers must have expertise in the entry procedures, admissibility requirements, classification, valuation, and the rates of duty and applicable taxes and fees for imported merchandise. Should you need your containers to arrive safely, fast and on time to their destination, trust Transcontinental Ltd. Mr Pedro Salmo Fernando, is an experienced businessman with a extensive knowledge about clearing customs in Luanda and who will devote his extensive experience to offer you the best of service.

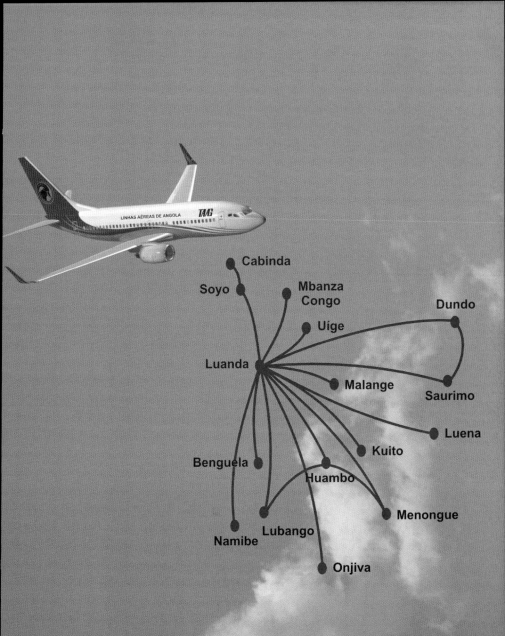

Cabinda
Soyo
Mbanza Congo
Dundo
Uige
Luanda
Malange
Saurimo
Luena
Kuito
Benguela
Huambo
Menongue
Namibe
Lubango
Onjiva

Sempre

33115

LEISURE

"Walking ten thousand miles of world is better than reading ten thousand scrolls of books."

Angolan proverb

OVERVIEW

The Republic of Angola is located in sub-Saharan Africa and has an area of 1,246,700 km, made up of 18 provinces. The north borders with the Republic of Congo Brazzaville, the east with the Democratic Republic of Congo and Zambia, the south with Namibia and Botswana, while to the west lies the Atlantic Ocean.

The national flag has three colours (red, black and yellow), a machete, a star and half a cogwheel:

• Red represents the blood spilled by Angolans during the war of national liberation.
• Black represents the African continent.
• Yellow represents the natural resources of the country.
• The machete is the symbol of the peasants, their fight for liberation and agricultural production.
• The star is the symbol of progress and international solidarity.
• The cogwheel symbolizes industrial production and the workers.

The Angolan population is estimated at between 14 and 16 million inhabitants, figures that will be confirmed after collation of the latest electoral census.

The official language is Portuguese, but more than 42 languages are spoken, of which Umbundo, Kimbundo, Oxikuanyama and Mbunde are predominant.

The official currency is the Kwanza (Kw).

A visa issued in the country of origin is required to enter the country.

The official time is GMT +1 and does not vary during the year.

HISTORY

The Angolan territory has been inhabited since pre-history and remains have been found in the provinces of Luanda, Namibe, Benguela and the Congo.

For centuries great migrations of the Bantu peoples occurred, who formed kingdoms and had a greater presence in the interior of the country.

When the Portuguese arrived in Angola towards the end of the fifteenth century, they established commercial relations with the Kingdom of the Congoja Matamba and the Ndombomuita, and they only entered the interior of the country later in the seventeenth century.

However, the partition of Africa between European countries towards the end of the nineteenth century at the Conference of Berlin determined the borders of each African country.

The slave trade soon appeared after the colonial occupation, and ended with the abolition of slavery and the independence of Brazil.

The patriotic wars date from the nineteenth century and grew more intense throughout the twentieth century from the 1960s, successfully bringing to an end the Portuguese colonial rule. As a result, the independence of Angola was declared on 11th November 1975. The leader of the MPLA – Popular Movement for the Liberation of Angola – Dr Agostinho Neto, was the first President.

President Agostinho Neto died four years later and was succeeded by José Eduardo Dos Santos, who has remained President through to the present day.

From 1975 to 2002, the date of the signature of the peace accords, the country suffered a civil war that destroyed all the territorial infrastructure and split up Angolans.

These times have come to an end and since 2002 the country has achieved renewed economic growth, stability and development. It has seen significant increases of its GDP, and it has stabilized its macroeconomic policies. These successes are recognized internationally.

TOURISM

NATURAL RESOURCES

Tourism in Angola has grown with the increase of both internal tourism and business-oriented tourism, which is a very important aspect for the development of the sector.

The primary resources of tourism are those natural resources that can be used in a sustainable way. Angola is without a doubt a country with a great natural heritage and an important and diversified environment, such as:

• Landscape diversity (mountain ranges, forests, desert, waterfalls, rivers)

• Ecological attractions
• Natural parks with specific fauna and flora
• Navigable rivers rich in fish resources
• Ethnographic and cultural heritage
• Hospitality of the population
• White sand beaches
• Temperate sea
• Sea with a variety of waves and rich in maritime fauna.

Angola has 37 protected areas, including the national and regional parks, forest, integral and partial reserves and coutadas (hunting grounds) that correspond to 15.1% of the national territory.

The fauna is diversified and includes the 'Big Five' mammals, some endemic species, such as the Palanca Negra (national icon), which can be found in the National Park of Kangandala in the province of Malange, the White Rhinoceros, a very rare species, and indigenous bird species, which can be observed in the province of Cuanza Sul.

CULTURAL RESOURCES

Angola has great potential for cultural tourism based on the distinctive historical and cultural factors of the people who inhabit it and, with over 500 years of colonial occupation, a series of monuments, fortresses, forts, churches, slave prisons and slave routes.

An important aspect of the history of Angola and its heritage relates to the foundation of the country, that is to say the Kingdom of the Congo established between the fifth and sixth centuries, whose remains can be found in the city of Mbanza Kongo.

All over the country, notable remains exist of cave art, an exceptional example being the archaeological site of Tchitundu-Hulo (Stone Age) in the province of Namibe.

There are 300 classified monuments that are in the process of being restored.

The church of the Muxima is the oldest in Angola and is located in the province of Bengo about 60 km from Luanda and dates from the sixteenth century.

Some other examples of the rich cultural heritage in Angola are:

• Fortress and Church of Muxima that date from the 16th century located in the province of Bengo.
• Church of Our Lady of the People established on 1st November 1548 in the province of Bengo.
• Fortress of Roçadas Forts and the monument of Mufilo in the province of Cunene.
• Fort of Silva Porto and embala Ndulo in the province of Bié.
• Forts of Kissala and of King Ekuikui II in the province of Huambo.
• Fortress of Caconda constructed in 1682 and the fort of Humbe constructed in 1857 in the province of Huíla.
• Fortress of São Fernando and the old prison in Namibe.
• Ruins of the fortress of Pungo-A-Ndongo of 1671 and evangelical church of the Quêssua in Malanje.

Roadside food stalls provide a cheaper option for eating

• Cave ruins of the fortress of Kibala and paintings in the Kibala–Luanda route.

• Cemetery Dos Reis of Cabinda (Mbuco-Mbuadi) and the church of S. Tiago de Lândana in Cabinda.

• Fortress of Mbembe and the tomb of the great King and Mbianda-Ngunga Warrior in Uíge.

• Funerary architecture and the site of Muacawewe, where the footprints of Txinguri and dog are found in Lunda Sul.

• Fortress of S. Pedro da Barra and the Palace of Iron in Luanda.

• Biggest museum of Angola and the Bala-Bala archaeological site in Lunda Norte.

• Sixteenth-century fortress of Massangano and the eighteenth-century fortress of Kambambe.

• Prison of Missombo and the ruins of the Muene Vunongue fort.

• Fort of Dilolo and the ruins of Moxico Velho in the province of Moxico, among others.

FOOD AND DRINK

In Angola food is based on the cassava and maize that is processed to make fuba. This in turn allows the making of funge or pirão, food eaten all over the country, which is one of the main accompaniments to go with meat and fish, and forms the basis of calulu, moamba, dry meat, cabidela, ginguinga, etc.

 Ice: As in all African countries, be careful with ice. Try to always get your drinks chilled, so ice is not necessary.

Grilled river and lagoon fish are very popular, such as the famous Cacusso, known for its odd taste.

Other frequently used elements of Angolan cooking are vegetables such as cabbage, leaves of sweet potato, bean leaves, jimboa, pumpkin leaves, gumbos, inhame, etc., which are used in the preparation of other accompaniment foods such as quizaca, machanana, mingeleca, usse, lombi, fúmbua, muteta, kapande, etc. eaten all over the country, and prepared in different ways according to the regions.

The best-known national drinks are ocisangua from sugar cane, ovingundu (mead), txikele, n'zuji, maruvo, quissangua, kacipembe or owalende from sugar cane, sweet potato, mango, banana, etc.

OTHER CULTURAL AND ETHNIC RESOURCES

Music and Dance

Music and dance are popular cultural means of showing feelings that characterize the beautiful country that is Angola.

Along with a diversity of musical styles, such as kilapanga, semba, rebita kuduro and others, Angola has the nationally and internationally known semba, sung and played all over the country and by artists of various age groups.

Dance forms include xinganji, txianda, maringa, massemba, rebita, muquixi, ngoma, marimba, quissanje, among others.

Artisan Industry

Basket making and weaving of mats are of Bantu origin and the raw materials used are staple fibres, stems, leaves and straw. To a great extent weavers use a basket-making technique called 'crossed and twisted'. Colours also predominate.

Fabric Weaving

In the past fabrics were made from rafia and cotton, but nowadays these have gone out of fashion. Currently the weaving production is starting to become more important, with the local inhabitants of the region of Buenga making fine items from the maiamba palm.

Sculpture

The art of sculpture in Angola is generally focused on the nude form. This cultural expression finds its greatest splendour in the province of Cabinda. The items that can be

found country wide are masks, wall paintings, sculptures and statuettes and the raw material is wood, ivory and xistóides plates. There is also religious art, such as crucifixes and religious figures in wood, brass and copper.

Musical Instruments

Angola is considered a very rich country from the musical point of view and recognizes its musical heritage. Percussion instruments abound, usually made from wood, such as kissanges (hand piano), rattles, 'violins' and some models of guitar.

For rhythm, there is also the reco-recos, whistles, xylophones, flutes, along with other models such as the marima, the N'Pungo (a sort of tube) to mention a few, that invite us to a discovery of strange noises.

Religious Festivities

There are two great pilgrimages in Angola, the Muxima (Bengo) and the Nossa Senhora do Monte (Lubango).

Great Events

Angola has experienced a resurgence of Carnival, the most important being in Luanda in terms of its exoticism, joy, rhythm, many colours and many people.

CAPITAL AND ENVIRONS

Luanda is the capital of the Republic of Angola, initially called São Paulo Assunção de Loanda, and was established on 25th January 1575 by captain Pablo Dias de Novais, who when disembarking on the island of Cabo found quite a numerous native population. The first Portuguese settlement was established there. He brought about 700 people with him, of which 350 were men of arms, priests, merchants and servants.

One year later, recognizing that it was not the best place for the capital of the conquest, he advanced to the mainland and established the village of São Paulo de Luanda. He laid the first stone for the construction of the church

dedicated to S. Sebastião in the place where the Museum of the Armed Forces is today. Thirty years later, with the increase in the European population and the growth of construction, the village of São Paulo de Loanda took on the role of city, with the township of S. Miguel extending to the plaza in front of the hospital Maria Pia (currently Josina Machel).

The Axiluanda (men of the sea) developed their own culture, while remaining part of the Ambundu ethnic group. The Axiluanda carried on cultural traditions of great importance, such as the traditional carnival, dances and parties. Among the typical dress, those of the fisherman, the grocer and the bessangana stand out. In dedicating customary rites to the Kianda (goddess of the sea), they favoured the carnival dances like the semba, rebita and kazucuta.

• Capital: city of Luanda

• Political/administrative division: the province has nine cities – Maianga, Ingombotas, Samba, Sambizanga, Rangel, Viana, Cazenga, Kilamba Kiaxi and Cacuaco, spread over 2,257 km^2.

• The biggest ethnic group is the Ambundu.

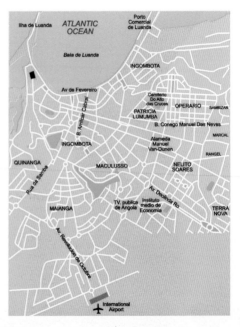

The Luanda Viewpoint

• The climate is tropical and dry and the annual average temperature is 25 °C.

• Luanda International Airport 4 de Fevereiro and the port of Luanda are the points of entry for sea and air travellers.

TOURIST ATTRACTIONS

Nature

The Cuanza River rises in the central plateau and flows into the Atlantic Ocean to the south of Luanda and is the country's biggest river.

The Island of Mussulo has a good beach for walking and beach sport. The waves are calm and the sea is good for diving. Its natural beauty and the viewpoints for taking photographs attract many tourists.

The Island of Luanda is the province's main attraction, due to its location and the beautiful beaches surrounded by beautiful coconut palms. To the right the sea is calm and excellent for swimming; to the left the waves are stronger, but even so are inviting for a good dive.

This place is ideal for leisure, with tents, snack bars and craft workshops among other attractions of interest.

The Cuanza delta, situated to the south of Luanda, is a place of paradise that offers a vast flora as well as a wonderful spectacle where the sea dunes join with the river estuary.

Artisan fishing is one of the main sources of income for the Luandan population who live along the sea coast and in the creeks of the Cuanza and Bengo.

Nice beach in Mussulo Island

The integral natural reserve of the Ilhéu dos Pássaros was established as a natural reserve on 21st December 1973, and its 1.7 km² area is famous for the diversity of migratory and water birds – and also mosquitoes!

History and Culture

The Church of NS de Nazaré, situated in the Praça do Ambiente, was built in 1664 and has a pink marble altar.

The Church of NS do Carmo is situated in the Irene Cohen plaza. It was built in 1669 and the ceiling was painted by hand.

The Church of NS dos Remédios, situated in the Rua Rainha N'Ginga, was built in the seventeenth century.

The Palácio de Ferro was built by Gustave Eiffel, dating from the late 1800s. It came to Luanda between 1901 and 1902 after the world exhibition, where it was bought by the Companhia Comercial de Angola. It needs restoration.

The Museum of Natural History is a building from 1956. It has two permanent exhibition halls, displaying mammals and fish. It also has an auditorium, a hall for temporary exhibitions and a library. It is closed on Mondays.

The Museum of Anthropology is located in the Rua Friedrich in an old colonial house and has an interesting collection of African art. It is open at weekends.

The National Museum of Slavery is situated 18 km south of Luanda in an old factory. It shows the history of and the route taken by slaves. It is open at weekends.

The National Museum of the Armed Forces at the Fortress of S. Miguel is located in Avenida 4 de Fevereiro and is currently dedicated to cultural activities.

The Hospital Josina Machel (formerly Maria Pia), inaugurated in 1886, is the main hospital of Angola and has been completely restored.

The Historical Landmark 4 de Fevereiro marks the beginning of the armed struggle against colonialism and is located in the most populous city of Angola, Cazenga.

The Mausoleum is being built in memory of the first President of Angola, Dr António Agostinho Neto.

The National Bank of Angola is a building constructed at a moment of strong economic growth in Angola. It is situated in Avenida 4 de Fevereiro, conceived by the architect Vasco Regalieira and inaugurated in 1956.

Where to Stay

NOTICE! Be aware that since late 2004, business in Luanda has picked up, there are a lot of conferences being held in the city and also many business trips, therefore we do recommend that you book your hotel room in advance, well before arriving in Luanda, as you risk not finding one.

Hotel Alvalade
Rua Emílio M'Bidi
Alvalade, Luanda
Tel: +244-222-327470
Fax: +244-222-327480
Email: hotelalvalade@netangola.com
Situated in a renovated and attractive zone of the city of Luanda, and near the International Airport 4 de Fevereiro, the Hotel Alvalade is the newest hotel in the country. It has 202 rooms, including 14 suites, a restaurant that offers varied dishes from international cuisine to the exotic Angolan traditional flavours, bars, four conference rooms, private parking and the full range of services worthy of a four-star hotel.

Hotel Avenida
Rua Cerqueira Lukoki, n° 120
Luanda
Tel: +244-222-334726

Fax: +244-222-334727
Email: havenida@netangola.com

RECOMMENDED

Hotel Continental
Rua Rainha N'Ginga n° 18–21
PO Box 5150, Luanda
Tel: +244-222-334243 / 396599
Fax: +244-222-392735
Email: reservas@hcontinental.org
Website: www.hcontinental.org
Situated in downtown Luanda, the Continental Hotel has a panoramic view of the Bay. It is 1 km from the Island of Luanda and 5 km from the International Airport 4 de Fevereiro, and one of the oldest hotels in the country. The hotel has 71 rooms, including 7 suites, and all the rooms are equipped with air conditioning, satellite TV, telephone with direct access to local and international networks, private safe and mini bar. There is a restaurant with à la carte service and international and regional cuisine, two conference rooms, a business centre, car hire, etc.

Hotel Forum
Rua Ho Chi Min, Luanda
Tel: +244-222-321858 / 324344 / 324348
Fax: +244-222-322193
Email: hotelforum@netangola.com

Hotel Marinha
Largo Morthala Mohamed
Ilha do Cabo, Luanda
Tel: +244-222-309399 / 304400

Hotel Mundial
Rua Conselheiro Júlio de Vilhena, n° 14
Tel: +244-222-390561 / 337239
Fax: +244-222-390460 / 390555
Email: novohotelmundial@hotelmundial.com

Hotel Tivoli
Rua da Missão, n° 85
PO Box 2049, Luanda
Tel: +244-222-392292 / 393890 / 393897
Fax: +244-222-335644 / 391128
Email: htivoli@ebonet.net

Hotel Trópico

Rua da Missão, nº 103, Luanda

Tel: +244-222-370070

Fax: +244-222-393330 / 391798

Email: tropico@netangola.com

Right in the centre of the city, only a few minutes from the International Airport 4 de Fevereiro, the Hotel Trópico offers the space needed for business meetings, conferences or for a pleasant stay. It has 280 rooms, including 8 suites, two restaurants, with highly specialized professionals and well-selected and prepared foods, offering a variety of international cuisine, six conference rooms, a business centre, private garage and all the services for a pleasant stay with the comfort required nowadays.

Hotel Presidente

Largo 4 de Fevereiro, Luanda

Tel: +244-222-311717 / 311449

Fax: +244-222-310607

Email: hpresidente@netangola.com

Aldeamento Turístico Roca das Mangueiras

Mussulo

Tel: +244-222-370731

Fax: +244-222-371030

Email: rocadasmangueiras@snet.co.ao

Complexo Hoteleiro da Endiama

Rua Houari Boumediene, nº 66–68

PO Box 5589, Miramar, Luanda

Tel: +244-222-447954 / 449852

Fax: +244-222-446937

Email: complexo2@snet.co.ao

Complexo Turístico Onjango

Mussulo

Tel: +244-222-638503

Fax: +244-222-638555

Email: onjango.pelicano@jembas.com

Website: www.jembas.com

Bungalows, restaurant, bars, discussion room and sports fishing. Visitors can participate in water sports, sports fishing and Island boat trips.

Complexo Turístico Turitanga

Barra do Dande

Mobile: +244-912-502719 / 204400

Email: turitanga@hotmail.com

It has bungalows, a restaurant, live music, camping, horse riding, river fishing, swimming pool, etc.

Where to Eat

Restaurante Abdeson

RECOMMENDED

Avenida Murtala Mohamed, nº 47, r/c

Ilha do Cabo, Luanda

Tel: +244-222-309587

Mobile: +244-923-424456

Surely one of the best and finest restaurants in town. Asian specialities, original and inventive food mixing different Asian influences. Beautiful indoor and outdoor setting and excellent service and attention to detail. Spend a nice day on the beach enjoying the cosy terrace. A must: try the Teppanyaki Asia for an unforgettable dinner.

Restaurante Arcádia

Av. 4 de Fevereiro, 134

Tel: +244-222-338474

Restaurante Bahia

Av. 4 de Fevereiro

Restaurant-Bar-Terrace

À la carte and self-service, with traditional cuisine and snacks, with background music and parking for 100 cars.

Bamboo Imperial, Snack Bar

RECOMMENDED

Rua General Roçadas, nº 43

Maianga, Luanda

Tel/Fax: +244-222-394716

Mobile: +244-923-962508

Email: bambooimperial@snet.co.ao

Brand new weight-watchers paradise! You can enjoy your lunches and dinners at this Snack Bar without losing your athletic figure. Perfect for quick lunches or to grab a snack at any point of the day without worrying about calories! The best beauty and relaxation salon in the city. You can have a snack while you wait for a nice massage or an impeccable manicure and pedicure or hair cut. Do not forget to try the multi-fruit shakes and enjoy the tasty light sandwiches and risk-free salads!

Restaurante Bordão

Av. Morthala Mohamed, 236

Tel: +244-222-337799 / 309028

Fax: +244-222-337799

Email: bordao@snet.co.ao

Restaurante Buraco da Floresta

Largo Gamal Abdal Nasser

Tel: +244-222-396319

Restaurante Cais de 4

Avenida Murtala Mohamed

Ilha do Cabo, Luanda

Tel: +244-923-315757

Email: caisdequatro@hotmail.com

Enjoy the view of Luanda harbour from its fantastic veranda. Do not miss the mouth-watering chocolate cake.

Restaurante Caribe

Avenida Murtala Mohamed, Ilha do Cabo, Luanda

Tel: +244-912-202887 / 923-446662

If you long for a tasty barbecue, this is the place to come for either lunch or dinner. If after the delicious meal you feel like relaxing, just stay and enjoy the live band that plays every Friday evening.

Restaurante Chez Wou

Av. Mortala Mohamed nº 50, r/c, Ilha do Cabo, Luanda

Tel: +244-222-309517

Fax: +244-222-309583

Mobile: +244-924-237190

Genuine food in a truly Chinese atmosphere served by friendly and efficient waiters.

Restaurante Chimazé

Rua Pedro F. Machado

Tel: +244-222-333376

ABDESON Restaurant, for unforgettable dinners

Restaurante Coconuts

Av. Murthala Mohamed, Ilha do Cabo, Luanda

Tel: +244-912-205777 / 923-581333

Relax by the sea in this nicely decorated bar. Try the excellent veal carpaccio or choose from the choice of cocktails. Very good service by friendly staff.

Restaurante Embaixador

Rua Clube Maritimo Africano, nº 72, Luanda

Tel: +244-222-396979 / 397157

Enjoy the fish in this nicely decorated classic restaurant.

Restaurante Esplanada Swim Bar

Piscina do Alvalade

Tel: +244-222-328133

Restaurante Fisch Paradise

Rua Paralela a Massano de Amorim, 11

Tel: +244-222-309175 / 309856

Restaurante Fortaleça de San Miguel

Fortaleça de San Miguel, Avenida 4 de Fevereiro Marginal de Luanda

When you visit this Fortress built by the Portuguese, after going for a walk among its walls and visiting the museum and enjoying the excellent view over the city, you can come and have a nice lunch at the Fortaleça Restaurant. We recommend sitting at their fabulous garden.

Restaurante Miami Beach

Av. Murthala Mohamed

Ilha do Cabo, Luanda

Tel: +244-923-573053 / 330700

Pleasant restaurant–bar by the sea. Come and join the salsa nights on Saturdays and dance until dawn or, if you prefer a more relaxing plan, sip a cool caipirinha while listening to live music on Thursdays and Sundays.

Restaurante O Garfo

Rua Emílio M'Bidi, nº 66

Tel: +244-222-320350

Restaurante Petisqueira

Rua João Morais

Tel: +244-222-333682

Restaurante Pimm's

Rua Emilio Mbindi, nº 102, Luanda

Tel: +244-222-326290 / 321970

In this restaurant the delicious traditional Portuguese cuisine is wisely combined with the chic decor.

Restaurante Pintos

Rua Atlético, nº 3, Luanda

Tel: +244-222-335-322

Fax: +244-222-392-358

A classic, now renovated. Very cosy bar and excellent cod fish.

Restaurante Saint Jorge

Ilha de Luanda

Tel: +244-222-309812

Restaurante San João

Rua Fernão Sousa, 8

Tel: +244-222-324368

À la carte service and take-away as well as typical Angolan cuisine specialities, shellfish, grilled and buffet food, with lively background music. It has a band at the weekends.

Restaurante Sanghai Baia

Av. Murthala Mohamed

Ilha do Cabo, Luanda

Tel: +244-222-309198

Fax: +244-222-309103

Mobile: +244-923-788188 / 924-296666

Email: shanghai_baia@yahoo.com.cn

Great place with a nice view of the bay, newly decorated in a trendy fashion. VIP rooms. Traditional Asian food.

RECOMMENDED

Restaurante Tambarino

Rua Amílcar Cabral, 23, r/c

Tel: +244-222-397343 / 396884

À la carte and take-away service. The cuisine specialities are varied with traditional, typical and buffet food. It has background music every day, and on Wednesdays and Fridays it has live music. For us, the best restaurant in Luanda. Chic, elegant décor and absolutely gorgeous food. The restaurant prides itself on its cod fish, but the meat dishes are also delicious. To end your meal, indulge yourself in the unforgettable desserts buffet. Excellent wine list and service. In the evening, you can enjoy a drink or two and some music in the cosy downstairs bar. The best and most professional catering in town. This should be your first choice for a pleasant dinner.

Restaurante & Catering Veneza
Rua Che Guevara n° 116–120, Luanda
Tel:+244-222-320954 / 328184 / 328283
Mobile: +244-912-200135 / 923-401900
Email: rest.veneza@netangola.com
Golden Award Tourism – Gastronomy Section (Troféu de Ouro de Turismo, Hotelaria – Gastronomia)
New Millennium – Spain 2005 (Premiação do Novo Milénio – Madrid Espanha 2005)

Amazing gastronomic experience! If you come to Luanda and do not try Veneza, you'd better not come to Luanda! We are not exaggerating! With the best quality, prices and

quantities in the city, the portions serve at least two very hungry people! Portuguese and Mediterranean cuisine. Do business or chat with friends over a dish of tasty home-made feijoada or delicious and unique Bife na pedra. Excellent take-away and home delivery in the near future.

Restaurante XL
Rua Ho Chi Minh
Tel: +244-222-321002 / 325993
À la carte service, self-service and take-away. The main specialities are fast food, pizzas and some types of buffet. It caters for baptisms and weddings and has background music.

Entertainment

Nightlife in Luanda is very animated and lots can be found to do on the island of Luanda and in the city, such as restaurants and terraces with live music, as well as pubs and discos with a variety of styles of music, not only Angolan, such as kizomba, semba and rebita, but also from

Angola is well known for its excellent hospitality

other African, American and European countries. There are also cinemas, shows and cultural centres, especially:

Casa 70
Rua da Liberdade 70, Vila Alice
Live shows with artists of national and international repute, enterprise festivals, banquets, weddings, anniversaries, events, and various celebrations.

Café del Mar
Avenida Murtala Mohamed
Ilha do Cabo, Luanda
Tel: +244-222-309241 / 309554
Mobile: +244-912-205777 / 923-581333
Enjoy a delicious caipirinha or a refreshing tutti-frutti juice while feeling the sea breeze. If hungry, just nibble the excellent club sandwich or go for the Sunday brunch. Make yourself comfortable in their wide, cushioned seats and make the most of the relaxing, summery atmosphere.

Other cultural venues:

- Centro Cultural Kilamba
- Centro Cultural Chá de Caxinde
- Centro Cultural Agostinho Neto

- Disco-Pub Chillout
- Discoteca Chihuahua
- Discoteca Bingo
- Miami Beach
- Disco Palós
- Salas de Cinema Atlântico
- Salas de Cinema Karl Max
- Teatro Avenida

Nightlife

For comedy:

Boite Adão, Clube Montana, Discoteca Acuarium, Animatografo, Brasília, Chavarote, Contencioso, Copacabana, Rex.

For a good night out in Luanda:

Bay In
Avenida Murtala Mohamed
Ilha do Cabo, Luanda

Peixe Grelhado; Batata e Feijão de Olio de Palma

Chill Out

Av. Murthala Mohamed

Ilha do Cabo, Luanda

Tel: +244-912-202887 / 923-446662

One of Luanda's most beautiful places at the beach. A great place to chill out in the afternoons and go partying when night comes. Special parties on Thursdays, Fridays and Saturdays. You can also have some dinner here.

Palos

Rua Frederick Engels, 10, Luanda

Tel: +244-222-394957

The most well-known disco in town. International music and ambiance. Unique! Nice open-air club in the centre of town. Often has themed parties and Latino nights on Thursdays to kick off your weekend in the best way possible. Come and make the most of the city's nightlife.

REGIONS

The regions in Angola are not specifically defined as zones for particular activities, not least tourism. The country is going through a development phase.

The following is a summary of cultural and leisure attractions in the various regions:

NORTH

Made up of the provinces of Cabinda, Zaire and Uíge, this region has the particularity of being the only province that is linked to the rest of the country only by air or sea, due to the flow of the Zaire River and to the fact of having to cross the Democratic Republic of the Congo.

CABINDA

Cabinda is the province of the country located furthest north and its main activity is oil exploration and drilling. However, there are other activities such as the wood industry, agriculture and traditional fishing.

Nevertheless, as in all the other provinces of the country, it has natural social and historical attractions likely to attract people, once equipped with support infrastructure.

• Capital: city of Cabinda

• Political/administrative division: the province has four cities – Cabinda, Buco-Zau, Belize and Cacongo, distributed over 7,270 km^2.

• The dominant ethnic group is the Bakongo.

• The climate is tropical and humid and the average temperature is 25 °C.

TOURIST ATTRACTIONS

Nature

The Maiombe Forest, with 290,000 hectares of tropical forest, is the main attraction of the province of Cabinda. It is crossed by major rivers. There are trees of more than 50 metres high, allowing the harvesting and processing of wood, mainly blackwood, ebony, ironwood, rarewood and African sandalwood.

The forest reserve of the Kakongo, with an area of 650 km^2, is situated next to the border with the Democratic Republic of Congo and is also delimited by the Luali and Inhuca Rivers.

The Chiloango River, navigable over a great length for small transport boats, is the most important of the province, which also has the rivers Lucola, Luango, Lulondo, Luali, Fubo, lagoons such as Bumelambuto and Tchiuksi, and lakes such as Sassa-Zau and Nkukulu that will be of great interest to tourists.

As with the other provinces of the coast, it also has beautiful beaches such as Malembo, Futila, Chinga, Capelo and others.

History and Culture

Place of the Signature of the Treaty of Simulambuco – owing to its cultural and historical value, and its location near the city of Cabinda, the place is very much visited.

Regional Museum of Cabinda (Building in Rock) – an important centre for research and collection of traditions relating to the province.

Ruins of old fortress of Cabinda – imposing historical monument with great cultural value.

Due to the Portuguese settlement of Cabinda, it also has great examples of religious architecture:

• Church of the Mission of Lucula Zenze.
• Church of the Mission of St° António.
• Church of S. Tiago Maior.
• Church NS Rainha do Mundo.

Cabinda also has great examples of funerary architecture, such as:

• Mbuco-Mbuadi Cemetery – cemetery dedicated to the kings of Cabinda, with huge sculptures that decorate the tombs.
• Tombs of the noblemen of Cabinda.
• Tombs of the Duke of Chiázi.
• Tomb of Macongo.
• Archaeological remains of the Ngóio.

WHERE TO STAY

Hotel Pôr-do-Sol
Rua das Mangueiras
Tel: +244-231-222684 / 222685
Fax: +244-231-224687
Email: hotelpordosol@supernet.ao
This hotel's main customers are the oil companies. It has 24 rooms, a restaurant, a swimming pool and a conference room.

Complexo Turístico Simulambuco
Rua do Comercio
Tel: +244-231-224648 / 224645
Fax: +244-231-224686
Composed of individual accommodation units, restaurant, bar and terrace, this tourist complex is well known for its conference room.

Hotel Maiombe
Rua Dr Agostinho Neto – Caixa Postal 95
Tel: +244-231-222572 / 224351
Fax: +244-231-224353

Where to Eat
Restaurante Ouro Verde
Rua Irmão Ventura
Tel: +244-231-220298
Fax: +244-231-220299

ENTERTAINMENT

• Dancing Samba Bar
• Discoteca As Tantas Há
• Discoteca Tchiowa

ZAIRE

Zaire is also a province where the main activity is oil, but it has other activities such as agriculture and local fishing.

• Capital: the city of M'banza Congo was once the headquarters of the magnificent and powerful Kingdom of the Congo, the old city of S. Salvador do Congo that was the entry point for the Portuguese in 1482 when Diogo

Cuanza River

Cão arrived at the estuary of the Zaire River and established relations with the Kingdom.

- Political/administrative division: the province has six cities – M'banza Congo, Cuimba, Noqui, Nzeto, Soyo and Tomboco, occupying an area of 40,130 km².
- The dominant ethnic group is the Bakongo. The climate is tropical and humid with an average temperature between 24 °C and 26 °C.
- The province is reached by air to the airports of M'Banza Congo and Soyo and Tomboco and by land from Luanda through the province of Bengo.

TOURIST ATTRACTIONS

Nature

The Pedra do Feitiço situated in Soyo is a place of great tourist value.

The Caves of the Zau Evua are located 80 km from the city of M'banza Congo.

Yala Nkuw (Tree of the Force) is the only example in Africa and was the place where the King of the Congo executed sentences.

As in all the provinces of the coast, Zaire also has attractive beaches such as the Sereia and the Pobres.

The Falls of Rio Mbdrige, as well as some lagoons, are good for bathing.

History and Culture

The ruins of the Old House of the King (today Kulumbimbi Museum) is located in M'Banza Congo.

The first cathedral ruins of the Catholic church of Angola, constructed in 1491, are in M'Banza Congo. They were visited by Pope John Paul in 1992.

The Ponta do Padrão is the landmark of where the first Portuguese missionaries disembarked in Angola in 1485.

Porto Rico is the port that was used for exporting slaves.

Porto do Pinda is an old slavery port.

WHERE TO STAY

Hotel Porto Rico
Localizado no Soyo
Tel: +244-233-278049

Hotel Estrela do Congo
Located in M'Banza Congo

UÍGE

Uíge province, a traditional farming area and a great centre of plantation and production of coffee, contributed greatly to the development of Angola in colonial times.

• Capital: city of Uíge.
• Political/administrative division: the province has 16 cities – Maquela do Zombo, Quimbele, Damba, Mucaba, Bungo, Bembe, Songo, Milunga, Buengas, Sanza Pigeon, Ambuíla, Uíje, Negage, Puri, Cangola and Quitexe, covering 58,698 km².
• The dominant ethnic group is the Bakongo.
• The climate is tropical and humid, with an annual average temperature of 24 °C.
• It is reached by air, via the airports of Uíge and Negage, and also by land. From Luanda the route is through the province of Bengo.

TOURIST ATTRACTIONS

Nature

The falls of the Cuilo River in Sanza Pombo, the falls of Mbombo of the same river, the lagoon of Luzamba and Mavoio, the lagoon of Sacapate, are places with very strong tourist potential.

The forest reserve of Beu, with an area of 1,400 km², has a diverse vegetation with a dense forest. The north is bounded by the border with the Democratic Republic of Congo, the west by the Zadi River, the east by the Beu River and the south by the town of Beu.

The Lagoa do Feitiço, and the legend that surrounds it, is presented as a great cultural attraction.

The most important rivers are the Zadi, the Lucala, the Dange and the Luvulu, which are normally navigable by small boats.

The lagoons of Luzamba and Mavoio are good for bathing.

History and Culture

The bust of the hero N'bemba, an old landmark of the city, is situated at the entrance of the N'Bemba N'Gango quarter.

The Pedra do Tunda is situated in Negage and is where criminals were judged.

The tomb of Mekabango, the great warrior in the resistance against the colonial occupation.

The tomb of King M'Bianda-N'Gunga, great king and warrior of the resistance against the colonial occupation.

The Church of S. José, next to the rocks of Encoje, dates from the eighteenth century.

The fortress of Bembe, constructed in the twentieth century, is situated next to the church of S. José.

WHERE TO STAY

Hotel Residencial Chave d'Ouro
Rua do Comércio
Tel: +244-233-220815

CENTRE NORTH
BENGO

Bengo is a province located on the coastal strip and has agriculture as its main activity, as well as sea and river fishing, which occurs mostly in the Bengo and Dande Rivers and produces two species of fish looking very much like catfish and cacusso. In the area of Ambriz and Cabo Ledo, the sea fishing is very rich for crustaceans (shrimp, prawns and lobsters).

The province has an extensive river network, with the Cuanza River being the most important in the country. There are also the rivers Onzo, Dande, Bengo and Longa flowing through the province.

Bengo has a variety of lakes and lagoons, with most of them in the cities of Dande and Icolo and Bengo.

The lagoons of Ibéndoa, Cabiri and Ulua are well known and appreciated.

Both the rivers and the streams offer wonderful environments that are highly suitable for tourist investment. The rivers are largely navigable, allowing tourist trips to appreciate the beautiful nature that the province holds.

The natural beauty of the 7-km beach of Pambala in the Libongos and the beaches of Cabo Ledo and Ambriz leave no doubt that Bengo is one of the provinces that have some of the most beautiful beaches in the country.

• Capital: city of Caxito.
• Political/administrative division: the province has seven cities – Caxito, Kibaxe, Catete, Ambriz, Muxiluando Muxima, Nambuangongo and Icolo and Bengo, covering 33,016 km².
• The dominant ethnic group is the Ambundu.
• The climate is tropical and humid, with an average temperature of 26 °C.
• Bengo links the whole country to the capital with its road network. Although it has a small airport, air travel is hardly used.

TOURIST ATTRACTIONS

Nature

The Barra do Dande is a scenic area with several beautiful lagoons and lakes, and provides great tourist opportunities.

The Barra do Cuanza has a rich natural landscape and features the bridge that crosses the river with the same name to the south of the province.

The locality of Cabo Ledo is distinguished by white, clean beaches located to the south of the province, and has good sea fishing.

The lagoons of Ibendoa, Cabiri, Ulua do Sungui are well worth a visit, and offer good eating out opportunities. The Ibendoa Lagoon is considered the mother of the lagoons and on 26th and 27th July each year there is a ritual to the god Kianda to ask for blessing and greater productivity in the local fishing activity.

The Quissama National Park, a major attraction in the province, is currently going through a process of repopulation of its animal life. Located to the south of the province, it has lodge accommodation. With 999,000 hectares it is considered one of most extensive national parks in the world.

The beaches of Ambriz and Pambala located in the north of the province are pristine.

History and Culture

The Church of NS da Muxima dates from the sixteenth century and is well known for the miracles that have happened there. It is also a very popular place for both national and foreign pilgrimages.

The Fortress of Muxima was built following the battle between the Portuguese and the Dutch in the sixteenth century XVI and is situated at the top of a mountain behind the Church of NS da Muxima.

Ruins:

• Fostuir da Quissama
• Farol de Cal de Bom Jesus
• Ruínas da Antiga Residência do Chefe de Posto do Bom Jesus
• Antiga Igreja de Jesuitas da Barra do Dande
• Sítio Arqueológico do Ambriz.

WHERE TO STAY

Quissama National Park (Lodge)
Tel: +244-222-440855
Mobile: +244-923-589879

WHERE TO EAT

Restaurante Mangais – Veranda dos Mangais Hotel & Restaurant

Barra do Cuanza – Clube de Golfe, Eco-turismo

Info in Luanda: Rua Major Canhangulo, n° 3 B, Ingombota, CP 1889

Tel: +244-222-391653 / 394825

Fax: +244-222-336633

Mobile: +244-923-408667

Website: www.mangais.com

Typical Village in Cuanza Region

For a top weekend! Full assorted Angolan buffet to start with before passing to the main menu, where you can try the freshest seafood you have ever eaten. It is bought fresh every morning at the local port fish market. Try the Kitetas in a superb sauce and the super-fresh Langosta (lobster buffet). The wines are good too. Keep some space for the wonderful desserts. Excellent service and attention to detail. Elegant atmosphere and incomparable environment. Before lunch you can have a ride on a horse-carriage and afterwards you can enjoy a nice boat trip in the Cuanza River. For a perfect weekend, and a wild and romantic time, you can stay at the resort's bungalows. You will definitely come back for more.

Restaurante da Pousada da Barra do Cuanza;

Barra do Cuanza

The boat trip along the river Cuanza is one of the services provided.

Restaurante Pescaria do Queirós

Cabo Ledo

It specializes in dishes based on shellfish and fish as a great attraction.

CUANZA NORTE

Cuanza Norte is a rich agricultural province, having arable lands mainly for producing coffee and cotton.

The province has a great industrial park at Cambambe, where the hydroelectric power dam with the same name is located. It supplies the provinces of the north of Angola, including Luanda, with electric energy.

Cuanza Norte has a long stretch of the river Cuanza, the biggest river of Angola.

A place of great cultural and historical value in the province is the tomb of Queen N'Ginga M'Bandi.

- Capital: city of N'Dalatandu
- Political/administrative division: the province has nine sities – Ambaca, Banga, Bolongongo, Cambambe, Cazengo, Golungo Alto, Ngonguembo, Lucala, Quiculungo, Samba Cajú, over an area of 24,110 km^2
- The dominant ethnic group is the Kimbundu.
- The climate is tropical and humid, with annual average temperatures between 22 °C and 24 °C.
- Although the province has an aerodrome and an airport for small/medium aircraft transport, travel by land is more common, with road and rail links.

TOURIST ATTRACTIONS

Nature

The beach of Kiamafulo results from the low volume of the river Cuanza and is good for swimming and sports.

The lagoons of Golome number almost 50 and are located in the district of Nguimbi-Songue in the city of Kambambe. They offer local fishing to visitors, an activity that has existed since the sixteenth century.

The forest reserve of Golungo Alto, with an area of 558 km^2, is excellent for a wide variety of hunting, due to the abundance of some animal populations.

Another one is the forest reserve of Caculama that is completely bounded by rivers and has an area of 800 km^2

The Botanical Centre of Kilombo is another attraction with its diversity of flora, including some rare species.

The Falls of Rio Muebenje are situated 10 km from the city of Cazengo, with waterfalls crashing down from a height of 110 metres and cascading onto an immense green plain.

The province has beaches along the river Cuanza, mainly in the city of Dondo.

History and Culture

The great tourist attraction of the province is the Fortress de Massangano situated in the city of Cambambe, alongside the river Cuanza, and constructed in 1583. It served as the starting point for the Portuguese when they faced the Dutch who occupied the city of Loanda.

WHERE TO STAY

There are no hotels at present.

WHERE TO EAT

Restaurante Oasis

Cuanza river bank

CUANZA SUL

Cuanza Sul is a province bounded on the north by the river Cuanza and has agriculture as its main activity. Fishing, mainly of crustaceans, also has quite a relevant role.

• Capital: city of Sumbe.

• Political/administrative division: the province has 12 cities – Sumbe, Porto-Amboim, Quibala, Mussende, Libolo, Conda, Ebo, Cassongue, Quilenda, Waku-Kungo, Eku-Seles and Anboim, covering an area of 55,660 km^2. There are a number of ethnic groups due to migration in search of arable land by various peoples. The ethnic groups Kibalas, N'Goias, Musseles, Mussumbas and Bailundos predominate.

• The climate is tropical and humid and the annual average temperature varies between 24 °C and 28 °C.

• The province has an airport at Waku Kungo and two aerodromes, one in Sumbe and another one in Porto Amboim. However, normally overland travel is used for the interior of the province.

TOURIST ATTRACTIONS

Nature

Cuanza Sul has a range of natural attractions such as the rivers Keve, Longa, Cambondo and Cubal, as well as the forest and caves of Sassa, the spa waters of Tokota, the medicinal waters of Waco, the caves of Kicombo, the waterfalls of Binga and the estuary of the river Keve.

The estuary of the river Keve or Cuvo is located between the cities of Sumbe and Porto Amboím, towards the Atlantic Ocean.

The river Keve or Cuvo is deep and navigable and offers excellent conditions for water sports, fishing and hunting ducks.

Its 6 km has nice beaches and there is beautiful vegetation along its banks, with regional plants. It would be well suited to the construction of a tourist complex.

The Quedas de água das Cachoeiras (waterfalls) are a truly wonderful sight. The Binga waterfalls are located along the Sumbe–Gabela road and offer a panoramic view, inhabited by beautiful flocks of birds and many plants.

The forest and caves of Sassa is a place of geographic and archaeological interest, located 5 km downtown from Sumbe, and is an area with much vegetation, offering a highly attractive and scenic forest where it is possible to view the caves and the environment around you.

The caves of Sumbe, formed by limestone stalactites and stalagmites, are some 11 km from the city of that name and can be considered one of the best in the world for their size.

The Bay of Kicombo, situated 15 km from Sumbe, is a real spectacle.

With its natural attractions the province enjoys favourable conditions for camping. There are three camp sites, one in Sumbe, one in Gabela and another in Wuako Kungo.

History and Culture

The province is a great source of religious, funerary, civil and military architecture, with monuments, archaeological fortresses and remains of great cultural and historical interest.

The Fortress of the Libolo has evidence of the revolt of Libolo in 1917 between the colonial population and forces in the Pedra Escrita.

Other sites of interest:
• Ruins of the Fortim of Kicombo
• Ruins of the Fortress of Kibala
• Ruins of the old Military Barracks of Novo Redondo
• Fortress of Amboim
• Fortress of Seles
• Wall of the Kariango
• The Mother Church

WHERE TO STAY

Hotel Ritz
Rua Marginal no Sumbe
Tel: +244-236-230761

Hotel Sôl Nacional
Rua Marginal no Sumbe
Tel: +244-236-230440

WHERE TO EAT

Restaurante O Príncipe
Rua Marginal no Sumbe
Tel: +244-236-230079

Restaurante Salão de Chá
Largo Dr Agostinho Neto
Tel: +244-236-220261

MALANJE

Malanje province's main activity is agriculture, but it is also know for its craft work. There are three craft work centres in the province in the cities of Marimba, Quirima and Massango.

Of strong historical and cultural interest is the Massacre da Baixa de Kassanje, the first great moment of the Angolan nationalistic rebellion, where on 4th January 1961 workers of the Cotonang firm rebelled against the Portuguese colonialists and in response they suffered an act of repression, particularly from the air force.

• Capital: city of Malanje.
• Political/administrative division: the province has 14 cities – Malanje, Massango, Marimba, Calandula, Caombo, Cunda Dia Baze, Cacuso, Kiwaba Nzoji, Quela, Mucari, Cangandala, Kambundi Katembo, Quirima and Luquembo, over 97,602 km^2.
• The dominant ethnic groups are the Ambundu, Kimbundu and Kikongo.
• The climate is tropical and humid, with annual average temperature of 22 °C.
• The province has an airport in the city of Malanje and

an aerodrome in Kapanda. From Luanda, Malanje is reached by a road crossing the provinces of Bengo and Cuanza Norte.

TOURIST ATTRACTIONS

Nature

Malanje has the benefit of two river basins, of the rivers Cuanza and Zaire.

One of the most beautiful sites in the world is here – the Falls of Kalandula are outstanding. Among other attractions are the falls of Luondo in Cangandala, the island of Cuanza in Cangandala, and the fast falls of the Lui in Kumba-dia-Base.

The Black Rocks of Pungo-A-Ndongo not only have natural but also historical and cultural value because the foot-prints of Queen N'ginga M'Bandi, her dog and the prints of her cane are marked there.

Malanje also has the privilege of having a rare species in its territory – the Giant Palanca Negra – an inhabitant of the National Park of Kangandala, which has an area of 600 km^2 and was established as a national park in 1970.

History and Culture

From a historical and cultural point of view, Malanje's major attractions include the tomb of Ngola Mbandi and the cemetery of Kambundi Katembo.

The Furnas de Cacolo are ruins of primitive habitations underneath rocks, and natural graves are found here.

The Evangelical Church of Quêssua is also an important cultural reference in the province.

WHERE TO STAY

Hotel Gigante
Rua Praça do Comércio
Tel: +244-251-232208

Hotel Palácio Regina
Rua Henrique de Carvalho

WHERE TO EAT

Restaurante Kukina
Rua Comandante Dangereux
Has a disco.

Restaurante Marcos
Rua Comandante Dangereux

Restaurante Piquenique
Rua Comandante Dangereux
Tel: +244-251-222634

ENTERTAINMENT

Discoteca Cantinho da Marimba
Rua Cândido dos Reis

A giant Palanca Negra in Malanje

CENTRE SOUTH

BENGUELA

Benguela is a province with its own specialities, such as the influence of the cold current of Benguela that comes from the Antarctic, the climate and the economic importance of the Port of Lobito and the Benguela Railway, along which goods move from the interior to the coast and vice versa, crossing the country from east to west and crossing the borders of the Democratic Republic of Congo and the Republic of Zambia.

Due to its location, it has become the connecting point between several regions of the country.

Situated on the Benguela coast it has famous beaches such as Lobito, Caotinha, Caota, etc.

Benguela has two airports, one in Benguela and another one in Catumbela, and besides access by road, it is possible to arrive by sea through the port of Lobito, where there are movements of large cargo and passenger ships.

• Capital: Benguela.
• Political/administrative division: the province has nine cities – Benguela, Lobito, Bocoio, Caimbambo, Cubal, Chongoroi, Ganda, Baía-Farta and Balombo over an area

Pedras Negras de Pungo A Ndongo, Malanje

of 37,802 km².   ming, bathing, fishing and water sports.

• The dominant ethnic group is the Ovimbundu with
some predominance also of the Nganguela. Offshore fishing allows catches of fish with great sport-
• The tropical barren climate is influenced by the cold current ing value such as the large catfish, tuna, daurade and the
of Benguela and the annual average temperature is 24 °C. hogfish, among others.

TOURIST ATTRACTIONS

Nature

The Regional Park of Chimalavera is the main nature reserve of the province, with a diversified fauna and an area of 150 km².

Benguela has a variety of natural attractions such as its The Reserva Parcial of the Buffalo was created in 1974, beaches, the Lobito sandbank, the river Catumbela and and owes its name to the black buffalo that predominates nature reserves. Such beaches are favourable for swim- nates, covering an area of 400 km².

Lovely sunsets & beautiful beaches are synonymous with great tourist attractions

The Praia Morena extends for some kilometres and is a favourite with courting couples, with its white sand beaches.

The Praia da Caota is located 10 km from the centre and extends for 400 metres. Its waters are clean and quite calm. The Caota combines sand and pebbles and is becoming an ideal place for underwater fishing.

The Praias do Lobito are easy to find due to the proximity of places to stay. The beaches of Restinga, Compao, Cabaia and Liro are notable.

The rivers and lakes of Cavaco, Capilongo, Catumbela, Gunge, Coringe, Unchi, among others are part of the hydrographic network of the province.

History and Culture

The Church of NS do Pópolo was built in 1748 in the baroque style and is considered a national monument.

The Ermida da NS dos Navegantes was built in 1957, on the crest of the mountain, and the architecture includes a cross that can be seen from afar when illuminated.

The Capela da NS da Graça is situated in the district of Cavaco, 3 km north of Benguela. Even today there are great festivities in honour of NS da Graça.

The Ponta do Sombreiro is a lighthouse located in the western part of the Bay of Benguela about 10 km west of the city, positioned high up in the form of a sombrero. The Palace of the Government, located in Lobito, is an example of old colonial architecture.

See also the Church of NS da Arrábid and the Quilve Lighthouse in Lobito.

WHERE TO STAY

Benguela
Hotel M'ombaka
Rua Massano de Amorim, n° 33

Hotel Luso
Av. Aires de Almeida Santos
Tel: +244-272-23668 / 231292
Fax: +244-272-236680
It has 30 rooms, 10 suites, restaurant, leisure area and cyber café.

Hotel Praia Mar
Complexo Turístico Baia Azul

Hotel Navegante
Rua 25 de Abril, Lobito

Notel Términus
Praça 11 de Novembro

Hotel Turimar

WHERE TO EAT

Restaurante Gunga
Rua 15 de Agosto, n° 9, r/c, Lobito

Restaurante O Escondidinho
Rua Cândido Reis, Benguela
Tel: +244-272-233206

Restaurante Sombra
Rua Ilha da Madeira, Benguela
Tel: +244-272-233152

Restaurante Tan-Tan
Rua 10 de Fevereiro, Benguela
Tel: +244-272-234174

Restaurante Zulo
Restinga do Lobito
Mobile: +244-923-437610

Restaurante Cabana
Ponta da Restinga, Lobito

Restaurante Sol e Mar
Ponta da Restinga, Lobito

Restaurante Bambus
Rua Neves Ferreira, Catumbela

Restaurante Chicoil
Aeroporto de Benguela

HUAMBO

Located in the central plateau of Angola, Huambo has as its main attraction the Morro do Moco, at 2,620 m high the highest point in Angola, in a beautiful location to the north of the city of Ekunha.

Agriculture is the main economic activity of the province, which has a large industrial park and the second-biggest hotel network in Angola closely following Luanda.

The province has an airport that is one of the best in the country. It has a runway of about 2,800 m. Two national highways link Luanda to Huambo. One goes via Calulo and another via Sumbe and Benguela.

• Capital: city of Huambo.
• Political/administrative division: the province has 11 cities: Huambo, Londuimbale, Bailundo, Katchiungo, Thicala Tcholohanga, Ucuma, Ecunha, Mungo, Tchinjenje, Longonjo and Caála, over an area of 34,270 km².
• The main ethnic group is the Ovimbundu.
• The climate is tropical and upland with a dry, cold season and another rainy one, where it is hardly ever warm, therefore the precipitation is constant. The annual average temperature is lower than 19 °C.

TOURIST ATTRACTIONS

Nature

Another great tourist attraction is the Ilha dos Amores in Ekunha, also known for its fantastic landscape.

The mountain of Hama is another natural attraction for its climate, the cleanliness of its rivers and for the mineromedicinal water that it produces – the spa waters of Hama.

Another place of interest is the fish reservoir, integrated into the Centre of Studies of the Sacahala, near the road to the province of Bié.

Other attractions are:
• Very pure waters of the Lépi
• Greenhouse of Grania
• Regional Forest of Sacahala
• Green Forest of Chianga and its lagoons
• Cave of Bela Vista
• Landscape Cave of Chinhama.

History and Culture

Embala Grande do Huambo is a historical site that is a mixture of walls, underground areas, caves, and brooks that strangely disappear under rocks, reappearing later at another point of their mysterious journey.

The Municipal Museum has sections on ethnography, pictures and photographs.

The Nine Statues spread over the gardens of the city show a little cultural wealth of the province.

The ruins of Embala Grande, with its walls, is 20 km from Huambo.

The Underground Tunnel was where Soba Candumbo sheltered.

The Mount of Santo António do Bailundo is the place of King Ekuikui's tomb.

WHERE TO STAY

Hotel Nino
Rua 5 de Outubro
Tel: +244-241-222780 / 222787 / 222799
Fax: +244-241-222788
It has 55 rooms, 5 suites, restaurant and bar.

Hotel Konjevi

Pensão Ekumbi

WHERE TO EAT

Restaurante Petisco GiGi
Rua Dr Lacerda
Tel: +244-241-220258

Restaurante Novo Império
Rua Dr Lacerda
Tel: +244-241-223176

ENTERTAINMENT

Some discos exist and also a leisure centre. The city feasts are on 21st September.

BIE

Bié is interesting because its location determines the centre of the country.

The province has agriculture as its main activity, which takes advantage of an extensive hydrographic network, especially the rivers Cuanza, Luando, Kunhinga and Cune.

Bié has an airport at Kuito and aerodromes at Andulo, Kuemba, Nharea, Chitembo and Kamacupa.

Five roads link the province to five other provinces.

• Capital: city of Kuito.
• Political/administrative division: the province has nine cities: Kuito, Kunhinga, Andulo, N'harea, Chinguar, Chitembo, Katabola, Kamacupa and Kuemba, over an area of 70,314 km².
• The biggest ethnic group is the Ovimbundu.
• The climate is tropical and humid upland and has an annual average temperature of 19 °C.

TOURIST ATTRACTIONS

Nature

Bié is one of the highest points in Angola, and is crossed by some rivers that provide attractive fluvial beaches such

as Andulo (blue beach), Kunhinga (green beach) and the beach of Kuito.

The fact of the Cuanza, the biggest river in Angola, having its source there is the main notable fact.

The forest zone around the river Kuquema is a reserve bordered by the rivers Cune, Cuanza and Chimandianga and has an area of 4,500 km².

Other places of interest:
• Lagoons of Chitende and Senogue
• Thermal waters of Chitocota
• Palaeolithic cave
• Bombo, Hundo, Lungundua and Kalijongo caves.

History and Culture

Buildings of interest include the residence of the sadly missed Dr Agostinho Neto, the first City Council of Silva Porto, the National Bank of Angola of Silva Porto and the Catholic Church of Embala Jamba.

The Jardim Pouca Vergonha is situated in the centre of the city and owes its name to a statue of a naked woman.

The Statue of Christ the King (Centre of Christ King) demarcates the geographic centre of Angola in the city of Camacupa.

Other places of interest:
• Forte de Silva Porto
• Forte de N'harea
• Forte de Munhango
• Antiga Cadeia dos Indígenas.

ENTERTAINMENT

The festivities of the city start on 15th August and finish on the 31st of the same month. Other related regional festivities in the life of the community exist such as the Evamba (feast of circumcision), the Ayele (traditional feast with clowns and dances and banquets) and the Uvala (wedding feast), among others.

SOUTH
HUÍLA

Huila is a province whose main activity is cattle and agriculture. It has a high tourist potential for places of interest and wonderful small farms.

The province has an airport at Lubango. There are three runways for small aircraft in Jamba, Matala and Caluquembe.

The province is reached by road from Benguela, Namibe, Huambo and Cunene. By rail you cross from Namibe to Matala.

Senhora do Monte Huila

- Capital: city of Lubango.
- Political/administrative division: the province has 13 cities – Quilengues, Lubango, Humpata, Chibia, Gambos, Quipungo, Caluquembe, Caconda, Chicomba, Matala, Jamb, Chipindo and Kuvango over an area of 275,002 km^2.
- The predominant ethnic group is the Nyaneka-Nkumbe.
- The climate is tropical, wet upland and the average temperature is 19 °C.

TOURIST ATTRACTIONS

Nature

Huíla is crossed by the river Cunene to the east and the river Caculevar to the south. It has some lakes such as the Lake of Quipungo, the Lake of Tchivinguiro and the Lake of Arimba. Other lake formations come from two dams of the Tundavala and the das Neves.

The fauna is very rich with elephant, lion, palanca, olongo and guelengue predominating, and more particularly the black buffalo.

From the top of the mountain the Tundavala Rift in Lubango gives a panoramic view of the city of Namibe. The national park of Bicuar, with an area of 7,900 km^2, was established as a natural hunting reserve in 1938, where you can find various species of animals and a diversified flora.

The forest reserve of Guelengue and Dongo is completely bounded by rivers and has a 1,200 km^2 area.

The Leba Mountain Range has a tarred road that links the cities of Lubango and Namibe and is extremely tortuous.

Other places of interest:
- Caves and Lago Ondimba
- Lagoon of Tchivinguiro
- Lagoon of Quipungo
- Boca da Humpata viewpoint
- Bimbe viewpoint
- Das Neves dam
- Cascade of Huíla
- Cascade of the Humpata Animal Station.

History and Culture

The old Palace of the Government was built in 1887.

The old City Hall was built between 1900 and 1915.

The old Railway Station was built between 1905 and 1923.

The Chapel of Our Lady of the Mount, situated in Lubango, was built in 1919.

The Fortress of Caconda was built in 1682.

The Fort of Huíla was built in 1845 by Lieutenant João Francisco Garcia in the immediate vicinity of the Huíla waterfall.

Cristo Rei in Huíla

The Cathedral was built in 1939.

The Monument of Christ the King was built where the founders of the city were welcomed in 1884–1885.

The Barracões is a historical place where the founders of city were welcomed in 1884–1885.

WHERE TO STAY

Grande Hotel da Huíla
Avenida Dr Agostinho Neto
Tel: +244-261-220512

Complexo Turístico Ondyelwa Lodge
Tel: +244-261-220159

Complexo Turístico Munhonguera Lodge
Nossa Senhora do Monte
Tel: +244-261-220183

Hotel Amigo

Hotel Império
Rua Deolinda Rodrigues

WHERE TO EAT

Restaurante A Cubata
Complexo Nossa Senhora do Monte
Tel: +244-261-221442

Restaurante Restauração
Prédio do Comercio Interno
Tel: +244-261-221947

Restaurante Cascata
Rua Hoyji Ya Henda

Tirol Restaurant

ENTERTAINMENT

Boite Diplomata
Casino da Nossa Senhora do Monte
Clube Desportivo Ferroviário
Clube Desportivo Sport Lubango e Benfica
Complexo da Nossa Senhora do Monte
Dancing Amigo
Inter Club do Lubango
Sala de Jogos 'o Bingo'.

NAMIBE

Namibe is the biggest fishing centre of the country and the Port of Namibe is the starting point of the Mocamedes railway line (CMF) that links the coast to the iron mines of Jamba.

The main economic activity of the population is fishing, although agriculture and cattle have some importance in the economy of the province.

The province has an airport, but also it has road and sea access.

• Capital: city of Namibe.
• Political/administrative division: the province has five cities: Namibe, Camucuio, Bibala, Virei and Tombwa over an area of 58,137 km^2.
• The climate is tropical barren with an annual average temperature of 21 °C.

TOURIST ATTRACTIONS

Nature

The coastal desert allows Namibe to offer one of the best climates, if not the best, of the coast of Angola.

The estuary of the river Cunene offers fabulous freshwater beaches, along with several others such as Bonfim, Amélia, Farolin Noronha, the Moçâmedes bay beach, etc.

From the estuary of the river Cunene up to the north coast of the province, the conditions for fishing, water sports and underwater hunting are favourable.

Cave Paintings in Namibe Province

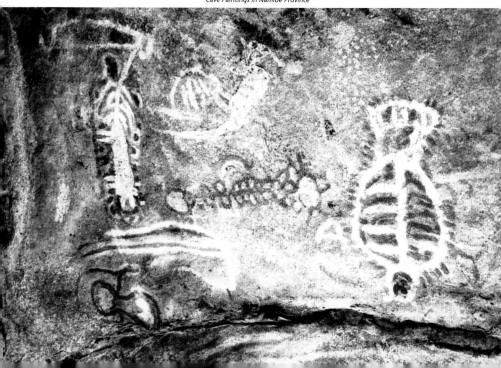

Despite all these attractions, the Namibe desert also occupies its place in the world due to the existence there of the rare exotic plant Welwitchia Mirabilis.

The national park of Iona was established as a national park in 1964. It has an area of 15,150 km^2 and the animals that stand out in importance are the quelengue and mountain zebra.

The special reserve of Namibe was established as a special reserve in 1957. It has an area of 4,450 km^2 and the animals that stand out are the black ostrich, rhinoceros, mountain zebra, suricat and quelengue.

HISTORY AND CULTURE

The Quipola Chapel is in the area of Benfica, in the city of Namibe.

The Chapel of the Amélia Beach is 2 km from the city of Namibe.

The Fortress of S. Fernando (current military unit of the navy) is situated in the city of Namibe.

The Fortress of Kapangombe is in the city of Bibala and was used to house slaves before embarking for the Americas. It is the current army barracks.

The Government Palace is located in the centre of the city, on the Marginal do Namibe.

WHERE TO STAY

Hotel Moçâmedes
São João
Tel: +244-264-261165

Hotel Residencial Mariner
Avenida Eduardo Mondlane
Tel: +244-264-260145

WHERE TO EAT

Restaurante da Alice
Campos Cabral
Tel: +244-264-262664

Restaurante Tic Tac
Tel: +244-264-260287

CUNENE

Cunene is a province that has the distinction of having the biggest baobab tree in Africa, in the region of Peupeu.

The predominant economic activity is cattle and agriculture.

The province has airports at Cahama and Ondjiva. Cunene is also reached by road via some provinces of Angola and from the Republic of Namibia.

• Capital: city of Ondjiva.
• Political/administrative division: the province has six cities: Cuanhama-Ondjiva, Cuvelai, Namacunde, Ombandja-Xangongo, Cahama and Curoca-Oncócua over an area of 87,342 km^2.
• The natives of Cunene belong to the great Ambó group.
• The climate is tropical semi-arid and the annual average temperature is 23 °C.

TOURIST ATTRACTIONS

Nature

The falls of Ruacaná on the river Cunene, on the border with Namibia, drop about 100 m and are well worth a visit. They also offer spectacular landscape views.

The Mupa National Park is another natural resource of great importance. It is situated in the north of the province and has an area of 660,000 hectares. It was given the status of national park on 26th December 1964, and hunting reserve on 16th April 1938.

The Kuroca Caves are another outstanding natural beauty.

The waterfalls of the river Cunene can also be seen at the Ruacaná dam in the region of Kalueke and in the black mountain (Epupa) region of Kuroka.

History and Culture

The Fortes Roçadas Fortress in Xangongo in the colonial past served as a military base for attacks and occupation of the areas to the south of Xangongo. It is situated in Xangongo, on the right bank of the river Cunene.

The Mufillo Monument symbolizes the great battles and victories of King Mandume, helped by King Tchetekela of Cuamato, against the Portuguese in the nineteenth century.

The Vau-do-Penbe Monument symbolizes the memory of the Portuguese overthrown in the act of passage to the river Cunene due the resistance of the nationalists there.

The Memorial Complex of King Mndume, located in the city of Namacunde 42 km from Ondjiva, is surrounded by woods that symbolize the heroism of the Kwanyama people.

The Ombala Grande is the historical burial site of the kings. It was the political centre of the Kwanyama Kingdom where the 11 kings lived, except King Mandume who was not circumcised.

WHERE TO STAY

Complexo Memorial ao Rei Mandume
Oihale
Mobile: +244-923-452695

Hotel Vila Okapale
Ondjiva
Tel: +244-265-250001

CUANDO CUBANGO

Cuando Cubango's fauna is the biggest tourist attraction of the province, which is why it participates in the Okavango Project that includes other countries of the southern region of the continent.

It is the second-biggest province of Angola and has agriculture as its main economic activity.

The province has an airport at Menongue and three more airfields at Cuito Cuanavale, Mavinga and Rivungo.

• Capital: city of Menongue.
• Political/administrative division: the province has nine cities – Menongue, Calai, Cuangar, Cuchi, Dirico, Cuito-Cuanavale, Mavinga, Nancova and Rivungo in an area of 199,049 km².
• The predominant ethnic group is the N'ganguela.
• The climate is tropical upland and the annual average temperature is 20 °C.

TOURIST ATTRACTIONS

Nature

The Parcial do Luiana Reserve was established as a reserve in 1966, with an area of 8,400 km² of diversified flora and fauna, where a great concentration of elephants is a highlight. It is located close to the borders with Zambia and Namibia.

The Parcial de Mavinga Reserve was established as a reserve in 1966. It has area of 5,950 km² and among its animals mention must be made of the rhinoceros, lion, elephant, black palanca and kaku, among others.

Other places of interest:
• Manlova Mountain
• Maculungongo Falls
• The river Kutato Falls
• The Mucusso, Luengue, Lomba, Luiana and Mavinga hunting grounds
• The river Kuebe swimming pool
• The Kambumbe dam.

History and Culture

The Campo Político do Missombo is situated 15 km from the city of Menongue.

The ruins of the Fort Muene Vunongue are situated on

the outskirts of the city of Menongue.

There are two battle sites of interest – Cuito Cuanavale battle site and Mavinga battle site.

WEST

This region is very strong in terms of historical culture, with notable sites such as the biggest museum in Angola and the statue of Samanhonga, known throughout the world as 'The Thinker'.

LUNDA NORTE

Lunda Norte is a province with great importance for the economy of the country due to the predominant activity: exploration and extraction of diamonds, which are abundant in the alluvial beds of some of the rivers that flow through the province.

This activity also influences other sectors of the economy.

The province has two large airports at Lucapa and Dundo. It is served by two national roads, the highway 180 that leaves Chitato and in the north–south direction goes through the city of Lucapa to Saurimo, Luena and follows south-west, and the 230 that comes from Saurimo in the direction east–west, and later goes through Capenda-Camulemba and Xá-Muteba on its way to Malanje and Luanda.

• Capital: city of Lucapa.

• Political/administrative division: the province has nine cities: Lucapa, Tchitato, Cambulo, Cuilo, Caungula, Cuango, Lubalo, Capenda-Camulemba and Xa-Muteba, over an area of 102,783 km^2.

• The biggest ethnic group is the Cokwe.

• The climate is tropical and humid, with an annual ave-

When buying local souvenirs do not forget to ask for the national label stamp

rage temperature of 24 °C.

LUNDA SUL

TOURIST ATTRACTIONS

Nature

The province of Lunda Norte has a rich hydrographic network, crossed from south to north by a series of rivers that are tributaries of the majestic river Zaire.

Places of interest:

• Archaeological site of Bala-Bala

• Archaeological site of Luaco

• Archaeological site of Candala.

History and Culture

Cultural tourism is key in this province, exploiting the fact of the biggest museum in Angola being located there, the National Museum of Dundo, which has a rich share of the culture of the country.

Other places of interest:

• The Government Palace

• The CTT Buildings

• Regional Museum of Dundo.

Lunda Sul is a province that has a rich historical and cultural tradition and was the home of one of the biggest empires of the region – Lunda Cocwe Empire.

One of the most important historical events was the war by the brothers Txinguri and Txinhama against their sister, Queen Lueji, for having married Txipinda Ilunga, a hunter of inferior ethnic group, thus breaking the law of the empire

It also has diamond mining as main activity, agriculture and fishing being only subsistence activities.

A main airport exists in the province. A national road links Luanda and Saurimo.

• Capital: city of Saurimo.

• Political/administrative division: the province has four cities: Saurimo, Dala, Muconda and Cacolo, covering an area of 77,637 km^2.

• The population is mainly composed of the Lunda Cocwe ethnic group.

• The climate is tropical and humid and the annual average temperature is between 21 °C and 23 °C.

Traditional body painting in Lunda Sul

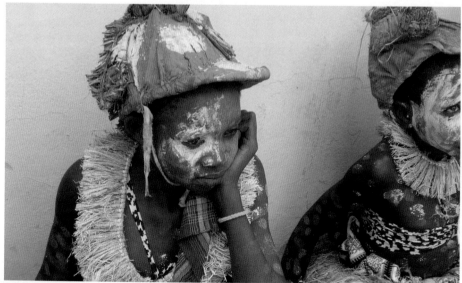

TOURIST ATTRACTIONS

Nature

The abundance of rivers in this province, such as the Luachimo, Chicapai, Cuango, Mombo, Luó and Cassai, offers the province natural attractions such as the falls they provide, and some of them offer good fishing.

The river Chimbwe in the city of Dala gives the province a very attractive island.

Other places of interest:
• Falls of the Luachimo
• Falls of the river Chicapa
• Falls of the river Chihumbwe
• Falls of Samussanda
• Poligno Forest of the river Muanguês
• Luari Lagoon
• High Chicapa Lagoon.

Another attraction is the dense, evergreen forests, following the water courses.

History and Culture

The province has some notable historical places where battles took place against the Portuguese forces, like Mona Quimbundo, Sueji and Itengo.

Other small places of interest also exist:
• Old seat of government
• Residence of the former employees of the public administration
• Building of the CTT
• Delegation of Endiama
• Religious monument of Our Lady of Lourdes
• Religious monument of the Catholic Mission.

WHERE TO STAY

Residencial Clínica
Saurimo

Where to Eat

Restaurante 17 de Setembro
Rua da Liberdade
Tel: 253-250462

Restaurante da D. Fernanda

Restaurante Mobil

MOXICO

Moxico is a province that has agriculture as its main economic activity, though the local population also practises hunting and fishing for a living.

This region has a rich flora with a great diversity of trees. After Cabinda, Moxico is the biggest timber producer in the country.

Moxico is reached by air through the airports of Luena, Cazombo and Lumbala N'Guimbo.

• Capital: city of Luena.
• Political/administrative division: the province has nine cities: Luena, Kamanongue, Léua, Luacano, Luau, Luchazes, Alto Cauele, Lumbala Nguimbo and Lumege, and is the biggest province of the country with an area of 223,023 km^2.
• The most predominant ethnic group is Cokwe.
• The climate is tropical wet upland, with an annual average temperature of 21 °C.

TOURIST ATTRACTIONS

Nature

With its diverse flora, the environment is good for camping.

The forest reserve of Katupe is completely bounded by rivers and has an area of 150 km^2.

The forest reserve of Lucusse is also bounded by rivers and has an area of 2,450 km^2 with woods and dense forests.

349

Another attraction is the national park of Cameia, one of the most unspoilt of the country, with species of fish such as caqueia, mussata, missogi, etc. It has an area of 14,450 km².

History and Culture

At the archaeological remains of the Rio Cassai-Cawéwé there are rocks with footprints of people and animals, among other impressions.

Other places of interest:
• Forte de Dilolo
• Ruins of Moxico Velho.

WHERE TO STAY

Hotel Luena
Luena

Residencial Horizonte
Bairro Nzagi
Tel: +244-254-260077

WHERE TO EAT

Restaurante Lago Dilolo
Bairro Saydi Mingas
Tel: +244-254-260034

ENTERTAINMENT

There are tourist recreation areas along the rivers Lumege, Pinto, Luena and Sacassange.

ITINERARIES

• 4 Days, 3 Nights: Feel and Live the Wonders of Cuanza Sul

The excellent beaches of Cuanza Sul are the main attraction of the region.

In the south of the province are the beautiful Gabela Waterfalls, about one hour north of Sumbe, where you can relax in the leisure park with a view of the falls and take spectacular photos. Following the same road towards Gabela, you will be able to enjoy warm waters in the Conda region.

Wako-Kungo is two hours' inland from the city of Sumbe and is a fertile region for farming. Taking the road south towards the estuary of the river Cubal (about 10 km) you will be able to visit the beaches of Tambi, Cambimba, Kuicombo, Barrote, Kibeijulo, Affection, Cabeça da Baleia, Sousa Dui and Chitamba that are known for being clean and secluded.

In the capital you can enjoy the beautiful coastal road, where you can find hotels, restaurants and bars and appreciate the cuisine of the region and its shellfish.

Contact your travel and tourism agency or the Tourist Institute for the Promotion of Angola (Infotur) for more details.

• 3 Days, 2 Nights: Bengo, Meeting Up with Nature Again

The Kissama Park is about 120 km south of Luanda and is known as one of the greatest of Angola, with a dramatic landscape and a variety of animal species, and is without doubt the main attraction of the province of Bengo. The famous rivers that run through the region are excellent for fishing, an activity that has not yet reached its potential in Angola.

For your enjoyment, the beautiful province has welcoming beaches in Cabo Ledo, Pambala and Ambriz. Caxito is the liveliest city of Bengo, with discos and restaurants. Historical monuments mark the region's history.

Following the Barra do Cuanza road, you will be able to enjoy a stroll to Muxima. The Bom Jesus is a place you must visit. It lies about 60 km from Luanda, on the road from Viana to Catete. It is essentially a farming zone with an industrial region in development on the banks of the river Cuanza. Contact your travel and tourism agency or the Tourist Institute for the Promotion of Angola (Infotur) for more details.

On our way to Barra do Dande

• Short Itinerary: Lubango–Namibe

1. The park of Our Lady of the Mount is a tourist complex with various leisure facilities, including restaurants and lodgings.

2. The viewpoint of the Mouth of the Humpata allows you to contemplate the panorama of the city of Lubango at an altitude of 1,100 metres.

3. The viewpoint of Christ the King is one of the most enviable points to contemplate the panoramic area of the city of Lubango, at an altitude of 1,310 metres. The statue in homage to Christ the King is located there.

4. In the district of Palanca, some 7 km from the crossing, is the Kulioko Restaurant, which has excellent service, as well as the Palanca Negra Motel, well known for its vast structure, accommodation services, refreshment and conference rooms.

5. A little before the Palanca crossing is the fisheries zone of the Humpata poligno forest, specializing in growing trees for planting in the province of Huíla.

6. Barely 500 metres from the main road there is the 'da Chela' mineral water plant. The sour and fresh milk and cheese plant of Chavele is located in the same zone, as well as the Jamba Fazenda, dedicated to farming, and the Humpata slaughterhouse.

7. At least 22 km away we visit the Town Hall of Humpata, and 4 km north of this is the Falcope and Barragem das Neves Tourist Centre.

8. After the Town Hall of Humpata, we visit the local market selling a variety of products.

9. After another 12 km or so on the main road, we get to Tchivinguiro, where we find the former school of agricultural overseers, the modern day Intermediate Institute of Agronomy, which trains the country's technicians.

10. Further along the breathtaking Leba road we can admire the Chela mountain range. Only a stone's throw further on to the left we can see the magnificent viewpoint of Leba at an altitude of 2,100 m.

11. After descending the precarious road in the Chela mountain range, taking 20 minutes at least, we arrive at the square of Leba, a place that more or less is the border of the two provinces. In the market 5 km from the provincial border we end up in the main square where people sell a variety of drinks, refreshments, cookies and snacks.

12. In Chiculungira there are two crossroads where we continue to the Town Hall of Bibala.

13. Caraculo is another of the town halls of Namibe, like Bibala. There we stop for some refreshment services.

14. Rio Giraúl has one of the most appreciated structures of human workmanship – the bridge with solar bulbs or lights. Rio Giraúl is an oasis in the desert because all the way through Chiculongiro it is dry. It only flows in the rainy season.

TRAVEL AGENCIES AND TOUR OPERATORS

Atlántida

Rua Engracia Fragoso,n° 61 , Luanda

Tel: +244-222-390320 / 390668 / 393001

Fax: +244-222-395275 / 390466

Email: geral@atlantidaviagens.co.ao

Atlántico Azul – Imbondex Turística, Lda.

Rua de Cafago, n° 2, 1st Floor, Kinaxixi, Luanda

Tel: +244-222-396536

Email: imbondexturistica@ebonet.net

Atlas Viagens, Lda.

Rua Amilcar Cabral, n°159, Luanda

Tel: +244-222-331631

Fax: +244-222-396694

Email: reservas@atlasviagens.com

Charme Tours

Rua 1° Congresso MPLA, n° 33 / 35, Luanda

Tel: +244-222-397499 / 699

Fax: + 244-222-331576

Email: charme.tours@netangola.com

Chik-Chik

Rua Hoji Ya Henda, n° 40, Luanda

Tel: +244-222-442042 / 440819

Fax: +244-222-448946

Email: chik@ebonet.net

 RECOMMENDED PARTNER Etram Travel Agency

Rua da Missão, 93, R/c, Luanda

Tel: +244-222-334173

Fax: +244-222-337497

Email: etagencia@snet.co.ao

Eurostral

Rua Marechal Broz Tito 27, 1st Floor, Kinaxixi, Luanda

Tel: +244-222-441617 / 398059 / 399091

Fax: +244-222-443022

Mobile: +244-923-30145

Email: eurostral@snet.co.ao

 RECOMMENDED PARTNER Expresso, Viagens e Turismo S.A.

Rua Amilcar Cabral, n° 172

PO Box 1359, Luanda

Tel: +244-222-331719

Fax: +244-222-336755

Mobile: +244-923-416431

Email: luanda@expressoangola.com

Website: www.expressoangola.com

 RECOMMENDED PARTNER HULL BLYTH Angola - HBA Travel - Viagens e Turismo, Lda.

Avd. 4 de Fevereiro, n° 5/7

PO Box 1214, Luanda

Tel: +244-222-311421 / 310044

Fax: +244-222-310043

Mobile: +244-912-504424

Email: hbaviagens@gmail.com

hbenquiries@hull-blyth.com

Internacional Travel

Rua Gastao de Sousa Dias, Luanda

Tel: +244-222-326258 / 326263

Intours – Viagen e Turismo, Lda.

Rua Martin Luther King, n° 57/67

PO Box 2464, Luanda

Tel: +244-222-393777 / 396650

Fax: +244-222-394297

Email: intours.agencia@ebonet.net

Kissama Tour – Agência de Viagens

Rua Guilherme Pererita Inglês, n° 40, Luanda

Tel: +244-222-332171

Fax: +244-222-339786

Paccitur Travel

Rua Liga Nacional Africana, n° 27-A

Aeroporto Intern, 4 de Fevereiro, Luanda

Tel: +244-222-448634 / 351166

Fax: +244-222-449547

Email: paccitur@snet.co.ao

TRAVEL AGENCIES AND TOUR OPERATORS

RECOMMENDED PARTNER Prismatur, Lda. Agência de Viagens e Turismo

Comandante Eurico n°45 R/C B
Patrice Lumumba, Luanda

Tel: +244-222-445488

Fax: +244-222-445336

Mobile: +244-912-514337/923-401440

Email: prismatur@mail.com

Website: www.prismatur.com

Reino Limitada

Rue Mota Feo n° 14 , 3° Floor, Luanda

Tel: +244-222-311550 / 310580

Somitour

Rua Rainha Ginga, Luanda

Tel: +244-222-398059

RECOMMENDED PARTNER Transcontinental Viagens & Turismo

Rua Travesa da Sorte, n° 22, Maianga, Luanda

Tel: +244-222-338003 / 339836

Fax: +244-222-331395 / 310313

Mobile: +244-912-943773

Email: tcv@snet.co.ao

Tropicana

Av. Comandante Valodia 199, Luanda

Tel: +244-222-444099 / 448924 / 449902

Mobile: +244-912-506330 / 912-514945 / 912-514944

Fax: +244-222-440-283 / 442-748/ 396-365

Email: tropicana@ebonet.net

World Travel Agency

Avenida 4 de Fevereiro, n°39 R/c, Luanda

Tel: +244-222-310972

Fax: +244-222-310717

Email: wta.resa@wtangola.com

Zepa - Agência de Viagens, Lda.

Rua Álvares Maciel, n° 5

PO Box 2524, Luanda

Tel: +244-222-337240/41/42

Fax: +244-222-337236

BASIC VOCABULARY

Hello	Bom dia	I can't speak Portuguese	Não falo Português
Hello (informal)	Olá	Do you speak English?	Fala Inglês?
Thank you (said by a man)	Obrigado (ob-ree-GAH-doo)	Is there someone here	Há aqui alguém que
Thank you (said by a woman)	Obrigada (ob-ree-GAH-dah)	who speaks English?	fale Inglês?
How are you?	Como está? / Tudo Bem?	Help!	Socorro!
Fine, thank you	Bem, obrigado / a	Good day	Bom dia
What is your name?	Como se chama?	Good evening	Boa tarde
My name is ____	(O) meu nome é ____	Good night	Boa noite
Nice to meet you	Muito prazer em conhecê-lo	I don't understand	Não compreendo
Please	Por favor (pohr fa-VOHR)		
You're welcome	De nada (je NAH-dah)	1	um / uma
		2	dois / duas
Yes	Si	3	três
No	Não	4	quatro
Excuse me / I'm Sorry	Desculpe	5	cinco
Goodbye	Adeus	6	seis (seysh)
Goodbye (informal)	Tchau	7	sete
See you later	Até logo	8	oito

BASIC VOCABULARY

9	nove	Evening	Use afternoon ("tarde") for early evening,
10	dez	and night ("noite") for late evening. Unlike English, "boa	
11	onze	noite" is used as an initial greeting and not just to say	
12	doze	goodbye.	
13	treze		
14	catorze	Today	hoje
15	quinze	Yesterday	ontem
16	dezasseis	Tomorrow	amanhã
17	dezassete	This week	esta semana
18	dezoito	Last week	a semana passada
19	dezanove	Next week	próxima semana
20	vinte	Sunday	domingo
21	vinte-um/uma	Monday	segunda-feira
22	vinte-dois	Tuesday	terça-feira
23	vinte-três	Wednesday	quarta-feira
30	trinta	Thursday	quinta-feira
40	quarenta	Friday	sexta-feira
50	cinquenta	Saturday	sábado
60	sessenta		
70	setenta	January	Janeiro
80	oitenta	February	Fevereiro
90	noventa	March	Março
100	cem	April	Abril
200	duzentos	May	Maio
300	trezentos	June	Junho
500	quinhentos	July	Julho
1000	mil	August	Agosto (AGOSH-too)
2000	dois mil	September	Setembro
1,000,000	milhão	October	Outubro
		November	Novembro
Number	número	December	Dezembro
Half	metade		
Less	menos	A table for one person	Uma mesa para uma
More	mais	/two people, please.	/duas pessoa(s), por favor.
		Can I look at the menu?	Posso ver o menu, por favor?
Now	agora	Breakfast	pequeno-almoço
Later	depois		
Before	antes de (ANtesh deh)	Lunch	almoço
Morning	manhã	Supper	jantar
Afternoon	tarde	I want _____.	Quero _____.
Night	noite	Chicken	frango
		Beef	bife

BASIC VOCABULARY

Fish	peixe	Butter	manteiga
Ham	fiambre	May I have a glass of __?	Quero um copo de __?
Sausage	salsicha	May I have a cup of __?	Quero uma chávena de __?
Cheese	queijo	May I have a bottle of __?	Quero uma garrafa __?
Eggs	ovos	Coffee	café
Salad	salada	Tea (drink)	chá
Vegetables	vegetais	Juice	sumo
Fruit	fruta	(Bubbly) water	água com gás
Bread	pão	Water	água
Toast	torrada	Beer	cerveja
Rice	arroz	red/white wine	vinho tinto/branco
Salt	sal	The check, please.	A conta, por favor.
Black pepper	pimenta negra		

USEFUL WEBSITES

These are some of the main useful websites should you be travelling or doing business in Angola

Angola Acontece: www.angolaacontece.com

AngoNoticias: www.angonoticias.com

Angola Trade Directory: www.dcda.net

Expo Angola: www.expo-angola.snet.co.ao

Journal of Angola: www.jornaldeangola.com

Luanda Commercial Antenna: www.ebonet.net/lac/

National Broadcasting: www.rna.ao

National Press Agency: www.angolapress-angop.ao

Semanario Angolense: www.semanarioangolense.net

Public Television: www.tpa.ao

Radio Ecclesia: www.recclesia.org

www.aavota.com

www.africaaction.org

www.africa-ata.org/angola.htm

www.alfandegas.com

www.angola-consulate.org

www.angolaemb.se

www.angola.org

www.angola.org.uk

www.anip.ao.co

www.arenaangola.com

www.cia.gov

www.comesa.int

www.cplp.org

www.damisela.com

www.dnci.net

www.ec.europa.eu

www.embajadadeangola.com

www.embajada-online.com

www.eventseye.com

www.flysn.be

www.fesa.og.ao

www.folha8news.com

www.forummercadodecapitais.com

www.globalsecurity.org

www.guiadelmundo.com

www.hmnet.com

www.hotelsuperportal.com

www.iie-angola-us.org

www.loc.gov/law/guide/angola.html

www.luanda.usembassy.gov

www.mind-angola.com www.minfin.gv.ao

www.netangola.com

www.oefre.unibe.ch.html

www.paginasdouradas.co.ao

www.quantum-capital.net

www.sidestep.com

USEFUL WEBSITES

www.state.gov

www.travelblog.org

www.travelnotes.org

www.travelnow.com

www.travelzoo.com

www.trekearth.com

www.unitedworld-usa.com

www.us-angola.org

www.vozdeangola.tk

www.wikipedia.com

www.winne.com

www.worldbank.org

www.worldlii.org/catalog/2674.html

www.worldinfozone.com

www.un.org

www.worldroom.com

www.worldtravelserver.com

www.wto.org

SOURCES

Ango-Accommodation: www.angoalojamento.com

Angola-Hosting: www.angolahosting.com

ANIP-Angolan National Agency of Private Investment: www.investinangola.com, www.iie-angola-us.org

Angola-Press Agency: www.angolapress-angop.ao

Commercial Directory of Angola: www.dcda.net

National Bank of Angola: www.bna.ao

Ministry of Finance: www.minfin.gv.ao

Ministry of Public Administration, Employment and Social Security: www.mapess.gv.ao

National Directory of Internal Commerce: www.dnci.net

Luanda-Online: www.luandaonline.com

Official Republic of Angola Website: www.angola.org

US-Angola Chamber of Commerce: www.us-angola.org

National Encyclopedia: www.nationsencyclopedia.com

Travel Note: www.travelnotes.org

Vector – Images: www.vector-images.com

WIKIPEDIA: www.wikipedia.com

TOP COMPANIES
(in alphabetical order)

AAA
Agrinsul
Águas do Bom Jesus
Air Gemini
Alcatel
Angoalissar
Angola Telecom
Angolauto SARL
Ascorp
Auto-Sueco
Avis Rent-A-Car (Angola)
BAI - Banco Africano de Investimento
Banco Comercial Angolano
Banco de Comércio e Indústria
Banco de Fomento de Angola
Banco de Poupança e Crédito
Banco Espirito Santo Angola
Banco Nacional de Angola
Bivac International
BP Exploration Angola Ltd
British American Tobacco Angola
Café GINGA
Caminhos de Ferro de Benguela
Catermar (Angola)
Chela
ChevronTexaco
Coca-Cola Bottling (Luanda) SARL
Constroi-Angola
Cuca BGI
De Beers Angola Holdings SARL
Deloitte
EKA - Empresa Angolana de cervejas
Emaxicom Lda
Empresa de Desenvolvimento Urbano
Empresa de Tabacos de Angola SARL
Empresa Nacional de Electricidade
Enana
Endiama
ENEP
Ensa - Seguros de Angola SARL
Entreposto Comercial e Industrial Lda
Epal
Ernst & Young
Esso Exploration Angola
FAMO
FDES
Fina Petroleos de Angola SARL
GAM(Grupo António Mosquito)
Gestao de Fundos SARL
Ghassist SARL

Grinaker (Angola) Lda
Grupo Arosfram
Grupo Importrading
Intertransports Centre SARL
ITM Mining
Jembas Assistência Médica
KPMG
Lactiangol
M'Bakassy & Filhos
Macon - Transportes Lda
Maersk (Angola), Lda
Millennium BCP
Misbubishi Corporation-Luanda
Mota-Engil Engenharia
Movicel - telecomunicações Lda
Multichoice Angola
NCR - Informática Lda
NDS - Nile Dutch Africa Line
Nexus - Telecomunicações e Serviços
NGR - Materiais de Construção
Nocal
Nokia
Norsk Hydro Angola SA
Nova Cimangola
Nova Sotecma SARL
Odebrecht
Pagena
Petrobras
Porto de Lobito
Porto de Luanda
Porto do Namibe
Price water house coopers
Robert Hudson Lda
Rocha Monteiro Lda
Secil Maritima
Shell Development Angola B.V
Sicasal Angola
Sistec
Soares da Costa
Somague Engenharia - Angola
Sometal
Sonangol
TAAG
Teixeira Duarte
Tintas CIN de Angola SARL
Total E&P Angola
Toyota de Angola SARL
Uniao Comercial de Automóveis SARL
Unicargas E.P.
Unitel SARL

COMPANY INDEX

AGRICULTURE

CAMPOTEC ....PAGE 101
INSTITUTO NACIONAL DEL CAFÉ - INCA ....PAGE 101
INSTITUTO NACIONAL DOS CEREAIS - INCER ....PAGE 102
INSTITUTO NACIONAL DE DESENVOLVIMENTO AGRARIO - INDA..PAGE 103
INSTITUTO NACIONAL DAS FLORESTAS - IDF ....PAGE 106
INSTITUTO NACIONAL DE PESCA ....PAGE 108
NOVA SOTECMA ....PAGE 109

ENERGY & OIL

ANGASES ....PAGE 115
EDEL..PAGE 116
ELECNOR ....PAGE 116
ENEL..PAGE 117
EPAL..PAGE 118
GAMEK ....PAGE 119

AKER KVAERNER ....PAGE 119
BP ....PAGE 120
CHEVRON ANGOLA ....PAGE 120
ENI ....PAGE 122
GALP ENERGIA ....PAGE 123
HALLIBURTON ....PAGE 123
HYDRO ANGOLA ....PAGE 124
OCTOMAR SERVIÇOS MARITIMOS ....PAGE 124
PARAGON ANGOLA...PAGE 125
PETROBRAS ....PAGE 125
PETROMAR...PAGE 127
SCHLUMBERGER OILFIELD SERVICES ....PAGE 127
SONANGOL HOLDING ....PAGE 128
SONANGOL RESEARCH & PRODUCTION ....PAGE 133
SONANGOL LOGISTICS...PAGE 135
SONANGOL – GAS ....PAGE 137
SONANGOL – TELECOMMUNICATIONS ....PAGE 139
SONANGOL – SGDPS ....PAGE 141
SONANGOL – SOCIAL ....PAGE 145
SOMOIL ....PAGE 146
STATOIL ANGOLA ....PAGE 146
TOTAL E&P ANGOLA ....PAGE 147
WAPO ....PAGE 148

FINANCE

AAA ....PAGE 156
BANCO BAI ....PAGE 157
BANCO DE COMERCIO E INDUSTRIA - BCI...PAGE 157
BANCO ESPIRITO SANTO – BESA ....PAGE 158

COMPANY INDEX

BANCO BIC ....PAGE 158
BFA - BANCO DE FOMENTO ANGOLA ....PAGE 159
BANCO MILLENNIUM ....PAGE 159
BNA - BANCA NACIONAL DE ANGOLA ....PAGE 161
BPC - BANCO DE POUPANÇA E CREDITO ....PAGE 161
BIVAC INTERNATIONAL ....PAGE 164
DELOITTE ....PAGE 164
DNV - DET NORSKE VERITAS ....PAGE 165
ERNST & YOUNG ....PAGE 165
G + A, GLOBAL ALLIANCE ....PAGE 166
INE - INSTITUTO NACIONAL DE ESTATISTICA ....PAGE 166
KPMG ....PAGE 167
NOSSA SEGUROS ....PAGE 169
PWC ....PAGE 169
QUANTUM CAPITAL...PAGE 170
RIDGE SOLUTIONS ....PAGE 171

INDUSTRY & TRADE

AGUAS DE BOM JESUS - MITC ....PAGE 177
AIA - ASSOCIAÇÃO INDUSTRIAL DE ANGOLA ....PAGE 178
AGENCIA NACIONAL PARA O INVESTIMENTO PRIVADO, ANIP......................................PAGE 178
ANGONABEIRO...PAGE 179
AROSFRAM...PAGE 180
BRITISH AMERICAN TOBACCO, BAT ....PAGE 180
COCA-COLA..PAGE 181
CUCA_EKA_NOKAL ....PAGE 182
EAL, EDIÇOES DE ANGOLA..PAGE 182
ENEPA ....PAGE 183
EXECUTIVE CENTER ....PAGE 184
FATA ....PAGE 184
FEPEL ....PAGE 185
GRUPO BARTOLOMEU DIAS ....PAGE 187
GRUPO CHICOIL ....PAGE 188
GRUPO SOGEC ....PAGE 188
GUE, GUICHE UNICO DE EMPRESAS...PAGE 189
ICELAR, REPLICA..PAGE 189
IDIA - INSTITUTO DESENVOLVIMENTO INDUSTRIAL ....PAGE 196
LACTIANGOL ....PAGE 196
PINTO BASTO ....PAGE 197
REFRIANGO ....PAGE 198
SAGRES BEER ....PAGE 199
SILNOR ....PAGE 199

MINING

ALROSA ....PAGE 205
ASCORP ....PAGE 206
CATOCA..PAGE 206
DE BEERS ....PAGE 208

COMPANY INDEX

ENDIAMA E&P ....PAGE 208
1-ENDIAMA P&P..PAGE 209
2-FUNDACION BRILLANTE ....PAGE 210
3-SODIAM ....PAGE 210
ITM..PAGE 211
SDM ....PAGE 212
SOCIEDADE MINEIRA DO CHITOTOLO, LDA. ....PAGE 212
SML, SOCIEDADE MINEIRA DO LUCAPA, LDA. ....PAGE 215

PUBLIC SERVICES

AGOSTINHO NETO UNIVERSITY ....PAGE 229
CATHOLIC UNIVERSITY OF ANGOLA ....PAGE 229
IL - INSTITUTO DE LENGUAS ....PAGE 230
UNIVERSITY JEAN PIAGET..PAGE 230

CLINICA BIODENTE ....PAGE 231
CLINICA CLIDOPA..PAGE 232
CLINICA SAGRADA ESPERANÇA..PAGE 233
CLINICA SOCLIMEDIC...PAGE 234
INSS ....PAGE 235

ALFA 5 ....PAGE 236
ANGO ATENTA...PAGE 236
ANGO PATRULHA...PAGE 238
AP SERVICES...PAGE 239
COPEBE ....PAGE 241
DSL..PAGE 241
LINCE ....PAGE 242
MAMBOJI..PAGE 244
PROTECTOR ....PAGE 245
SECURITAS ....PAGE 247
TELESERVICES ....PAGE 249

WORKS & HOUSING

EDURB ....PAGE 255
MOTA ENGIL ....PAGE 256
NOVA CIMANGOLA ....PAGE 256
ODEBRECHT ....PAGE 257
PAGENA ....PAGE 258
SOARES DA COSTA ....PAGE 258
TEIXEIRA DUARTE...PAGE 261

TOURISM

AAVOTA...PAGE 267
AHORESIA ....PAGE 267
AGENCIA ATLAS VIAGENS, LDA. ....PAGE 268

COMPANY INDEX

AGENCIA EUROSTRAL ....PAGE 269
AGENCIA EXPRESSO VIAGENS ....PAGE 270
AGENCIA DE VIAJES HULL BLYTH...PAGE 271
AGENCIA PRISMATUR ....PAGE 272
AGENCIA TRANSCONTINENTAL ....PAGE 272
BAMBOO IMPERIAL ....PAGE 273
DNAT ....PAGE 274
FITNESS CLUB...PAGE 274
FORUM HOTEL ....PAGE 275
INFOTOUR ....PAGE 276
MADIBA RESORT ....PAGE 278
MANGAIS, ECOTURISMO ....PAGE 278
TAMBARINO RESTAURANTE & CATERING ....PAGE 282
VENEZA RESTAURANTE & CATERING ....PAGE 283

TRANSPORT & COMMUNICATIONS

MOVICEL ....PAGE 290
ANGOLA TELECOM ....PAGE 290
ARENA DIRECT ....PAGE 292
CITELFONICA ....PAGE 293
DREAD LOCKS ....PAGE 293
JEMBAS ASSISTENCIA TECNICA (JAT) ....PAGE 294
MSTELCOM – NEXUS ....PAGE 294
SISTEC ....PAGE 295
UNITEL ....PAGE 296

ATS ....PAGE 298
CARGO TEAM ....PAGE 299
DHL ....PAGE 299
DIRECCAO NACIONAL DAS ALFANDEGAS ....PAGE 300
ENANA ....PAGE 301
FACAR ANGOLA...PAGE 301
HULL BLYTH-CARGO ....PAGE 303
MAERSK & SEALAND ....PAGE 303
PANALPINA..PAGE 303
PUERTO DE LOBITO ....PAGE 304
PUERTO DE LUANDA ....PAGE 305
SDV ....PAGE 305
TAAG ....PAGE 306
TRANSCONTINENTAL ....PAGE 307

THE TOOL TO REACH INTERNATIONAL BUSINESS GOALS...

THE PREMIER GUIDEBOOK FOR BUSINESS GLOBETROTTERS

B.eBiz

eBiz *guides*

L.eBiz

All you need to know to do business and have fun

...AND ENJOY THE BEST LEISURE DESTINATIONS

THE PREMIER GUIDEBOOK FOR BUSINESS GLOBETROTTERS

We are looking for worldwide sales representatives

Join a successful team
around the world

www.eBizguides.com   info@ebizguides.com

All you need to know to do business and have fun

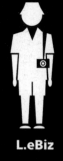

Your
compass
to investment

www.winne.com

Online since 1996 and reporting about investment opportunities in emerging markets. The best database available on the ne

WORLD INVESTMENT NEWS

The Multimedia Information Company